Embedded Ethernet and Internet Complete

Designing and Programming
Small Devices for Networking

Jan Axelson

Lakeview Research LLC
Madison, WI 53704

Lakeview Research LLC   info@Lvr.com
5310 Chinook Ln.   www.Lvr.com
Madison, WI 53704

14 13 12 11 10 9 8 7 6 5 4 3 2 1

ISBN 1-931448-00-0   Printed and bound in the United States of America

Contents

Contents

Contents

Introduction

This is a guide to designing and programming embedded systems to communicate in local Ethernet networks and on the Internet.

An embedded system is a device that has computer intelligence and is dedicated to performing a single task, or a group of related tasks. Embedded systems often perform monitoring and control functions such as gathering and reporting sensor readings or controlling motors and switches. They're called embedded systems because the program code is an integral part of, or embedded in, the devices.

Ethernet is the networking technology used in many offices and homes to enable computers to communicate and share resources. Many Ethernet networks also connect to a router that provides access to the Internet.

For many years, embedded systems and Ethernet networks existed in separate worlds. Ethernet was available only to desktop computers and other large computers. Embedded systems that needed to exchange information with other computers were limited to interfaces with low speed, limited range, or lack of standard application protocols.

But developments in technology and the marketplace now make it possible for embedded systems to communicate in local Ethernet networks as well as on the Internet. Network communications can make an embedded system more powerful and easier to monitor and control. An embedded system can host a Web site, send and receive e-mail, upload and download files, and exchange information of any kind with other computers connected via a network interface.

One development that has made Ethernet feasible for embedded systems is the availability of inexpensive controller chips to handle the details of Ethernet communications. The CPUs that provide the processing power for embedded systems have also gotten faster and more capable of handling the demands of communicating with the controllers. Internet protocols provide standard, well-documented ways of exchanging data. Both Ethernet and the Internet protocols are free and open standards available for use without royalties or licensing fees.

Technologies and Protocols

Designing and programming an embedded system for networking can require skills and knowledge in a variety of areas in electronics, programming, and networking.

To interface an Ethernet controller to a CPU, you'll need to know about hardware design.

To write the program code that controls the system, you'll need to know how to write and debug code for your system's CPU.

To build the network, you'll need to know how to select and use cables, repeater hubs, switches, and other network hardware.

To enable sending and receiving data over the local network, you'll need to be familiar with the Ethernet protocol.

To enable sending and receiving data over the Internet and some local networks, you'll need to be familiar with Internet protocols.

To serve Web pages, you'll need to know about Web-page design.

To keep your system and its data safe, you'll need to know how to implement measures that provide network security.

This book brings together all of these fields of knowledge with a focus on how they relate to the networking of embedded systems. Creating a Web page for a major corporation's Web site is very different from creating a home page for a device with limited resources. But designing for small systems isn't just a matter of scaling back. For example, a Web page hosted by an embedded system will almost certainly want to display more than basic pages with static, unchanging text. Instead, the pages typically provide real-time information and may want to accept and act on user input as well.

This book shows how to meet the networking and application needs of embedded systems in spite of their hardware and software limitations of small devices. In many cases, you can choose to simplify the tasks involved by using hardware and software modules that do much of the work for you.

Who should read this book?

This book is for anyone who wants to design, program, or learn about networking with embedded systems.

These are some of the questions this book answers:

What are the advantages and limits of using Ethernet with embedded systems? Find out whether Ethernet is the right technology for your project.

What hardware and program code do I need to connect an embedded system to an Ethernet network? There are many options for creating an Ethernet-capable embedded controller, from buying a module with hardware and software support for networking to putting it all together from scratch. This book will help in selecting the components for your systems.

How do I build a network? An Ethernet-capable device can't communicate if it doesn't have a network to connect to. Find out how to select network cables and hubs and use them to put together an Ethernet network

How can I connect my device or network to the Internet? An Internet connection can extend a device's reach to the entire Internet. Find out how to obtain an Internet connection for your device and ensure that your network is configured to enable your device to perform the communications it requires.

How can my devices send and receive messages over the local network or the Internet? The Internet and many local networks use the TCP/IP suite of Internet protocols to send and receive messages of all types. This book will show you how embedded systems can use these protocols to exchange messages.

How can I host a Web site on my embedded system? Even a very basic embedded system can function as a Web server, which responds to requests from other computers for Web pages. Find out what a device requires to function as a Web server and how to create the pages your device will serve.

How can my Web server's pages include dynamic, real-time content and respond to user input? This book will show how an embedded system can display up-to-date information and respond to text and other input from users.

How can my embedded system send and receive e-mail, exchange files with an FTP server, or host an FTP server that other computers can access? This book includes examples for each of these applications.

How can I ensure that the programming and other information in my devices is secure on the Internet? Good security practices can ensure that unauthorized users can't change configuration settings or view private information in your device. Security practices can also help to prevent problems due to careless or accidental mistakes. Find out what you need to do to keep your device and the local network it resides in secure and functioning properly.

This book assumes you have a basic knowledge of digital circuit design and microcontroller or microprocessor programming for embedded systems. I don't assume any knowledge of networking.

About the Example Applications

The example applications in this book use two Ethernet-capable modules: a TINI module from Dallas Semiconductor and a RabbitCore module from Rabbit Semiconductor. Both are capable and well-supported products that will enable you to get your projects up and running quickly. You won't go wrong using either of these modules.

The TINI examples use the Java programming language. The Rabbit examples use Dynamic C, Rabbit Semiconductor's implementation of the C programming language for embedded systems. Every application in the book has both a TINI and RabbitCore example. The book also discusses a number of other components that are suitable for many projects.

How This Book Is Organized

Each of the chapters in this book has two sections: Quick Start and In Depth. The Quick Start section gives practical information and examples that you can put to work right away. The In Depth section has more detail about the protocols and technologies used in the Quick Start examples.

The order that you read the sections may vary depending on your needs and preferences. You can read the book straight through for an understanding of each of the topics in turn. Or to get something up and running quickly, you might read the Quick Start sections first, referring to the In Depth material as needed. Or if you prefer to gain a background in a topic before delving into implementation details, you can read a chapter's In Depth section before the Quick Start.

Updates, Corrections, and Additional Resources

The first place to look for more information on the topics covered in this book is my Embedded Ethernet page at *www.Lvr.com,* which is the Web site of this book's publisher, Lakeview Research. At this location, you'll find the following:

- Complete source code for all of the TINI and Rabbit applications in the book.
- Windows applications for communicating with the TINI and Rabbit applications.
- Corrections and updates to the book.
- Links to additional resources relating to Ethernet networks and embedded systems.

The text of this book refers to many other information sources, including standard and specification documents and books with more information about the topics covered.

Acknowledgments

This book would not be the same without the advice, suggestions, corrections, additions, and other input provided by many capable experts. In particular, I want to thank Carrie Maha, Owen Magee, and Norman Rogers of Rabbit Semiconductor; Kris Ardis and Don Loomis of Dallas Semiconductor; Bruce Boyes of Systronix; Fred Eady of EDTP Electronics; Pete Loshin, author of *TCP/IP Clearly Explained;* Shawn Silverman, creator of the Tynamo Web server; and Charles Spurgeon, author of *Ethernet: The Definitive Guide.*

I hope you find the book useful! Comments invited.

Jan Axelson

jan@Lvr.com

1

Networking Basics

Some computers are independent units, with little need to exchange information with other computers near or far. At most, these computers may use local interfaces such as USB or RS-232 to communicate with printers or other devices close at hand.

But with a network connection, a computer can reach beyond its local interfaces to send and receive information of any kind, over distances large and small, via wires or through the air. Computers of different types can communicate using network protocols supported by all. In a network of embedded systems, each system can communicate with the other systems in the network, sharing information and sending and responding to requests as needed. Desktop computers in the network can monitor and control the operation of the embedded systems.

Many local networks follow the networking standard popularly known as Ethernet. Ethernet networks are capable and flexible. Many products designed for use in networks have support for Ethernet built in. A router, or gateway, enables an Ethernet network to communicate with computers in other networks, including computers on the Internet.

Two or more computers that share a network connection form a local area network, or LAN. The smallest network links just two computers. For example, a data logger might connect to a remote computer that receives and displays the logger's data. Or a personal computer (PC) may use a network connection to monitor and control a piece of equipment. At the other extreme, the Internet is the largest network. With an Internet connection, the computers in a local network can access resources on the Internet and make local resources available to any computer on the Internet.

To design and program embedded systems for networking, you need to understand the elements that make up a network, so this chapter begins with the basics of how networks are structured. Following this is an introduction to Ethernet, including its capabilities and how Ethernet networks manage network traffic.

Quick Start:
The Elements of a Network

All computer networks have some things in common. Every network must have the physical components that enable the computers in the network to exchange data. And in every network, the computers must agree about how to share the data path that connects the computers, to help ensure that transmitted data gets to its destination.

Components

All networks include the following physical components:

- Two or more computers that need to communicate with each other. In the networks described in this book, at least one of the computers is an embedded system, which is a device that contains a computer dedicated to a specific task or a series of related tasks.

- A defined physical interface, to ensure that the output of a transmitting computer is compatible with the inputs of the receiving computers. For Ethernet networks, the Ethernet standard specifies this interface.

- Cables or wireless transceivers to connect the computers. Ethernet networks have several options for cables. An Ethernet interface may also connect to a device called a wireless access point, which enables the embedded system to access a wireless network.

The computers in the network must also agree on the following aspects of sharing the network:

- Rules for deciding when a computer may transmit on the network. When multiple computers share a data path, whether in a cable or wireless medium, the computers need to know when the path is available for transmitting. The Ethernet standard contains rules that specify when a computer may transmit.

- A way of identifying a transmission's intended destination. In Ethernet networks, multiple computers may receive a message intended for one computer in the network. When a message arrives at a computer's network interface, the computer needs to know whether the message is intended for itself or another computer. Every communication in an Ethernet network includes a hardware address that identifies the Ethernet interface of the intended receiver. Some communications also use Internet protocols that contain additional addressing information, such as an addresses that identify the sending and receiving computers on the Internet and a port, or process, that receives the communication at the destination computer.

- A defined format for the information sent on the network, so a computer can understand and use the information it receives from the network. In Ethernet networks, all data travels in structures called frames. Each frame includes fields for data, addressing, and other information that helps the data reach its destination without errors. The information in a frame's data field may also use protocols that help the receiver of the frame decide what to do with the received data.

Modular Design

To make designing and maintaining a network as easy as possible, most networked computers use modules, or components, that work together to handle the job of network communications. Each module is responsible for a single task or a small set of related tasks. Each module knows how to exchange information with one or more of the other modules, but the modules don't need to know details about how the other modules accomplish their tasks.

The modular approach has a couple of benefits. If each module is as independent as possible, it's easier to make changes when needed, possibly even swapping in a different module entirely, without requiring changes in the other modules. And isolating problems is easier when a single module contains all of the code to perform a function.

A module may consist of hardware, software, or a combination. A software module may be as small as a procedure or subroutine within a larger application or unit of code. Or a module may be a library of routines or a class or package of classes in a separate file.

In an embedded system, the program code may be referred to as firmware, which typically means that the code is stored in Flash memory or another nonvolatile memory chip, rather than on a disk drive. In general, with software stored on a drive, users can install, run, and uninstall applications as needed. In contrast, firmware tends to be an integral, seldom-changing part of the device. Users may have the ability to load new firmware into a device, but the new firmware is typically an update or upgrade to existing code, rather than an entirely different type of application.

The Network Protocol Stack

You can think of the modules used in networking as being stacked in layers, one above another. A computer's network protocol stack consists of the modules involved with networking. Figure 1-1 shows an example of a net-

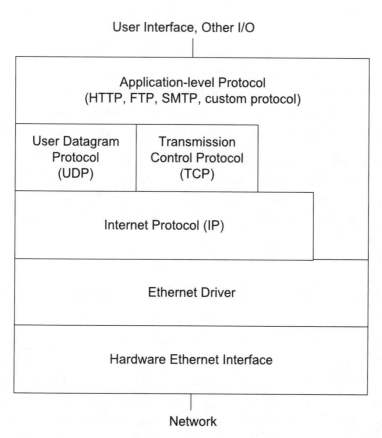

Figure 1-1: The networking support in most computers uses a layered model, where a variety of components each manage a portion of the job of network communications.

work protocol stack for a computer that connects to an Ethernet network and supports common Internet protocols.

(To prevent confusion, I should point out that this use of the term stack has nothing to do with the internal stack of a computer's central processing unit (CPU). A CPU's stack is a special area of memory for temporary storage. This type of stack has no direct relation to networking.)

At the bottom of the stack is the hardware interface to the network cable. At the top of the stack is a module or modules that provide data to send on the network and use the data received from the network. In the middle there may be one or more modules involved with addressing, error-checking, and providing and using status and control information.

In transmitting, a message travels down the stack from the application layer that initiates the message to the network interface that places the message on the network. In receiving, the message travels up the stack from the network interface to the application layer that uses the data in the received message.

The number of layers a message passes through can vary. For some messages that travel only within a local network, the application layer can communicate directly with the Ethernet driver. Messages that travel on the Internet must use the Internet Protocol. Messages that use the Internet Protocol can also use the User Datagram Protocol or the Transmission Control Protocol to add error checking or flow-control capabilities.

The Application: Providing and Using Network Data

The application provides data to send on the network and uses data received from the network. An application often has a user interface that enables users to request data from a computer on the network or provide data to send on the network. In an embedded system, the user interface may just enable basic configuring and monitoring functions, while the system performs its network communications without user intervention.

The data that the application sends and receives may be anything: a single byte; a line of text; a request for a Web page; the contents of a Web page; a file containing text, an image, binary data, or program code; or anything that a computer wants to send to another computer in the network.

The data sent by an application follows a protocol, or set of rules, that enables the application at the receiving computer to understand what to do with the received data. An application may use a standard protocol such as the hypertext transfer protocol (HTTP) for requesting and sending Web pages, the file transfer protocol (FTP) for transferring files, or the simple mail transfer protocol (SMTP) or Post Office Protocol (POP3) for e-mail messages. Applications may also send and receive data using application-specific protocols.

In an embedded system, the application might be a module that periodically reads and stores sensor readings or the states of other external signals, or an application might use received data to control motors, relays, or other circuits. An embedded system can function as a Web server that receives and responds to requests for Web pages, which may enable users to provide input or view real-time data. Embedded systems can send and receive information via e-mail and in files via FTP.

An application layer may support multiple processes, or tasks. For example, a single system might host a Web page and also provide an FTP server that makes files available for downloading. Port numbers can identify specific processes at the destination computer.

TCP and UDP: Error Checking, Flow Control, and Ports

A network communication often includes additional information to help data get to its destination efficiently and without errors. A module that supports the Transmission Control Protocol (TCP) can add information for use in error checking, flow control, and identifying an application-level process at the source and destination computers.

Error-checking values help the receiver detect when received data doesn't match what was sent. Flow-control information helps the sender determine when the receiver is ready for more data. And a value that identifies an application-level port, or process, can help in routing received data to the correct process in the application layer.

TCP performs all of these functions. Many Internet and local-network communications such as requests for Web pages and sending and receiving e-mail use TCP. Windows and other operating systems have support for TCP built in. Development kits for network-capable embedded systems often include libraries or packages with TCP support.

In sending data using TCP, the application layer passes the data to send and values that identify the data's source and destination to a TCP layer. The TCP layer creates a TCP segment that consists of a header followed by the application data (Figure 1-2). The header is a defined structure with fields

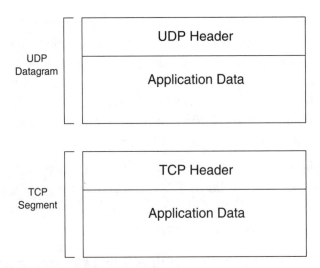

Figure 1-2: The UDP and TCP layers add a header to the data payload before passing the data down the stack. In the opposite direction, the UDP and TCP layers strip the headers before passing the data up the stack.

containing information used in error checking, flow control, and routing the message to the correct port at the destination. The TCP layer doesn't change the message to be sent. It just places the message in the data portion of the TCP segment. The TCP segment encapsulates, or provides a container for, the data received from the application layer. The TCP layer then passes the segment to the IP layer for transmitting on the network.

In the other direction, the TCP layer receives a segment from the IP layer, strips the TCP header, and passes the segment to the port specified in the TCP header.

A simpler alternative to TCP is the User Datagram Protocol (UDP). Like a TCP segment, a UDP datagram has a header, followed by a data portion that contains the application data. UDP includes fields for specifying ports and optional error-checking, but no support for flow control. Windows and many development kits for embedded systems include support for UDP.

Chapter 5 has more about TCP and UDP.

In some networks, communications may skip the TCP/UDP layer entirely. For example, a local network of embedded systems may have no need for flow control or additional error-checking beyond what the Ethernet frame provides. In these cases, an application may communicate directly with a lower layer in the network protocol stack, such as the IP layer or Ethernet driver.

IP: Internet Addressing and Routing

The Internet Protocol (IP) layer can help data get to its destination even if the source and destination computers are on different local networks. As the name suggests, the Internet Protocol enables computers on the Internet to communicate with each other. Because IP is closely tied to TCP and UDP, local networks that use TCP and UDP also use IP.

The term *TCP/IP* refers to communications that use TCP and IP. The term can also refer more broadly to the suite of protocols that includes TCP, IP, and related protocols such as UDP.

In Ethernet networks, a unique hardware address identifies each interface on the network. IP addresses are more flexible because they aren't specific to a network type. A message that uses IP can travel through different types of networks, including Ethernet, token-ring, and wireless networks, as long as all of the networks support IP.

In sending a message, the TCP layer passes the TCP segment and the source and destination addresses to the IP layer. The IP layer encapsulates the TCP segment in an IP datagram, which consists of a header followed by a data portion that may contain a UDP datagram or a TCP segment (Figure 1-3). The header has fields for the source and destination IP addresses, error checking of the header, routing, and a value that identifies the protocol, such as TCP or UDP, used by the data portion.

In a similar way, a UDP layer may pass a UDP datagram to the IP layer.

In receiving a message, the IP layer receives an IP datagram from a lower level in the network stack. The IP layer performs error-checking and uses the protocol value to determine where to pass the contents of the data portion.

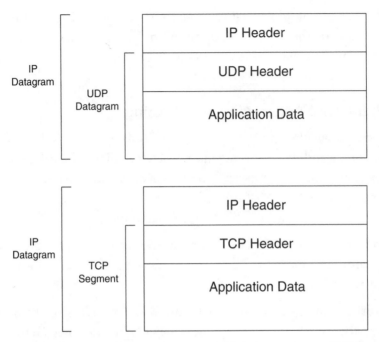

Figure 1-3: The IP layer adds a header to a UDP datagram or TCP segment before passing the data down the stack. In the opposite direction, the IP layer strips the IP header before passing a UDP datagram or TCP segment up the stack.

In the IP header, the source and destination IP addresses identify the sending and receiving computers. Each computer in a network that uses IP addresses must have an address that is unique within the network or networks that the sending computer can communicate with. Local networks can use addresses in three blocks reserved for local networks. A computer that communicates over the Internet must have an address that is different from the address of every other computer on the Internet. The Internet Corporation for Assigned Names and Numbers (ICANN) assigns blocks of addresses to Internet Service Providers and others who may in turn assign portions of their addresses to other users.

Three protocols often used along with IP for assigning and learning IP addresses are the dynamic host configuration protocol (DHCP), the domain name system (DNS) protocol, and the Address Resolution Protocol (ARP).

A computer functioning as a DHCP server can use DHCP to assign IP addresses to the computers in a local network. A computer that wants to learn the IP address of a domain such as *Lvr.com* can use the DNS protocol to request the information from a computer functioning as a DNS server. And a computer that wants to learn the Ethernet hardware address that corresponds to an IP address in a local network can broadcast an ARP request for this information.

Chapter 4 has more details about IP and related protocols.

A communication in a local network that doesn't use TCP or UDP may not require IP. Instead, the application layer may communicate directly with a lower layer such as the Ethernet driver.

The Ethernet Driver and Controller: The Hardware Interface

In an Ethernet network, the interface to the network is an Ethernet controller chip and its driver. The Ethernet driver contains program code that manages communications between the controller chip and a higher level in the network protocol stack. To send an IP datagram over an Ethernet network, the IP layer passes the datagram to the Ethernet controller's driver. The driver instructs the Ethernet controller to transmit an Ethernet frame containing the datagram, preceded by a header that contains addressing and error-checking information (Figure 1-4).

In receiving an IP datagram from the network, the Ethernet controller checks to see if the destination address matches the interface's hardware address or a multicast or broadcast address that the controller is configured to accept. If there is a match, the controller checks for errors and the driver passes the datagram or an error indication to the IP layer.

Chapter 3 has more about Ethernet controllers.

Clients and Servers

In some networks, the computers may send messages to other computers in the network at any time. For example, a computer that performs monitoring functions might send an alarm notification to a master computer as soon as

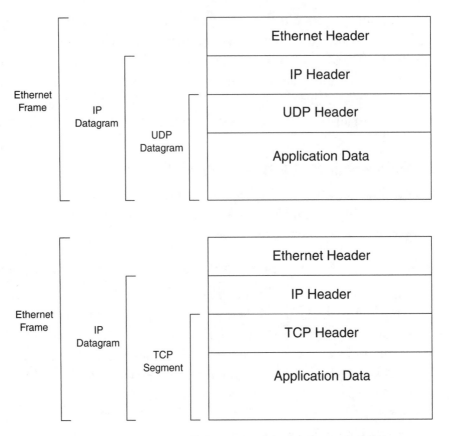

Figure 1-4: The Ethernet controller adds a header to an IP datagram before sending the datagram on the network. In the opposite direction, the Ethernet controller strips the Ethernet header before passing a datagram to the IP layer.

the condition causing the alarm occurs. The computer doesn't have to wait for the master computer to request the information.

In contrast, many other network communications are between a client computer, which requests resources, and a server computer, which provides the resources on request. A resource may be a Web page, a file, or any other information the server makes available. By running multiple processes, a single computer can function as both a client and a server.

The client and server must agree on a protocol for requesting and sending resources. For common tasks, there are standard protocols such as HTTP,

FTP, and SMTP, and POP3. The computers typically send the requests and responses in the data portions of TCP segments.

When you use a browser to view Web pages, the browser is functioning as a client, requesting pages from server computers that store Web pages. To function as a server that provides Web pages on request, a computer must be running server software. Server software for PCs includes Apache Software Foundation's Apache HTTP Server and Microsoft's Personal Web Server. Embedded systems can function as servers with the addition of program code that decodes and responds to received requests.

Another use for the terms client and server is to refer to computers that have established a TCP connection, which enables the computers to exchange messages using TCP. The client is the computer that initiated the connection, while the server is the computer that accepted the request to connect. Once the connection is established, either computer can send messages to the other, though a higher-level protocol may limit what each computer can do.

Requirements for Internet Communications

To communicate on the Internet, a computer in an Ethernet network has additional requirements. Internet communications of course require a physical connection to the Internet. And messages sent on the Internet must use the Internet Protocol.

Large businesses and schools are likely to have Internet access available. For others, obtaining an Internet connection involves contracting with an Internet Service Provider (ISP). The ISP provides an IP address that identifies the computer on the Internet.

Domain names such as *rabbitsemiconductor.com* and *dalsemi.com* provide a more user-friendly way to request a resource on the Internet, compared to using numeric IP addresses. Domain names are available from a variety of registrars for a yearly fee.

Local networks that connect to the Internet typically have a firewall, which is hardware, software, or a combination that protects the local network by limiting the types of communications that local computers can send and receive. To make a server or other resource available on the Internet, you may need to configure your firewall to permit receiving requests or other communications from outside the local network.

ilipThe focus of this book is Ethernet networks, but a computer doesn't have to have an Ethernet connection to connect to the Internet. Another option is to use a modem and a dial-up connection to an ISP, using the Point-to-Point Protocol (PPP).

Chapter 4 has more about obtaining an Internet connection.

A Word about Web Servers

Many networked embedded systems function as Web servers, which respond to requests for Web pages from browsers in the network. The pages hosted by embedded systems are likely to display dynamic content that can change each time the page is requested. Examples of dynamic content include sensor readings, date and time information, or counts of Web-page visitors. Some pages may also enable users to provide data to the server, which can process the data and perhaps return a result on a Web page.

There are several ways to support dynamic content in Web pages. Applications programmed in C often use common gateway interface (CGI) and server side include (SSI) programming. Applications programmed in Java often use Java servlets. A few products, such as Netmedia's SitePlayer, support product-specific methods that may involve defining variables and inserting codes in the Web page to cause the values of the variables to display on the page. Chapter 6 and Chapter 7 have more about Web pages and dynamic content.

In Depth: Inside Ethernet

Ethernet isn't the only way to network embedded devices, but it's a popular choice. It's possible to put together and use an Ethernet network without knowing much about its inner workings. Hardware and software compo-

14

nents with built-in Ethernet support can shield you from the details. But a little knowledge about Ethernet can help in selecting network components, writing the software that exchanges data over the network, and trouble-shooting any problems that come up.

This section discusses Ethernet's advantages and limits and how Ethernet uses frames and media-access control to help get data to its destination. Chapter 2 covers Ethernet's media systems (such as 10BASE-T), which allow a choice of cable type and network speed.

Advantages

There are many reasons why Ethernet is popular and useful for networks of embedded systems and other computers.

It's Versatile

Ethernet is versatile enough to suit many purposes. Probably the best known use for Ethernet is in linking desktop computers in offices, but that's not its only use. Ethernet can transfer any kind of data, from short messages to huge files. An Ethernet communication can take advantage of existing higher-level protocols such as TCP and IP, or it can use an application-specific protocol. Ethernet doesn't require a large or fast computer. With the addition of an Ethernet controller chip, even an 8-bit microcontroller can communicate in an Ethernet network.

It's Easy to Use

With Ethernet, much of the work has been done for you. All of the computers in the network follow standard Ethernet specifications for interconnecting, managing network traffic, and exchanging data. You don't have to design the hardware interface or invent the rules from scratch. Yet Ethernet is flexible enough to allow choices. For example, a network may use twisted pair, fiber-optic, or coaxial cable. The requirements for each cable type and speed are specified, so all you need to do is decide which cable type best fits your application and select cable of that type.

A Wide Selection of Products Is Available

Hardware, software, and debugging tools for Ethernet are readily available. Ethernet's popularity means that components and tools are easy to find and inexpensive. Many PCs and other desktop computers have Ethernet support built in. At most, a PC requires an expansion card or adapter to provide the hardware interface. Windows and other operating systems include software support for Ethernet networking.

Designers of embedded systems have a good selection of modules with Ethernet capability. Many modules include a CPU, while others contain just a controller chip and an interface that you connect to your own CPU. Or you can put together your own circuits by selecting a CPU, Ethernet controller, and related components. Code to support TCP/IP, and related protocols is available from a variety of sources. Many vendors of Ethernet-capable modules also provide support for TCP/IP. Debugging tools such as bus analyzers are readily available.

The Hardware Controls Network Access

With Ethernet, the hardware manages the network traffic, so there's no need for software to control network access. In a network that uses half-duplex interfaces, the computers share a transmission path, and all computers have equal access when the network is idle. When a computer has something to send, its Ethernet controller waits for the network to be idle and then attempts to transmit. If two or more interfaces try to transmit at the same time, the interfaces detect a collision and each delays a random amount of time, then tries again. In a network that uses full-duplex interfaces, each computer has its own transmission path to an Ethernet switch, which manages the traffic to each connected computer.

It's Fast

Ethernet is fast. It supports speeds from 10 Megabits per second (Mb/s) to 10 Gigabits per second (Gb/s). Ten Mb/s is adequate for many embedded systems. The hardware to support slower speeds is generally less expensive, but the higher speeds are there if needed.

It Can Span Long Distances

A single twisted-pair cable between two computers or between a repeater hub or switch and a computer can be 100 meters. A half-duplex segment of fiber-optic cable in a 10-Mb/s system can be as long as 2000 meters, while a full-duplex segment can be as long as 5 kilometers. With repeater hubs or switches, a network can span even longer distances. A router can enable a network to communicate with other networks, including the entire Internet.

Interfaces are Electrically Isolated

Every Ethernet interface must be electrically isolated from its network cable. The isolation protects the computer's circuits from damaging voltages that may occur on the network. Isolation transformers meeting the standard's requirements are readily available. Fiber-optic cable doesn't conduct electricity, so connections to fiber-optic networks are isolated by definition.

The Cost Is Reasonable

Because Ethernet and TCP/IP are popular, hardware and software are available from a variety of sources at reasonable cost, and sometimes for free. Support for Ethernet and TCP/IP is built into or easily added to computers of all types, including development boards for embedded systems.

Limits

Ethernet isn't the answer for every embedded system's communications needs. For some systems, there are simpler, cheaper, or otherwise more appropriate ways to network.

Cost

If keeping the cost to an absolute minimum is essential, there are cheaper interfaces that are suitable for some applications. For example, the EIA-485 interface, popularly known as RS-485, requires only very inexpensive transceivers and can use the asynchronous communications port available in most microcontrollers. RS-485 supports communications at up to 10 Mb/s and distances of up to 4000 feet, though the maximum distance decreases with speed.

A downside is that the RS-485 specification doesn't define protocols for addressing or for determining when a computer can transmit on the network, so the developer needs to provide these.

Another alternative for inexpensive short-distance networks is synchronous interfaces such as I^2C, Microwire, and Serial Peripheral Interface (SPI). Philips Semiconductor's P82B715 I^2C bus extender chip adds buffering that enables longer cables in an I^2C network. Maxim Semiconductor's 1-Wire network is another option for shorter links. Interfaces such as the Universal Serial Bus (USB) and IEEE-1394 (Firewire) provide a way for PCs to communicate with multiple peripherals.

While each of these interfaces is appropriate for some applications, none matches the combination of flexibility, speed, ease of use, and wide support that Ethernet offers.

Real-time Limits

Ethernet alone doesn't guarantee real-time transfers, or transfers that will occur with minimal delay or at precise times or intervals. Because a device may have to wait to transmit on the network, a device can't know exactly when a message will transmit. Generally though, Ethernet transmissions have minimal delays unless the network is extremely busy.

If an application requires greater control over when a transmission takes place, there's nothing in the Ethernet standard that prevents adding a protocol to support greater control within a local network. For example, a master interface could query each of the other interfaces in a local network in turn, with these interfaces transmitting only when requested by the master. With this arrangement, the master can ensure that the network is idle when an interface tries to transmit.

For some applications, the computers in the network must collect or act on data with minimal delays, but the transfer of the data in the network doesn't have to be in real time. For example, an embedded system may collect periodic measurements, then transmit a block of measurements at its leisure to a PC.

Efficiency

Ethernet isn't very efficient when transferring small amounts of data. All Ethernet data travels in structures called frames. Each frame must have between 46 and 1500 data bytes. Along with the data, each frame includes 26 bytes of synchronizing, addressing, error-detecting, and other identifying information. So to transmit a single byte of data, the frame that contains the byte must also include 26 bytes of overhead plus 45 bytes of padding. Other protocols such as TCP and IP add more overhead that a specific application may not need.

Still, all that really matters is that messages get to their destination on time, and unless the network traffic is very heavy, it generally doesn't matter if the data format isn't as efficient as possible.

Power Consumption

Ethernet isn't the best solution if your device must be extremely low power. Power consumption for an Ethernet controller chip can be 50 milliamperes or more at 5 volts. Most chips support a low-power mode that can reduce power consumption when data isn't transmitting. Still, I^2C and some EIA-485 interfaces can have much lower power consumption overall.

Using a PC for Network Communications

An option worth considering for some embedded systems is to let a PC handle the network communications. The embedded system can connect to the PC using any appropriate local interface (USB, RS-232, or parallel port). The PC can then provide the network connection and an application that transfers data between the embedded system and the network. For example, an embedded system might monitor environmental conditions and use a USB connection to send the readings to a PC. The PC might host a Web page that displays the readings. With this arrangement, the embedded system doesn't have to directly support network communications at all.

The IEEE 802.3 Standard

Just about every popular computer interface has a standard, or specification document, that serves as an ultimate reference that defines what circuit designers and programmers need to know in order to use the interface. At minimum, a standard defines the electrical characteristics of the interface's signals. A standard may also specify data formats, software protocols, connectors, and cables.

The Institute of Electrical and Electronics Engineers (IEEE) is responsible for the specification popularly known as Ethernet. The IEEE's members participate in developing and maintaining many computer-related standards. The Ethernet standard and related documents are available from *www.ieee.org*.

A Brief History

Ethernet originated at Xerox Corporation in the 1970s. An early description appeared in the article *Ethernet: Distributed Packet Switching for Local Computer Networks*, in the July 1976 issue of *Communications of the ACM*, a publication of the Association for Computing Machinery. The article was by Robert M. Metcalfe and David R. Boggs of the Xerox Palo Alto Research Center.

In 1980, Digital Equipment Corporation (DEC), Intel Corporation, and Xerox Corporation formalized Ethernet's description in a document titled *The Ethernet, a Local Area Network: Data Link Layer and Physical Layer Specifications*. Another name for this standard is DIX Ethernet, from the first letters of the companies involved. Xerox gave up its trademark rights to Ethernet, allowing the DIX standard to be an open standard not under the control of a single company.

In 1985, the IEEE released its own edition of the standard. The interface described in the IEEE standard is very similar to the DIX interface and is backward-compatible with it, so networks that comply with the DIX standard also comply with the IEEE standard.

The *Ether* in Ethernet refers to luminiferous ether, which is the name given to a hypothetical medium that was once thought to serve as the propagation medium for electromagnetic waves. The existence of ether has since been disproved, but the name lives on in the term Ethernet.

The 802.x Series

Although the Ethernet name continues in popular use, the IEEE standard uses the word sparingly. The document that describes Ethernet is IEEE Std. 802.3, with the unwieldy title of *Part 3: Carrier sense multiple access with collision detection (CSMA/CD) access method and physical layer specifications.* CSMA/CD is the method Ethernet uses for sharing the network, as described later in this chapter.

Ethernet is one in a group of IEEE standards that describe technologies for use in local and metropolitan area networks. A local network typically exists in a single room or building, while a metropolitan area network (MAN) might span a campus or city. Ethernet's main use is in local networks, though recent standards and usage have expanded its scope to larger networks such as MANs and Wide Area Networks (WANs).

All of the standards in the 802 series share the numbering convention of 802.x. The 802 signifies that the standard relates to local or metropolitan area networking, and *x* represents one or more digits that identify the specific standard.

The Ethernet standard is one of several 802-series standards that define alternate approaches for a network's physical layer and method of media-access control, which defines how computers share a network. The physical layer described in the standard includes the electrical specifications of the transceivers and the electrical and physical specifications of the connectors and cables. Media-access control includes how each computer knows when it can transmit and how the computers identify the intended receiver of a transmission.

Over the years, the IEEE has published a variety of supplements to the original Ethernet standard. In periodic updates of the main standard, the IEEE incorporates the supplements into the main standard. For example, the supplement for Gigabit Ethernet, 802.3z, is now part of the 802.3 standard.

The 802.3ae amendment, approved in 2002, adds support for 10-Gigabit Ethernet.

Options for Ethernet cables in the 802.3 standard include coaxial, twisted-pair, and fiber-optic cables. The 802.11 standard is a separate document that covers methods of wireless networking.

The 802.3 standard allows four network speeds. The original standard supported only 10 Mb/s. The standard now also supports 100 Mb/s, often called Fast Ethernet, 1 Gb/s (Gigabit Ethernet), and 10 Gb/s (10-Gigabit Ethernet, also called 10GbE).

Frames

All data in an Ethernet network travels in structures called frames. An Ethernet frame has defined fields for data and other information to help the data get to its destination and to help the destination computer determine whether the data has arrived intact.

The Ethernet controller's hardware places information to be sent in frames for transmitting, and extracts and stores the information in received frames.

Table 1-1 shows the fields in an IEEE 802.3 Ethernet frame. The fields add synchronizing bits, addressing information, an error-checking sequence, and additional identifying information to the data being sent.

Preamble and Start Frame Delimiter

The Preamble and Start Frame Delimiter fields function together. They provide a predictable bit pattern that enables the interfaces on a 10-Mb/s network to synchronize to, or match the timing of, a new frame being transmitted.

In any data link, the receiving interface needs to know when to read the bits in the transmitted data. Some interfaces, such as I^2C, are synchronous interfaces that include a clock line shared by all of the devices. With I^2C, the transmitting device writes bits when the clock is low, and a receiving device reads the bits when the clock is high.

Table 1-1: An IEEE 802.3 Ethernet frame has seven fields.

Field	Length in bytes	Purpose
Preamble	7	Synchronization pattern.
Start Frame Delimiter	1	End of synchronization pattern.
Destination Address	6	Ethernet hardware address the frame is directed to.
Source Address	6	Ethernet hardware address of the sender.
Length or Type	2	If 1500 (05DCh) or less, the length of the data field in bytes. If 1536 (0600h) or greater, the protocol used by the contents of the data field.
Data	46 to 1500	The information the source wants to send to the destination.
Frame Check Sequence	4	Error-checking value.

Other interfaces, such as Ethernet, are asynchronous, which means that the interfaces don't share a clock. RS-232 and other serial interfaces that use a UART (universal asynchronous receiver transmitter) are asynchronous. Each transmitted word begins with a Start bit. The receiver uses the leading edge of the Start bit as a timing reference to predict when to read each of the bits that will follow. An RS-232 character typically has eight or nine bits that follow the Start bit.

In contrast, a single Ethernet frame may contain over 1000 bits. Detecting a single voltage change at the beginning of a frame isn't enough to enable the interface to reliably predict when to read all of the bits that follow.

For 10-Mb/s Ethernet, the solution is to begin each frame with a known bit pattern that contains many transitions. Receiving interfaces use the pattern to synchronize to, or lock onto, the transmitted frame's clock.

The Preamble and Start of Frame Delimiter fields provide this pattern. The Preamble consists of seven identical bytes, each with the value 10101010. The Start Frame Delimiter follows the Preamble, and consists of the byte 10101011. After detecting the first transition in the Preamble, a receiving interface uses the transitions of the following bits to synchronize to the timing of the transmitting interface. The final two bits in the Start Frame Delimiter indicate the end of the Preamble.

The faster Ethernet interfaces use different methods to synchronize, but include the Preamble for compatibility.

In the earlier DIX standard, the Preamble frame is 64 bits and includes the Start-of-Frame byte, while the 802.3 standard defines the Start of Frame as a separate field. The transmitted bit patterns are the same in both cases.

Destination Address

Every Ethernet interface has a 48-bit physical, or hardware, address that identifies the interface on the network. The Destination Address field contains the physical address of the intended receiver of the frame. The receiver may be an individual interface, a group of interfaces identified by a multicast address, or a broadcast address to all interfaces in the network.

Every interface in the network reads the destination address of a received frame. If the address doesn't match the interface's physical address or a multicast or broadcast address the interface has been configured to accept, the interface ignores the rest of the frame.

The first two transmitted bits in the address have special meanings. The first bit is 0 if the address is for a single interface, and 1 if the address is a multicast or broadcast address. A broadcast address is all 1s and is directed to every interface in the network. Multicasting provides a way for an interface to communicate with a selected group of interfaces. The interfaces in the multicast group are configured to accept frames sent to a specific multicast address.

The second bit of the destination address is zero if the address was assigned by the manufacturer of the interface, which is the usual case. In the 802.3 standard, the second bit is 1 if the address is administered locally. In the DIX standard, the second bit is always zero.

Chapter 4 has more about how a sending interface learns the destination's address.

Source Address

The Source Address field contains the 48-bit physical address of the transmitting interface. See Destination Address above for more about Ethernet addresses.

Length/Type

The Length/Type field is 16 bits that can have one of two meanings. The field can indicate the number of bytes of valid data in the data field or the protocol used by the data in the field that follows.

If the value is less than or equal to 1500 decimal (5DCh), the value indicates length. The data field must contain between 46 and 1500 bytes. If there are less than 46 bytes of valid, or usable, data, the length field can indicate how many of the bytes are valid data.

If the value is greater than or equal to 1536 decimal (600h), the Length/Type field indicates the protocol that the contents of the data field use. On on-line database at the Internet Assigned Numbers Authority's Web site (*www.iana.org*) specifies values for different protocols. The value for the Internet Protocol (IP) is 800h.

Values from 1501 to 1535 decimal are undefined.

The DIX standard defined this field as a type field only. The original IEEE 802.3 standard defined the field as a length field only. The current 802.3 standard allows either use.

Data

The contents of the data field are the reason why the frame exists. The data is the information that the transmitting interface wants to send.

The data field must be between 46 and 1500 bytes. If there are fewer than 46 bytes of data, the field must include pad bytes to increase the size to 46 bytes. If the transmitting interface has more than 1500 bytes to send, it uses multiple frames.

As explained earlier in this chapter, the data field often contains additional information besides the raw data being sent. This information is typically in headers that precede the data. The Ethernet frame doesn't care what's in the data field, as long as it meets the length requirements.

Another term for the contents of the data field is the message. The data payload, or message body, is the message minus any headers or other supplemental information in the data field.

Frames with a full 1500 data bytes are the most efficient because they have just 26 bytes, or less than 2 percent, of overhead. At the other extreme, a frame with just one data byte plus 26 bytes of headers and the required 45 bytes of padding has 71 bytes of overhead.

An Ethernet frame must be at least 512 bits (64 bytes) not including the Preamble and Start-of-Frame bits. This is the size of a frame with the minimum 46 data bytes. Receiving interfaces ignore frames that are shorter than this minimum size.

Frame Check Sequence

The Frame Check Sequence (FCS) field enables the receiving interface to detect errors in a received frame.

Electrical noise or other problems in the network can corrupt a frame's contents. A receiving interface can detect corrupted data by using the 32-bit cyclic redundancy check (CRC) value in the frame check sequence field. The transmitting interface performs a calculation, called the cyclic redundancy check, on the bytes to be sent and places the result in the frame check sequence field. The receiving interface performs the same calculation on the received bytes. If the results match, the frame's contents are almost certain to be identical to what was sent.

The Ethernet controller's hardware typically performs the CRC calculations on both ends. On detecting an error in a received frame, the controller typically sets a bit in a status register.

Media Access Control: Deciding When to Transmit

In Ethernet networks that use half-duplex interfaces, only one interface at a time can transmit, so the interfaces need a way of deciding when it's OK to transmit. The Ethernet standard refers to the method of deciding who gets to transmit as *media access control*.

There are several ways to achieve media access control. In some networks, one computer is the master, and the other computers transmit only after receiving permission from the master. The USB interface uses this type of media-access control. In a token-passing network, the computers take turns. The token can be as basic as a register bit or sequence of bits that a computer sets to indicate possession. Only the computer holding the token can transmit. When a computer finishes transmitting, it passes the token to another computer. The token-ring network described in IEEE standard 802.5 is an example of a token-passing network.

Ethernet uses a media-access control method called *carrier sense multiple access with collision detection*, or CSMA/CD. This method allows any interface to attempt to transmit any time the network is idle. If two or more interfaces try to transmit at the same time, both wait a bit, then retry.

One way to understand how CSMA/CD works is to examine the words that make up the term. *Carrier* comes from the world of radio, where audio broadcasts ride on, or are carried by, a higher frequency called the carrier. Ethernet doesn't have a carrier in this sense. Instead, the carrier is said to be present whenever an interface is transmitting. *Carrier sense* means that an interface that wants to transmit must monitor the network and sense, or detect, when the network is idle, indicated by the absence of a carrier.

Multiple access means that no single interface controls the network traffic. Any interface can attempt to transmit on a network that has been idle for at least the amount of time defined as the interframe gap (IFG). In a 10Mb/s network, the IFG equals 96 bit times, or 9.6 microseconds.

The Ethernet controller's hardware normally handles the sending and receiving of frames, including detecting collisions and deciding when to try again after a collision. The CPU writes the data to send into memory that the controller can access, and the controller stores received data in memory that the CPU can access. The CPU uses interrupts or polling to learn of the success or failure of a transmission and the arrival of received data.

Responding to Collisions

A collision results when two interfaces in the same *collision domain* try to transmit at the same time. In half-duplex Ethernet networks, the computers connect to repeater hubs that provide attachment points for multiple interfaces. All of the interfaces that connect via repeater hubs share a collision domain, which means that every network transmission goes out to all of the interfaces. Interfaces that connect directly via coaxial cable also share a collision domain.

Another option for connecting interfaces is to use switching hubs, popularly called Ethernet switches, or just switches. Like repeater hubs, Ethernet switches provide attachment points for multiple interfaces, but interfaces that connect via switches don't share a collision domain. Instead, the switches are responsible for managing the storing and forwarding of traffic received from connected interfaces. Chapter 2 has more about repeater hubs and switches and the options for connecting interfaces.

On detecting a collision, the transmitting interface doesn't stop transmitting immediately. Instead, it continues long enough to be sure that the other transmitting interface(s) have time to detect the collision. A transmitting interface that has detected a collision always finishes sending the 64 bits of the Preamble and Start of Frame Delimiter if these haven't transmitted yet. Following these, the interface sends an additional 32 bits called the jam signal, then stops transmitting. The jam signal can be any arbitrary data except the previous frame's CRC value.

Delaying before Retransmitting

After an interface stops transmitting due to a collision, the next task is deciding when to try again. If two interfaces wait the same amount of time and then retry, another collision will occur. Instead, the Ethernet standard defines a backoff process where each interface selects a randomly chosen delay time before attempting to retransmit. This reduces the chance that two interfaces will retry at the same time, although multiple retries may be needed at times.

The delays before retrying are multiples of the interface's slot time, which is specified in units of bit times. For 10-Mb/s and Fast Ethernet, the slot time is 512 bit times, which works out to 51.2 microseconds at 10 Mb/s and 5.12 microseconds at 100 Mb/s. For Gigabit Ethernet, the slot time is 4096 bit times, or 4.096 microseconds.

For the first retry, an interface chooses randomly between retrying immediately or waiting one slot time before retrying. If the first retry results in a collision, the interface tries again, randomly selecting a delay of 0, 1, 2, or 3 slot times.

Each new attempt, up to ten tries, selects from a larger range of backoff times, as Table 1-2 shows. The formula for determining the number of slot times to choose from is 2^x, where x is the number of the retry. In the first retry, the interface selects between 2^1, or 2, slot times (0 or 1). The second retry selects from 2^2, or 4, slot times (0, 1, 2, or 3). And so on up to 2^{10}, or 1024 slot times (0 to 1023), which the interface uses for the final seven retries if needed. After 16 tries, the interface gives up and reports a failure, typically with an interrupt.

Network Limits to Ensure Collision Detection

To prevent an interface from trying to use a frame that has experienced a collision, a transmitting interface must be able to detect the collision and abandon the frame before transmitting for one slot time. The IEEE 802.3 standard specifies slot times and maximum cable lengths to ensure that a transmitting interface will always be able to detect a collision in time.

For 10-Mb/s and Fast Ethernet, one slot time equals the time required to transmit 512 bits, which is the minimum frame size minus the Preamble and Start Frame Delimiter.

For Gigabit Ethernet, the minimum frame size is still 512 bits, but the slot time is 4096 bits and a valid transmission must have at least 4096 bits. To extend a short frame to 4096 bits, the transmitting interface has two options. It can follow the frame with carrier extension bits, which are non-data symbols that keep the carrier present for the required time. Or for

Table 1-2: For each retry after a collision, the Ethernet controller selects from a larger number of delay times.

Retry number	Possible delay times, in units of slot time, chosen randomly
1	0 or 1
2	0, 1, 2, 3
3	0 to, 1, 2, 3, 4, 5, 6, 7
4	0, 1, 2, 3, 4, 5, 6, 7, 8, 9, 10, 11, 12, 13, 14, 15
5	0, 1, 2, 3, 4, 5, 6, 7, 8, 9, 10, 11, 12, 13, 14, 15....30, 31
6	0, 1, 2, 3, 4, 5, 6, 7, 8, 9, 10, 11, 12, 13, 14, 15.... 62, 63
7	0, 1, 2, 3, 4, 5, 6, 7, 8, 9, 10, 11, 12, 13, 14, 15....126, 127
8	0, 1, 2, 3, 4, 5, 6, 7, 8, 9, 10, 11, 12, 13, 14, 15....254, 255
9	0, 1, 2, 3, 4, 5, 6, 7, 8, 9, 10, 11, 12, 13, 14, 15....510, 511
10	0, 1, 2, 3, 4, 5, 6, 7, 8, 9, 10, 11, 12, 13, 14, 15....1022, 1023
11	0, 1, 2, 3, 4, 5, 6, 7, 8, 9, 10, 11, 12, 13, 14, 15....1022, 1023
12	0, 1, 2, 3, 4, 5, 6, 7, 8, 9, 10, 11, 12, 13, 14, 15...1022, 1023
13	0, 1, 2, 3, 4, 5, 6, 7, 8, 9, 10, 11, 12, 13, 14, 15....1022, 1023
14	0, 1, 2, 3, 4, 5, 6, 7, 8, 9, 10, 11, 12, 13, 14, 15....1022, 1023
15	0, 1, 2, 3, 4, 5, 6, 7, 8, 9, 10, 11, 12, 13, 14, 15....1022, 1023
16	0, 1, 2, 3, 4, 5, 6, 7, 8, 9, 10, 11, 12, 13, 14, 15....1022, 1023
17	report failure

all frames after the first, the interface may send a burst of additional frames to fill the slot time.

Full-duplex Interfaces

An Ethernet interface can be half duplex or full duplex. With a half-duplex interface, the computer can't send data while receiving. With a full-duplex interface, the computer can transmit and receive at the same time.

Full duplex has several advantages. A full-duplex Ethernet segment doesn't need to support collision detecting because there are no collisions to detect. With two data paths available, a full-duplex segment can theoretically support twice the traffic of a half-duplex segment at the same speed. For fiber-optic links, the maximum allowed segment lengths are much greater for full duplex. In half-duplex segments, the data's round-trip travel time must be short enough to ensure that collisions are detected in time. The length of full-duplex fiber-optic segments are limited only by optical losses in the fiber.

A full-duplex segment can link two computers, a computer and a switch, or two switches. Full-duplex segments are common in high-speed links between switches. Inexpensive Ethernet switches have made full-duplex links popular for segments that connect computers to their networks as well.

The cabling to support full duplex is present in all of the popular twisted-pair and fiber-optic media systems. Most full-duplex Ethernet media systems use a separate cable pair or fiber strand for each direction. Twisted-pair Gigabit Ethernet systems use hybrid circuits that enable simultaneous transmitting and receiving on the same wires.

To use full duplex, the interface's Ethernet controller must support full-duplex mode. Many controllers have options to configure the controller to support half or full duplex or to auto-negotiate, using full duplex if possible and half duplex otherwise. If you're using a module with provided Ethernet-controller software, the software will need to support full-duplex mode and auto-negotiation if you want to use these capabilities in the controller.

Physical Addresses

To send an Ethernet frame on the network, a computer places its physical address in the Source Address field and the places destination's physical address in the Destination Address field. The physical address has two parts, a 24-bit Organizationally Unique Identifier (OUI) that identifies the interface's manufacturer and an additional 24 bits that are unique to the piece of hardware.

For a fee, the IEEE grants the rights to use an OUI. At this writing, it's a one-time fee of $1650. An interface card purchased for a PC or an embedded-system module with an Ethernet interface typically has a physical address programmed into the hardware. If you use an address provided in this way, you can be just about 100% sure that the physical address won't match the address of any other interface your interface might communicate with. (And if it does, it's not your fault.)

If you want to assign a different, locally administered address, some products enable changing the address.

The physical address is often expressed as a series of six hexadecimal bytes:

00-90-C2-C0-D3-EA

In the above example, 00-90-C2 is the OUI and C0-D3-EA is the unique value assigned by the owner of the OUI to a specific piece of hardware.

Each byte has a decimal value from 0 to 255. The IEEE 802.3 standard and other network standards use the more precise term *octet* instead of byte. In common usage, both terms refer to 8-bit values, but an alternate definition for byte is "the data size sufficient to hold a character," and this value can vary with the computer system.

Sometimes the sending computer doesn't know the receiving computer's physical address. To learn the physical address that corresponds to an IP address in the local network, a computer can send a broadcast message using the address resolution protocol (ARP). To obtain the IP address that corresponds to an Internet domain name, the sending computer can use the DNS protocol to send a request to a domain name server.

When transmitting to a computer outside its local network, including on the Internet, an interface sends the Ethernet frames to a router in the local network, and the router does what is needed to send the message on its way. Chapter 4 has more on ARP, domain name servers, and routers.

Using a Protocol Analyzer to View Ethernet Traffic

In troubleshooting network problems, it's often helpful to be able to view the network traffic to find out exactly what is (and isn't) transmitting. A protocol analyzer makes this possible and can be extremely helpful in tracking down problems. A protocol analyzer may be software only or it may be a hardware device that runs analyzer software.

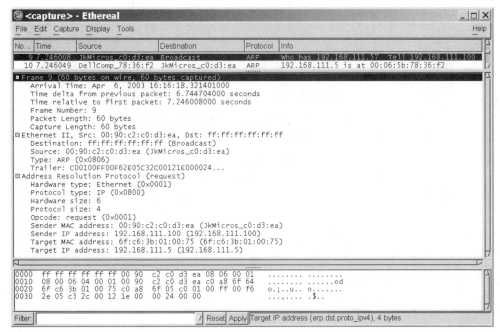

Figure 1-5: The Ethereal Network Protocol Analyzer decodes and displays Ethernet traffic.

The Ethereal Network Protocol Analyzer

The Ethereal Network Protocol Analyzer is a full-featured and free protocol analyzer from Gerald Combs and others, available from *www.ethereal.com*. You can use Ethereal to view the contents of Ethernet frames along with timing and other information. The software decodes data for over 300 network protocols. Figure 1-5 shows data captured by Ethereal during a response to an ARP request for a computer's Ethernet hardware address.

You can run Ethereal from any PC in the network you're monitoring. To ensure that the frames you want to see are visible, the PC running Ethereal should be in the same collision domain as the computer whose traffic you're monitoring.

Other Options

Ethereal is one of a variety of software-based protocol analyzers for Ethernet. Another option for viewing network traffic is to use a hardware analyzer that you plug into an available port in the network. An example is Agilent Technology's J6800A Network Analyzer. The J6800A is a portable system that contains an embedded PC running network analyzer software. You can control the analyzer remotely over a network or dial-up connection. A traffic generator enables you to specify traffic to place on the network. Two time-synchronized data acquisition systems enable comparing two locations at once.

2

Building a Network: Hardware Options

Putting together an Ethernet network requires making choices about network speed, cable type, and methods of connecting the computers to the network. The options are the same whether the network connects PCs, embedded systems, or a combination. If you're adding an embedded system to an existing network, you need to ensure that your system's speed and cabling are compatible with the network.

In developing a networked embedded system, it's likely that you'll want to connect the system to a PC at some point. A Web browser or other application on a PC can provide a handy way to monitor and control the operation of embedded systems. Even if the final configuration doesn't require PC communications, a PC can be useful for testing device firmware before you add other network computers or an Internet connection.

This chapter begins with a guide to using Ethernet to connect an embedded system to a PC. Following this is a discussion of the options for cable types, network speeds, and methods of interconnecting computers in Ethernet networks.

Quick Start: Connecting to a PC

If you don't yet have an embedded system with an Ethernet interface, learning how to connect a system to a PC may seem to be a little ahead of the game. But understanding something about network configurations and options can be useful in deciding what cable type and speed an embedded system's interface should support.

Components and Configurations

A popular configuration for networked embedded systems follows the specification for the 10BASE-T media system in the Ethernet standard. A 10BASE-T network uses twisted-pair cables with a network speed of 10 Mb/s. Many Ethernet-capable modules have built-in support for 10BASE-T networking, and any recent-vintage standard PC with Ethernet support will support 10BASE-T as well.

To connect a PC to an embedded system in a 10BASE-T network, you need the following components:

A PC with Ethernet support and a 10BASE-T interface. To find out what kind of network support a PC has, look in Windows' Device Manager under Network adapters (Figure 2-1). To view the Device Manager in Windows XP, click in order **Start, Settings, Control Panel, System, Hardware**, and **Device Manager**. Or in any recent Windows edition, from the Windows desktop, press **F1** and search for *Device Manager*. The adapter's name usually includes the supported speed or speeds. An **Advanced** tab may also offer choices under Media Type. For example, you may be able to configure a multi-speed, autoswitching card to use one speed only. (This option can be useful if your PC connects to a multi-speed repeater hub and you want to view network traffic at another speed in a protocol analyzer.)

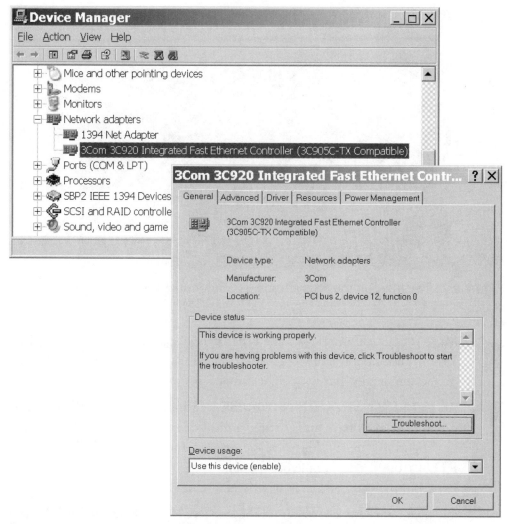

Figure 2-1: In Windows' Device Manager, the Network adapters category shows any installed Ethernet adapters.

For PCs that don't already have a 10BASE-T interface, there are several options. You can add a network interface card that plugs into the computer's internal PCI bus. Or you can use a USB/Ethernet adapter that attaches to a USB port or an Ethernet/PC Card adapter that plugs into a PC Card (PCMCIA) slot.

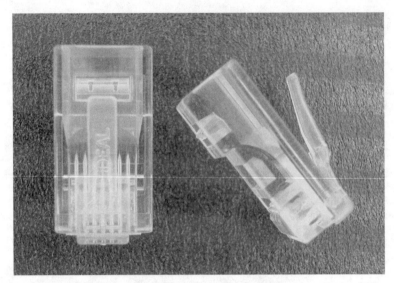

Figure 2-2: Twisted-pair media systems use 8-conductor RJ-45 connectors.

Most 10BASE-T interfaces, like other twisted-pair Ethernet interfaces, use RJ-45 connectors (Figure 2-2). These are similar in design to modular telephone connectors, but with eight contacts instead of four.

An embedded system with a 10BASE-T Ethernet interface. The embedded system must have an Ethernet controller, which may be a discrete chip or a portion of a chip that performs other functions. The Realtek RTL8019AS is an example of a popular controller chip for 10BASE-T systems, but there are others, as described in Chapter 3.

Chapter 3 also describes several Ethernet-capable modules that each have an Ethernet controller and related components. If you're designing your own circuit from the ground up, the companies that produce controller chips generally provide example schematics and application hints for using the chips.

A cable to connect the PC and embedded system or a repeater hub or Ethernet switch and cables to connect to it. The number and type of cables depends on whether you're connecting the PC and embedded system

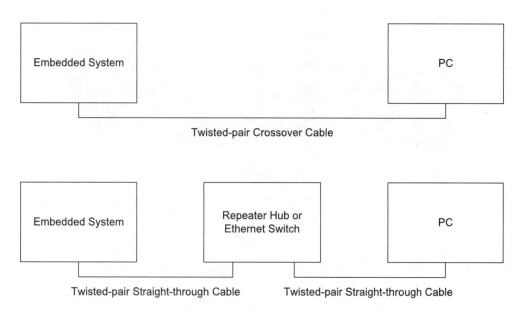

Figure 2-3: To connect an embedded system to a PC's 10BASE-T Ethernet interface, you can use a direct connection with a crossover cable or a repeater hub or switch with straight-through, or 1-to-1, cables.

to each other directly or through a repeater hub or switch. Figure 2-3 shows both options.

Twisted-pair Ethernet cable is available in two wiring configurations: straight-through, also called 1-to-1, and crossover. In a straight-through cable, the connections on both connectors are the same. For example, on both connectors, pin 6 connects to the green wire, and pin 2 connects to the orange wire. In a crossover cable, the pin connections for some of the wires are swapped from one of the cable to the other. For example, on one connector, pin 2 connects to the orange wire and pin 6 connects to the green wire, while at the other end of the cable, pin 2 connects to the green wire and pin 6 connects to the orange wire. The In Depth section of this chapter has more about crossover cables.

To connect an embedded system directly to a PC, all you need is a crossover cable rated as Category 3 or higher. For use at higher speeds, the IEEE 802.3 standard recommends Category 5e cable, and Category 5e or Category 6

39

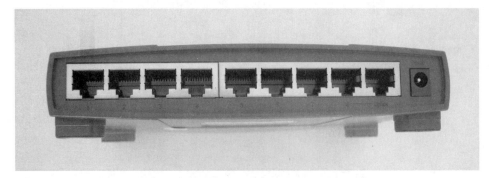

Figure 2-4: A hub has multiple ports for connecting interfaces to a network.

cable can be a good investment if you might eventually use a higher speed. Category 5 cable is also acceptable. In some electrically noisy environments, Category 5 may be preferable, as explained later in this chapter.

Crossover cables are widely available. The cable should have an RJ-45 plug at each end and can be up to 100 meters long.

If your PC is already in a network, or if you want to connect more than one embedded system to the PC, use a repeater hub or Ethernet switch. These are devices with connection points for multiple cables (Figure 2-4). To connect an embedded system to a PC through a repeater hub or Ethernet switch, use straight-through cables rated as Category 3 or higher. Again, Category 5, Category 5e, or Category 6 cable is also acceptable.

Additional PCs or embedded systems can attach to the remaining ports of the repeater hub or Ethernet switch. Repeater hubs and switches are widely available. Generally, to use a repeater hub or switch, you just attach the cables, apply power, and the device is ready for use.

Other Options

Although 10BASE-T networks are popular, they don't suit every purpose. Some networks require faster communications or a different cable type.

If 10 Mb/s isn't fast enough, you can upgrade to Fast Ethernet, at 100 Mb/s. Use cables rated as Category 5 or better. Gigabit Ethernet uses the same cables, but because the interface is newer, the selection of controller chips and other hardware is more limited. To gain the full advantage of a higher speed, any repeater hubs or switches between the computers that are communicating must support the higher speed as well.

Fiber-optic cable has advantages over twisted-pair cable, including immunity to electrical interference and lightning damage, immunity to security breaches due to monitoring by direct or magnetic coupling, and greater maximum cable length. The down side is more expensive cables, repeater hubs, switches, and interfaces. Converter modules are available if you need to connect an embedded system with a twisted-pair interface to a repeater hub or switch with fiber-optic connectors.

Another option for 10 Mb/s networks is coaxial cable. Coaxial cable has fallen out of favor for Ethernet because it's limited to 10 Mb/s and because twisted-pair networks are less expensive and easier to work with. But if you're adding to an existing network that uses coaxial cable, you'll need compatible interfaces for the devices you connect to the network. Some repeater hubs include a BNC connector for coaxial cable in addition to RJ-45 jacks, to make it easy to add twisted-pair interfaces to a coaxial network.

In Depth:
Cables, Connections and Network Speed

A network interface can't do much without a connection to the other computers in the network. This section has more detail about the choices for cabling and other hardware required for interconnecting computers in networks of different speeds.

Cable Types for Different Uses

The Ethernet standard allows the use of three cable types: twisted-pair, fiber-optic, and coaxial cable. Table 2-1 summarizes the features of each cable type.

Table 2-1: Ethernet allows a choice of three types of cable.

Cable Type	Twisted Pair	Fiber Optic	Coaxial
Maximum data rate (Mb/sec.)	1000	10,000	10
Maximum length per segment (meters)	100+	2000 (half duplex, 10 Mb/s), 5000 (full duplex, 10 Mb/s)	500 (thick coax), 185 (thin coax)
Cost	low	high	moderate
Noise immunity	good	excellent	good
Ease of Installation	excellent	good with prefabricated cables, fair/poor if attaching connectors on raw cable	fair/poor

Twisted-pair cable is popular because it's inexpensive yet performs well. Fiber-optic cable is immune to electromagnetic interference and can carry signals much longer distances, but at higher cost. Coaxial cable was the original cable type for Ethernet and isn't recommended for new networks. Transceivers for coaxial-cable systems can be hard to find.

The IEEE 802.3 standard defines a variety of *media systems* that each use a particular cable type at a specific bit rate. For example, the 10BASE-T media system uses unshielded twisted pair cable at 10 Mb/s.

If you're connecting your embedded systems to an existing network, and if the embedded system uses a different media system than the network, cable converters and multi-speed repeater hubs and switches are available.

Cable Categories

To simplify the task of selecting a cable type, various documents define cable categories according to performance, interconnection method, and other characteristics. The IEEE 802.3 standard in turn references these categories. This way, instead of having to find a match between a manufacturer's products and a series of specifications, you can just look for cable of the category recommended for your network's cable type and speed. Many cable manufacturers specify when a product is suitable for a specific media system, such as fiber-optic cable that meets the requirements for a 10BASE-FL media system.

An important document for specifying networking cable is *TIA/EIA 568: Commercial Building Telecommunications Cabling Standards*. The document's sponsors are two trade groups: the Telecommunications Industry Association (TIA) and the Electronic Industries Association (EIA).

The TIA/EIA-568-B edition of the standard, released in 2001, covers fiber-optic and twisted-pair cable. The earlier (-A) edition also covered coaxial cable, but the new edition doesn't recommend coaxial cable for new installations.

The IEEE 802.3 standard also references *ISO-IEC 11801: Information Technology - Generic Cabling For Customer Premises*. This standard is a product of the International Organization for Standardization (ISO) and the International Electrotechnical Commission (IEC). The standard duplicates much of the contents of TIA/EIA 568, with minor differences and the addition of information relating to components used primarily in Europe.

For fiber-optic cable, the IEEE 802.3 standard references documents from the IEC and the American National Standards Institute (ANSI).

All of the documents are available from Global Engineering Documents (*www.global.ihs.com*).

In addition to these standards, for fire safety, the U.S. National Electric Code (NEC) rates cables according to flammability, heat resistance, and visible smoke on exposure to flame. Three categories specify permitted uses. General-purpose cable is for use on a single floor, but not for routing through floors or ceilings. Riser cable may pass between floors but may not be routed through a plenum, which is any area that functions as a part of the heating, ventilation, and air conditioning (HVAC) system. Plenum cable is suitable for all locations, including routing through plenums. Non-plenum cable may be allowed in plenum spaces if enclosed in metal conduit. Local building codes may have additional requirements.

This book doesn't attempt to cover the craft of cable routing. A good guide is *Cabling: the Complete Guide to Network Wiring* by David Grott, Jim McBee, and David Barnett (Sybex).

Attaching Connectors

For all cable types, you can buy cables with connectors attached or attach connectors to raw cable yourself. Attaching connectors to twisted-pair cable is fairly straightforward and requires just a few tools. Attaching connectors to fiber-optic cable is more complicated and requires a greater investment in materials and equipment.

Twisted Pair Cable

Twisted-pair cable is popular because it's inexpensive, yet it can carry signals over long distances. The twists reduce noise in the cable in two ways: by reducing the size of the magnetic field that emanates from the wires and by canceling any noise the wires pick up via magnetic coupling.

Cable Categories

Networks of all three speeds can use cable that meets the Category 5e specification defined in EIA/TIA-568-B. A Category 5e cable contains four unshielded twisted pairs (UTPs) of wires. Each pair consists of two insulated conductors that spiral, or twist, around each other, with about one to three twists per inch (Figure 2-5). Varying the number of twists per inch from pair to pair helps to reduce noise in the wires. The wire diameter is 24 or 22 AWG. An outer layer of insulation surrounds the pairs.

The conductors may be solid or stranded. A stranded conductor, which consists of many small-diameter wires, can withstand repeated flexing and is a good choice for patch cords and other uses where you're likely to move or reroute the cable frequently. A solid conductor, which is a single, larger-diameter wire, has better electrical performance but may break after repeated flexing. Solid conductors are a good choice inside walls and in other locations where the wiring doesn't move once installed.

In the EIA/TIA-568-B standard, Category 5e cable replaces the Category 5 cable recommended in earlier editions of the standard. Although Category 5 cable is acceptable for all three Ethernet speeds, Category 5e cable has

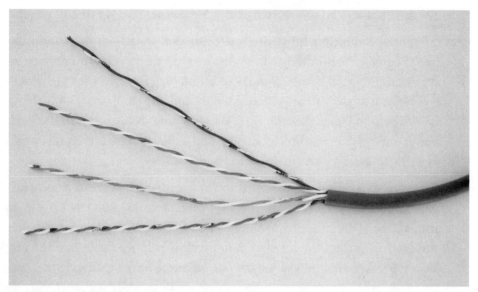

Figure 2-5: Twisted-pair cable for Ethernet contains four pairs of wires, with the wires in each pair twisted around each other.

stricter manufacturing and testing specifications, and the standard recommends it for new installations. In 2002, an addendum to the standard defined a new cable type, Category 6 cable, which has improved performance over Category 5e. Category 6 cable is suitable for all twisted-pair Ethernet networks with the exception of some networks in industrial environments, as explained later in this chapter.

For 10-Mb/s Ethernet, you can use lower-quality Category 3 cable, but Category 5 or greater doesn't cost much more and won't need changing if you later upgrade to a faster speed.

A 10-Mb/s or Fast Ethernet cable segment uses two of the four pairs in a cable. One pair carries data in each direction. In a 10-Mb/s segment, phone wiring can use the other two pairs, though there is some risk of interference and the wires will need to be moved if you upgrade to a higher speed. So it's best to use separate cables for phone lines and networking if possible. Gigabit Ethernet uses all four wire pairs in a complex signaling protocol that enables all eight wires to transmit and receive at the same time.

All three speeds can use twisted-pair cable segments of up to 100 meters.

The usual connectors for twisted-pair Ethernet are RJ-45 plugs and jacks. A cable segment's performance is no greater than the lowest rating of the cable, its connectors, and the jacks the connectors plug into. To gain the benefit of a cable's rated performance, the cable should use connectors with the same or better rating, and the connectors should plug into jacks with the same or better rating. For example, Category 5e cable should use connectors and jacks rated as Category 5e or Category 6.

Ethernet transceivers are designed to work with cables that have a characteristic impedance of 100 ohms. A cable's characteristic impedance is the input impedance of an infinite, open line. The value varies with the wire diameter, the spacing of the wires in relation to each other in the cable, and the insulation type. A line's physical length has no effect on its characteristic impedance. There are techniques for calculating or measuring characteristic impedance, but you shouldn't have to resort to these. Cable manufacturers specify the characteristic impedance of cables suitable for networking.

Category 3 through Category 6 cable all have 100-ohm characteristic impedance. Using cable with a different characteristic impedance can degrade signal quality and result in data errors.

The wires in the twisted-pair cables are color-coded (Table 2-2), with a color (blue, orange, green, or brown) assigned to each twisted pair. One wire in the pair is predominantly white with colored stripes or splashes and the other wire in the pair is predominantly colored, with optional white stripes or splashes. For example, if one wire in a pair is blue, the other wire in the pair is predominantly white with blue stripes.

The electrical interface for twisted-pair cable uses differential signaling, which requires two wires to carry a signal. The voltage on one wire is the negative, or complement, of the voltage on the other wire. The receiver detects the difference between the voltages, and any noise that is common to both wires cancels out. A line that uses differential signaling is called a balanced line.

Table 2-2: Category 5 cable contains four color-coded twisted pairs.

Pair Number	Predominant Color	Stripe or Splash Color
1	White	Blue
	Blue	White or none
2	White	Orange
	Orange	White or none
3	White	Green
	Green	White or none
4	White	Brown
	Brown	White or none

Shielded Twisted-pair Cable

Unshielded cables aren't the only choices available for twisted-pair cables. Ethernet networks can also use shielded cable. A shield can reduce noise due to capacitive, electromagnetic, and high-frequency magnetic coupling. The TIA-EIA-568 standard specifies requirements for two shielded-cable types suitable for Ethernet networks: 100-ohm screened twisted-pair (ScTP) cable and 150-ohm shielded twisted-pair (STP) cable.

In ScTP cable, the shielding consists of a layer of plastic and metal tape surrounding the pairs and a conductive drain wire or braid contacting the metal side of the tape. In STP cable, each pair has its own shield as well. STP cable requires $100\Omega{:}150\Omega$ transformers for impedance matching between the 150-ohm cable and the 100-ohm network interface.

Connectors for shielded cable must also be shielded, with a continuous shield from the cable to the connector. The shield should be grounded at one end only.

Shielded cable is more expensive and many networks don't need it. For 10-Mb/s networks, the IEEE 802.3 standard doesn't forbid shielded cable but says that unshielded twisted pairs meet most networks' requirements. A Fast Ethernet cable segment may use unshielded or shielded twisted-pair cable. For Gigabit Ethernet, the standard just says that the use of shielded cable is outside the scope of the document.

Connector Wiring

There are two common pinouts for the RJ-45 connectors used with twisted-pair cable: T568A and T568B (Table 2-3). The TIA/EIA-568-B standard allows either, but recommends T568A. (The similarity in names between the TIA/EIA-568-B standard and the T568B pinout is coincidental.)

As the illustration shows, the only difference between the two pinouts is the swapping of the wires in pairs 2 and 3.

Within a cable (except for crossover cables), both ends must use the same pinout. The only difference between the two pinouts is the color of the wires at the pins. With T568A, pins 1 and 2 are the green pair and pins 3 and 6 are the orange pair, while with T568B, pins 1 and 2 are the orange pair and pins 3 and 6 are the green pair. At 10 and 100 Mb/sec., pins 1 and 2 always carry traffic from an interface, and pins 3 and 6 always carry traffic to an interface. You can use cables with different pinouts in a network, but to avoid confusion when troubleshooting, it's best to standardize on a single pinout and use it throughout if possible.

Most RJ-45 connectors are designed for use with either solid or stranded conductors, but not both. If you're making your own cables, be sure to use connectors that match the conductor type and are rated for your cable category or better. If you use shielded cable, use shielded connectors as well.

Crossover Cables

A crossover cable enables connecting two twisted-pair 10-Mb/s or Fast Ethernet interfaces directly, without going through a repeater hub or switch. Another use for crossover cables is to connect two repeater hubs or switches when neither has an available uplink port, as described later in this chapter. The cable swaps the green and orange pairs. In other words, at one end of the cable, pins 1 and 2 are the green pair and pins 3 and 6 are the orange pair, and at the other end, pins 1 and 2 are the orange pair and pins 3 and 6 are the green pair. This also happens to be the only difference between the T568A and T568B pinouts, so if you wire one connector as T568A and the other as T568B, you have a crossover cable.

Table 2-3: The only difference between the wiring of a T568A and T568B connector is which pairs connect to pins 1 and 2 and pins 3 and 6.

Pin Number	Wire Color	
	T568A	T568B
1	white with green stripe/splash	white with orange stripe/splash
2	green	orange
3	white with orange stripe/splash	white with green stripe/splash
4	blue	blue
5	white with blue stripe/splash	white with blue stripe/splash
6	orange	green
7	white with brown stripe/splash	white with brown stripe/splash
8	brown	brown

To avoid mix-ups, label crossover cables prominently. You can avoid having to use crossover cables by using switches that have auto-crossover capability. These switches detect the need for a crossover and perform the crossover internally and automatically when needed.

Adding Connectors to Twisted-pair Cables

Category 5 and higher cables with connectors attached are readily available in a variety of lengths. Some vendors will make cables of custom lengths. Manufactured cables are convenient and reliable. But there are occasions when adding your own connectors to raw cable is quicker or less expensive. For example, you may need a cable quickly and don't have the desired length on hand, or you may need to replace a bad connector on a cable that runs inside walls and is inconvenient to replace.

To make cables, you'll need the following:

• Cable of the desired type and fire rating, such as Category 5e, solid conductor, general-purpose.

• Connectors with the same or better rating as the cable, and suited for solid or stranded cable as needed.

• A cable crimper for attaching the connectors.

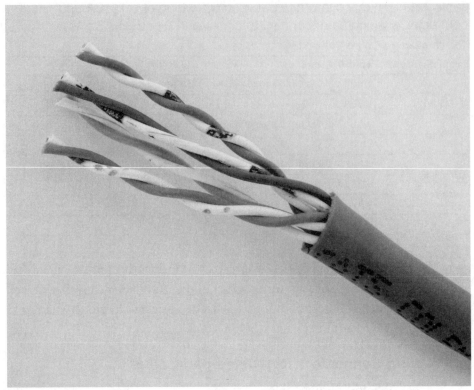

Figure 2-6: Stripping the outer jacket reveals the four twisted pairs.

- A cable stripper for removing the outer cable jacket. In a pinch, a utility knife will do.
- A cable cutter to cut the cable and trim the conductors in the cable.
- A cable tester to verify the connections.

These are the steps in attaching connectors to a cable:

1. Cut a length of cable equal to the needed length plus an appropriate amount of slack to allow for changes or rerouting and a few inches to allow for attaching the connectors.

2. Use the cable stripper to remove about an inch of the outer jacket from the end of the cable (Figure 2-6). After stripping, inspect to be sure you didn't nick the insulation on the conductors. If you did, cut off the ends and

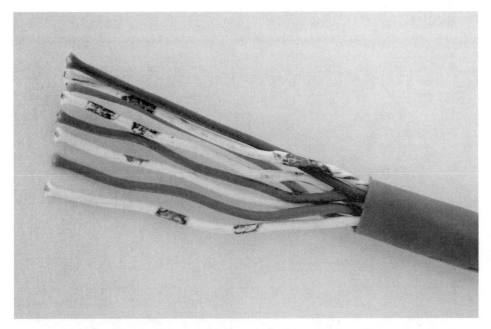

Figure 2-7: Separate and straighten the wires for inserting in a connector.

start over. You don't need to strip the insulation on the individual conductors.

3. Separate and straighten the conductors (Figure 2-7). Align the conductors in a row to match the connector pinout you'll be using, such as the 568A pinout.

4. Keeping the conductors aligned, trim the ends so about 1/2 inch of each extends beyond the jacket (Figure 2-8). To prevent crosstalk, no more than half an inch of the conductors should be untwisted.

5. With the conductors aligned, push the conductors all the way into the connector. Each conductor fits into a groove in the connector. All of the conductors should reach the end of the connector and at least 1/4 inch of the jacket should be inside the connector. Even though 10-Mb/s and Fast Ethernet systems don't use all eight wires, connect them all to allow for upgrades, to avoid unterminated wires that can lead to crosstalk, and because it's easier to crimp them all. Examine the connector to be sure that

51

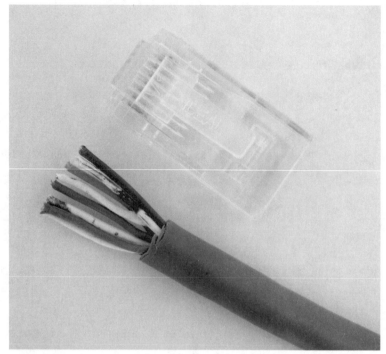

Figure 2-8: Trim the wires to fit the RJ-45 connector.

the conductors are lined up properly and that all extend to the end of the connector. If not, remove the cable from the connector, realign or trim the conductors as needed, and try again.

6. Insert the connector into the crimping tool and squeeze the handle to crimp the connector to the cable (Figure 2-9).

7. Examine the result (Figure 2-10). If the conductors aren't aligned correctly, cut off the connector and try again.

8. Repeat these steps for the cable's other end. A cable tester (Figure 2-11) can verify that all of the connections are good. Some testers perform additional tests of cable quality.

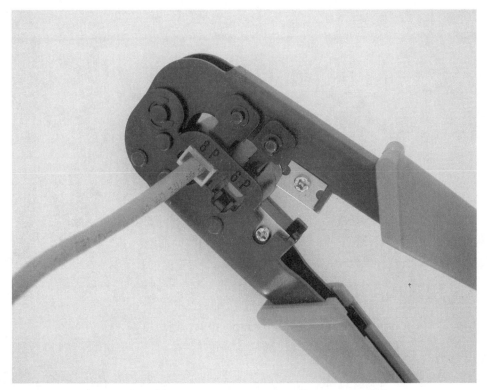

Figure 2-9: A crimping tool attaches the connector to the cable.

Fiber Optic Cable

In the copper wires of twisted-pair cable, the data signals are electrical volt-ages. In fiber-optic cable, signals transmit as pulses of light. In this book, the term *light* refers to electromagnetic radiation of visible wavelengths as well as the slightly longer, invisible wavelengths of infrared energy. Fiber-optic com-munications may use visible or infrared light.

As with twisted-pair networks, fiber-optic networks use repeater hubs and switches to connect interfaces to the network.

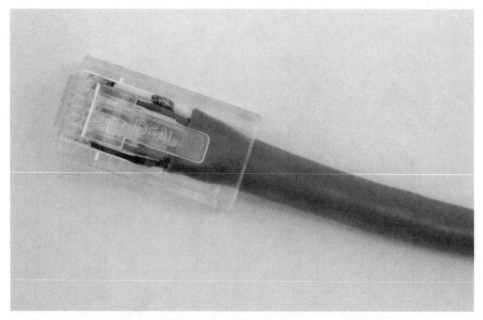

Figure 2-10: A cable with RJ-45 connector attached.

Advantages

Using light instead of electrical signals to transmit data has several advantages:

Ability to carry data long distances. For twisted-pair media systems, the maximum length of a cable segment is around 100 meters. For fiber-optic media systems, the maximum length of a segment ranges from a few hundred meters to 2000 meters for half duplex and 5000 meters for full duplex.

Immunity to electromagnetic interference. When a copper wire carries data, the varying currents in the wire cause a magnetic field to emanate from the cable. If a conductor's magnetic field overlaps another conductor's magnetic field, the signals couple, or link together via magnetic induction. This in turn induces currents that appear as noise in the signals being transmitted. Fiber-optic cables don't use electrical current, so there are no magnetic fields or magnetic coupling.

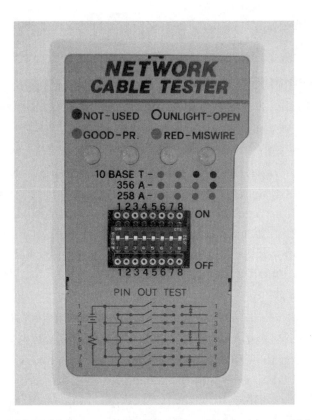

Figure 2-11: A cable tester can verify the correct wiring in a cable.

Security from eavesdropping. Signals in copper wire can be monitored either by tapping into the cable directly or by coupling to the cable's magnetic field. Neither of these methods works with fiber-optic cable.

Small diameter. For a cable that carries traffic between two interfaces, the cable diameter is likely to be the same (around 5mm) whether using twisted-pair or fiber-optic cable. But if you need to route a dozen or more connections along a common path, a single fiber-optic cable that contains many strands will have a much smaller diameter than the equivalent in twisted-pair cables.

Immunity to damage from lightning or other sources of large voltages or currents. Electrical signals in the environment have no effect on the signals in fiber-optic cable. Fiber-optic cable can be routed next to power cables with no ill effects.

Disadvantages

The main disadvantage to fiber-optic cable is the added cost, in dollars and in time if you attach your own connectors rather than buying fabricated cables or hiring someone to make the cables for you.

In addition to paying more for the cables themselves, components such as repeater hubs, switches, routers, and interface cards tend to be expensive in comparison to equivalent components for twisted-pair networks. Many Ethernet controller chips can interface to twisted-pair cable with few additional components, while an interface to fiber-optic cable requires an added media attachment unit (MAU) or physical layer device (PHY), as described later in this chapter.

Adding connectors to fiber-optic cables is more difficult than crimping connectors on twisted-pair cables. The process can involve many steps, including stripping the cable, filling the connector with epoxy, inserting the fiber in the connector, crimping the cable onto the connector, drying the epoxy, removing excess fiber from the tip, and polishing.

Some manufacturers offer connectors that take varying approaches to simplifying or speeding up the process of attaching fibers. Some connectors use a fast-curing adhesive in place of epoxy. Others use crimp-on connections with no epoxy or adhesive at all. A connector may have pre-injected epoxy that only requires heating of the connector to soften the epoxy before inserting a fiber. Yet another approach is a connector that contains a fiber stub and a built-in crimping mechanism that enables the installer to easily splice the stub to a fiber strand. The down sides to these time-saving methods can be reduced reliability and greater expense.

For short cable runs, an alternative to all of these methods is to buy standard or custom cables with connectors attached. The cables will be more expensive, but you won't have to buy tools, equipment, and supplies for attaching connectors or spend time making the cables.

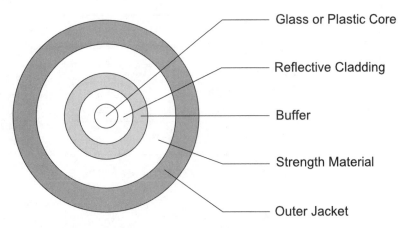

Figure 2-12: A fiber-optic cable has several protective layers surrounding the core and cladding.

Construction

A typical fiber-optic cable with one fiber strand contains a flexible glass or plastic core surrounded by a reflective cladding and a protective coating (Figure 2-12). The protective coating contains a buffer to protect the core and its cladding, a strength material to enable pulling cable during installation without stretching the fiber, and an outer jacket to protect the entire assembly.

A single cable may contain multiple strands of fiber in a single jacket. Duplex cable has two strands and is useful for Ethernet segments, which require a strand for each direction.

At each end of an Ethernet fiber-optic cable segment are a transmitter and receiver (Figure 2-13). A transceiver module contains a transmitter and a receiver in a single unit.

The transmitter converts electrical signals to optical signals to be carried by a strand of fiber. The module contains a light source, an electrical interface, and either a connector or a fiber pigtail (a short length of fiber) for splicing to a strand of fiber.

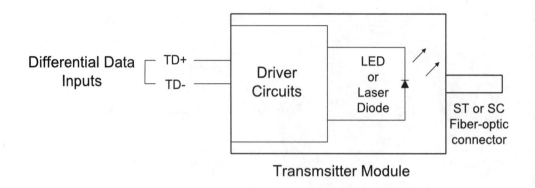

Differential Data Inputs

TD+

TD-

Driver Circuits

LED or Laser Diode

ST or SC Fiber-optic connector

Transmsitter Module

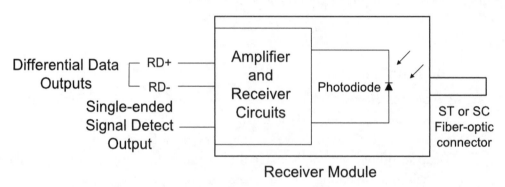

Differential Data Outputs

RD+

RD-

Single-ended Signal Detect Output

Amplifier and Receiver Circuits

Photodiode

ST or SC Fiber-optic connector

Receiver Module

Figure 2-13: A typical fiber-optic transmitter module converts differential data to light, while a receiver module converts light to differential data and a signal-detect output. Each module has a fiber-optic connector and pins that connect to inputs or outputs and power and ground.

The light source may be a light-emitting diode (LED) or a semiconductor laser. Lasers generally have faster switching times, while LEDs are cheaper. The transmitter may generate pulses of light in either of two ways. The transmitter may switch the light source on and off by switching the input current to the light source. Or the light source may be on all of the time, with circuits that modulate, or control, the transmitter's output by alternately blocking the light and letting it pass. Modulated outputs are more complex but can have very fast switching times.

A fiber-optic receiver contains a photodetector, an electrical interface, and a connector, sometimes with a fiber pigtail attached. The photodetector is a photodiode or phototransistor that converts received optical signals to electric current. Additional circuits in the module convert the current to voltages.

Sources for transmitter, receiver, and transceiver modules include Agilent Technologies and Micro Linear Corporation. The vendors provide documentation, evaluation kits, and application notes, often with complete schematic diagrams and even circuit-board layouts for Ethernet interfaces.

Length limits for fiber-optic cable are due to attenuation and dispersion of the signals in the cable. Causes of attenuation are absorption, scattering, and leakage of the light as it travels in the fiber. Dispersion is the gradual widening of pulses as they travel along a fiber, eventually making it hard to distinguish the transitions between pulses. In half-duplex segments, the need to detect collisions limits the round-trip travel time of data and further limits the maximum segment length.

Specifications

Specifications for fiber-optic cable include whether the cable is single mode or multimode and the diameters of the core and cladding.

A mode is a stable pattern, or path, that light may take as it propagates through a fiber. The diameter of a fiber strand and the composition of the fiber's core and cladding limit the number of paths. Single-mode fiber has just one path and can carry signals at high bit rates and over long distances. In multimode fiber, a signal may use any of multiple modes to travel in the fiber. Multimode fiber is less expensive and is adequate for most Ethernet networks. The IEEE 802.3 standard requires multimode fiber for 10-Mb/s and Fast Ethernet. Gigabit Ethernet may use multimode or single-mode fiber.

The diameters recommended by the IEEE 802.3 standard for multimode fiber are 62.5 μm for the core and 125 μm for the cladding. This type of cable is referred to as 62.5/125 cable. The standard also provides guidelines for systems that use 50/125 cable, which can have better performance at a

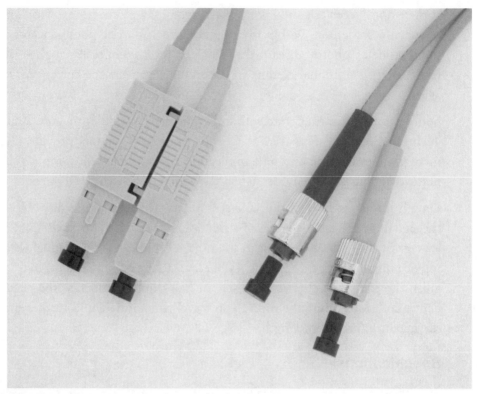

Figure 2-14: Two popular connectors for fiber-optic cables are the Low Cost Fibre Optical Interface, or SC, connector (left) and the BFOC/2.5, or ST, connector (right).

similar price. The single-mode fiber available as an option for Gigabit Ethernet is 10/125 cable.

Connectors

The IEEE 802.3 standard recommends specific connector types for use in segments of different speeds. For 10-Mb/s segments, the standard requires the BFOC/2.5 connectors commonly known by the trademarked name ST connector (Figure 2-14). For Fast Ethernet, the standard recommends using Low Cost Fibre Optical Interface Connectors, known by the trademarked name of duplex SC connector. The publication *Connectors for optical fibres and cables* (IEC 60874) contains specifications for these connectors. The document *Fiber Optic Connector Intermateability Standard Type SC* (TIA/EIA-604-3) uses the term *568SC connectors* to refer to the SC connectors.

The ST connectors are also acceptable for Fast Ethernet. Gigabit Ethernet segments use SC connectors.

Where saving space is important, small-form-factor (SFF) connectors are available. The SFF LC connectors introduced by Lucent Technologies are available from a variety of sources. In a duplex connection, LC connectors are half the size of SC connectors. The connectors use the same latching mechanism as RJ-45 connectors. The LC Alliance Web site at *www.lcalliance.com* has more information about the connectors and where to obtain them. Another option is MT-RJ connectors, which are about one third the size of SC connectors and also use a latching mechanism.

For permanent connections between two strands, splicing kits contain the tools and materials for joining two strands by melting, gluing, or clamping the ends together.

Coaxial Cable

The third option for Ethernet cabling is coaxial cable (Figure 2-15). A coaxial cable, or coax for short, consists of a copper core surrounded by an insulating sleeve, a solid or braided metal shield, and a protective jacket. The copper core is the conductor, and the shield serves as a ground return. The term coaxial refers to the way that the core and the shield that surrounds it are symmetrical around a line, or axis.

Coaxial cable was the only cable type specified in the original Ethernet standard, but coax isn't common in new networks for several reasons. First, you can use coaxial cable only in 10-Mb/s networks. If you use coax and later want to upgrade to a faster speed, you'll need new cables. With twisted-pair or fiber-optic cable, you can use the same cables if you change speeds.

Also, compared to coaxial cable, twisted-pair cabling is cheaper and easier to connect, and fiber-optic cable allows longer cable segments and has other

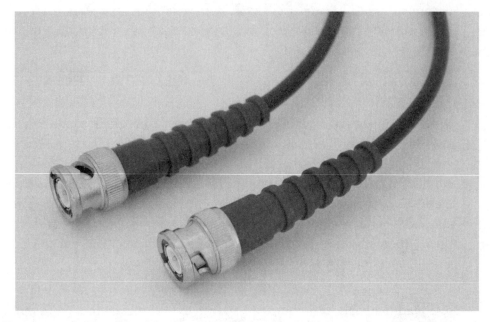

Figure 2-15: Coaxial cable was the original cable type used in Ethernet networks. Of Ethernet's two options for coaxial cable, the thin coax above was easier to use and more popular than thick coax.

benefits. So about the only reason for using coaxial cable is for compatibility with an existing system.

With that said, the IEEE 802.3 standard allows the use of two types of coaxial cable, commonly known as thick coax, at about 10mm in diameter and thin coax, at about 5mm in diameter. For each, the standard specifies maximum segment length, methods of attaching interfaces, and other requirements.

Of the two, thin coax was more popular. A segment of thin coax can be between 0.5 and 185 meters long. The cables use BNC connectors (Figure 2-15).

To attach interfaces to thin coax, a network may use a single cable segment with "T" connectors, multiple segments that connect to repeaters, or a combination. A segment of thin coax may consist of multiple lengths of cable connected in series via T connectors, with the third leg of each T connector attached to an interface. A segment may have up to 30 interfaces connected in this way. The stub from a T connector to an interface must be no more than 4 cm. A network can also use a repeater with attachment points for multiple cables.

Thick coax is much less convenient to set up. Each interface must have a transceiver that attaches directly to the cable, typically via a "vampire" tap that clamps onto the cable. A stub of up to 50 meters connects the transceiver to the interface. To reduce reflected voltages, the taps must be attached at multiples of 2.5 meters along the cable. The cable is bulky compared to thin coax. A segment of thick coax can be up to 500 meters, however, with up to 100 interfaces attached to it.

Both types of coaxial cable have a characteristic impedance of 50 ohms and require a 50-ohm termination at each end of a cable segment. For both, the shield is grounded at one end only. The IEEE 802.3 standard has additional specifications for coaxial cable.

Connections for Harsh Environments

The recommendations so far have all assumed that the cabling and other equipment will be in an office or equivalent setting where the environment doesn't present any special challenges to the cables, connections, and data being transmitted. But some embedded systems must function where the components are subjected to one or more of the following:

- Electromagnetic interference (EMI) from motors and other industrial equipment.
- Extreme temperatures (hot or cold).
- Vibration.
- Liquids, including water, oil, and corrosive substances.
- Dust or dirt.

For these environments, industrial-grade cables and connectors are available.

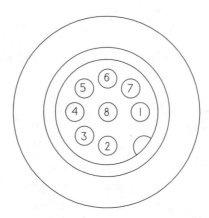

Figure 2-16: The M12 connector provides a secure connection for harsh environments.

Cables

To reduce problems caused by electromagnetic interference, use fiber-optic cable or shielded twisted-pair cable. In environments where there is high-frequency electrical noise, Category 5 cable may be a better choice than Category 5e or Category 6 cable, which are more sensitive to high-frequency noise.

The TIA is developing a standard for industrial-grade twisted-pair cable, tentatively called Category 5i cable.

Connectors

Harsh environments may also require ruggedized connectors to replace the usual office-grade RJ-45 connectors. One option is the M12 connector (Figure 2-16) available from Lumberg Inc. and others. The connector is about 12mm in diameter and has four or eight contacts, with one contact in the center and the rest arranged in a circle around the center. A threaded housing secures the connector on the enclosure and protects the contacts from environmental hazards. For use with systems that use RJ-45 connectors, there are adapters that connect an RJ-45 jack to an M12 connector and cables that have an RJ-45 plug on one end and an M12 connector on the other. Another option is to place an RJ-45 connection in a sealed housing.

The Siemon Company's Industrial MAX plug and outlet is an example of this type of connection.

Enclosures

A system that operates in a harsh environment will also need an enclosure that shields the circuits from electrical noise and environmental hazards. Circuits in dusty environments often can't use fans for cooling, but low-power components and circuits can eliminate the need for a fan.

Supplying Power

Many embedded systems are located near reliable power sources. At most, a system near a power source needs a rectifier to convert alternating current (AC) to direct current (DC) and one or more voltage regulators to provide the DC voltages required by CPU and other components.

For systems that aren't located near a power source, one option is to use battery power and either replace the batteries as needed or recharge the batteries via solar cells or another energy source. Another option is to provide power over the same cabling that connects the system to the network.

For systems that want to receive power over the network cables, the 802.3af amendment to the IEEE 802.3 standard specifies methods of providing moderate amounts of power over the same twisted-pair cabling used for network data. This amendment, titled *Data Terminal Equipment (DTE) Power via Media Dependent Interface (MDI)* was approved in 2003. A term often used to describe the technology in the amendment is Power Over Ethernet.

Twisted-pair interfaces at 10, 100, and 1000 Mb/sec. can use the methods described in the amendment. As Figure 2-17 shows, the Power Sourcing Equipment (PSE) that provides power can be in either of two locations. An Endpoint PSE is inside the repeater hub or switch that connects to the powered device (PD). A Midspan PSE is a separate device that connects between a repeater or switch and the powered device. Segments at 1000 Mb/s can use Endpoint PSEs only.

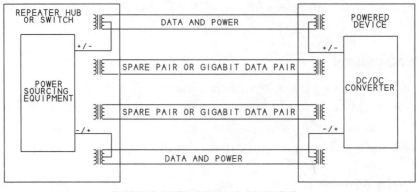

ENDPOINT POWER SOURCING EQUIPMENT
USING DATA WIRES

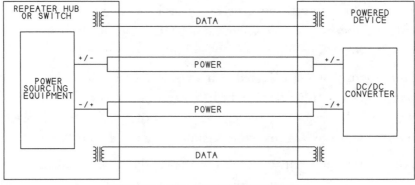

ENDPOINT POWER SOURCING EQUIPMENT
USING SPARE WIRES (10 AND 100 MB/SEC ONLY)

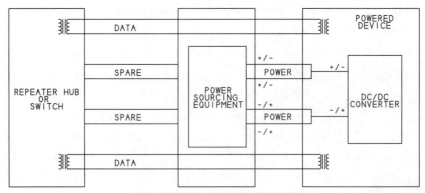

MIDSPAN POWER SOURCING EQUIPMENT
USING SPARE WIRES (10 AND 100 MB/SEC ONLY)

Figure 2-17: Ethernet devices can receive power over the same twisted-pair cables that carry data.

The PSE can supply power over unused wire pairs in a cable or on the same wire pairs used for data. Only 10- and 100-Mb/sec. systems have unused pairs. To use data wires, the PSE applies a DC voltage to the center tap of a pair's isolation transformer.

The PSE detects a device that requires power, supplies power as needed, monitors power use, and reduces or removes power when no longer required. A PSE can supply about 13 Watts (350 milliamperes at 37V).

For information about products that implement the 802.3af amendment, see *www.poweroverethernet.com*.

Going Wireless

Sometimes you don't want to use cables at all. This book's focus is Ethernet, which by definition is a wired interface. It's possible, however, to connect a system with an Ethernet interface to a wireless network.

The term *wireless Ethernet* usually refers to a network that follows one of the IEEE 802.11 standards. The main 802.11 standard, like Ethernet's 802.3 standard, specifies a physical layer and a method of media-access control for networking. The physical layer may use radio-frequency (RF) transmissions in the 2.4 Gigahertz frequency band or infrared transmissions. Both allow transmitting data at 1 or 2 Mb/s.

A variety of supplements to the standard describe additional options for the physical layer at higher speeds. A popular standard for wireless networks has been the 802-11b supplement, which describes the interface known as *Wi-Fi*, for wireless fidelity. An 802-11b interface transmits at up to 11 Mb/s in the 2.4 Gigahertz band. The 802-11g supplement approved in 2003 enables transmitting at 54 Mb/s in the same band and can fall back to the 802-11b rate when needed. Networks that use the physical layer described in the 802-11a supplement transmit at up to 54 Mb/s in the 5 Gigahertz band.

The easiest way to connect a device with an Ethernet interface to a wireless network is to use a wireless access point. The access point has an 802-11b or other wireless interface and connects via a cable to an interface that wants to communicate over the wireless network. Initial configuration of the access point typically requires a PC, but once the access point is configured, the network administrator can usually change the configuration via a Web page hosted by the access point.

Media Systems

The media systems defined in the IEEE 802.3 standard each use a particular cable type at a specific network speed. So for example, a 10-Mb/s twisted-pair network uses a different media system than a Fast Ethernet twisted-pair network or a 10-Mb/s fiber-optic network. For each media system, the standard specifies the electrical characteristics, signaling protocol, and methods of connecting to an interface.

Some of the media systems defined in the standard are rarely used. This chapter focuses on the more popular ones, which Table 2-4 lists.

The standard uses a system of identifiers to distinguish the media systems. Each identifier has three elements. The first number is the network speed in Megabits per second (10, 100, 1000) or bits per second (10G). Then the word BASE or BROAD indicates the type of signaling used, baseband or broadband. All of the popular media systems use baseband signaling, which means that the cable carries only Ethernet data and signaling. A broadband media system carries multiple types of data and signaling.

The final value identifies either the cable type or the maximum length of a cable segment. In more recently defined media systems, the value indicates the cable type. For example, in the identifier 10BASE-T, the *T* signifies twisted-pair cable. The maximum cable length per segment as specified by the standard is 100 meters, but the identifier doesn't contain this information. In identifiers defined earlier in Ethernet's history, the third value indicates maximum cable length. For example, in the identifier 10BASE-5, the maximum segment length is 500 meters. The media type is coaxial cable, but the identifier doesn't contain this information.

Table 2-4: Each media system uses a particular cable type and data rate.

Media System	Cable Type	Speed (Mb/s)
10BASE-T	twisted pair, Category 3 or higher	10
100BASE-TX	twisted pair, Category 5 or higher	100
1000BASE-T	twisted pair, Category 5 or higher	1000
10BASE-FL	fiber optic, multimode	10
100BASE-FX	fiber optic, multimode	100
1000BASE-SX	fiber optic, multimode	1000
1000BASE-LX	fiber optic, multimode or single mode	1000
10BASE-2	thin coax	10
10BASE-5	thick coax	10

Encoding

One of the characteristics specified by the media system is how the data is encoded for transmitting. The encoding method helps to ensure that the data reaches its destination without errors. The encoding defines what voltages or light levels correspond to different values. In addition, for some media systems, the encoding defines code symbols to represent groups of bits. The controller chip's hardware handles the encoding and decoding. You don't need to understand how the encoding works to design and program a network, so this book includes only brief descriptions of the methods and the reasons for their use.

Block Encoding

Fast Ethernet and Gigabit Ethernet media systems use methods of block encoding. Block encoding groups bits to be transmitted into blocks that are typically 4 or 8 bits each, then converts each block into a set of bits called a code symbol.

Block encoding can ensure frequent transitions in transmitted data, to help in keeping the transmitting and receiving interfaces synchronized. Another advantage is the availability of additional code symbols. After assigning code symbols to all of the possible groups of bits, extra symbols remain. A protocol can specify any use for these, and typically uses the symbols to provide status or control information.

A code symbol is longer than the bits it represents. In the 4B/5B block encoding used in Fast Ethernet, a 5-bit code symbol represents 4 data bits. Each code symbol contains one or more transitions. In the 8B/10B block encoding used in fiber-optic Gigabit Ethernet, a 10-bit code symbol represents 8 data bits. In both cases, the extra bits increase the maximum transition rate in the cable by 25 percent.

In addition to ensuring that there are sufficient transitions, 8B/10B encoding attempts to maintain a DC balance by ensuring that the number of transmitted zeros is roughly the same as the number of transmitted ones over time. The encoding accomplishes this by assigning two possible code symbols to some 8-bit values, with the two symbols containing different numbers of zeros and ones. The transmitter maintains a *disparity value* that is a measure of the number of transmitted zeros versus ones over time. When the ratio of transmitted zeros to ones gets out of balance, the transmitter switches to the set of code symbols that will restore the balance.

Twisted-pair Gigabit Ethernet uses block encoding along with pulse amplitude modulation and transmitting on all four wire pairs at once. The result is an interface that can transmit at a very high bit rate without requiring a very high bit rate in the cable. The code symbols are 5 bits, with each symbol representing 2 bits.

Transmitting the Bits

The different media systems use different encoding methods in transmitting the data bits or code symbols that represent the data bits.

Ten-Mb/s systems use a method called Manchester encoding (Figure 2-18). In a logic 1, the signal is a low voltage or low light level for the first half of the bit period and a high voltage or high light level for the second half of the bit period. A logic 0 is the reverse: the signal is high for the first half of the bit period and low for the second half.

The advantage to Manchester encoding is that it guarantees a transition in each bit, and this makes signals easy to synchronize to. The down side is that the maximum rate of transitions is twice the bit rate, and hardware that can handle higher bit rates tends to be more expensive.

In Fast Ethernet systems, the bits in a code symbol transmit using a method of encoding called multi-level transition 3, or MLT-3. Instead of specifying two voltage ranges that correspond to logic 0 and logic 1, MLT-3 uses three voltage ranges. For each bit time, a change from one logic level to the next signifies a logic 1, while no change signifies a logic 0. The data in Fast Ethernet systems is also scrambled before transmitting to provide bit patterns that reduce electromagnetic emissions.

In twisted-pair Gigabit Ethernet, instead of serially transmitting the bits in the code symbols, which would take five bit times, the transmissions use a

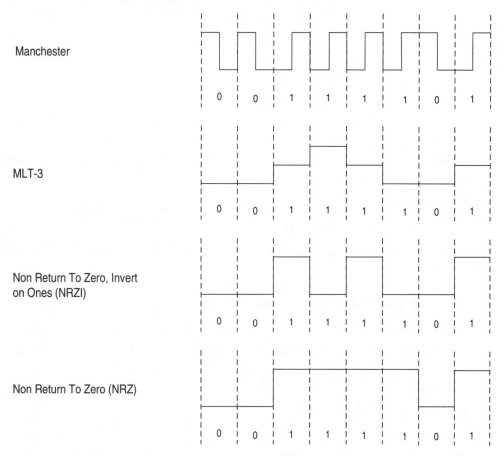

Figure 2-18: Different media systems use different methods of encoding data before sending it on the network.

system of 5-level pulse-amplitude modulation. A code symbol is one of five defined voltage levels, and each level represents a 2-bit value. In this way, two bits of data transmit in one bit time on each pair of wires.

With each transition representing two bits and four signal pairs transmitting at once, each bit time transmits 8 bits of information. Transmitting a Gigabit per second, the maximum transition rate is 125 transitions per microsecond, which is the same maximum transition rate as in Fast Ethernet.

Twisted-pair Gigabit systems also uses error correcting, digital signal processing, and other techniques to ensure signal quality. An Idle symbol transmits when there is no other traffic.

Fiber-optic segments for Fast Ethernet transmit the individual bits in a code symbol using a method of encoding called non-return to zero, invert on ones (NRZI). A logic 0 results in no change in light level; if light transmitted during the previous bit's time period, light continues to transmit for the logic-0 bit that follows. A logic 1 results in a change in light level: if light transmitted during the previous bit's time period, light doesn't transmit for the logic-1 bit that follows, and if light didn't transmit during the previous bit's time period, light does transmit for the logic-1 bit that follows.

Gigabit fiber-optic segments transmit the individual bits in the code symbols using non-return-to-zero (NRZ) encoding. NRZ is the simplest encoding: light transmits to indicate a logic 1 and light doesn't transmit to indicate a logic 0.

Twisted-pair Media Systems

The identifiers for popular twisted-pair media systems are 10BASE-T, 100-BASE-TX, and 1000BASE-T. Below is basic information about each.

10BASE-T

Bit rate: 10 Mb/s.

Cable Type: Category 3 (also known as telephone twisted pair) or higher. Category 5e or higher recommended.

Connector Type: RJ-45.

Maximum length of a cable segment: A 10BASE-T cable segment can be 100 meters or more. The main limiting factor for the cable is attenuation as signals travel through the cable and connectors. The maximum allowed attenuation is 11.5 decibels. The exact length limit varies with the cables and components, but generally, a segment that uses cables and connectors rated as Category 3 or better should have no trouble transmitting 100 meters.

Maximum number of transceivers per cable segment: 2.

Encoding: Manchester.

Comments: A workhorse for low-cost communications.

100BASE-TX

Bit rate: 100 Mb/s.

Cable Type: Category 5 or higher. Category 5e or higher recommended.

Connector Type: RJ-45.

Maximum length of a cable segment: 100 meters

Maximum number of transceivers per cable segment: 2.

Encoding: 4B/5B block encoding.

Comments: Also known as twisted-pair Fast Ethernet.

1000BASE-T

Bit rate: 1000 Mb/s.

Cable Type: Category 5 or higher. Category 5e or higher recommended.

Connector Type: RJ-45.

Maximum length of a cable segment: 100 meters.

Maximum number of transceivers per cable segment: 2.

Encoding: block encoding with pulse amplitude modulation. All four wire pairs carry data at the same time.

Comments: Also known as twisted-pair Gigabit Ethernet.

Fiber-optic Media Systems

The identifiers for popular fiber-optic media systems are 10BASE-FL, 100-BASE-FX, 1000BASE-SX, and 1000BASE-LX. Below is basic information about each.

10BASE-FL

Bit rate: 10 Mb/s

Cable Type: multimode, 62.5/125 (recommended), 50/125 and other cables allowed.

Connector Type: BFOC/2.5, also known as ST connectors.

Maximum length of a cable segment, half duplex: 2000 meters (with two or fewer repeaters); full duplex: 5 kilometers. Cables under 5 meters may require filters or attenuators.

Maximum number of transceivers per cable segment: 2.

Encoding: Manchester.

Comments: Allows very long cable segments in half- and full-duplex modes.

100BASE-FX

Bit rate: 100 Mb/s

Cable Type: 62.5/125 or 50/125 multimode.

Connector Type: Low Cost Fibre Optical Interface Connectors (SC or 568SC type) recommended. BFOC/2.5 (ST type) Media Interface Connector (MIC) also permitted.

Maximum length of a cable segment: half duplex: 412 meters; full duplex: 2 kilometers.

Maximum number of transceivers per cable segment: 2.

Encoding: 4B/5B block encoding.

Comments: Full duplex allows very long segments.

1000BASE-SX

Bit rate: 1000 Mb/s.

Cable Type: 62.5/125 or 50/125 multimode.

Connector Type: Low Cost Fibre Optical Interface Connectors (SC type).

Maximum length of a cable segment, half duplex: 220 to 316 meters, depending on cable type; full duplex: 220 to 550 meters, depending on cable type. Minimum: 2 meters.

Maximum number of transceivers per cable segment: 2.

Encoding: 8B/10B block encoding.

Comments: Because of the encoding, the maximum transition rate is 1.25 Gigabaud for a data rate of 1 Gigbit per second. This high rate requires the use of lasers as the light source. The SX in the name refers to a short-wavelength light source.

1000BASE-LX

Bit rate: 1000 Mb/s.

Cable Type: 62.5/125 or 50/125 multimode or 10/125 single-mode.

Connector Type: Low Cost Fibre Optical Interface Connectors (SC type).

Maximum length of a cable segment, half duplex: 316 meters; full duplex: 5000 meters with single-mode fiber, 550 meters with multimode fiber. Minimum: 2 meters.

Maximum number of transceivers per cable segment: 2.

Encoding: 8B/10B block encoding.

Comments: Because of the encoding, the maximum transition rate is 1.25 Gigabaud for a data rate of 1 Gigabit per second. This high rate requires the use of lasers as the light source. The LX in the name refers to a long-wavelength light source.

Coaxial-cable Media Systems

The identifiers for coaxial-cable media systems are 10BASE-5 and 10BASE-2. Below is basic information about each:

10BASE5

Bit rate: 10 Mb/s.

Cable type: 50-ohm coaxial cable rated for use in 10BASE-5 networks, approximately 10mm in diameter.

Connector Type: Type N connectors (IEC 60169-16) or coaxial tap connectors.

Maximum length of a cable segment, half duplex: 500 meters. Minimum 2.5 meters.

Maximum number of transceivers per cable segment: 100.

Encoding: Manchester.

Comments: Not recommended for new networks.

10BASE-2

Bit rate: 10 Mb/s.

Cable type: 50-ohm coaxial cable rated for use in 10BASE-2 networks, approximately 5mm in diameter.

Connector Type: BNC.

Maximum length of a cable segment, half duplex: 185 meters. Minimum 0.5 meter.

Maximum number of transceivers per cable segment: 30.

Encoding: Manchester.

Comments: Not recommended for new networks.

Interfacing to Ethernet Controllers

The different cable types and speeds require different hardware interfaces to Ethernet controller chips. The Ethernet standard defines several types of interfaces for connecting a computer's media access control (MAC) layer, which manages the sending and receiving of network data, to the physical layer, which contains the components that are specific to a cable type or speed.

Depending on the cable type and network speed, the physical layer may contain little more than transceivers, some filtering, and a connector, or the layer may include circuits that encode and decode data and convert between serial and parallel interfaces.

Many Ethernet controllers have an on-chip interface for twisted-pair cables and require only filtering circuits and a connection to an RJ-45 connector.

Figure 2-19 shows some options for cable connections.

In Figure 2-19A, a 10-Mb/s controller uses an attachment unit interface (AUI) that connects to a media attachment unit (MAU) that in turn interfaces to the network cable. The MAU is a separate unit that attaches to the controller's 15-pin AUI interface. The MAU provides an interface to an Ethernet connector, a collision-detect output, and jabber-detection circuits to prevent a malfunctioning interface from continuously transmitting. With an AUI, you can switch between coaxial, twisted-pair, and fiber-optic cable by swapping the MAU.

In Figure 2-19B, a 10- or 100-Mb/s Ethernet controller uses a medium-independent interface (MII) that connects to a physical layer device (PHY), which in turn connects to the network cable. The PHY may be on the same circuit board as the Ethernet controller or a separate unit. The MII converts between the network's serial data and a 4-bit data bus that connects to the Ethernet controller. Some Ethernet controller chips include a PHY core for twisted-pair interfaces. An Ethernet controller that includes an embedded PHY typically requires external filtering circuits between the PHY and network connector.

In Figure 2-19C, a Gigabit Ethernet controller uses a Gigabit medium-independent interface (GMII) that connects to a Gigabit PHY, which connects to the network cable. Because of Gigabit Ethernet's speed, the GMII can't use a cable to connect to the Ethernet controller, but must be on the same

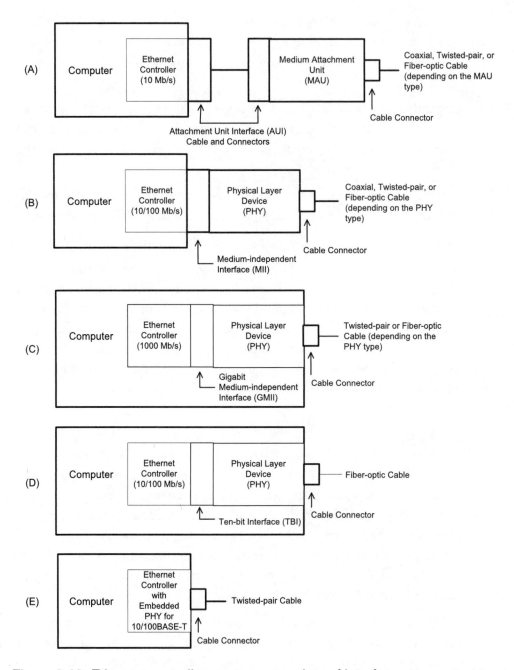

Figure 2-19: Ethernet controllers can use a variety of interfaces to connect to the network cable.

circuit board or a daughter board. The GMII converts between the network data and an 8-bit data bus that connects to the Ethernet controller.

Another option for a Gigabit Ethernet controller used with fiber-optic cable is a Ten-Bit Interface (TBI) (Figure 2-19D), which connects to a Gigabit PHY, which connects to the network cable. The TBI converts between the network data and a 10-bit data bus that connects to the Ethernet controller.

Figure 2-19E shows an Ethernet controller that contains an embedded PHY for use with twisted-pair cable.

Using Repeater Hubs, Ethernet Switches, and Routers

Ethernet networks have several options for interconnecting the computers in a network.

As Chapter 1 explained, repeater hubs and switches have attachment points for two or more cables that can connect to other interfaces in a local network. Both repeater hubs and switches repeat, or regenerate, traffic received on one port to the other ports. A repeater hub repeats all traffic to all ports, with the exception of some multi-speed repeater hubs that convert traffic between speeds only when necessary. A switch examines the destination of all received traffic and when possible, forwards the traffic only to the port on the path to the destination.

A note on terminology: the Ethernet standard uses the terms *repeater hub* and *switching hub* to distinguish between the two device types. However, in popular use, *hub* by itself generally refers only to repeater hubs, while *switch* refers to switching hubs. To prevent confusion, this book uses the standard's term *repeater hub* but avoids using *switching hub* in favor of *switch* or *Ethernet switch*.

Repeater hubs and switches make it easy to add and remove network interfaces. Each repeater hub or switch has multiple ports. To add an interface, you just attach the interface's cable to an available port on the repeater hub or switch. With most media systems, you can add more ports by connecting additional repeater hubs or switches to available ports on existing repeater hubs and switches. As explained earlier, networks that use coaxial cable have other options such as T connectors, but twisted-pair and fiber-optic networks must use repeater hubs or switches to connect more than two interfaces.

Communicating with other networks, including the Internet, requires an additional piece of equipment: a router.

Repeater hubs, switches, and routers are readily available as off-the-shelf products. A network of embedded systems can use the same devices as networks that link PCs. For Internet communications, a local computer may connect via a modem to a router at an Internet Service Provider.

Repeater Hubs

A repeater hub can connect multiple interfaces and helps to ensure reliable communications by detecting collisions, regenerating missing preamble bits, and blocking traffic from failed interfaces. The IEEE 802.3 standard specifies the functions of repeater hubs that support a single speed but doesn't forbid hubs that support multiple speeds. On receiving traffic from an interface, the repeater hub repeats the traffic, passing it to each of the other attached interfaces. In a network that uses repeater hubs, each interface sees all of the traffic from the other interfaces, with two exceptions. Repeater hubs block traffic from failed interfaces. And a multi-speed hub may convert between speeds only when necessary.

Connecting Interfaces

Ethernet cable segments have maximum permitted lengths, depending on the media system. Repeater hubs enable increasing the distance between interfaces by connecting two or more segments in series. The hub regenerates the signals, enabling them to travel farther than the maximum length of a single segment.

Besides repeating what it receives, a repeater hub also detects and responds to collisions and prevents traffic from misbehaving interfaces from reaching the other interfaces in the network.

As Chapter 1 explained, when two or more interfaces try to transmit at the same time, the transmitting interfaces have to be able to detect the collision before the number of bits in a minimum-size frame has transmitted. When a repeater hub increases the distance between interfaces, the time it takes for signals to travel from one end of the network to the other increases as well. This longer travel time means that it can take longer for a transmitting interface to detect a collision. So to ensure that interfaces can detect collisions in time, repeater hubs must detect collisions and on detecting a collision, send a jam signal to all attached interfaces. A repeater hub also extends received frame fragments when necessary by adding alternating 1s and 0s to the end of the fragment.

A repeater hub cuts off traffic from a failed interface or network segment so the rest of the network can continue to operate normally. The hub stops repeating an interface's traffic if the port has either a large number of collisions or collisions that persist longer than normal. When the hub is no longer repeating the traffic from an interface, the offending interface is said to be *partitioned* from the rest of the network. Meanwhile, the rest of the network can communicate.

After partitioning an interface, a repeater hub continues to attempt to send traffic to the interface. If the interface begins working properly again, the hub resumes repeating traffic from the interface.

In a similar way, a repeater hub also cuts off communications with an interface that is jabbering, or continuing to transmit longer than the maximum time allowed for a frame.

How Many Repeater Hubs?

In addition to limiting the length of cable segments, the IEEE 802.3 standard limits the number of repeater hubs allowed between two interfaces. The two factors that determine the maximum number of repeater hubs and the maximum length of cable segments are the interframe gap, or time between frames, and the round-trip propagation delay, or how long it takes a bit to travel the length of the network and back.

As cable length increases, the time required for a bit to travel the length of the network increases, so the time required to detect a collision in the worst case increases as well. Also, the interframe gap may shrink as signals pass through repeater hubs. If for any reason a repeater hub doesn't receive all of a frame's Preamble bits, the hub regenerates the bits when it repeats the frame, and these added bits shorten the gap between the current and next frames.

The maximum number of repeater hubs varies with the media system. For 10BASE-FL networks, adding repeaters can also shorten the maximum allowed segment length. Ethernet switches, described later in this chapter, can extend a network beyond what's possible with repeater hubs.

The IEEE 802.3 standard provides two transmission-system models to use as guides in configuring a system that meets the requirements. Model 1 specifies maximum numbers of repeater hubs and maximum segment lengths for different media systems. The guidelines are conservative. If you want to exceed what Model 1 allows, Model 2 has calculation aids for determining whether a particular configuration meets the requirements.

The Model 1 guidelines say the following:

In a 10BASE-T or 10BASE-FL network, the transmission path between two interfaces may contain up to five segments and four repeater hubs (Figure 2-20). A network may have more than four repeater hubs as long as the path between any two interfaces has no more than four repeater hubs.

A 10BASE-FL network has additional restrictions on segment length in some configurations. With two or fewer repeater hubs, the maximum segment length is 2000 meters. With three repeater hubs, the maximum segment length between repeaters is 1000 meters, and the maximum distance between a repeater hub and an interface is 400 meters. With four repeater hubs, the maximum length of each segment is 500 meters. So using repeater hubs, the maximum distance between interfaces in a 10BASE-FL network is 6000 meters, using two repeaters hub and three 2000-meter segments.

In a 100BASE-TX or 100BASE-FX network, a transmission path between two interfaces can have one Class I repeater hub or up to two Class II repeater hubs. A Class I repeater hub converts as needed between encoding methods. A network that contains only 100BASE-TX and 100BASE-FX

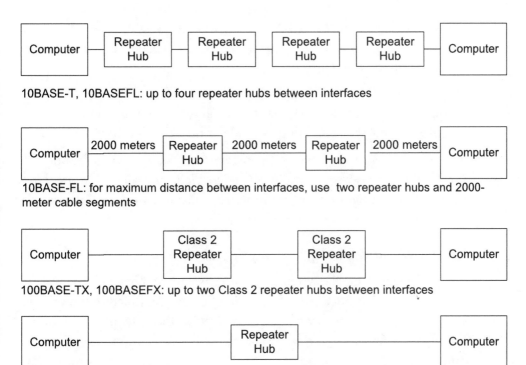

10BASE-T, 10BASEFL: up to four repeater hubs between interfaces

10BASE-FL: for maximum distance between interfaces, use two repeater hubs and 2000-meter cable segments

100BASE-TX, 100BASEFX: up to two Class 2 repeater hubs between interfaces

1000BASE-TX, 1000BASE-FX: zero or one repeater hub between interfaces

Figure 2-20: The Model 1 guidelines specify the maximum number of repeaters between interfaces in different media systems

interfaces doesn't need converting because both media systems use the same encoding.

In a 1000BASE-TX or 1000BASE-FX network, a transmission path between two interfaces can have only one repeater hub. Virtually all Gigabit Ethernet systems use switches instead of repeater hubs.

Auto-negotiating

With the addition of 10-Gb/s Ethernet, an Ethernet interface can support up to four speeds, as well as half duplex and full duplex communications. The IEEE 802.3 standard defines a protocol for auto-negotiating that enables an interface to automatically use the fastest speed and duplex mode available without requiring manual configuring in hardware or software.

When two interfaces that support auto-negotiating connect to each other, they exchange a series of handshaking signals to determine the fastest configuration supported by both.

When an interface that supports auto-negotiating connects to an interface that doesn't support auto-negotiating, the auto-negotiating interface detects and matches the speed and duplex mode of the other interface.

To use auto-negotiating, the Ethernet interface's hardware must support the protocol and auto-negotiating must be enabled, typically in configuration registers, and supported by the Ethernet controller's driver software. The hardware then handles the details of auto-negotiating.

Crossover and Straight-through Cables

For all Ethernet media systems except twisted-pair Gigabit systems, each interface has a dedicated pair of wires or a fiber strand for communicating in each direction. When a computer transmits on the network, the transmitting wires or fibers need to be routed to the receivers on the receiving computers.

For twisted-pair media systems, the repeater hub or switch normally performs the crossover. The interfaces that connect to the repeater hub or switch transmit on pins 1 and 2 and receive on pins 3 and 6. The repeater hub or switch routes data received on pins 1 and 2 to pins 3 and 6 at the hub or switch's ports.

But what if you need to add ports or extend a 10- or 100-Mb/s network by connecting two repeater hubs or switches in series? If the first device's port transmits on pins 3 and 6 and the second device's port expects to receive on pins 1 and 2, a connection between the devices requires a crossover cable. An alternative is to use the uplink port available on many repeater hubs and switches. An uplink port is identical to the device's other ports except that it doesn't have an internal crossover. So if you connect two repeater hubs or switches using an uplink port on one of the devices, you can use a straight-through cable. Figure 2-21 illustrates.

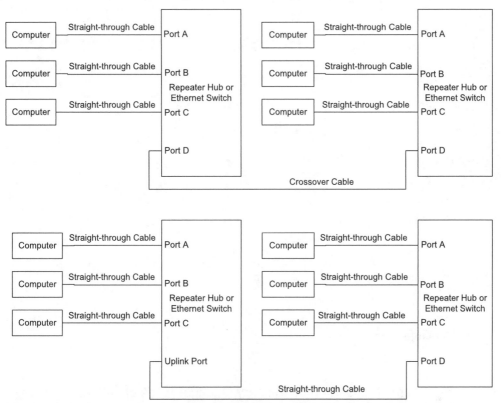

Figure 2-21: To connect two repeater hubs or switches in a twisted-pair network at 10 or 100 Mb/s, use a crossover cable or a straight-through cable with an uplink port.

Some switches have auto-crossover capability and will swap the pairs automatically as needed.

Multi-speed Repeater Hubs

An enhancement to the single-speed repeater hub is the multi-speed hub, which can connect interfaces of different speeds. A popular type of multi-speed repeater hub supports 10BASE-T and 100BASE-TX media systems. The ports typically configure themselves automatically for the speed of an attached interface. A multi-speed repeater hub contains a repeater hub for 10 Mb/s and a repeater hub for 100 Mb/s, with an internal switch that connects the hubs.

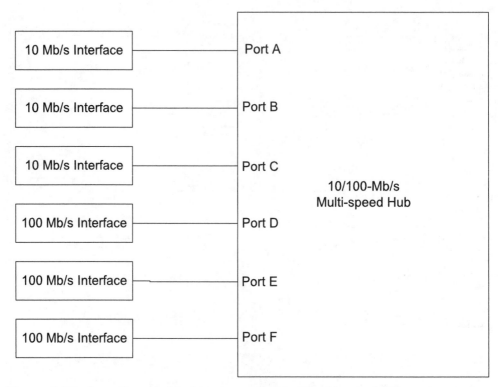

Figure 2-22: A multi-speed hub can connect to interfaces of different speeds and will convert traffic to another speed as needed.

Most multi-speed repeater hubs convert between speeds only as needed. In Figure 2-22, the interfaces at ports A, B, and C are 10 Mb/s and the interfaces at ports D, E, and F are 100 Mb/s. If the interface at port A sends a frame to the interface at port B, the repeater hub may detect that the frame is destined for a 10-Mb/s interface and thus may decide not to convert and pass the traffic on to ports D, E, and F. If the interface at port A sends a frame to the interface at port D, the repeater hub must do the conversion.

Ethernet Switches

Like a repeater hub, an Ethernet switch provides attachment points for connecting interfaces to a network. A switch can do everything a repeater hub can, with one big advantage. Instead of sending all frames to all ports, a switch examines each received frame and if possible, sends the frame only to the port that connects directly to the frame's destination or to a repeater hub, switch, or router on the way to the destination. Switches generally cost little more than repeater hubs and can improve network performance by isolating some of the network traffic.

Ethernet switches use the bridging technology and protocols described in *IEEE 802.1D: Part 3: Media Access Control (MAC) Bridges.*

Understanding the benefits of Ethernet switches requires understanding the concept of collision domains. As Chapter 1 explained, a collision domain consists of all of the interfaces connected either via repeater hubs or on the same segment of coaxial cable. If two interfaces in a collision domain try to transmit at the same time, a collision results and both must retry later. On a switch, each port is in a separate collision domain, so the interfaces connected to one port don't see traffic between the switch's other ports.

In many networks, the multiple collision domains provided by switches result in a less congested network. In Figure 2-23, when Interface 1 sends a frame to Interface 2, Repeater Hub 1 repeats the frame to Interfaces 2 and 3 and to Port A on the switch. If the switch determines that the destination interface is available from Port A, the switch doesn't send the frame out Port B or C. Interfaces 4–7 don't see the frame and are free to exchange other traffic. If Interface 4 and Interface 7 both attempt to send a frame at the same time to Interface 1, neither interface sees a collision. The switch receives the frames on its Port B and Port C and forwards the frames in sequence out Port A.

On receiving a frame, a switch uses the frame's destination address to decide where to send the frame. To make this decision, the switch has to know which ports correspond to which addresses.

The IEEE 802.1D standard defines a way for an Ethernet switch to learn recently used addresses without requiring any user setup or configuring. The switch learns addresses by reading the source address of every frame it receives. The switch stores these addresses in a table, with each entry containing the source address, the port that received the frame, and when the

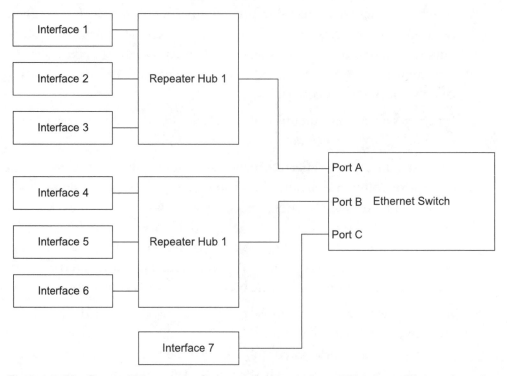

Figure 2-23: On an Ethernet switch, each port is in a different collision domain.

switch received the frame. In some cases, the source address will match the address of one of the interfaces that connects directly or via a repeater hub to one of the switch's ports. In other cases, the source address will be for an interface that is one or more switches or repeater hubs away.

When a frame arrives, the switch looks for a match between the frame's destination address and the addresses in the switch's table. On finding a match, the switch sends the frame only to the designated port. If there is no match, the switch sends the frame to all of its ports, in a process called flooding.

This method of learning addresses and filtering traffic according to their destination addresses can dramatically reduce the amount of traffic that an individual interface sees. To keep the table from overflowing, the switch removes entries that have had no recent traffic.

A switch may also connect interfaces of different speeds. On a typical switch, the ports use auto-negotiation to automatically configure themselves to support the speed of an attached interface.

Handling Traffic

Because each port on a switch has its own collision domain, a switch may at times receive more traffic than it can handle right away. For example, if two ports on a switch each receive a frame destined for a third port, the switch can only transmit one frame immediately, and must store the other. Switches contain buffer memory for this purpose.

No matter how big the buffer memory is, it's possible that on a busy network, the buffer will be full when a new frame arrives. When this happens, the switch drops, or ignores, the frames it can't handle. The IEEE 802.1D standard doesn't specify a way to notify the sending interface when a frame is dropped. If the sending interface needs to know that the data arrived at its destination, the sender can use a higher-level protocol such as TCP, which requires the receiver to return an acknowledgment on receiving a frame. The acknowledgment travels in a new frame sent by the receiver of the original data. Chapter 5 has more on TCP.

How Many Switches?

The IEEE 802.1D standard recommends a maximum of seven switches between interfaces, to limit the total time required for a transmission to reach its destination. In practice, messages that use the Internet Protocol (IP) are likely to get to their destinations even if there are more switches between the interfaces.

Routers

A router can do everything an Ethernet switch can do, including providing attachment points for interfaces and forwarding traffic. But an Ethernet switch can only work with Ethernet frames. If your Ethernet network wants to communicate with a different kind of network, or with another Ethernet network, or over the Internet, a router can provide access beyond the local network. Another term for a router is gateway.

When a computer with an Ethernet interface wants to send a message on the Internet, the computer places the message in an Ethernet frame and sends it to a router that can communicate on the Internet. The router does what's needed to send the message toward its destination. In the opposite direction, the router receives messages from the Internet and sends them in Ethernet frames onto the local network.

Messages that travel on the Internet uses the Internet Protocol to identify the receiving interface. As Chapter 1 explained, an Ethernet frame's data field can contain an IP datagram. When a router receives an Ethernet frame from the local network, it looks inside the IP datagram's header in the frame's data field to read the destination's IP address.

Like switches, routers maintain tables of recently used addresses and where to route traffic to them. For an unfamiliar address, the router sends the data to a designated default router.

Routers don't forward broadcast data. Chapter 4 has more about using a router to connect a device to the Internet.

For more details about the hardware in Ethernet networks, a good reference is *Ethernet: The Definitive Guide* by Charles Spurgeon (O'Reilly).

3

Design Choices

When you're ready to begin designing an embedded system for networking, you'll need to make some decisions about the device hardware and the programming code that will control the hardware. At one extreme, you can do it all yourself, interfacing an Ethernet controller chip to a CPU and writing code to support Ethernet communications and the Internet protocols the device uses. Or you can save a lot of time by starting with a module that contains a CPU, Ethernet interface, and software support for Ethernet communications and Internet protocols. Or you can choose a middle path, such as using a provided software library but designing your own circuits.

This chapter begins by introducing a sampling of products available for networking embedded systems. Whether or not you ultimately select one of the products described, reviewing the options can help in determining how to approach a project.

Every computer in an Ethernet network must have an Ethernet controller, and there are choices here as well. This chapter's In Depth discussion describes the capabilities and operation of popular Ethernet controllers.

Quick Start:
Selecting Components

As with any project, familiarity can make a big difference in how easy it is to get something up and running. On the software side, both C and Java are popular languages for programming networked embedded systems. If you have experience in one of these languages, it makes sense to stick with it. On the hardware side, if you have experience with a particular CPU family, it often makes sense to stay with it if possible as well. At the same time, if there is a product that suits your purpose perfectly but will take some time to master, it may be worthwhile to dig in and learn something new, especially if you can use the knowledge in additional projects in the future.

This book doesn't have room to describe every possibility, and new and updated products continually become available. For links to the latest information about the products described and others, visit Lakeview Research's Embedded Ethernet page at *www.Lvr.com*.

Complete Solutions

Some products are complete solutions that provide both the hardware and program code for Ethernet and Internet communications. The hardware typically includes a circuit board with a CPU, Ethernet controller, and related components. The program code includes support for Ethernet, TCP/IP, and other Internet protocols.

Beyond these basics, the options vary. Different products use different CPUs, and the type and amount of memory and I/O options vary. A product may support programming in assembler, C, Java, or a combination of languages. Some circuit boards are suitable for use in projects as-is, while others are designed mainly as development systems for projects that will eventually be moved to a project-specific circuit board. Some products may require additional investments in programming hardware and debugging tools, while others include these or enable using free software tools.

The documentation and other sources of help and examples provided by a vendor or other parties can make a big difference in how easy it is to get a project up and running. For the hardware, complete schematic diagrams help in interfacing to the module and troubleshooting. For programming, some vendors make the source code available so you can examine and change or adapt the code if you wish. Others offer only the rights to use provided code in executable form.

In this book, I've included example programs for two popular modules that provide complete solutions: Rabbit Semiconductor's RCM3200 RabbitCore C-programmable Module with Ethernet and Dallas Semiconductor's DSTINIm400 Networked Microcontroller Evaluation Kit. The capabilities of the modules are similar in many ways, but each takes a different approach both in the included hardware components and in programming. The following descriptions summarize the features and capabilities of these and a selection of additional modules.

Rabbit Semiconductor RCM3200

At a glance: A fast Z80-derivative CPU with plenty of I/O, low EMI, and a complete development system, including a C compiler.

Ethernet support: 10BASE-T and 100BASE-TX.

Source: Rabbit Semiconductor (*www.rabbitsemiconductor.com*).

Hardware. The RCM3200 RabbitCore C-programmable Module with Ethernet (Figure 3-1) is a circuit board that contains Rabbit Semiconductor's Rabbit 3000 microprocessor, which is a much improved and enhanced derivative of ZiLOG, Inc.'s venerable Z80 microprocessor. The circuit board is smaller than a business card and supports a variety of I/O interfaces.

The Rabbit 3000 microprocessor has seven 8-bit I/O ports. Many of the bits can have special functions, including six serial ports for asynchronous and synchronous communications and Infrared Data Association (IrDA) protocols, a bidirectional parallel port, two input-capture channels, four pulse-width-modulation (PWM) outputs, and two quadrature encoder units with inputs for optical incremental encoder modules.

In addition to the I/O ports, there is an external memory bus with 8 data bits and 20 address lines. The power supply can range from +3.6V to as low

Figure 3-1: Rabbit Semiconductor's RCM3200 Ethernet Core Module contains a CPU, Ethernet controller, and RJ-45 connector. (Photo courtesy of Rabbit Semiconductor.)

as +1.8V. A counter that functions as a real-time clock has a separate power pin to make it easy to provide battery backup. The chip is in a 128-pin LQFP (low profile quad flat pack).

The Rabbit 3000 is an obvious choice for systems that must obtain Federal Communications Commission (FCC) certification or comply with other regulations that limit electromagnetic interference (EMI). The chip's designers have gone to great lengths to create a CPU whose internal architecture and external interfaces make it easy to design systems that pass EMI tests. An article on Rabbit Semiconductor's Web site has details.

The Rabbit 3000 also has several features for applications that must conserve power. Lowering the supply voltage can reduce power consumption by 75 percent. Slowing the clock reduces power consumption as well. The CPU can switch between a fast clock (up to 54 Megahertz) and a second clock that can run at 32 kilohertz. The CPU can use the slow clock while waiting for a specified time to elapse or an event to occur, then switch to the faster clock when processing power is needed. With a low supply voltage and a slow clock, current consumption can be as low as a few hundredths of a milliampere.

The RCM3200 module contains a Rabbit 3000 clocked at 44.2 Megahertz along with memory and components to support Ethernet communications. There are 512 kilobytes of Flash memory for storing programs, 512 kilobytes of fast RAM for loading code for execution, and 256 kilobytes of RAM for storing data. One of the serial ports uses a special programming cable to load firmware from a PC into RAM or Flash memory.

The module's Ethernet controller is an ASIX AS88796 3-in-1 Local Bus Fast Ethernet Controller, which interfaces to the CPU's external data bus. The module has an RJ-45 connector for 10BASE-T and 100BASE-TX Ethernet media systems. Two headers on the bottom of the board provide access to the I/O bits and other signals.

The RCM3200's development kit includes an RCM3200 module and a prototyping board with a power-supply connector, a voltage regulator, a prototyping area, and switches and LEDs for experimenting (Figure 3-2). The RCM3200's headers plug into sockets on the board.

Figure 3-2: For project development, the RCM3200 attaches to a prototyping board. (Photo courtesy of Rabbit Semiconductor.)

The RCM3200 is one of several modules offered by Rabbit Semiconductor. If you don't need the speed of 100BASE-TX, take a look at the RCM2100 module, which supports only 10BASE-T Ethernet. The RCM2100 contains a Rabbit 2000 microprocessor, a slower but still very serviceable CPU with the same instruction set at the Rabbit 3000. The module's Ethernet controller is a Realtek RTL8019AS Full Duplex Ethernet Controller. The Rabbit 3000 and 2000 microprocessors are also available for use on circuit boards of your own design.

Software. Rabbit Semiconductor's Dynamic C is a complete environment for writing and editing code, compiling and linking, loading compiled code into the RCM3200's RAM or Flash memory, and debugging (Figure 3-3). The compiler also supports in-line assembly code.

For networking, Dynamic C includes drivers for the Ethernet controller and libraries that support TCP/IP communications and other networking protocols. The libraries provide support for an HTTP server, an FTP client and server, and sending and receiving e-mail with SMTP and POP3. A file system supports storing information in files in Flash memory or battery-backed RAM.

Additional library modules are available, including a module that implements the open-source, real-time MicroC/OS-II operating system. An Advanced Encryption Standard (AES) module supports encrypting network data using the Rijndael Advanced Encryption Standard cipher. (See Chapter 10 for more about encryption.) Other modules support the Point-to-Point protocol (PPP) and Simple Network Management Protocol (SNMP).

Source code for all of the libraries is provided. Dozens of short, well-commented example programs illustrate how to use the functions in the libraries.

Two code modules perform basic functions for all Dynamic C programs. Compiled code automatically includes the Virtual Driver module, which performs initialization and timer functions. The Rabbit BIOS is compiled separately and handles startup, shutdown, debugging communications, and other basic tasks. Dynamic C loads the BIOS into the RCM3200's memory

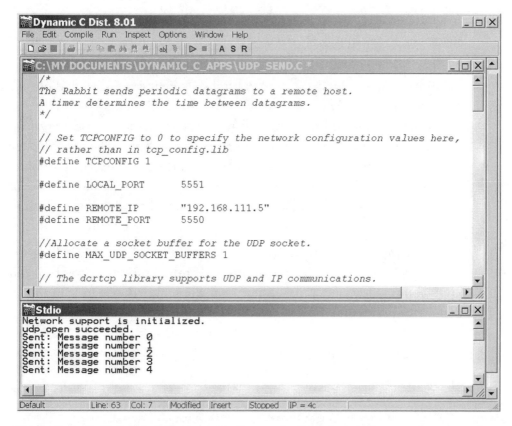

Figure 3-3: Rabbit Semiconductor's Dynamic C is a complete environment for programming, loading and running programs, and debugging.

automatically using the Rabbit 3000's bootstrap mode and programming cable. The Virtual Driver and Rabbit BIOS are fully documented, with source code available.

Dynamic C has built-in support for multitasking for tasks that each require CPU time on a regular basis. A system may use cooperative or preemptive multitasking.

In cooperative multitasking, the tasks must agree to cooperate to not use more than their share of processor time. Dynamic C achieves cooperative multitasking through the use of costatements and cofunctions.

A costatement is a list of statements with a pointer that keeps track of which statement to execute next. A costatement typically functions as one statement in a list of statements that execute in sequence in a loop.

Within a costatement, a waitfor control statement can test to find out if a function has completed or a timeout has occurred. If waitfor returns true, the costatement continues with the next statement in the list. If waitfor returns false, the costatement jumps to its closing brace. The next time the costatement executes, the costatement begins at the waitfor that previously returned false. In this way, the code can make its way through a series of statements without being blocked by a statement that takes a long time to execute. A waitfor statement can call any function that returns a value.

In the example below, an endless for loop alternates between calling the tcp_tick() function, which performs background processing for TCP and UDP communications, and a costatement whose function is to send a datagram once per second.

```
for(;;) {
  tcp_tick(NULL);
  costate {
    //wait DelaySec seconds between sends.
    waitfor(DelaySec(1));
    //send a datagram to the remote host.
    send_datagram();
  }
}
```

The first time the costatement executes, the waitfor(DelaySec(1)) statement executes and saves a value that indicates the current time. The statement returns false and execution jumps to the costatement's closing brace, then to the top of the for loop. Each time through the loop, waitfor(DelaySec(1)) executes, returning False until one second has elapsed. On returning true, execution continues with the send_datagram() statement. This statement calls the application's send_datagram() function, which sends a datagram to a remote host. Program execution then loops back to the waitfor() statement, which restarts the delay timing.

Dynamic C's cofunctions are similar to costatements, but can accept and return arguments.

Costatements and cofunctions are convenient for many applications, but it's also possible to achieve cooperative multitasking with state-machine based programming. State machines can be useful when the program code repeatedly performs a series of tasks, but not always in the same order.

A C switch statement can implement a state machine. For example, a TCP server can use a switch statement to decide what code to execute depending on the current state of a connection. Possible states might be initializing a socket, waiting for a connection, receiving a request, receiving headers, sending a response, and waiting to close a connection. Rabbit Semiconductor's *state.c* example illustrates this approach.

In preemptive multitasking, each task is guaranteed processor time. There's no need to depend on the other tasks to yield. Dynamic C's slice statement enables preemptive multitasking by running a task for a time slice, or period, measured in units of 1/1024 second. At the end of the slice, the task suspends. If all of the tasks in a program's main loop use slice statements, you can determine how often each task receives its slice from the total number of slices.

A limitation to using slices with TCP/IP communications in Dynamic C is that all TCP/IP functionality must take place in a single slice. The MicroC/OS-II library module provides another way to achieve preemptive multitasking.

The documentation for Dynamic C and the hardware modules includes an extensive series of detailed manuals. Rabbit Semiconductor's Web site hosts a tech-support Bulletin Board. In addition, a *rabbit-semi* e-mail discussion list for developers is available at *www.groups.yahoo.com*.

Another programming option for Rabbit modules is the WinIDE Integrated Development Environment from Softools, Inc. (*www.softools.com*). Like Dynamic C, WinIDE includes an editor, a compiler and linker, the ability to load compiled code into RAM or Flash memory, and a debugger. The Control Cross C compiler is a full Standard C compiler. Compiled code is smaller and faster than code compiled with Dynamic C.

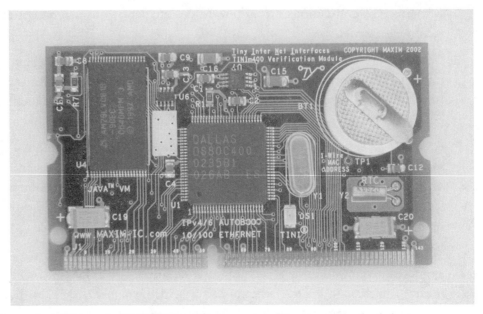

Figure 3-4: Using the DSTINIm400, you can create a networked device programmed in Java.

Dallas Semiconductor DSTINIm400 (TINI)

At a Glance: A fast microcontroller with an enhanced 8051 architecture, plenty of I/O, an operating system, and a Java virtual machine (JVM).

Ethernet support: 10BASE-T, 100BASE-TX

Typical Uses: applications that need speed, lots of I/O, or a CAN interface.

Source: Dallas Semiconductor (*www.dalsemi.com*). Dallas Semiconductor is a wholly owned subsidiary of Maxim Integrated Products.

Hardware. TINI stands for Tiny InterNet Interface. Technically, the TINI isn't a CPU or a circuit board, but a platform that consists of a CPU and related components, support for networking, and a Java runtime environment.

The DSTINIm400 Networked Microcontroller Evaluation Kit (Figure 3-4) is a module that implements the TINI platform. The module's circuit board contains a Dallas Semiconductor DS80C400 Network Microcontroller, which is a much enhanced, high-speed derivative of Intel Corporation's long-popular 8051 microcontroller.

The high speed comes from a fast clock and the ability to execute instructions in fewer clock cycles than an 8051. The maximum clock speed is 75 Mhz. To decrease EMI, the chip can use a slower clock with an on-chip clock multiplier.

The '80C400 contains over 9 kilobytes of RAM and can address 16 Megabytes of external memory.

The chip has eight 8-bit I/O ports. Many of the port bits can function as data and address lines for an external memory bus with 8 data bits and 22 address bits. Most of the other port bits have alternate functions as well. There are three asynchronous serial ports and a programmable output clock for an Infrared Data Association (IrDA) interface. A 1-Wire-net Master can control communications on a 1-Wire net, or MicroLAN, which connects components using a single data line plus a ground line. A Controller Area Network (CAN) 2.0B controller enables communicating over a CAN network, which is a serial interface and protocol that's popular in automotive, industrial, and medical applications. If you don't need a port bit's alternate function, you can use the bit as a generic I/O bit.

The '80C400 chip includes a programmed 64-kilobyte ROM that contains three firmware components. A networking stack supports TCP/IP and related protocols, including IP version 6 (described in Chapter 4). A preemptive task scheduler enables sharing CPU time among multiple tasks. For remote storage of firmware and easy firmware upgrades, the NetBoot component enables the TINI to automatically locate, load, and run program code from the local network or the Internet.

The chip also contains hardware support for Ethernet, including an Ethernet controller for 10-Mb/s and 100-Mb/s networks. An on-chip MII must connect to an external PHY that provides the physical interface to a 10- or 100-Mb/s network.

The DS80C400 chip requires a +1.8V Core Supply Voltage and a +3.3V I/O Supply Voltage. The DSTINIm400 module requires a +3.3V source and contains a regulator to provide +1.8V to the '80C400. For connecting to external circuits, the module has a 144-contact SODIMM (Small Out-line Dual In-line Memory Module) connector with connections to the address and data lines, other signals, and power pins.

On the DSTINIm400 module, additional memory includes two Megabytes of Flash memory for program code and one Megabyte of battery-backed RAM.

Not surprisingly, all of the other integrated circuits on the module are from Maxim or Dallas Semiconductor. A DS1672 Low-Voltage Serial Timekeep-ing Chip contains a 32-bit counter that counts seconds for use as a base for a real-time clock. The DS2502-E48 is a 1-Wire Add-Only Memory chip that contains a factory-programmed, write-protected Ethernet hardware address. The remaining bytes in the 1-kilobyte chip are available for storing informa-tion that will never or seldom change. (The contents of the Add-Only Memory's PROM can be added to or patched, but not erased.) A MAX1792 low-dropout linear regulator provides 1.8V for the '80C400's Core Supply Voltage input. Two MAX6365 Supervisory Circuits and a 3V lithium bat-tery provide battery backup for the RAM chips.

For project development, the DSTINIs400 Sockets Board Evaluation Kit (Figure 3-5) is a circuit board with components and connectors that make it easy to communicate with the DSTINIm400 module. The module plugs into a SODIMM socket on the board.

On the DSTINIs400, an Intel LXT972A Fast Ethernet Transceiver and fil-tering circuits provide an interface between the DS80C400's MII and an RJ-45 jack that can connect to a 10BASE-T or 100BASE-TX network.

A MAX560 +3.3V Transceiver provides a TIA/EIA-562-compatible inter-face for two of the '80C400's serial ports. TIA/EIA-562 is similar to TIA/EIA-232 (also known as RS-232), but with smaller minimum voltage swings. The minimum outputs for a TIA/EIA-232 interface are ±5V, while TIA/EIA-562 requires just ±3.7V. Over short distances, TIA/EIA-562 inter-faces can connect directly to TIA/EIA-232 interfaces with no problems. The DSTINIs400 board includes DB-9 connectors for these ports.

Figure 3-5: The DSTINIs400 Sockets Board Evaluation Kit contains a socket for the DSTINIm400 module and an Ethernet transceiver for communicating with a 10BASE-T or 100BASE-TX network

For interfacing to the '80C400's CAN controller, the DSTINIs400 has a CAN transceiver with connections to a header. Another header connects to two '80C400 port bits that can function as an I²C interface for synchronous serial communications.

Solder pads for an iButton clip connect to the '80C400's 1-Wire Master interface. An iButton is a computer chip inside a round, coin-style, stainless-steel battery case. The base, which consists of the sides and bottom of the case, are ground, and the lid is the data connection. Communications with an iButton use the 1-Wire interface. Uses for iButtons include providing identification, generic data storage, temperature data, and real-time-clock information.

A DS2480B Serial Port to 1-Wire Interface Bridge enables using serial port 1 on the '80C400 to communicate with 1-Wire devices.

The board includes solder pads for a Xilinx XC2C64 CoolRunner II complex programmable logic device (CPLD). The CPLD interfaces to the '80C400's data and address buses and adds 48 I/O bits that are brought out to headers on the board.

The board requires a regulated +5V supply. A MAX1692 Step-down Regulator on the board provides a +3.3V supply for the DSTINIm400 and other components.

The '80C400's predecessor is the '80C390, a slower and less-full-featured but still very powerful chip. The DS-TINI-1 module contains an '80C390, Flash memory, and battery-backed RAM. A 72-contact Single In-line Memory Module (SIMM) connector provides access to the address and data buses, Ethernet signals, port bits, and other signals. For Ethernet communications, the module has Standard Microsystems Corporation (SMSC)'s LAN91C96 Ethernet controller. A Maxim DS2433 EEPROM with a 1-Wire interface stores the Ethernet hardware address. An advantage of the DS-TINI-1 is that the complete Ethernet interface, except for the RJ-45 connector, is on the module, while the DSTINIm400 module requires an external Ethernet transceiver. The '80C390 doesn't contain a programmed ROM, but uses external Flash memory to store a bootstrap loader and runtime environment as well as application programs.

Dallas Semiconductor isn't the only source for TINI hardware. Systronix (*www.systronix.com*) has a variety of offerings. The TStik (Figure 3-6) is a DS80C400 module that uses the same SIMM connector as the DS-TINI-1. Unlike the DSTINIm400, the TStik includes an Ethernet transceiver and filtering circuits, so there's no need to provide these on a separate board. Two editions of the TStik are available, with and without an external memory bus. Systronix also offers a variety of development boards for use with the DS-TINI-1 and TStik.

The Software. The TINI Software Developers Kit (SDK), available for free downloading from Dallas Semiconductor's Web site, includes the TINIOS

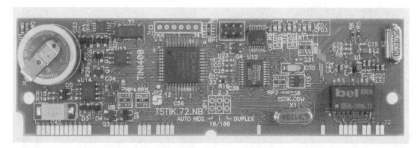

Figure 3-6: The TStik from Systronix is a TINI that contains a DS80C400 on a circuit board with a 72-pin SIMM connector. (Photo courtesy of Systronix.)

operating system and a Java Virtual Machine (JVM). The operating system enables running multiple tasks by scheduling the tasks in time slices. The operating system supports a file system and includes memory and I/O managers. The JVM contains an interpreter that executes Java programs and communicates with the operating system. Every Java-capable computer must have a JVM. The DSTINIm400's JVM uses about 40 kilobytes of memory.

Two useful programs for use in developing TINI applications are the JavaKit utility available from Dallas Semiconductor and a Telnet application.

The JavaKit utility runs on a PC and communicates over a serial-port link with a TINI (Figure 3-7). Typing e at the JavaKit prompt causes the TINI to start its JVM and run the slush command shell. After logging on with a user name and password, you can use slush commands to run programs, view directories, and execute commands such as ipconfig, which can set a static IP address or specify that the TINI should use DHCP to receive its IP address.

When the TINI has been configured for network communications, you can log onto slush over the network using a Telnet application such as Windows' HyperTerminal. To use Hyperterminal for a Telnet session, set up the connection to connect to the TINI using TCP/IP.

A .startup file in the TINI's /etc directory can name applications to run when slush starts.

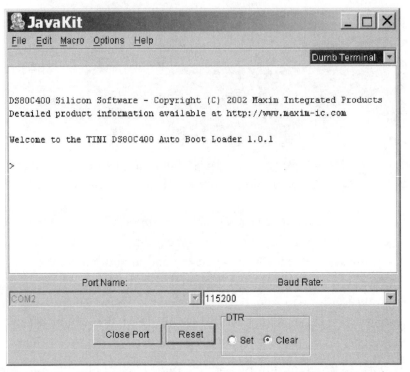

Figure 3-7: The JavaKit utility enables you to start the TINI's JVM and run the slush command shell.

Java programs for TINI can access the standard core Java packages *java.lang, java.io, java.net,* and *java.util.* The TINI implements most of the JDK version 1.1.8 distribution. This isn't the latest distribution, but is still plenty capable for use in embedded-systems applications.

The TINI also supports a series of TINI-specific classes. Several of the classes relate to networking. The TININet class sets and gets network parameters such as the Ethernet address, IP address, and subnet address. The HTTPServer class implements a basic Web server. The DHCPClient and DNSClient classes enables the TINI to use DHCP and the DNS protocol.

The HTTPServer class only supports Web pages with static content. To function as a Web server that serves dynamic content, the TINI can use additional software such as the Tynamo Web server from Shawn Silverman or Smart Software Consulting's TiniHttpServer. Both of these include support for Java servlets.

To compile Java programs, you can use just about any Java compiler and Java development system, including the compiler in the free Java Development Kit (JDK) from Sun Microsystems (*java.sun.com*). Borland's JBuilder environment (*www.borland.com*) includes a compiler and graphical interface for developing. JBuilder comes in several editions, including a free Personal Edition.

After compiling a *.java* file to a *.class* file, an additional step creates the binary file required by the TINI. The TINIConvertor utility converts *.class* files to *.tini* files, which contain the byte codes, or machine instructions, that the TINI's JVM interprets. A *.tini* file is essentially the same as a *.class* files, but with redundant information removed for a smaller file size.

To copy *.tini* files from a PC to a TINI, you can use any generic FTP client program configured to access the TINI's IP address.

The source code for the operating system and Java API aren't available. Dallas Semiconductor and Maxim Integrated Products grant users a no-charge license to load the binary file containing the code into a TINI system.

Dallas Semiconductor provides application notes and many short examples that you can use in writing custom applications. The book *The TINI Specification and Developer's Guide* by Don Loomis, the lead architect and developer of TINI, has additional TINI information and examples. The book is available in printed form from Addison Wesley or as a free download from Dallas Semiconductor. Another book that focuses on the DSTINI-1 is *Designing Embedded Internet Devices* by Dan Eisenreich and Brian DeMuth (Newnes). Other support includes an e-mail discussion list sponsored by Dallas Semiconductor and a variety of Web pages maintained by TINI users.

Although the TINI was created as a Java computer, it's possible to program the DSTINIm400 in C or assembly code using Keil Software's uVision2 C compiler.

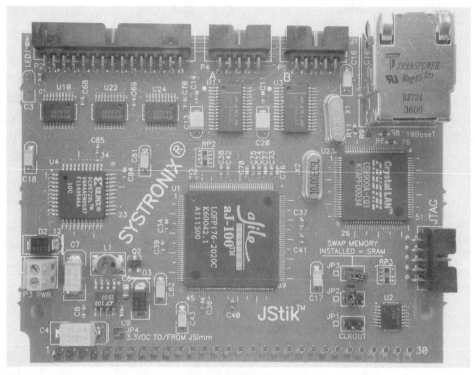

Figure 3-8: Systronix's JStik board contains an aJ-100 microcontroller with native execution of Java bytecodes. (Photo courtesy of Systronix.)

Systronix JStik

At a glance: direct execution of Java bytecodes eliminates the need for an interpreter.

Ethernet support: 10BASE-T

Typical use: Applications that use Java and require speed.

Source: Systronix (*www.systronix.com*).

Hardware. The TINI isn't the only option for Java programmers. Systronix's JStik board (Figure 3-8) contains aJ-100 microcontroller from aJile Systems Inc. The aJ-100's native execution of Java bytecodes results in very fast performance. The chip is based on the JEM processor developed at Rockwell Collins.

The JStik adds a high-speed I/O bus that can operate at bursts of 50 Megabytes per second, two RS-232 ports, and SPI and I²C interfaces. The board fits into a 60-contact SIMM socket and has an RJ-45 plug and additional I/O connectors.

Software. Systronix provides aJile's Jem Builder tool and Charade debugger for building, loading, and testing applications. You can use other Java environments and tools with the JStik as well.

Netburner MOD5282 Processor Module

At a glance: Fast Ethernet and a fast 32-bit CPU with lots of memory and I/O.

Ethernet support: 10BASE-T and 100BASE-TX

Typical use: Applications that need speed and abundant resources

Source: Netburner, Inc. (*www.netburner.com*)

Hardware. Netburner's MOD5282 Processor Module contains Motorola's 32-bit ColdFire MCF5282 processor. The MCF5282 supports a subset of the Motorola 68000 CPU's instruction set. The chip has 512 kilobytes of Flash memory and 64 kilobytes of RAM.

For I/O interfacing, the MCF5282 has three UARTS, a CAN interface, an I²C controller, a queued serial peripheral interface (QSPI) for synchronous serial communications, and an 8-channel, 10-bit analog-to-digital converter.

The chip is in a 256-pin mold array process ball-grid array (MAPBGA) package that contains the media-access control circuits for 10BASE-T and 100BASE-TX Ethernet in addition to the CPU.

The MOD5282 includes 8 Megabytes of SRAM and connections for a 16-bit data bus and 16-bit address bus. For networking, the board includes a PHY for 10-Mb/s and 100-Mb/s Ethernet and an RJ-45 connector.

Applications are compressed and stored in Flash memory. At startup, the application loads into and runs from RAM.

The Module 5282 Development Kit contains a MOD5282 board, a power supply, connectors, and other components for prototyping and testing.

Software. Also included in the Module 5282 Development Kit are software support for Ethernet and Internet protocols, an operating system based on the freeware μC/OS, the freeware GNU C/C++ compiler, a debugger, and configuration utilities.

All of the software included with the development kit includes complete source code. The software supports TCP/IP, and related protocols, including code that enables NetBurner modules to function as Web servers and to send and receive e-mail.

Microchip Technology PICDEM.net Demonstration Board

At a glance: An aid to developing networking applications for Microchip Technology's PICMicro microcontrollers.

Ethernet support: 10BASE-T

Typical use: Projects that require minimal resources or any PICMicro-based project with an Ethernet interface or support for Internet protocols.

Source: Microchip Technology (*www.microchip.com*).

Hardware. The PICDEM.net Demonstration Board contains a microcontroller, Ethernet controller, related components, and a breadboarding area. The board is intended mainly for developing and testing, rather than as a plug-in module for use in a product.

The microcontroller is a PIC16F877, a member of Microchip Technology's popular PICMicro family The PIC16F877 has Flash memory that can store 8192 14-bit words, 368 bytes of RAM, and 192 bytes of EEPROM. There are 33 I/O bits. Many of the bits have alternate functions, including an eight-channel, 10-bit analog-to-digital converter, an asynchronous serial port, a synchronous serial port, and a parallel interface. The clock speed is 19.6608 Megahertz.

The microcontroller is in a 40-pin DIP socket, and can be replaced by other members of the PIC family, including the PIC18C452 and PIC18F452. The board also contains a 32-kilobyte serial EEPROM for storing Web pages the microcontroller will serve. For experimenting, the board provides LEDs, a pushbutton, potentiometers, and an LCD module. The Ethernet controller is a Realtek RTL8019AS. The interface to the controller uses the CPU's parallel port and five additional I/O bits.

For loading programs, there is a connector for use with Microchip's MPLAB In-Circuit Debugger, which can program the microcontroller's Flash memory. You can use the serial port and a terminal emulator such as Windows' Hyperterminal to load network configuration information into the EEPROM.

Software. The microcontroller comes programmed with firmware to support networking and serve a sample Web page. The source code is on the accompanying CD. The networking code is from Iosoft, and is described in detail in the book *TCP/IP Lean: Web Servers for Embedded Systems* by Jeremy Bentham (CMP Books). The source code is available to anyone who buys the book. Commercial use of the code requires paying a licensing fee to Iosoft.

Special-Purpose Modules

In addition to products that provide a complete generic system for networking, a variety of modules and chips are available to handle specific tasks. Some products can interface to just about any CPU. If you have an existing product or a CPU that you want to use, one of these modules may provide a way to add networking capability. This section describes a selection of products.

Lantronix Device Server

At a glance: enables any device with an asynchronous serial port to communicate over a network.

Typical use: any device or system that communicates over a serial port and requires network access.

Ethernet support: 10BASE-T, 100BASE-TX

Source: Lantronix, Inc. (*www.lantronix.com*)

Hardware: Lantronix offers its Device Servers in a variety of packages, including devices in enclosures, circuit boards and chips for incorporating into other devices, and a server squeezed into a slightly extended RJ-45 connector. Each server has a TTL-compatible asynchronous serial port for communicating with an external device or system and an RJ-45 connector for connecting to an Ethernet network. Firmware is stored in Flash ROM. The CPU varies depending on the product. Two of the options are AMD's AMD186ES and Lantronix's DSTni-LX, which contains a CPU, serial ports, Ethernet controller, and RAM.

Software: The Device Servers contain firmware to support Ethernet and Internet protocols, including UDP, TCP, IP, and HTTP. User firmware manages communications between the serial port and the server. For programming, the DSTni-LX Development kit includes a development board and the Paradigm C++ Professional development toolkit. The USNET TCP/IP software suite and a real-time operating system are also available separately for use in your own hardware. USNET is compatible with Intel 80x86, Motorola 68K, and other microprocessors. Source code is included.

Ubicom IP2022 Wireless Network Processor

At a glance: A CPU optimized for networking with software-configurable peripherals and wireless support.

Typical use: Web servers and wireless networking

Ethernet support: 10BASE--T

Source: Ubicom, Inc. (*www.ubicom.com*)

Hardware. Ubicom's IP2022 Wireless Network Processor is a CPU optimized for networking functions. The chip contains two configurable Serializer/Deserializer blocks. Using software modules provided by Ubicom, each block can support Ethernet, USB, a General Purpose Serial Interface (GPSI), a Serial Peripheral Interface (SPI), or a UART. The CPU uses a 120-Megahertz clock obtained from a 4.8-Megahertz crystal.

The Universal Device Networking Kit contains a development board, an adapter for in-circuit programming, and software. The Advanced Wireless

Figure 3-9: Ubicom's Universal Device Networking Kit contains the IP2022 Wireless Network Processor. (Photo courtesy of Ubicom, Inc.)

Kit adds support for IEEE 802.11b wireless networking on a PC Card with supporting firmware. The Phantom Server is a Web server module with an IP2022 CPU, 512 kilobytes of Flash memory for storing Web pages, and support for CGI and SSI.

Software. Project development uses Ubicom's integrated development environment and GNUPro, a software development suite that includes a C compiler. The suite is built around the open-source GNU standard and is available from Red Hat (*www.redhat.com*). The IP2022's Core Software Development Kit includes support for Ethernet and Internet protocols.

Netmedia SitePlayer Ethernet Web Server

At a glance: a very inexpensive module that can serve Web pages and perform UDP communications with a minimum of user programming. Requires a serial link to a CPU to update Web page data and receive data from clients.

Ethernet support: 10BASE-T

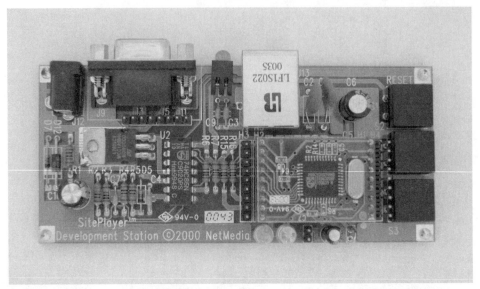

Figure 3-10: Netmedia's SitePlayer and development board provide a Web server with Ethernet and RS-232 interfaces.

Typical use: Basic monitoring and control tasks.

Source: Netmedia (*www.netmedia.com*)

Hardware. The main purpose of Netmedia's SitePlayer(Figure 3-10) is to provide a very low-cost platform for serving Web pages, including pages with dynamic content. For most projects, the SitePlayer communicates with an external CPU over a serial link. The SitePlayer can place data received from the CPU in its Web pages and can send data from a form or a hyperlink on a Web page to the CPU. The CPU can also use the SitePlayer to send and receive UDP datagrams over a network. In some very basic applications, you can use the SitePlayer without a connection to a CPU, such as applications where users click buttons on a Web page to toggle pins on the SitePlayer's board.

The SitePlayer contains just two chips: a Philips 8051-compatible P89C51 microcontroller and a Realtek RTL8019AS Ethernet controller. Two 10-pin headers provide access to the Ethernet interface, an asynchronous serial interface, an output for indicating status of the Ethernet interface, a reset input, and eight I/O pins.

The microcontroller's Flash memory stores the program code that runs the SitePlayer and the Web pages the SitePlayer serves. The SitePlayer can store up to 48 kilobytes of Web pages.

The SitePlayer's development board contains a SitePlayer module and headers for monitoring or connecting to the SitePlayer's pins. Also included are an RJ-45 connector for the Ethernet interface, an RS-232 interface and connector for the asynchronous serial interface, a voltage regulator and power-supply connector, an LED controlled by the LINK output, a Reset button, and two additional LEDs and pushbuttons.

Software. A SitePlayer project requires a SitePlayer Definition file, which is a text file that contains setup parameters and variable definitions in a Siteplayer-specific format. The setup parameters include information such as whether the SitePlayer should receive its IP address from a DHCP server and if not, what IP address to assign to the SitePlayer. The definitions are for variables that will contain dynamic content in the Web pages. The SitePlayer's software manual explains the syntax to use in the Definition file.

The Web pages served by the SitePlayer are like any Web pages except that they may contain pointers to objects that correspond to variables in the Definition file. A "^" before a name indicates a pointer. For example, ^flow is a pointer to the variable flow. When the SitePlayer serves the Web page, it substitutes the current value of the named variable for the pointer.

Netmedia's SiteLinker utility assembles a Definition file into a SitePlayer Binary image and enables you to load the image and your Web pages into the SitePlayer. A SitePlayer Interface File enables receiving information provided by a user viewing a SitePlayer Web page.

The firmware inside the SitePlayer manages communications over the Ethernet and serial ports. The source code isn't available.

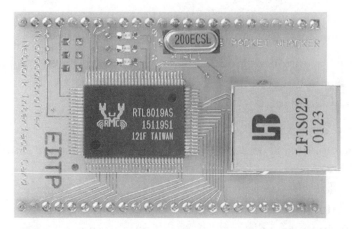

Figure 3-11: EDTP's PacketWhacker makes it easy to add an Ethernet interface to an external CPU. (Photo courtesy of EDTP Electronics.)

EDTP Electronics Packet Whacker

At a glance: An Ethernet interface on a circuit board with headers for connecting to a CPU.

Typical use: adding Ethernet to any microcontroller circuit.

Ethernet support: 10BASE-T

Source: EDTP Electronics (*www.edtp.com*)

Hardware. The Packet Whacker (Figure 3-11) from EDTP Electronics is an Ethernet interface only. The circuit board contains a Realtek RTL8019AS Ethernet controller, an RJ-45 connector, two headers that bring out the signals required to communicate with the Ethernet controller, and related components. You can use the Packet Whacker to add Ethernet to just about any microcontroller. EDTP Electronics has similar boards with other Ethernet controllers: the NICki has a Cirrus 8900A and the NICkita has an ASIX 88796L. The Whacked 8051 Development Board includes Packet Whacker circuits and adds a Philips P89C668 8051-compatible microcontroller and 64 kilobytes of Flash memory.

Software. EDTP provides example Packet Whacker firmware for UDP and TCP communications using a Microchip PIC16F877. The Whacked 8051

Development Board includes C and Basic (BASCOM-51) code for UDP, TCP, and other Internet protocols. The NICkita includes an e-book with information about using the ASIX 88796L controller.

Serial-to-Ethernet Bridge

At a glance: enables RS-232 and RS-485 devices to communicate over networks

Ethernet support: 10BASE-T

Typical use: remote communications with devices with serial interfaces.

Sources: Z-World (*www.zworld.com*), Netburner (*www.netburner.com*), R.E. Smith (*www.rs485.com*).

Hardware. Thousands of existing devices that don't support Ethernet have an RS-232 or RS-485 serial interface. With a serial-to-Ethernet bridge, you can communicate with these devices in an Ethernet network.

The bridge connects to the device's serial interface and to an Ethernet network. Computers anywhere in the network can then exchange data with the device. After being configured, the bridge transparently sends received serial data on the network in TCP segments and sends data received in TCP segments to the device's serial interface.

Two devices that connect to a network via bridges can communicate the same as if they were connected directly by a serial interface. The bridge converts between interfaces as needed.

Serial-to-Ethernet bridges are available from a variety of sources. Z-World's EM1500 Multipoint Serial-to-Ethernet Bridge supports four RS-232 ports and one RS-485 port. The board's CPU is a Rabbit 3000. R.E. Smith's ESPSX3 Serial Port Server has two RS-232 ports and one port that is configurable as an RS-232 port or an isolated RS-485 port. The board contains a Rabbit Semiconductor RCM2200 module. Netburner's SB72 Serial-to-Ethernet Device and Processor Board supports one RS-232 or RS-485 interface. The board's CPU is a Motorola ColdFire 5272.

Software. A Serial-to-Ethernet Server typically comes with an application that enables you to enter settings for your network and devices. Most also include a Web page that you can use for configuring when the device is on the network.

After configuring, computers on the network can use TCP/IP applications to communicate with the device.

In Depth:
Ethernet Controllers

An embedded system that supports Ethernet requires Ethernet controller hardware to provide the Ethernet interface. Many Ethernet controller chips are designed for use in desktop computers and include support for standard PC buses and Plug-and-Play functions. Small embedded systems typically don't need all of the capabilities of a PC's Ethernet controller. But because they're available and familiar, a few of the older, simpler PC controllers have found new life in embedded systems. More recently, controllers designed specifically for use in embedded systems have become available.

This section introduces some of the more popular controllers for embedded systems. If you buy a module with a controller on it, it's likely that it will use one of the chips described below. A module containing an Ethernet controller will probably include firmware support for communicating with the controller. In many cases you can use the firmware without having to know much about the controller's inner workings. Some vendors provide source code so you can customize if needed, while others release only the executable code.

Even if you don't need to program a controller directly, a basic understanding of how the controller works is helpful in selecting hardware and troubleshooting.

What the Hardware Does

Ethernet communications are typically handled by a combination of an Ethernet controller chip and device-driver code that communicates with the controller. Figure 3-12 shows the location of the Ethernet hardware and

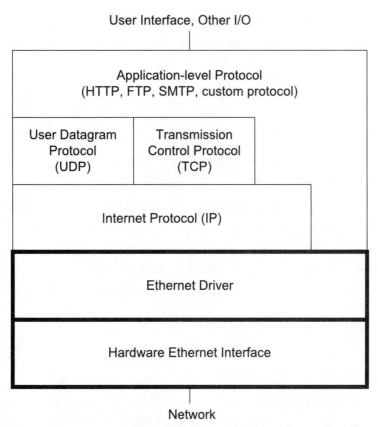

Figure 3-12: In the network protocol stack, the Ethernet driver communicates with the Ethernet controller hardware and either the IP layer or the application

driver in a network stack. Many embedded systems use IP with TCP or UDP, but for some applications, the Ethernet driver can communicate directly with the application layer.

The controller chip handles many of the details of sending and receiving Ethernet frames. In sending a frame, a controller typically does all of the following:

- Receives the message to send and the destination address from higher-level software.

- Calculates the Ethernet frame check sequence.

- Places data, addresses, and other information in the frame's fields.

- Attempts to transmit the frame when the network is idle.

- Detects collisions, cancels any transmitted frame with a collision, and retries according to the protocol specified in the IEEE 802.3 standard (half-duplex interfaces only).

- Provides an indication of success or failure of a transmission.

In receiving a frame, a controller typically does all of the following:

- Detects and synchronizes to new received frames.

- Ignores any frames that are less than the minimum size.

- Ignores any frames that don't contain the interface's address or a valid multicast or broadcast address in the Destination Address field.

- Calculates the frame-check-sequence value, compares the result with the received value, and indicates an error if they don't match.

- Makes the received frame's data and other information available to the receiving computer. Higher-level software reads the message and does whatever needs to be done with it.

Ethernet Controller Basics

In an Ethernet-capable embedded system, a CPU manages communications with the Ethernet controller. The minimum requirement for the CPU is a microcontroller with an external 8-bit data bus.

Some of the controllers that have been popular in embedded systems were designed for use on expansion cards for the ISA bus of early PCs. An embedded system that uses an ISA-compatible controller can ignore any unneeded interrupt, address, and status and control pins.

A shorthand term for a network interface controller is NIC. The same term can also refer to an expansion card that contains a network interface controller.

Related Components

A typical controller requires few additional components. For 10BASE-T and 100BASE-TX systems, the IEEE 802.3 standard requires an isolation transformer that also functions as a low-pass filter between the controller and the network's RJ-45 connector. Filters that comply with the standard are readily available. Examples include the FA163079 from YCL Electronics and the PM-1006 from Premier Magnetics. The appropriate filters vary with the controller chip or the MAU or PHY that connects to the filter. The vendors of these components typically provide recommendations and advice in selecting filters.

As explained in Chapter 2, many controller chips require few additional components to interface to twisted-pair cable, but fiber-optic or coaxial cable is likely to require additional MAU or PHY circuits.

Other typical required components include a timing crystal to clock the controller chip and decoupling capacitors for the power pins. Some controllers also support an interface to a serial EEPROM, which can provide non-volatile, read/write storage of configuration data such as the Ethernet hardware address. Most controllers also have status outputs for interfacing to LEDs.

NE2000 Compatibility

A term you're likely to hear in reference to program code for network controllers is NE2000-compatible. The NE2000 was an early and popular PC network interface card from Novell. The card contained National Semiconductor's DP8390 controller. Software for systems that use the '8390 or a compatible chip has come to be known as NE2000-compatible code.

A major feature of the '8390 is its set of internal registers. By reading and writing to the registers, a CPU can configure the controller, initiate transmitting of data on the network, and read received network data. The registers in the '8390 are arranged in two 16-byte pages. The CR register is at offset 00h on both pages. Writing to bits 6 and 7 in the CR register selects the current page. Offsets 01h through 0Fh on each page store additional register values. On power-up or reset, program code typically initializes the registers to desired values before Ethernet data transfers begin.

An NE2000-compatible chip should support all of the '8390's registers. Newer chips generally have additional register pages to support new features.

NE2000-compatible chips are also likely to support accessing buffer memory at addresses 4000h through 7FFFh. A portion of the memory forms a ring buffer for storing data received from the network, and the remainder of the memory stores data to be transmitted on the network.

Documentation

Many providers of controller chips have example code for setting up the registers and transferring frames. You may need to translate the code for use with a specific CPU. Source and executable code is also available from many vendors of modules that use the chips.

The documentation for the original DP8390 can be a useful supplement to the sometimes thin documentation provided for newer NE2000-compatible chips. National Semiconductor also has a couple of application notes. Note *AN-475: DP8390 Network Interface Controller: An Introductory Guide*, describes the processes of sending and receiving data. Note *AN-874: Writing Drivers for the DP8390 NIC Family of Ethernet Controllers*, focuses on programming, with example assembly code for a PC.

I won't attempt to duplicate the controllers' data sheets here. Instead, I'll concentrate on the features and capabilities that you'll want to know about in selecting a chip for a project. You can then go to the data sheet for the details.

The ASIX AX88796

An Ethernet controller designed for use in embedded systems is the AX88796 3-in-1 Local Bus Fast Ethernet Controller from ASIX Electonics Corporation. Rabbit Semiconductor uses this controller in its RCM3200 module. The controller supports Ethernet communications at 10 and 100 Mb/s.

The '88796 is NE2000-compatible. A major difference between the '88796 and the DP8390 is that the '88796 has an on-chip 16-kilobyte static RAM (SRAM) buffer for network data. The '88796 also has separate (not multiplexed) data and address buses and an interface to serial EEPROM.

Connections

Figure 3-14 shows the basic connections the RCM3200 module uses for the '88796. The chip is a 128-pin plastic light quad flat pack (PLQFP). The clock is a 25-Mhz crystal or oscillator. The power supply is +3.3V. Three outputs drive status LEDs.

Ethernet. For twisted-pair networks, the chip can connect through a filter to an RJ-45 jack. The RCM3200 uses a PulseJack module from Pulse Engineering, Inc. The module integrates the RJ-45 connector and filtering circuits in a single package. An on-chip MII enables using an external PHY to connect to other cable types at 10 or 100 Mb/s.

Bus Compatibility. The CPU0 and CPU1 pins configure the chip for use with one of four bus types that are popular in embedded systems: ISA, Intel 80186, Intel MCS-51 (8051), and Motorola 68000. The selected bus determines the functions of the pins that control reading and writing to the external data bus and the polarity of the interrupt output. For example, on a 68000 bus, pin 18 is a R/W input that controls bus reads and writes and pin 19 has no connection, while the ISA interface has separate read and write signals: pin 18 is IOWR and pin 19 is IORD.

SRAM. The controller's 16-kilobyte SRAM buffer holds packets waiting to transmit on the network and packets received from the network. With an 8-bit data bus, only 8 kilobytes of the SRAM are available.

Addressing. The chip has 10 address inputs, but not all systems need them all. The first five bits (SA0 through SA4) address the controller's internal registers. Every controller must have these lines connected to the CPU's address bus. Two of the registers (10h, 11h) are the Data Port, which enables the CPU to access the controller's 16 kilobytes of SRAM without using additional address lines.

In most systems, the Ethernet controller shares the data bus with other components, so the CPU needs a way to select the controller on the bus. Two ways to accomplish this are by using additional address lines to select a base address or by using the controller's Chip Select (/CS) input.

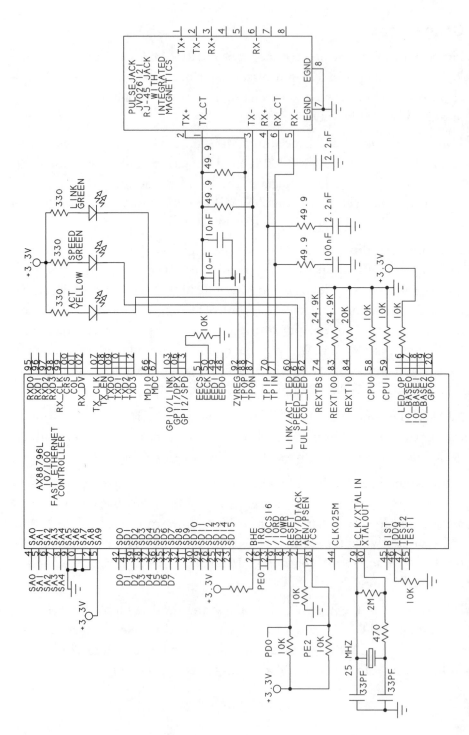

Figure 3-13: The ASIX AX88796 Ethernet controller supports communications at 10 and 100Mb/s. This schematic shows a portion of the circuits in Rabbit Semiconductor's RCM3200 module.

The 10-BASE0, 10-BASE1, and 10-BASE2 pins on the '88796 can select one of eight base addresses. Jumpers or CPU outputs can control the pins, or they can be hard-wired. The address values are compatible with PC hardware, but there's no reason you can't use them in other systems. For example, if the controller has a base address of 200h, the CPU accesses the chip's registers by reading and writing to the addresses 200h through 21Fh. To enable selecting the chip by address, the controller's address pins SA5 through SA9 must connect to the CPU's address bus.

If you instead use the Chip Select input to select the chip, you don't need to connect the controller's upper address lines to the bus, and you can select a base address in a higher address range than the options programmed into the chip. Rabbit Semiconductor's RCM3200 module uses the Chip Select along with firmware that configures the Rabbit 3000 CPU to strobe a port bit on I/O accesses to a specific address range.

When using Chip Select, SA5 through SA9 must match the selected base address in the controller. The RCM3200 module permanently enables base address 200h by tying SA9 high and tying SA5 through SA8 low at the controller.

Data. A register bit in the '88796 selects whether the controller uses 8 or 16 data lines. The data bus for the 68000 mode must be 16 bits, but the other buses can use 8 or 16 bits.

Interrupts. The IRQ interrupt output can request service from the CPU. The polarity of the signal depends on the selected bus type. A CPU that doesn't support or doesn't want to use interrupts can poll the interrupt line.

Serial EEPROM Interface. The '88796 has four pins that can interface to a serial EEPROM with a Microwire interface. The EEPROM can provide non-volatile storage for an Ethernet hardware address and other information. Unlike some other controllers, the '88796 doesn't automatically load information from the serial EEPROM into the controller's registers. Instead, the CPU must access the EEPROM's contents by reading and writing to the MII/EEPROM Management Register. The CPU can then copy the information it reads from the EEPROM to other registers.

If your system already has Flash memory or other non-volatile, read/write memory, you can save on component cost by using existing memory to store the configuration data instead of a serial EEPROM. This is the approach Rabbit Semiconductor uses in its RCM3200 module.

Transferring Data

Like the DP8390, the '88796 uses direct memory access (DMA) to automate transfers of network data into and out of the SRAM. The CPU reads and writes to the Data Port register, and the controller stores or retrieves the data at sequential addresses in the SRAM.

Receiving data. The '88796 stores data received from the network in a portion of the chip's SRAM reserved as a ring buffer. In a ring buffer, two pointers determine where to read and write next. The write pointer increments after each write to the buffer. After writing to the highest address, the pointer wraps back to the lowest address, forming a ring. Meanwhile, as the CPU reads the data from the buffer, the read pointer steps through the buffer in a similar way. To prevent lost data, the CPU must retrieve the data fast enough to keep the buffer from overflowing.

In the '88796, the Page Start Address Register (PSTART) and Page Stop Address Register (PSTOP) determine the buffer's size. Typically, half or more of the SRAM is reserved for the ring buffer, with the remainder left for the transmit buffer.

The ring buffer is structured as a series of 256-byte buffers, or pages. The Boundary Pointer register (BNRY) is the read pointer, which holds the page address of the next data packet for the CPU to read. The Current Page Register (CPR) is the write pointer, which holds the page address for storing the next data packet received from the network.

In storing a frame in the ring buffer, the controller reserves the first four bytes for storing the contents of the Receive Status Register (RSR), the address of the next packet to be stored in the buffer, and the number of bytes received.

The SRAM stores a received frame only if the destination address matches the controller's hardware address or another address the controller is configured to accept. The Physical Address Registers (PAR0–PAR5) contain the interface's Ethernet hardware address. In addition, the controller accepts frames sent to a multicast address specified in the controller's Multicast Address Registers (MAR0–MAR7), and the controller accepts broadcast transmissions if the Accept Broadcast (AS) bit is set in the Receive Configuration Register (RCR). The Receive Configuration Register also permits configuring the chip in promiscuous mode, which causes the controller to accept frames with any destination address.

On receiving a frame, the controller checks for CRC and frame-alignment errors and checks to be sure the frame is at least the minimum allowed frame size. The controller drops any frame that shows an error or isn't the minimum size.

When the contents of a frame are available in the ring buffer, the controller asserts an interrupt. The CPU can then use the controller's Remote Read command to retrieve the data from the ring buffer. The CPU reads all of the data from a single DMA-port address (10h) and the controller provides the bytes in sequence.

Sending data. Sending data on the network requires two steps: the CPU first copies the data to send to the SRAM and then instructs the controller to send the frame on the network. The CPU uses the controller's Remote Write command to write the data to transmit to the controller's SRAM. The CPU writes all of the data to the DMA-port address (10h), and the controller stores the bytes in sequence. Transmitting doesn't use a ring buffer because the CPU can control the transfer of data into the buffer.

After copying data to send to the SRAM, the CPU writes the starting page address of the data to the Transmit Page Start Register (TPSR) and writes the number of bytes to transmit to the Transmit Byte Count Registers (TBCR0, TCBCR1). When the CPU sets the TXP bit in the Command Register, the controller sends the specified bytes in a frame on the network.

The controller adds the preamble, start-of-frame delimiter, and CRC values in the appropriate locations in the Ethernet frame to be transmitted. The controller also decides when to attempt to send the frame on the network,

127

sends the bits to the network interface in sequence, and handles collisions and retries.

When a transmission is complete, an interrupt informs the CPU so it can prepare another frame to send or take other action.

Realtek RTL8019AS

For embedded systems with 10BASE-T support, one of the most popular controllers has been the RTL8019AS Full Duplex Ethernet Controller with Plug and Play Function from Realtek Semiconductor Corp. The '8019AS is another NE2000-compatible derivative of the DP8390. Like the ASIX '88796, the '8019AS has an on-chip 16-kilobyte SRAM and an interface to serial EEPROM.

The '8019AS is designed for use with the ISA bus, but the chip can also interface to other 8- and 16-bit buses. If you don't need support for Plug and Play, you can configure the chip to ignore it.

Connections

Figure 3-14 shows a portion of the schematic for Rabbit Semiconductor's RCM2100 module. The chip is a 100-pin quad flat pack (QFP). The clock is a 20-Mhz crystal or oscillator. Four outputs can drive status LEDs. The power supply is +5V.

Ethernet. For 10BASE-T networks, the chip can connect through a filter to an RJ-45 jack. The chip also contains an AUI to enable using other 10-Mb/s media systems.

SRAM. The controller's 16-kilobyte SRAM buffer holds packets waiting to transmit on the network and packets received from the network. When using 8-bit data, only eight kilobytes of the buffer are available.

Addressing. The address bus is 18 bits. The first five bits address the controller's internal registers. If the controller shares the bus with other chips, it can use additional address lines to select the chip on the bus. The chip allows a choice of 16 PC-compatible base addresses. The IORB and IOWB inputs control the read and write operations.

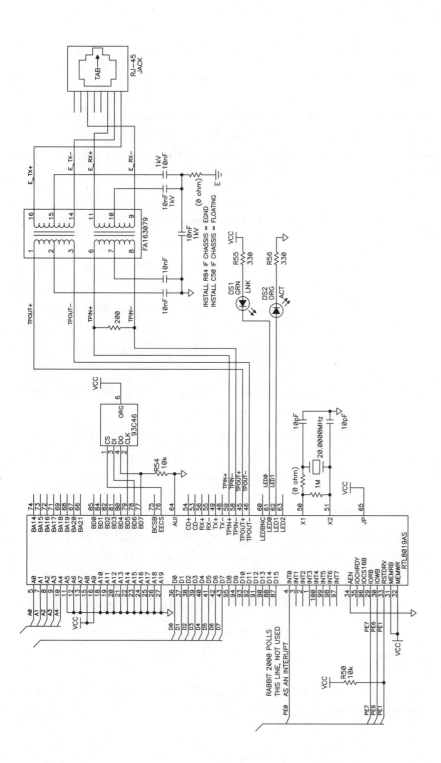

Figure 3-14: Realtek's RTL8019AS Ethernet controller provides an interface between a 10-Mbps Ethernet network and a CPU. (Courtesy of Rabbit Semiconductor Inc.)

Data. A register bit selects whether the controller uses 8 or 16 data lines.

Interrupts. An interrupt output can request service from the CPU. Three bits in the controller's CONFIG1 register select one of eight interrupt outputs on the controller. On an ISA card, seven of these outputs each connect to one of the IRQ lines on the ISA bus. This enables a PC to configure the card to use an available IRQ line by writing the appropriate value to the register.

The eighth output, INT0, has no assigned ISA-bus IRQ line. A small embedded system may wire IRQ0 directly to an interrupt on the CPU. A CPU can also poll IRQ0 to find out when an interrupt has occurred.

Serial EEPROM Interface. On power-up, the '8019AS can be configured to retrieve information from a serial EEPROM or another component with a compatible interface. Pins BD5, BD6, and BD7 can function as the clock, data input, and data output for a Microwire synchronous serial interface. These lines can connect to a 9346 serial EEPROM, which can store 1024 bits organized as 64 words of 16 bits each. The '8019AS has assigned EEPROM locations for initial values of configuration registers, an Ethernet address, and Plug and Play information.

If your system already has Flash memory or other non-volatile, read/write memory, you can save on component cost by using the existing memory to hold the configuration data instead of a serial EEPROM.

Transferring Data

The '8019AS manages network data much like the '88796, using DMA to transfer data into and out of the SRAM and storing received data in a ring buffer.

Realtek also offers controllers that support Fast Ethernet and Gigabit Ethernet.

SMSC LAN91C96

Another Ethernet controller designed specifically for embedded systems is Standard Microsystems Corporation (SMSC)'s LAN91C96 Non-PCI Full

Duplex Ethernet Controller with Magic Packet. Dallas Semiconductor's DS-TINI-1 module uses this controller. The '91C96 supports 10BASE-T Ethernet and has an AUI to support other 10-Mb/s media systems.

The chip is a 100-pin QFP or thin quad flat pack (TQFP). The power supply can be +5V or +3.3V.

Because it's not intended for use in PCs, the '91C96 doesn't have an ISA or PCI interface or support for Plug and Play. Instead it has a generic local-bus interface and also supports PC Card (PCMCIA) and Motorola 68000 buses. The configuration registers are not NE2000-compatible.

The chip can use 8 or 16 data lines and up to 20 address lines. An external serial EEPROM can store configuration information. A 6-kilobyte SRAM stores received network data and data waiting to transmit. The controller dynamically allocates the amount of memory used for transmitting and receiving according to the traffic. To ensure that some transmit memory is available, the chip can be configured to reserve a portion of memory for transmitting.

The chip supports Magic Packet, which is a power-conserving technology that enables the controller to wake from a sleep mode on receiving a special Magic Packet from the network. The Magic Packet contains a synchronization stream consisting of six bytes of FFh, followed by 16 repetitions of the controller's hardware address. AMD licenses the Magic Packet technology to chip manufacturers such as SMSC.

Cirrus Logic CS8900A

An older ISA-based controller that's suitable for some embedded systems is Cirrus Logic's CS8900A Crystal LAN ISA Ethernet controller. The '8900A is not NE2000-compatible. Instead it defines its own set of registers in on-chip SRAM that it calls PacketPage memory.

For 10-BASE-T networks, the chip can connect through a filter to an RJ-45 jack. An AUI port enables connecting to other 10-Mb/s media systems. There are versions for +5V and +3.3V power supplies. The package is a

100-pin TQFP. A serial-EEPROM interface enables the storing of addressing and other configuration data.

The PacketPage memory is 4 kilobytes. The first 350 bytes hold the contents of registers for configuring the bus interface, providing status and control information, initiating transmits, and address filtering. The rest of the memory holds received Ethernet frames and frames waiting to transmit. The amount of memory allocated for each direction can vary depending on the traffic.

The chip has 20 address lines. Although the controller supports both 8- and 16-bit data, there are several limitations with 8-bit data. When configured for 8-bit data, the controller doesn't support interrupts. The CPU must poll the chip to find out when a received frame is available, when a frame has finished transmitting, or when an error has occurred. With 8-bit data, there is no EEPROM interface, no support for DMA, and no auto-incrementing of the PacketPage pointer.

4

Using the Internet Protocol in Local and Internet Communications

The protocols in the IEEE 802.3 Ethernet standard enable the computers in a local network to exchange messages with each other. In practice, most Ethernet networks also use Internet protocols such as TCP or UDP and IP. These provide defined and well-supported methods for accomplishing common tasks such as flow control and flexible addressing and routing of messages.

Messages that travel on the Internet must use IP. And because TCP and UDP are designed to work along with IP, local communications that use TCP or UDP also use IP, even if they wouldn't otherwise require it.

This chapter begins with a guide to connecting embedded systems to the Internet. Following this is an introduction to the Internet Protocol, including when and how embedded systems can use it in local and Internet communications.

Quick Start: Connecting to the Internet

To communicate over the Internet, a computer must have three things: an IP address that identifies the computer on the Internet, the ability to send and receive IP datagrams, and a connection to a router that can access the Internet.

An Internet Service Provider (ISP) can provide one or more IP addresses and a connection to a router that can communicate over the Internet. Customers use a variety of ways to connect to ISPs. A high-volume user, including the networks at some large businesses, government offices, and schools, may have a dedicated, high-speed connection to an ISP. If your network is located at a facility that has this type of access, your network administrator can tell you if your system can use the connection. Connections that support low to moderate traffic typically connect to the ISP via a modem or other device that interfaces to a phone line or a cable from a cable-TV provider.

Considerations in Obtaining Internet Service

The type of Internet connection to use depends in part on its intended use. A computer that hosts a Web page that other computers can request has different requirements than a computer used only to request Web pages but not serve them.

In many Internet communications, one computer functions as a client, and the other as a server. A client requests resources from a server. A resource may be a Web page, file, or other data. In response to a request, a server sends the client the requested resource or a response such as an error message.

Microsoft's Internet Explorer and other Web browsers are clients. The text that you type or copy into the browser's Address text box (such as `http://www.Lvr.com` or `http://192.168.111.1`) identifies the resource you're requesting and the server you're requesting it from. The computers that host the resources are functioning as servers, which detect, interpret, and respond to requests from computers on the Internet or in a local network.

Many servers are huge systems that store thousands of files, but a server can also be a small embedded system that serves a few basic Web pages or other information on request. As Chapter 3 showed, many Ethernet-capable modules for embedded systems include software that enables the modules to function as Web servers.

If you want users on the Internet to be able to request Web pages, download or upload information, or access other resources on your system, you'll need three things: a computer that functions as a server, an Internet account that permits hosting a server, and network-security settings that enable the server to receive and respond to requests from other computers in the network without putting other local resources at risk.

When selecting a method of connecting, you need to consider the speed in both the upstream (towards the Internet) and downstream (from the Internet) directions. For many inexpensive accounts, the upstream speed is slower than the downstream speed. This arrangement is generally fine for home users, who tend to use Internet connections for activities such as Web surfing, where most of the traffic is downloads. Typical uploading activities for home users, such as sending moderate amounts of e-mail, aren't time-critical, so a slower upload speed is fine.

In contrast, a server sends most of its data upstream. Still, an embedded system that serves very basic Web pages or transfers moderate amounts of data may function fine with a slower connection.

To host a server, it's likely that you'll need a business, or commercial, account with your ISP. In addition to limited speed for upstream communications, accounts offered to home users typically forbid hosting servers because a server is likely to draw more traffic than the ISP can support at home-user prices. For home accounts, some ISPs block unsolicited requests to port 80, which is the default port where Web servers receive requests.

One option that uses a different approach is worth a mention for applications where an embedded system only needs to provide information periodically to a server on the Internet. Many ISPs and other companies offer Web hosting services that enable you to host Web pages on one of the company's servers. You upload the files, typically via FTP, to the server, and the server responds to requests to view the pages. For some applications, you can program a device to send files to the server as needed and let the server handle the work of serving requests on the Internet. With this arrangement, the device doesn't have to function as a server; it just needs to be able to transfer files as needed to a remote server.

Technologies for Connecting

There are several options for obtaining an Internet connection. A long-popular way for home users to connect to the Internet is via dial-up connections on phone lines. For higher speeds, alternatives are a Digital Subscriber Line (DSL), an Integrated Services Digital Network (ISDN) line, or a cable modem. Satellite connections are also possible. Table 4-1 compares the capabilities of the different methods. Not every connection type is available in all locations.

Depending on the type of access and the equipment that connects to the provider, Internet communications may use Ethernet, serial port (RS-232), or USB. Ethernet is fast and flexible, and an Ethernet network enables multiple computers to share a connection. Hardware support for RS-232 is very inexpensive. Most microcontrollers have an on-chip UART and require only a TTL-to-RS-232 converter. A computer that connects to the Internet via an RS-232 connection to a modem doesn't have to support Ethernet at all. Instead, the computer can use the Point-to-Point Protocol (PPP) to send and receive IP datagrams over the RS-232 connection.

Generally, a USB connection isn't practical for small embedded systems. USB modems must connect to a PC or other USB host, while most

Table 4-1: The speed of an Internet connection depends in part on the method of connecting. Downstream speeds are often faster than upstream.

Access Type	Downstream Speed (kb/s, typical maximum)	Upstream Speed (kb/s, typical maximum)	Transmission Medium
Dial up	56	56	phone line
ADSL	1500	384	phone line
SDSL	2000	2000	phone line
BRI ISDN	128	128	phone line
PRI ISDN	1500 (23 channels)	1500 (23 channels)	phone lines
Cable modem	1500, shared	384, shared	TV cable
Satellite	500	50	wireless

USB-capable embedded systems are USB devices. Also, USB modems typically come with driver software for Windows only.

Dial Up

A dial-up connection is available anywhere there is phone service. A modem provides an interface between a computer that wants to access the Internet and an ordinary phone line (Figure 4-1). To make a connection, the computer instructs the modem to dial a number that connects to a modem at the ISP. The ISP's modem in turn connects to a router with an Internet connection. A PC's modem may be on the motherboard or an expansion card, or the modem may connect to the PC via an RS-232 or USB port. An

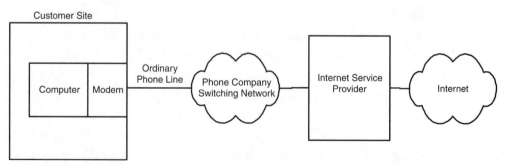

Figure 4-1: In a dial-up connection, the computer uses a modem to connect to an ISP over an ordinary phone line.

embedded system may also contain a modem or connect to an external modem, usually via RS-232.

The computer uses the Point-to-Point Protocol (PPP) to manage the modem connection and to send and receive IP datagrams over the serial link. Rabbit Semiconductor's Dynamic C has an optional module with libraries and example code for PPP communications. For TINI users, the `com.dalsemi.tininet.ppp` package supports PPP. *RFC 1661: The Point-to-Point Protocol (PPP)* defines the protocol.

Limitations of dial-up connections are a maximum speed of 56 kilobits per second and the need to provide a phone line for the connection. Advantages are low cost and availability anywhere there is phone service.

In general, a dial-up connection isn't the best option for a server because of limited speed. But dial up can be useful for some computers that occasionally communicate on the Internet. For example, a series of data loggers might periodically dial in to send readings to a central computer that is on the Internet and programmed to accept the communications from the data loggers. A system with a dial-up connection may also communicate by sending and receiving e-mail. Multiple systems can share a dial-up account if each calls in turn.

A computer that connects to an ISP via dial-up may also use Ethernet to connect to a local network.

DSL

DSL uses a conventional phone line with equipment at each end to enable the line to carry voice and Internet communications at the same time. Although the exact setup can vary with the provider, Figure 4-2 shows a typical configuration, where the customer's site has a DSL modem and a splitter. In the upstream direction, a splitter combines phone and Internet traffic on a single pair of wires. In the downstream direction, the splitter routes the phone and Internet traffic onto the appropriate wires inside the customer's premises. Another name for the splitter is network interface device (NID).

The line carrying Internet traffic in the customer's premises connects to a DSL modem, which has a USB or Ethernet connection to the customer's computer. At the phone company's central office, phone traffic is routed to and from the company's switching equipment, and Internet traffic is routed to and from a DSL Access Module (DSLAM). The DSLAM interfaces to the company's DSL equipment, which connects to the Internet.

DSL connections often use Point-to-Point Protocol over Ethernet (PPPoE). PPPoE requires logging on with a user name and password but doesn't require dialing a phone number to connect to the ISP. Dynamic C's PPP module supports PPPoE and includes an example application.

DSL has several variants with differing speed and distance limits. Not all providers offer all variants. Two popular options are asymmetric DSL (ADSL) and single-line, or symmetric DSL (SDSL). With ADSL, traffic in each direction has a different speed, with the downstream speed typically much faster than the upstream speed. Embedded systems that host busy Web or FTP servers will probably find SDSL, with equal speeds in both directions, more suitable.

The speed of a connection varies with the DSL variant, the distance from the phone company's central office, and the quality of the phone line. Theoretically, ADSL can support speeds as high as 6.1 Mb/s downstream and 1.5 Mb/s upstream. In practice, speeds are likely to be equal to or less than 1.5 Mb/s downstream and 384 kb/s upstream. The theoretical maximum for SDSL is 2 Mb/s in each direction. The maximum distance between the cus-

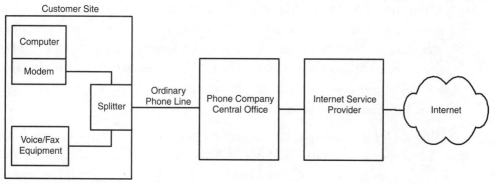

Figure 4-2: In a DSL connection, voice and fax lines can share the same phone line as data.

139

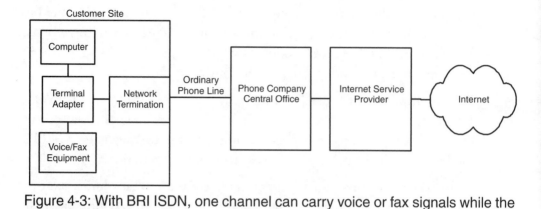

Figure 4-3: With BRI ISDN, one channel can carry voice or fax signals while the other carries data, or for a higher-speed connection, both channels can carry data.

tomer and the central office is around 18,000 feet for ADSL and 18,000 to 22,000 feet for SDSL.

ISDN

Like DSL, ISDN connections can use conventional phone lines. ISDN has two main variants. With Basic Rate Interface (BRI) ISDN, the phone line carries two 64-kb/s "B" channels that can be combined for a single 128-kb/s connection. A separate lower-speed "D" channel carries signaling information. As Figure 4-3 shows, the computer that wants to communicate over the Internet connects via Ethernet, RS-232, or USB to an ISDN terminal adapter, which in turn connects to a network termination. The customer's phone line connects the network termination to a switch at the phone company's central office, which routes the traffic to and from the ISP. It's also possible to use one ISDN channel for voice traffic and the other for a 64-kilobit Internet connection.

If BRI ISDN isn't enough, Primary Rate Interface (PRI) ISDN has 23 channels and speeds of up to 1.544 Mb/s. A BRI connection requires a T1 line, which is a special 4-wire phone line that carries digital data from the central office to the customer.

Cable Modem

A cable modem doesn't use phone lines, but instead uses a connection to a cable-TV provider that offers Internet access. The same cable can carry TV broadcasts and Internet traffic. As Figure 4-4 shows, the computer that wants to communicate over the Internet connects via Ethernet or USB to a cable modem. The cable modem in turn connects to a filter and splitter, then connects via coaxial cable to a neighborhood concentrator, which has a high-speed connection to the cable company's facility.

The cable's bandwidth is divided into channels. Each TV channel uses a 6-Mhz portion of the bandwidth. Internet traffic typically uses bandwidth above the TV channels for downstream traffic and bandwidth below the TV channels for upstream traffic.

With a cable modem, you share bandwidth with other customers in the neighborhood. So the performance of a cable-modem connection depends in part on the network speed provided by the account and in part on how much other traffic there is at the same time. Most cable-modem connections are asymmetrical, with higher downstream speeds. Typical network speeds for cable modems are from 256 kb/s to 1.5 Mb/s downstream and up to 384 kb/s upstream. Most providers encrypt the Internet traffic so customers who share a connection can't view each others' data.

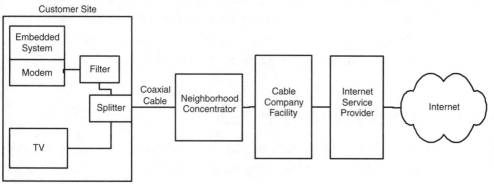

Figure 4-4: A cable-modem connection uses the same cable that carries TV programming.

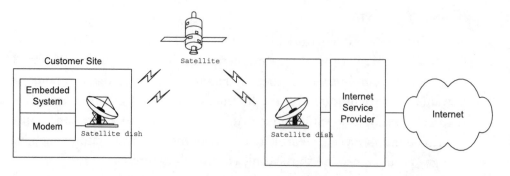

Figure 4-5: A satellite connection makes it possible to communicate from remote locations.

Because cable-TV providers market to residential customers, cable Internet may be unavailable at a business location. Because of the expense of running cable, cable Internet may be unavailable in remote locations.

Satellite

Another option for obtaining Internet access, especially for remote areas, is a satellite link (Figure 4-5). Early offerings of Internet access via satellite were downstream only, requiring a phone-line connection for upstream data. Newer systems offer 2-way communications via satellite. Download speeds range between 150 to 500 kb/s, with upstream speeds of around 50 kb/s. The low-speed upstream communications make satellite links less than ideal for hosting a server. The satellite dish requires a view of the southern sky. The satellite modem may connect via Ethernet or USB to a customer's computer.

Static and Dynamic IP Addresses

Every computer that communicates over the Internet must have an IP address, which the computer typically receives from its ISP. The IP address may be static or dynamic. A static IP address stays the same until someone explicitly changes it, while a dynamic IP address can change on every boot up or network connect (though the address typically changes only occasionally).

An embedded system may store a static IP address in non-volatile memory, either within an application or in memory where program code can retrieve the address when needed. Or the system may receive a static or dynamic IP address from a DHCP server on boot-up or network connect.

For hosting a domain, a static IP address is preferable because the name servers don't have to be updated unless the domain changes ISPs. If the computer hosting the domain has a dynamic IP address, the local name servers must be updated when the address changes, as described later in this chapter.

Connecting Multiple Computers to the Internet

A computer that connects to the Internet must have an IP address that is different from the addresses of all of the other computers on the Internet. When you contract with an ISP, you obtain the right for your computer to use one or more of the ISP's assigned IP addresses.

If you have a local network with multiple computers that need Internet access, it's often easier, more secure, and less expensive to have all of the computers share a single public IP address for Internet communications. Some ISPs charge for each connected computer whether or not they share an IP address, however.

Two ways to enable multiple computers to share a public IP address are with a router that supports the Network Address Translation (NAT) protocol and with a Windows PC configured as an Internet Connection Sharing host.

A router that supports the NAT protocol enables multiple computers to share a public IP address. The router connects to the ISP and to the computers in the local network. The router has two IP addresses: a public address for Internet communications and a local address for communicating with the local network. The router uses the NAT protocol to translate between the public and local addresses as needed.

To send a message on the Internet using a router with NAT support, a computer in the local network sends the message to the router's local address. The router creates a new IP datagram, placing the message in the datagram's data area and the router's public IP address in the datagram's Source Address field. The router than forwards the datagram to a router at the ISP, which sends the datagram onto the Internet. On receiving a datagram from the ISP's router, the local router uses information in the IP header to determine where to forward the message. The router then creates a new datagram with the appropriate local IP address in the datagram's Destination Address field and forwards the datagram to its destination.

A router with NAT support also helps to keep a local network secure, as described in Chapter 10.

If your local network includes a PC running Windows XP, there is another option. You can enable multiple computers to share a public IP address by configuring the PC as an Internet Connection Sharing host. The PC requires two network interfaces, one to the local network and one to the modem or other connection to the ISP. In Windows XP's Network Setup Wizard, select *This computer connects directly to the Internet. The other computers on my network connect to the Internet through this computer.* All Internet communications for the local network then go through the interfaces on this computer. Windows Help has more information on using Internet Connection Sharing.

Communicating through a Firewall

Any PC or other large computer with Internet access should have a firewall. All communications from outside the local network should pass through the firewall to reach a computer in the local network. The firewall protects the local network by controlling what local resources external computers can access. A firewall may be software only or a combination of hardware and software.

Without a firewall, a computer from outside the network might be able to retrieve private files, install a program that deletes files, or use another computer to launch attacks on other computers. A firewall can also defend against denial-of-service attacks, where a computer attempts to overwhelm a server by bombarding it with requests using forged, invalid source addresses.

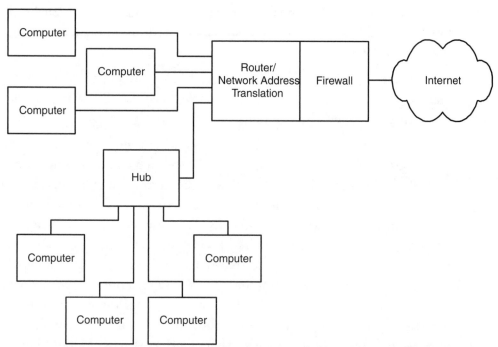

Figure 4-6: A firewall that supports the network address translation (NAT) protocol enables all of the computers in a local network to share a single public IP address.

In a local network, each computer may have its own firewall, or a single firewall may protect all of the computers in the network. The firewall may be software running on a PC or another general-purpose computer, or it may be a device designed specifically to function as a firewall. For networks that use a single firewall, the firewall is the only computer in the local network with a direct Internet connection. As Figure 4-6 shows, all of the other computers send and receive Internet communications by communicating with the computer that contains the firewall.

Some operating systems have firewall software built in. For example, Windows XP has an Internet Connection Firewall that you can configure for specific needs.

A hardware firewall for a small local network may provide additional capabilities, including functioning as a router with address translation and functioning as a DHCP server.

Even when an embedded system doesn't need a firewall to protect itself, many embedded systems are behind a firewall because they're in local networks that have firewall protection.

If your embedded system is behind a firewall, you may need to configure the firewall to enable your system to communicate. In a common setup, a firewall allows the local computers to request resources from computers on the Internet, but blocks all unsolicited incoming requests from the Internet. For example, the firewall typically enables local computers to request Web pages from computers on the Internet. The firewall stores information about each request, and when the computer returns an IP datagram containing the requested page, the firewall examines the header, determines that the datagram is in response to a previous request, and passes the datagram to the requesting computer. If the firewall doesn't recognize a datagram as a response to a previous request, the datagram doesn't pass through the firewall.

A computer that functions as a server available to all computers on the Internet must be able to receive unsolicited requests because the computer has no way of knowing where requests will come from. So you'll need to configure the firewall to allow the server to receive unsolicited communications on at least one port.

The details of how to configure a firewall vary with the product. Many stand-alone firewalls have a password-protected Web interface. Figure 4-7 shows an example configuration setup. Typically, to enable a specific computer to serve Web pages, you can configure the firewall to forward all open, or unsolicited, communications for port 80, which is the port used for HTTP requests, to the computer that serves the pages.

Chapter 10 has more about firewalls and security for networked embedded systems.

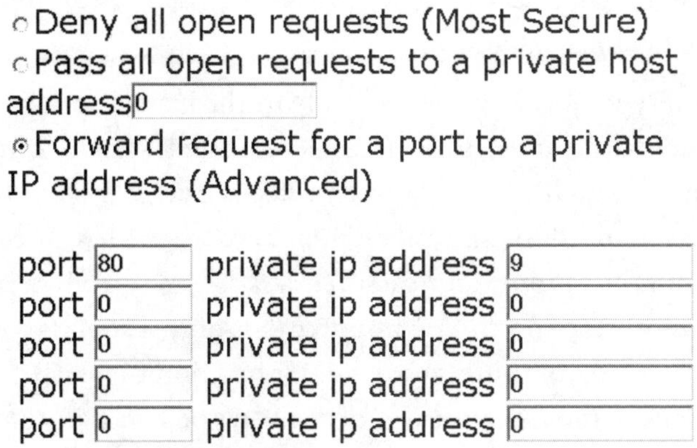

○ Deny all open requests (Most Secure)
○ Pass all open requests to a private host
address 0
◉ Forward request for a port to a private
IP address (Advanced)

port 80   private ip address 9
port 0   private ip address 0
port 0   private ip address 0
port 0   private ip address 0
port 0   private ip address 0

Figure 4-7: A firewall typically provides the option to forward unsolicited requests to a specific host or port on the host. In this example, all requests to port 80 are forwarded to host 9 in the subnet.

Obtaining and Using a Domain Name

After you obtain Internet access, connect your embedded system to the Internet, and configure your firewall to enable the embedded system to communicate, the system is ready to send and receive messages on the Internet.

Applications running on other computers on the Internet can access the embedded system by specifying its public IP address. For example, to view a server's home page, in the Address text box of a Web browser, you enter *http://* followed by the server's IP address.

Each IP address is 32 bits, typically expressed as four bytes in a format known as dotted quad, or dotted decimal, consisting of four decimal numbers separated by periods, or dots, as in 216.92.61.61.

An alternate, more human-friendly way to identify a computer on the Internet is with a domain name. Instead of remembering four numbers, users can provide a name such as *rabbitsemiconductor.com* or *dalsemi.com*. Another advantage of a domain name is that it can remain constant. The IP address of a particular Web page or other resource may change, either because the owner of the domain has changed ISPs or because the ISP uses dynamic IP addresses that change from time to time.

Just about every major Web site available to the general public on the Internet has a domain name. The tiniest embedded system can also have a domain name, though not every system needs one. A system that functions as a client has no need for an easily remembered name because the client initiates all communications, and each request received from a client includes the IP address to respond to. A computer that only responds to communications from selected computers that know the computer's IP address doesn't need a domain name either. But a domain name can be useful and convenient for an embedded system that functions as a server that's available to any computer on the Internet.

To obtain the right to use a domain name, you need to register the name and provide two name servers that will respond to requests for the domain's IP address, as described later in this chapter.

Understanding Domain Names

A domain name consists of a name that is unique within its root domain, followed by a dot and the name of the root domain. Some examples are:

rabbitsemiconductor.com
dalsemi.com
rfc-editor.org

The original defined root domains were *.com, .edu, .gov, .mil, .net,* and *.org*. In recent years, more have been added.

A domain name may also contain a country-code top-level domain after the root:

number-10.gov.uk

And one or more names to the left of the main domain may identify subset(s) of a domain:

minordivision.majordivision.example.com

The order of the names of the subsets indicates their hierarchy. In the example above, *majordivision* is a subset of *example.com*, and *minordivision* is a subset of *majordivision*.

The letters *www* preceding a domain name specify that the request should be routed to the domain's Web server:

www.Lvr.com

Many domains are configured so that including *www* is optional. On receiving an HTTP request that doesn't include the *www*, the domain's software passes the request to the Web server by default.

The major documents describing the Internet's Domain Name System (DNS) are *RFC1034: Domain names - concepts and facilities* and *RFC1035: Domain names - implementation and specification*. Both are incorporated in standard document *STD0013*. All are available from *www.rfc-editor.org*.

How a URL Specifies a Resource

When requesting a file or other resource from a computer on the Internet, a computer provides a uniform resource locator (URL) that helps in identifying the location of the resource and tells the server how to respond to the request. A URL specifies the protocol to use in reading the request, the name or IP address of the server that hosts the requested resource, the path to the file on the server, and the name of the requested resource (or no name to request a default file).

The document that defines URLs is *RFC 1738: Uniform Resource Locators (URL)*. At minimum, a URL specifies a *scheme* that identifies a protocol such as HTTP, followed by scheme-specific information such as a host name that identifies the location of a requested file. A host name is either an IP address in dotted-quad format or a domain name. Here is an example of a URL that requests a page from a Web server:

http://www.example.com:80/data/testdata.htm

http:// contains the scheme that tells the server to use the hypertext transfer protocol (HTTP) in responding to the request. Other schemes include *ftp* for FTP transfers and *mailto* for links to e-mail messages. Many browsers add *http://* if you omit the scheme when specifying a URL in the browser's Address text box.

example.com specifies the domain, and *www* specifies the Web server at the domain.

:80 specifies the port the client sends the request to. If the URL doesn't include a port number, the client uses the protocol's default port. RFC 1738 specifies default port numbers for standard protocols. The default for HTTP is port 80.

/data/ names a folder within the server's root folder. A small embedded system may store all of its files in the server's root folder. Forward slashes separate folder and file names even if the server's file system uses different separators.

The name of the requested file is *testdata.htm*. When a URL doesn't specify a filename, most Web servers are configured to serve a default home page, often titled *index.html*.

In many cases, you don't need to type the full URL in the browser's window. If you leave off the *http://*, most browsers insert it for you. Every domain should have a default page to serve if no page is specified. And many servers are configured to serve a Web page even if the URL doesn't contain *www*. So typing just the domain name, such as *example.com*, often causes the Web server at the specified domain to return the same default home page that would be returned by requesting *http://www.example.com:80/index.html*.

Registering a Domain Name

If you want to be able to access your embedded system by specifying a domain name, you must register the name with an appropriate authority. Registering in turn requires providing two name servers that respond to requests for the domain's IP address.

For all domains except those with country-code top-level domains, you can register the name with any of a number of domain name registrars accredited by the Internet Corporation for Assigned Names and Numbers (ICANN) at *www.icann.org*. The registrar pays a yearly fee to ICANN for each registered domain. The registrar in turn typically charges a yearly fee to the person or entity registering the domain. The domains managed by ICANN are available to registrants in any country.

In addition, each country-code top-level domain has a sponsoring organization for registering domains. The Internet Assigned Numbers Authority (IANA) at *ww.iana.org* has information about registering these domains.

Matching a Domain Name to Its IP Address

Name servers enable computers to match a domain name with the IP address required to access the domain's resources. Domain names are convenient for humans who are requesting resources, but each request ultimately must translate into one or more IP datagrams that contain the IP address of the datagram's destination. So a computer requesting a resource by domain name needs a way to learn the IP address that corresponds to the domain.

A system that communicates only with a defined set of hosts could store a lookup table that matches each host name with its IP address. If a host changes its IP address, the lookup table will need updating, however.

More commonly, matching a domain name to its IP address involves communications between one or more domain-name servers and a resolver. A domain-name server is a computer that stores records that match domain names with their IP addresses. The resolver is a program or process that uses the domain-name-system (DNS) protocol to communicate with name servers to find a match between a domain name and its IP address.

Each registered domain name must have two name servers that respond to queries for the domain's IP address. The ISP that provides the domain's IP address typically provides the name servers. Some registrars will provide name servers if you aren't ready to host the domain right away.

Once the name servers are set up and operating, the computers on the Internet need to learn about their existence. The Internet has a series of root name servers that store root zone files containing the IP addresses of the name servers for all registered domains. Each server stores records for one of the root domains such as *.com, .edu,* or *.mil.* To ensure that the information is always available even if a server fails, each root domain has multiple servers. The root name servers operate under the direction of IANA and are updated regularly. The servers are in varied locations and are owned by different entities.

To learn a domain's IP address, a computer uses the DNS protocol to send a query to a resolver, which may reside in the same computer that originated the query or elsewhere. The resolver first searches its own cache and returns the answer if found. If not, the resolver attempts to find the answer by querying a name server.

A local network may have an assigned local name server that functions as the resolver for queries from the local network. The local name server knows the addresses of the root name servers and maintains a database of information obtained from previous queries. If the local name server doesn't have the answer in its database, it queries a root name server or another server that it thinks may have the information.

On receiving a query, a name server may return the requested IP address or the IP address of another server that is likely to have the information. For example, to learn the IP address for *www.example.com*, a resolver may send a query to a *.com* root domain server that returns the address of the name server for *example.com*. The resolver can then query this name server for the address of *www.example.com*.

To learn the IP addresses of a local network's name servers, in Windows XP, click **Start** > **Run**, type **cmd**, and click **OK**. In the window that appears, type **ipconfig /all**. In the information displayed are the IP addresses of two DNS servers.

Although an embedded system with a domain name must have name servers that other computers can access to learn the domain's IP address, many embedded systems don't need to communicate with name servers themselves. An embedded system functioning as a server just needs to respond to requests that contain a source IP address to respond to. Other systems may communicate only with computers with known IP addresses. Systems that communicate only in a local network don't need to support domain names at all, though local computers may have locally assigned host names that correspond to local IP addresses.

In Depth:
Inside the Internet Protocol

The Internet Protocol (IP) helps data find its way to its destination even if the data must travel through other networks, including the many and varied networks that make up the Internet. Although it's called the Internet Protocol, local networks can use IP as well. Many communications in local networks use IP because they use its companion protocols, TCP and UDP.

This section introduces IP, including how computers obtain IP addresses, the format of IP datagrams, how IP and the domain name system help in getting messages to their destinations, and how embedded systems can use IP in communicating in local networks and on the Internet.

What IP Does

Figure 4-8 shows the place of the IP layer in network communications in the networking stack introduced in Chapter 1. In transmitting, the IP layer receives a message to send from a higher-level protocol layer such as TCP or UDP. The IP layer places the message in an IP datagram that consists of an IP header, followed by the message to send. The IP layer then passes the datagram to a lower layer such as an Ethernet driver, which sends the datagram on the network.

On the way to its destination, a datagram may pass through one or more routers. The router examines the destination's IP address and uses the address in deciding where to forward the datagram.

At the destination computer, the Ethernet layer or another network interface passes the IP datagram to the IP layer, which removes the IP header. Information in the header tells the computer what protocol layer, such as TCP or UDP, should receive the datagram's message.

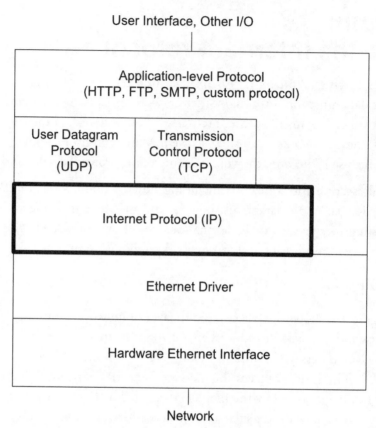

Figure 4-8: In an Ethernet network, the Internet Protocol layer communicates with the Ethernet driver and either a UDP or TCP layer or the application layer.

The Internet Protocol performs two major functions.

- It defines a way to specify source and destination addresses for use with any network interface and across networks that use different interfaces.

- It enables a datagram to pass through networks of varying capabilities by defining a protocol that allows a router to fragment, or divide, a datagram into multiple, smaller datagrams and enables the destination to reassemble the original message from the fragments.

Two things IP doesn't provide are flow control and error checking of the data payload. When needed, a higher-level protocol such as TCP can provide these. For local communications, Ethernet frames also provide error checking.

Two protocols can help in matching an IP address to a computer, or to be more precise, to a network interface (because a single computer can have multiple network interfaces). The Domain Name System (DNS) protocol described earlier in this chapter enables a computer to learn the IP address that corresponds to a domain name. And in Ethernet networks, the Address Resolution Protocol (ARP) described later in this chapter enables the sender of an IP datagram to match an Ethernet hardware address with an IP address in the local network.

The examples in this book use version 4 of IP (IPv4), which most networks are using at this writing. The expected replacement for IPv4 is IP version 6 (IPv6), which greatly increases the number of available IP addresses and adds other improvements for more efficient and secure transfers. It's likely that IPv6 routers will continue to support IPv4 for some time, so computers that support only IPv4 should have no trouble communicating with any destination.

The standards for IP and related protocols are the responsibility of the Internet Engineering Task Force (IETF) and its working groups (*www.ietf.org*). The IETF is open to anyone who has the necessary skills and abilities and wants to contribute.

The documents that define IP and many other networking protocols are available from the Request for Comments (RFC) Web site (*www.rfc-editor.org*). This book contains a number of references to RFC documents, so perhaps it's appropriate to say a few words about the documents and where they come from. The RFC Editor is a group funded by the Internet Society (ISOC). ISOC in turn is an organizational home for groups who are responsible for various standards relating the Internet's infrastructure.

The RFC Web site is a repository for RFC documents, which include standards-track documents as well as technical and organizational notes relating to networking and the Internet. The standards-track documents contain specifications that have undergone a review process to become approved standards.

Request for Comments may sound like an odd designation for an approved standard, and in fact, approved standards have alternate designations that use the STD prefix. For example, the document that defines IP is *RFC0791: Internet Protocol*. The standards-track document that includes RFC0791 and related documents is STD0005. The IETF's Internet Engineering Steering Group (IESG) is responsible for approving specifications as standards. A protocol doesn't have to be an approved standard before becoming widely implemented, however.

IP Addresses

A computer that uses the Internet Protocol must have an IP address. A network administrator may manually assign an IP address to each computer or the network may have a way of assigning addresses automatically to computers that connect to the network.

An IPv4 address is 32 bits. As explained earlier in this chapter, the conventional way to express an IP address is in dotted-quad format, such as 192.168.111.1.

Assigning Addresses

Each IP datagram includes the IP addresses of the datagram's source and destination. A computer's IP address must be unique within the network or networks that the computer can communicate with. In a local network with no direct connection to other networks, the address only needs to be different from the other addresses in the local network. In theory an isolated local network could use any IP addresses, but the IP standard reserves three blocks of addresses for local use.

For communicating over the Internet, the address must be different from the address of every other computer on the Internet. As described earlier in this chapter, the network administrator typically obtains the right to use one or more IP addresses from the ISP that supplies the network's Internet connection.

An ISP in turn obtains the right to use addresses via a system that involves a variety of organizations that manage the allocating and assigning of addresses. At the top is the Internet Corporation for Assigned Names and Numbers (ICANN), at *www.icann.org*. ICANN is a non-profit corporation that manages the top-level assigning and allocating of IP addresses. ICANN also manages the Internet's domain name system, the root server system that supports the domain name system, and the assigning of numbers to Internet protocols.

Under ICANN are several regional registries that manage the assigning and allocating of IP addresses in specific geographic areas. For example, the American Registry for Internet Numbers (ARIN) at *www.arin.net* allocates and assigns Internet addresses in North and South America and a few other areas. The regional registries assign and allocate addresses to some large end users and Internet Service Providers (ISPs). The ISPs may in turn assign some of their allocated addresses to end users and may allocate blocks of addresses to other ISPs, who may assign and allocate their addresses, and so on down the line.

The Network Address and Host Address

Each IP address has two parts: a network address, which is the same for all of the interfaces in the network, and a host address, which is unique to the interface within the network. The leftmost bits of the IP address are the network address and the rightmost bits are the host address.

Routers use network addresses to help in determining where to forward received datagrams. The hosts in a local network are generally located near each other physically. So a router can have a table entry that tells the router to forward all datagrams directed to a specific network address to a router that is physically closer to the network. Without network addresses, routers would have to have a separate entry for each IP address, which would quickly become unmanageable.

The number of bits allocated to the network address and host address depends on the network's size. A network with a 24-bit network address and 8-bit host addresses can have up to 254 hosts. (Host and network addresses of all zeros or all 1s have special meanings and can't be assigned to individual hosts or networks.) A network with an 8-bit network address and 24-bits host addresses can have over 2 million hosts.

To keep from running out of available IP addresses, network addresses should be as long as possible while still enabling every host on the Internet to have a unique host address. If every network had an 8-bit network address, there could be no more than 254 networks on the Internet. But if every network had a 24-bit network address, each network could have no more than 254 hosts.

There are two protocols for assigning network addresses on the Internet. The original protocol, called classful addressing, defines three network classes with network addresses of 8, 16, and 24 bits. By examining the first three bits of the IP address, a router can determine what class of network the host belongs to, and thus how many bits make up the network address.

Many networks with classful addressing are also divided into subnetworks, or subnets. For each subnet, the routers in the local network store an additional 32-bit value called the subnet mask, which enables routers to determine which subnet a datagram is directed to.

A newer, more flexible and efficient alternative to classful addressing is classless addressing, where a network address can be any number of bits. A value called the IP prefix, or network prefix, specifies the number of bits in the network address. Routers that support classless addressing use the IP prefixes in determining where to forward datagrams.

Classful Addressing

Table 4-2 shows the five network classes defined by RFC0791 for classful addressing. The most significant bits of an IP address indicates the class of the network the host belongs to and how many bytes make up the network address. You can identify the class from the decimal value of the first byte or from the binary value of the few most significant bits.

In a Class A network, the first byte is between 1 and 126, and the most significant bit is 0. The network address is 1 byte, leaving three bytes for the host address. There can be up to 126 Class A networks.

Table 4-2: A network's class determines how many hosts the network can contain.

Network Class	Most Significant Bit(s) in Network Address	Range of Most Significant Byte in Network Address	Number of Bytes in Network Address	Maximum Number of Networks	Number of Bytes in Host Address	Maximum Number of Hosts
A	0	1-126	1	126	3	16 million+
B	10	128-191	2	16,384	2	65,534
C	110	192-223	3	2 million+	1	254
D	1110	224-239	reserved for multicasting			
E	1111	240-255	reserved for future use			

In a Class B network, the first byte is between 128 and 191, and the two most significant bits are 10. The network address is 2 bytes, leaving two bytes for the host address. There can be up to 65,534 Class B networks.

In a Class C network, the first byte is between 192 and 223, and the three most significant bits are 110. The network address is 3 bytes, leaving 1 byte for the host address. There can be up to 16,777,214 Class C networks.

In a Class D network, the first byte is between 224 and 239, and the four most significant bits are 1110. Class D networks are reserved for multicasting, described later in this chapter.

In a Class E network, the first byte is between 240 and 255, and the four most significant bits are 1111. Class E is reserved for future use.

Using Subnets

Subnetting is the process of dividing a network into groups called subnetworks, or subnets. The hosts within a subnet are typically physically near each other and may belong to the same department or facility within an organization.

In the same way that routers use network addresses to decide where to route traffic on the Internet, routers can use subnet IDs to decide where to route traffic within a network.

A small, isolated local network doesn't have to concern itself with subnets. A large local network might use subnets for easier routing of messages. A public IP address obtained from an ISP is likely to be in a subnet, so even if your embedded system is in a small network, if the system connects to the Internet, the public IP address is likely to be in a subnet.

Besides helping in routing, subnetting helps to solve the shortage of available network addresses. With only three general-purpose network classes, many organizations requesting network addresses would have to request much larger blocks of addresses than needed. For example, a network of 300 hosts is too large for Class C, but with a Class B address, tens of thousands of addresses would be unused. With subnets, a 300-host network can reserve a portion of a Class B network, leaving the remaining addresses for other subnets.

In a subnet, the host-address portion of an IP address has two parts: a subnet ID and a host ID. The subnet ID is the same for all hosts in the subnet, while each host ID is unique in the subnet. The network-address portion of the IP address is the same for all of the hosts in all of the subnets in the network. A subnet ID can be any combination of bits in the host-address portion of the IP address, but in practice it's almost always the most significant bits.

Figure 4-9 shows an example. Three Ethernet networks are subnets in a Class B network. A hub in each subnet connects to a router that enables the computers in the subnets to communicate with computers in other subnets and on the Internet. In each of the IP addresses, the first two bytes (172.16) are the network address, the third byte is the subnet ID (1, 2, or 3), and the fourth byte is the host ID.

A subnet ID may use any number of the bits in the host address. For example, a Class C network that uses four bits for the subnet mask can have up to 14 subnets (2^4-2) and each subnet can have up to 14 hosts.

As explained earlier, you can determine how many bits of an IP address are the network address by examining the most significant bits in the address.

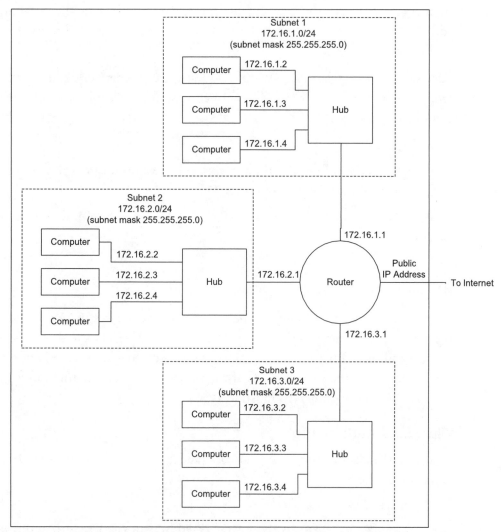

Figure 4-9: A router can enable multiple networks or subnets to communicate with each other and the Internet.

The Subnet Mask

Determining which bits in the host address are the subnet ID requires using a 32-bit value called the *subnet mask*.

In the subnet mask, the bits that correspond to the bits in the network address and the subnet ID are ones, and the bits that correspond to the bits in the host ID are zeros.

For example, in a Class B network, two bytes are the network address and two bytes are the host address. The subnet mask for a Class B network with eight bits of subnet ID is:

255.255.255.0

With eight bits of subnet ID, the network can have up to 254 subnets, and each subnet can have up to 254 hosts.

In a similar way, the subnet mask for a Class C network with four bits of subnet ID is:

255.255.255.240

(Decimal 240 equals binary 11110000.)

Program code can use the subnet mask to determine if a destination address is in the same subnet. To do so, perform a logical AND of the destination address and the subnet mask and compare the result to a logical AND of the host address and the subnet mask. If the values match, the destination is in the same subnet. Figure 4-10 illustrates.

Classless Addressing

With classless addressing, the network address and IP prefix are often expressed in the form:

```
xxx.xxx.xxx.xxx/n
```

where xxx.xxx.xxx.xxx is the lowest IP address in the network and n is the number of bits in the network-address portion of the IP address. For example, with a network address and IP prefix of 192.0.2.0/24, the network address is 192.0.2 (three bytes, or 24 bits), and the final eight bits in the IP address are the host address.

In routing datagrams for addresses that use classless addressing, routers use Classless Inter-domain Routing (CIDR) protocols defined in RFC 1519.

Example 1

```
Source address =                           192.168.0.229
Source subnet mask =                       255.255.255.224
Destination address =                      192.168.0.253
Subnet mask AND Destination address = 192.168.0.224
Subnet mask AND Source address =           192.168.0.224
192.68.0.224 XOR 192.68.0.224 =            0.0.0.0
```

The values match, so the destination address and the host are in the same subnet.

Example 2

```
Source address =                           10.2.1.3
Source subnet mask =                       255.255.0.0
Destination address =                      10.1.2.1
Subnet mask AND Destination address = 10.1.0.0
Subnet mask AND Source address =           10.2.0.0
10.1.0.0 XOR 10.2.0.0 =                     0.3.0.0
```

The values don't match, so the source and destination are not in the same subnet.

Figure 4-10: To determine whether a destination IP address is in the same subnet as the source IP address, perform a logical AND of each IP address with the source's subnet mask. If the two values are the same, the destination is in the same subnet and the source can use direct routing.

IP Addresses Reserved for Special Uses

Some IP addresses are reserved for special uses. A network address or host address can never be all zeros or all ones. So, for example, in a network with an IP address and IP prefix of 192.0.2.0/24, the hosts can have a host address of any value from 1 to 254, but not 0 or 255. There is no network at 255.255.255 or 0.0.0.0

The Local Host

The address 0.0.0.0 refers to the local host or network, also called "this" host or network. In a network with a DHCP server, a host sends a datagram with a source address of 0.0.0.0 to request the server to assign an IP address.

Broadcast Addresses

A destination address of all ones is a broadcast to all hosts in a network or subnet. A destination of 255.255.255.255 would appear to be a broadcast to the entire Internet, but in fact, Internet routers and most other routers ignore broadcasts, so the datagram only goes to the hosts in the local network or subnet. Individual hosts may also be configured to accept or ignore broadcasts.

A broadcast can also specify a network or subnet, with the host address and subnet ID, if any, set to all ones. For example, a network with this network address and IP prefix:

192.168.100.0/28

can have up to 14 hosts (192.168.100.241 through 192.168.100.254)

And a broadcast to:

192.168.100.255

is directed to all hosts in the network.

As Chapter 1 explained, an Ethernet frame with a destination address of all ones is another way to do a broadcast.

Loopback Addresses

Addresses with the most significant byte equal to 127 are loopback addresses reserved for loopback tests. On receiving data to transmit to a loopback address, the IP layer passes the data back up to the source instead of passing the datagram down for transmitting on the network. Transmitting to the loopback address can be a useful test of the local networking software.

Multicasting

Another option for sending datagrams to multiple hosts is multicasting, where a source addresses a datagram to a specific group of hosts that may reside in different networks and subnets. Uses for multicasting include sending audio and video to subscribers.

Classful addressing reserves the Class D addresses for multicasting. In practice, multicasting on the Internet has been uncommon because all routers between the source and destination must support multicasting, and many routers don't. Multicasting is feasible within local networks, however.

As explained in Chapter 1, in Ethernet networks, destination addresses can also identify multicast groups.

Local Addresses

In a local network that doesn't connect to the Internet, the IP addresses only have to be unique within the local network. An address range in each class is reserved for local networks that don't communicate with outside networks:

Class A: 10.0.0.0 to 10.255.255.255
Class B: 172.16.0.0 to 172.31.255.255
Class C: 192.168.0.0 to 192.168.255.255

These ranges are preserved with classless addressing as well.

The addresses are for use within networks where the network administrator can ensure that no two hosts have the same address. A network that uses addresses in these ranges should not connect directly to the Internet or to another local network that might use the same addresses. However, as explained earlier in this chapter, it's possible to connect computers with local addresses to the Internet by using a router that performs Network Address Translation (NAT).

Other Reserved Addresses

RFC 3330: Special-Use IPv4 Addresses lists other reserved ranges of IP addresses.

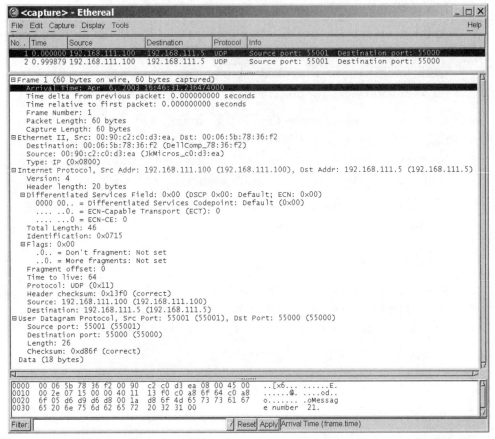

```
<capture> - Ethereal                                                        _ □ X
File  Edit  Capture  Display  Tools                                           Help

No. . Time       Source            Destination       Protocol  Info
    1 0.000000 192.168.111.100    192.168.111.5     UDP       Source port: 55001  Destination port: 55000
    2 0.999879 192.168.111.100    192.168.111.5     UDP       Source port: 55001  Destination port: 55000

⊟ Frame 1 (60 bytes on wire, 60 bytes captured)
     Arrival Time: Apr  6, 2003 16:46:31.236474000
     Time delta from previous packet: 0.000000000 seconds
     Time relative to first packet: 0.000000000 seconds
     Frame Number: 1
     Packet Length: 60 bytes
     Capture Length: 60 bytes
⊟ Ethernet II, Src: 00:90:c2:c0:d3:ea, Dst: 00:06:5b:78:36:f2
     Destination: 00:06:5b:78:36:f2 (DellComp_78:36:f2)
     Source: 00:90:c2:c0:d3:ea (JkMicros_c0:d3:ea)
     Type: IP (0x0800)
⊟ Internet Protocol, Src Addr: 192.168.111.100 (192.168.111.100), Dst Addr: 192.168.111.5 (192.168.111.5)
     Version: 4
     Header length: 20 bytes
   ⊟ Differentiated Services Field: 0x00 (DSCP 0x00: Default; ECN: 0x00)
        0000 00.. = Differentiated Services Codepoint: Default (0x00)
        .... ..0. = ECN-Capable Transport (ECT): 0
        .... ...0 = ECN-CE: 0
     Total Length: 46
     Identification: 0x0715
   ⊟ Flags: 0x00
        .0.. = Don't fragment: Not set
        ..0. = More fragments: Not set
     Fragment offset: 0
     Time to live: 64
     Protocol: UDP (0x11)
     Header checksum: 0x13f0 (correct)
     Source: 192.168.111.100 (192.168.111.100)
     Destination: 192.168.111.5 (192.168.111.5)
⊟ User Datagram Protocol, Src Port: 55001 (55001), Dst Port: 55000 (55000)
     Source port: 55001 (55001)
     Destination port: 55000 (55000)
     Length: 26
     Checksum: 0xd86f (correct)
  Data (18 bytes)

0000  00 06 5b 78 36 f2 00 90  c2 c0 d3 ea 08 00 45 00   ..[x6... ......E.
0010  00 2e 07 15 00 00 40 11  13 f0 c0 a8 6f 64 c0 a8   ......@. ....od..
0020  6f 05 d6 d9 d6 d8 00 1a  d8 6f 4d 65 73 73 61 67   o....... .oMessag
0030  65 20 6e 75 6d 62 65 72  20 32 31 00               e number  21.

Filter                                          ✓ Reset  Apply  Arrival Time (frame.time)
```

Figure 4-11: This capture from Ethereal shows an Ethernet frame whose data field contains an IP datagram. The data area of the IP datagram contains a UDP datagram.

The IP Header

An IPv4 header has twelve required fields and optional IP Options fields that precede the data, or message, being sent. Table 4-3 shows the fields in an IP header, and Figure 4-11 shows the contents of an example IP datagram. If you're using a provided library or other component for the IP layer, you normally won't have to concern yourself with the contents of most of the fields in the header, though the program code will need to provide

Table 4-3: Preceding the data portion of an IP datagram is a header with 12 or 13 fields.

Field	Number of Bits	Description
Version	4	IP version being used
Internet Header Length	4	Total length of the header in 32-bit words
Type of Service	8	Suggestions as to the importance of minimizing delay, maximizing throughput, and maximizing reliability in routing
Total Length	16	Total length of the datagram in bytes
Identification	16	Identifier for use in reassembling fragments
Flags	3	Information used in fragmenting
Fragment Offset	13	Position of a fragment in units of 64 bits
Time to Live	8	Maximum time or number of router hops a datagram may live
Protocol	8	Protocol identifier for the data portion of the datagram
Header Checksum	16	Error-checking value for the header
Source Address	32	IP address of source
Destination Address	32	IP address of destination
Options (optional)	varies	Additional information for security, routing, identification, and/or time stamping

source and destination IP addresses. Understanding the IP header can help in troubleshooting and in understanding IP's capabilities and limits, however. These are the functions of the fields in an IP header:

Version

The Internet Protocol has been through various revisions over the years. RFC0791, dated 1981, describes IP version 4, which is the version in popular use at this writing. Replacing IPv4 is IPv6, described in RFC2460. The field is 4 bits.

Header Length

The Header Length is the length of the datagram's header in 4-byte words. The length of the header can vary because of the optional IP Options field. The required fields use 20 bytes (for a Header Length of 5), and IP Options can use up to 40 additional bytes (for a Header Length of 15). The field is 4 bits.

Type of Service

The Type of Service bits offer a way for the sending process to advise routers how to handle the segment. The options are to maximize reliability, minimize delay, maximize throughput, or minimize cost. Routers may ignore these bits. The field is 8 bits.

Total Length of Datagram

The Total Length of Datagram field is the length of the header plus the data payload in bytes. The maximum is 65,535 bytes. The field is 16 bits.

Datagram Identification

The host that originates the datagram assigns a unique Datagram Identification value to the datagram. If a router fragments the datagram as it travels to its destination, each fragment will have the same Datagram Identification value. This field is 16 bits.

Flags

Two bits in the Flags field relate to fragmenting.

Bit 0 is unused.

Bit 1: Don't Fragment. If this bit is 1, routers should not fragment the datagram. If possible, a router should route the datagram to a network that can accept the datagram in one piece. Otherwise, the router discards the datagram and may return an error message indicating that the destination is unreachable. The IP standard requires hosts to accept datagrams of up to 576 bytes, so if the datagram may pass through unknown hosts and you want to be sure it won't be discarded due to size, use datagrams of 576 bytes or less.

Bit 2: More Fragments. When this bit is 1, the datagram is a fragment, but not the last fragment of the fragmented datagram. When the bit is 0, the datagram isn't fragmented or it's the final fragment.

The field is 3 bits.

Fragment Offset

The Fragment Offset field identifies the location of a fragment in a fragmented datagram. The value is in units of eight bytes, with a maximum of 8191, which corresponds to a 65,528-byte offset.

For example, to send 1024 bytes in two fragments of 576 and 424 bytes, the first fragment has a Fragment Offset of 0 and the second fragment has a Fragment Offset of 72 (because 72*8 = 576). The field is 13 bits.

Time to Live

If a datagram doesn't reach its destination in a reasonable time, the network discards it. The Time to Live field determines when it's time to discard a datagram.

Time to Live expresses the time remaining for the datagram, with each router decrementing the value by 1 or the number of seconds needed to process and forward the datagram, whichever is greater. In practice, routers typically take less than one second to process and forward a datagram, so instead of measuring time, the value measures the number of hops, or network segments between routers. The computer sending the datagram sets the initial value. The field is 8 bits.

Protocol

The Protocol field specifies the protocol used by the datagram's data payload so the IP layer will know where to pass received data. The document *RFC0790: Assigned Numbers* specifies the values for different protocols. TCP is 6. UDP is decimal 17. The field is 8 bits.

Header Checksum

The Header Checksum enables the receiver of a datagram to check for errors in the IP header only, not including the contents of the data area, or message. The checksum is calculated on the values in the header, with the Header Checksum bits assumed to be zero. Error checking of the message is required in Ethernet frames and TCP segments and optional in UDP datagrams. Figure 4-12 illustrates a checksum calculation.

To calculate a checksum on an IP header, do the following

1. Divide the header into a series of 16-bit words.

2. Add the first two words. If the result has a carry bit (if the result is greater than FFFFh), drop the carry bit and add 1 to the sum.

3. Add the next 16-bit word to the sum. Again, if the value has a carry bit, drop the carry bit and add 1 to the sum.

4. Repeat step 3 until all of the 16-bit words have been added in.

5. Find the one's complement of the result. To obtain the one's complement, in the binary value, change each 0 to 1 and change each 1 to 0. The result is the checksum.

RFC 791 says that the checksum appears to provide adequate protection, but may be replaced by a CRC calculation.

If you use software with built-in support for IP, you don't have to worry about providing code to calculate the checksum.

The field is 16 bits.

Source IP Address

The Source IP Address identifies the sender of the datagram. The receiver of a datagram can use this field to find out where to send a reply. The field is 32 bits.

Destination IP Address

The Destination IP Address identifies the destination of the datagram. The field is 32 bits.

Assigning an IP Address to a Host

A network may use any of a variety of ways of assigning IP addresses to its hosts. One approach is to have a network administrator configure the address at each host. This can work fine for small networks, especially if the

Contents of the IP header in Figure 4-11 expressed as 16-bit hexadecimal words:

```
4500
002E
0715
0000
4011
13F0  (checksum)
C0A8
6F64
C0A8
6F0F
```

Calculations to obtain the checksum:

```
4500 + 002E = 452E
452E + 0715 = 4C43
4C43 + 0000 = 4C43
4C43 + 4011 = 8C54
```
(Skip the checksum value.)
```
8C54 + C0A8 = 14CFC
14CFC - 10000 + 1 = 4CFD  (Drop the carry bit and add 1.)
4CFD + 6F64 = 6C61
6C61 + C0A8 = 17D09
17D09 -10000 + 1 = 7D0A  (Drop the carry bit and add 1.)
7D0A + 6F0F = EC0F
```
One's complement of EC0F = 13F0
The checksum is 13F0.

Figure 4-12: Calculating the checksum for this IP header verifies that the value is 13F0h.

hosts seldom change. But often, it makes more sense to have a single location in charge of assigning IP addresses. The Dynamic Host Configuration Protocol (DHCP) defines three ways of doing this.

DCHP: Three Options

The alternatives described in *RFC2131: Dynamic Host Configuration Protocol* are manual, automatic, and dynamic allocation. Table 4-4 compares the

Table 4-4: A network may use any of a number of methods to assign IP addresses to its computers.

Method of Assigning IP Addresses	Stores Addresses in a Single Server?	Method of Adding a Host	Method of Removing a Host	Requires the Host to Renew Its Lease Periodically?
Per Host Manual	no	manual	manual	no
DHCP Manual	yes	manual	manual	no
DHCP Automatic	yes	automatic	manual	no
DHCP Dynamic	yes	automatic	automatic	yes

capabilities of the Dynamic Host Configuration Protocol (DHCP)'s methods and manual assignment at the individual hosts.

All three DHCP methods require a computer that functions as a DHCP server. The other computers in the network are DHCP clients, which request IP addresses from the server. The server uses one of the three methods in responding to the requests.

On connecting to the network, a DHCP client uses UDP to broadcast a DHCPDISCOVER message to request an assigned IP address. Because the host doesn't have an IP address yet, it uses a source IP address of 0.0.0.0 in the request. The server must have another way of identifying the sender of the message. In an Ethernet network, the server can use the hardware address in the Source Address field of the Ethernet frame. The DHCP server responds to the DHCPDISCOVER message by returning an IP address to the requesting host, which uses the new address in future communications. RFC2131 and *RFC1533: DHCP Options and BOOTP Vendor Extensions* specify the format of DHCP requests and replies.

Manual Allocation

In manual allocation, the network administrator specifies an address for each host, but instead of configuring the addresses at each host, the administrator configures all of the addresses at the DHCP server. On receiving a DHCPDISCOVER message, the DHCP server returns the address assigned to the requesting host. For example, in an Ethernet network, the network administrator can provide the server with a table that matches an IP address to the Ethernet hardware address of each Ethernet controller in the network. The DHCP server reads the source's Ethernet address from the Ethernet frame, finds the corresponding IP address in the table, and returns the address to the requesting host's Ethernet address.

Manual allocation is more convenient than configuring an address at each host, but the allocation still requires the administrator to know each host's hardware address and to assign an address every time the network gains a new host.

Automatic Allocation

In automatic allocation, instead of maintaining a table of values matched to hardware addresses, the DHCP server begins with a list of available IP addresses. On receiving a DHCPDISCOVER message, the server selects any unassigned address to return to the requesting host and marks the address in the table as assigned to that host.

Dynamic Allocation

One thing that automatic allocation doesn't define is a way to reclaim addresses that are no longer in use. Reclaiming addresses is essential in networks that have more potential hosts than available IP addresses. For example, the hosts connected to an ISP at any one time will vary as different customers go on and off line. If the ISP assigns a permanent, or static, address to every computer that connects, it will eventually run out of addresses, even if only a few customers connect at once. A solution is to use dynamic allocation, which reclaims IP addresses that are no longer in use.

As with automatic allocation, in dynamic allocation, the DHCP server begins with a list of available IP addresses and returns addresses in response to DHCPDISCOVER messages. But instead of assigning a permanent address, the server leases the address to the client for a specified time. To keep an address, the client must periodically send a request to renew the lease. If the client disconnects from the network or for any other reason fails to renew its lease, the server is free to assign the address to another computer.

A client may request an infinite lease or suggest a lease time, but servers aren't required to comply with these requests. The lease time is a 32-bit value in seconds, with FFFFFFFFh indicating an infinite lease.

On receiving a request for an IP address, a DHCP server uses the previously assigned address for that host if available. A computer can also request a specific IP address. But with dynamic allocation, there is no guarantee that a request for an IP address will return a specific value. For some small embedded systems, it may be easier to store a static IP address in firmware. The DHCP server must then be configured to reserve this address.

Each network may have its own DHCP server, or multiple networks may use relay agents to share a DHCP server. A relay agent accepts DHCPDIS-COVER messages from hosts in a network and sends the messages to a DHCP server. The server replies to the relay agent, which then sends the message to the host that requested it.

In a network that has a NAT router that connects to a cable modem or DSL modem, the router typically can function as a DHCP server for the local network and as a DHCP client for the public network. The server can assign addresses to the hosts in the local network. The client enables the router to request an IP address from a DHCP server at the ISP.

Windows XP can function as a DHCP client for a server at an ISP or other location. Using Internet Connection Sharing, Windows XP can function as a DHCP server that assigns IP addresses to computers in a local network.

Considerations when Using Dynamic IP Addresses

When a domain's IP address changes, the DHCP server or other entity that changed the address must send an updated resource record to the domain's name servers.

If your ISP uses DHCP in assigning your network's public IP address and your embedded system has a domain name, you'll need to update the domain's name servers when the system's IP address changes. A way to achieve this is by using a service that handles the updates automatically. One provider of this service is Tzolkin Corporation (*www.tzo.com*).

To use Tzolkin's service with an embedded system, you'll need a PC in the same local network as the embedded system, and both computers must share a public IP address (using a NAT router as described earlier).

At the registrar where you registered the domain, you must change the registration to indicate that Tzolkin's name servers are the name servers for your domain.

On a PC that shares the embedded system's public IP address, run Tzolkin's application, which monitors the PC's current public IP address. When the address changes, the application automatically informs the name servers of the change. For best results, the PC running the Tzolkin application should be on line all of the time.

Matching an IP Address to an Ethernet Interface

Every IP datagram must include the IP address of its destination. A host can use a variety of ways to learn the IP address of a destination the host wants to communicate with.

A network administrator can provide each host with the IP addresses the host will communicate with. The hosts will need a way to update their lists when a host is added, removed, or changes its address, but if changes are rare, the updates can be done manually.

Some computers only need to reply to received communications using the source address in received datagrams. For example, a host that functions as a Web server that sends Web pages on request only needs to respond to received requests that include the IP address to reply to.

A host that wants to request a Web page or other resource or send other communications over the Internet must know the destination's IP address. As described earlier in this chapter, if a host knows only the domain name, a name resolver can query name servers to learn the IP address that corresponds to the domain name.

Using ARP

In a local network, the Address Resolution Protocol (ARP) can match an IP address with the Ethernet hardware address of the computer with that IP address. The document that defines ARP is *RFC 0826: An Ethernet Address Resolution Protocol: Or converting network protocol addresses to 48.bit Ethernet address for transmission on Ethernet hardware*, also available as standards-track document STD0037.

To learn the Ethernet hardware address that corresponds to an IP address, a host broadcasts an Ethernet frame containing an ARP packet. In the Ethernet header, the Type field contains 0806h, which indicates that the frame is carrying an ARP message. The destination address is all ones or a broadcast address for a specific network or subnet.

In a similar way, a computer can broadcast a RARP (reverse ARP) request to learn the IP address that corresponds to a hardware address, including the computer's own IP address. RARP is defined in *RFC0903: A Reverse Address Resolution Protocol*, also available as standards-track document STD0038.

In Chapter 1, Figure 1-5 showed an example ARP request captured with the Ethereal Ethernet analyzer. Figure 4-13 shows the request's reply.

ARP and RARP Format

ARP and RARP requests and replies transmit in the data fields of Ethernet frames. Each request or reply has nine fields. The purpose of each field is as follows:

Hardware address space. Indicates the hardware interface being matched to a protocol address. Ethernet=0001h. 2 bytes.

Protocol address space. Indicates the protocol being matched to a hardware address. IP=0800h (specified in RFC1010). 2 bytes.

Length in bytes of a hardware address. Ethernet hardware addresses are 6 bytes. 1 byte.

Length in bytes of a protocol address. IPv4 addresses are 4 bytes. 1 byte.

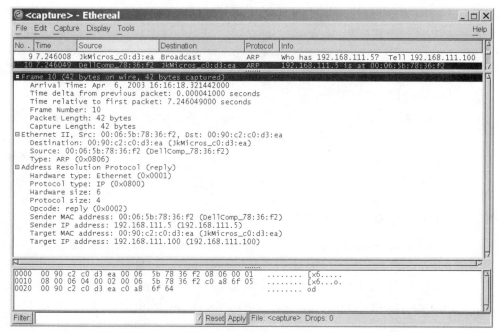

Figure 4-13: In this ARP response, the host with the specified target IP address responds with its Ethernet hardware address (00:06:5b:78:36:f2).

Opcode. Indicates the operation to perform:

1=ARP request
2=ARP reply
3=RARP request
4=RARP reply

2 bytes.

Source Ethernet hardware address. 6 bytes.

Source IP address. 4 bytes.

Destination Ethernet hardware address. For ARP requests, this value is undefined because it's the value being requested. For ARP replies, this value contains the hardware address for the request's IP address. For RARP requests and replies, this value is the hardware address whose IP address is being requested. 6 bytes.

Destination IP address. For RARP requests, this value is undefined because it's the value being requested. For RARP replies, this value contains the IP address that corresponds to the request's hardware address. For ARP requests and replies, this value is the IP address whose hardware address is being requested. 4 bytes.

To prevent having to send an ARP request before every communication to a host in the local network, a host can maintain a cache of ARP entries. To eliminate entries that are no longer valid, the cache must use timeouts or other methods.

How a Datagram Finds Its Way to Its Destination

When a host wants to send a message and knows the IP address of its destination, it's ready to send the IP datagram on the network. But how does the datagram find its way to its destination? The IP address contains no information about the physical location of the destination.

Direct Routing

Messages whose destination is within the local subnet, or within the local network when there is no subnet, use direct routing. In direct routing in an Ethernet network, the originating host sends an IP datagram in an Ethernet frame that contains the destination's Ethernet hardware address, as described in Chapter 1. The originating host uses ARP if needed to learn the destination's hardware address.

Within an Ethernet network, hosts connected by repeater hubs receive all valid frames sent by any of the hosts. An Ethernet switch forwards frames to a specific port if possible, and otherwise forwards the frame to all of the switch's ports.

Indirect Routing

Messages whose destination is outside the local subnet or network use indirect routing. With indirect routing, a designated default router accepts messages destined for outside the local subnet or network. An Ethernet network that connects to the Internet should have a default router for messages whose destination is outside the local network.

For example, if a computer in an Ethernet network wants to send a message on the Internet, the computer places the message in an IP datagram in an Ethernet frame. The destination address in the Ethernet frame is the default router's hardware address. The default router uses the destination address in the IP datagram to decide where to forward the datagram.

To decide where to forward the datagram, the router first checks its internal forwarding table for a matching IP address. Each entry in the table has the IP address of the router that is the next hop, or the next router on the way, for datagrams going to a specific address, network, or subnet.

A router builds its forwarding table by saving entries containing the source address of received datagrams and the router port that the datagram arrived on. To ensure that there's room for new entries, each entry has a timeout and is removed on timing out.

Of course, no forwarding table will contain an entry that matches every received destination address, if only because a router may begin with no entries other than a default router. On receiving a datagram with a destination address that isn't in the forwarding table, the router sends the datagram to another router designated as the first router's default router. In a similar way, the router that receives the datagram looks for a match in its forwarding table and sends the segment on either to a destination found in its forwarding table or to another default router.

An IP datagram may travel through a number of routers on the way to its destination. The source may have no way of knowing the maximum size of datagrams the routers or the destination can accept. If a datagram is too large for its destination, a router may send the data payload in multiple, smaller datagrams, with a portion, or fragment, of the data in each. On receiving the datagrams, the destination uses information in the IP header to put the fragments back together.

The Internet Control Message Protocol (ICMP)

Hosts that support IP must also support the Internet Control Message Protocol (ICMP) defined by *RFC 792: Internet Control Message Protocol.* ICMP is a basic protocol for sending messages. Some common uses for ICMP are to send a PING message to learn if a host is available on the network and to obtain the IP addresses of local routers.

ICMP messages travel in IP datagrams. The Protocol field in the IP header is 1 to indicate ICMP. The first byte in the data portion of the datagram is an ICMP Type code that determines the format of the data that follows. RFC 792, RFC 950, and RFC 1256 define the type codes listed in Table 4-5 and have further details about the message formats.

Table 4-5: ICMP is used for a variety of message types. Unless specified otherwise, all of the message types are defined in RFC 792.

Type Code	Message Type	Description
0	Echo Reply	Responds to an Echo message (Ping). Not all hosts respond to Echo requests.
3	Destination Unreachable	Indicates that a datagram won't be delivered because the destination IP address is unreachable or unavailable or because the datagram doesn't allow fragmenting and must be fragmented to reach its destination.
4	Source Quench	Requests a destination to reduce the traffic it is sending to a source.
5	Redirect	On receiving a datagram to forward, advises the source of a better router to use for that destination network in the future.
8	Echo	Requests a reply from the destination (PING).
9	Router Advertisement	Announces the availability of one or more routers (RFC1256).
10	Router Solicitation	Requests Router Advertisements (RFC1256).
11	Time Exceeded	Notifies that a datagram was discarded because the time-to-live field was zero or a fragmented datagram timed out before it could be reassembled.
12	Parameter Problem	Returns information about a datagram that was discarded due to a problem in the information in the header.
13	Timestamp	Provides a timestamp value containing the number of milliseconds since midnight in Universal Time or another, non-standard value.
14	Timestamp Reply	Returns the received timestamp value and a timestamp value containing the number of milliseconds since midnight in Universal Time or another, non-standard value. The value indicates the amount of time the original Timestamp message required to reach the destination.
15	Information Request	Enables a host to discover its network address. Obsoleted by RARP.
16	Information Reply	Enables a host to discover its network address. Obsoleted by RARP.
17	Address Mask Request	Requests the local subnet mask (RFC 950).
18	Address Mask Reply	Returns the local subnet mask (RFC 950).

5

Exchanging Messages Using UDP and TCP

This chapter shows how embedded systems can use the User Datagram Protocol (UDP) and the Transmission Control Protocol (TCP) to send messages over a network. The messages can contain any type of data. The systems must support IP, because TCP and UDP use IP addresses to identify a message's source and destination. The In Depth section of the chapter discusses UDP and TCP in detail, including when to use each and what's involved in supporting the protocols in an embedded system.

Quick Start: Basic Communications

UDP and TCP are standard, well-supported protocols for computers that need to send and receive messages within local networks or on the Internet. Many application protocols transfer information using UDP or TCP. For example, a computer that sends a request for an IP address to a DNS server places the request in a UDP datagram. A request to a server for a Web page and the page sent in response both travel in TCP segments. But you can also use UDP and TCP to transfer messages of any type, including information in application-specific formats.

In general, UDP is a simpler protocol to implement but has no built-in support for acknowledging receipt of messages, determining the intended order of messages, or flow control. If you use a module with support for both UDP and TCP, the programming effort to use the protocols is likely to be about the same for each. In some cases, TCP programming may be easier.

This section presents examples of UDP and TCP communications. The embedded systems in the examples are the Rabbit and TINI modules introduced in Chapter 3. For both modules, the amount of programming required to exchange messages is greatly simplified because of the supporting code provided with the modules.

Before using a Rabbit or TINI module in networking applications, you need to configure the module with the networking parameters appropriate for your module and network. This chapter has information about how to configure Rabbit and TINI modules to enable communicating on a network and the Internet.

And because many embedded systems communicate with PCs, I've included some tips for VB.NET programming on a PC that communicates with embedded systems. Even if there will be no PCs in your final network design, the display, keyboard, and programming resources of a PC can make it a useful tool in the initial stages of a project.

Configuring a Device for Network Communications

As Chapter 4 explained, communications that use UDP, TCP, or other Internet protocols must use IP addresses to identify the sender and receiver of the communications (with the exception that a UDP datagram doesn't have to specify a source address). In addition, sending a message using IP may require any or all of the following: a netmask value, the IP address of a gateway, or router, and the IP address of a domain-name server. The device firmware may specify these values, or the device may request the values from a DHCP server.

Rabbit Configuration

For Rabbit modules, Dynamic C supports several ways for a network interface to obtain an IP address and related values. An application can provide the values or obtain values from a DHCP server. The program code that specifies the values or how to obtain them can be in the main application or in a macro that the main program calls. Using a macro keeps the main program free of system-specific values, makes it easy to use the same configuration in multiple programs, and enables changing a configuration by just specifying a different macro.

Dynamic C's *tcp_config.lib* file defines constants for use in static configurations and macros for implementing a variety of common configurations. You can edit the file as needed for your devices and network, or you can provide your own configuration macros in a file you create called *custom_config.lib*.

To specify a configuration macro, the program code must include the following statement:

TCPCONFIG *macro_number*

where macro_number names the configuration in a configuration file. The statement must occur before the statement #use "dcrtcp.lib".

Configuring in the Application

The default macro, TCPCONFIG 0, does no configuring, so with this option, the main program has to provide the configuration information. TCPCONFIG 0 is the default, so a program that uses TCPCONFIG 0 doesn't require a TCPCONFIG statement at all. To use TCPCONFIG 0 with a static IP address, a program should define values for the constants below, as needed:

```
#define _PRIMARY_STATIC_IP  "192.168.111.7"
#define _PRIMARY_NETMASK    "255.255.255.0"
#define MY_NAMESERVER       "192.168.111.2"
#define MY_GATEWAY          "192.168.111.1"
```

The _PRIMARY_STATIC_IP and _PRIMARY_NETMASK strings should match the Rabbit module's IP address and the netmask of the subnet the Rabbit module resides in. If the module will access a domain name server, set MY_NAMESERVER to the IP address of the network's name server. If the module will communicate outside the local network, set MY_GATEWAY to the IP address of the subnet's gateway, or router, that connects to the outside world.

Using a Configuration File

To use static values defined in *tcp_config.lib*, use TCPCONFIG 1 in the application. The *tcp_config.lib* file defines the four constants above. Edit the statements with the values your system requires.

The following code in *tcp_config.lib* configures the interface using the values stored in _PRIMARY_STATIC_IP and _PRIMARY_NETMASK:

```
#if TCPCONFIG == 1
   #define USE_ETHERNET 1
   #define IFCONFIG_ETH0 \
     IFS_IPADDR,aton(_PRIMARY_STATIC_IP), \
     IFS_NETMASK,aton(_PRIMARY_NETMASK), \
     IFS_UP
#endif
```

The USE_ETHERNET macro is set to 1 to specify that the interface uses the system's first Ethernet port.

The IFCONFIG_ETH0 macro configures the first Ethernet port. The value of the macro is a parameter list, whose items are also macros. The IFS_IPADDR and IFS_NETMASK macros set the interface's IP address and netmask using the values defined earlier. The aton function converts strings in dotted-quad format to the binary values required by the macros. The IFS_UP macro brings up, or enables, the interface.

In a similar way, *tcp_config.lib* contains additional macros for other common configurations. For example, TCPCONFIG 3 specifies that the first Ethernet interface will obtain its IP address and other configuration values from a DHCP server. You can add your own custom configuration macros to the file as well.

TCPCONFIG values greater than 99 must be in a file called *custom_config.lib*. Create this file if you want to store custom configurations in your own file, rather than using *tcp_config.lib*.

Using ifconfig() to Set and Retrieve Network Settings

Dynamic C's ifconfig() function enables firmware to set and retrieve various network values at runtime. For example, on receiving a request to run a CGI program, a Web server might want to return a response containing a code that requests the browser to refresh the page. The response must include the URL of the page the browser should request. If the Rabbit's interface obtained its address from a DHCP server, a program can use ifconfig() to obtain the IP address to use in the URL.

Calls to ifconfig() can contain varying numbers of parameters. In the example below, the IFG_IPADDR macro returns the IP address for the default interface (IF_DEFAULT) in the variable my_ip_address. A sprintf() statement stores a URL containing the retrieved IP address in the character array redirect_to. The inet_ntoa() function converts the binary IP address returned by IFG_IPADDR to dotted-quad format.

```
longword my_ip_address;
char redirect_to[127];
char ip_dotted_quad[16];

ifconfig(IF_DEFAULT,
   IFG_IPADDR, &my_ip_address,
   IFS_END);

sprintf(redirect_to, "http://%s/index.shtml",
      inet_ntoa(ip_dotted_quad, my_ip_address));
```

Dynamic C's documentation has more details and examples for ifconfig().

Viewing Debugging Information

For debugging applications that use networking functions, the following directives are useful:

```
#define DCRTCP_DEBUG
#define DCRTCP_VERBOSE
```

DCRTCP_DEBUG enables debugging within the TCP/IP libraries. DCRTCP_VERBOSE prints debugging messages to Dynamic C's STDIO window. The global variable debug_on controls the number of messages, and thus the amount of detail revealed. To set debug_on from 0 (few messages) to 5 (maximum messages), set the third parameter in this ifconfig() statement:

```
ifconfig(IF_ANY, IFS_DEBUG, 5, IFS_END);
```

Use a lower value to decrease the number of messages and thus the amount of root memory required to display the messages. Another way to decrease the number of messages is to use directives that apply only to a specific library, such as FTP_DEBUG and FTP_VERBOSE.

When debugging is complete, remove the debugging directives and any related ifconfig() statements.

TINI Configuration

TINI modules can also configure their network interfaces using static values or values obtained from a DHCP server.

Using ipconfig

During project development, you can view and set the network configuration from within the JavaKit utility, using the command ipconfig. This ipconfig command is similar to the ipconfig utility that you can run from a command prompt under Windows.

Typing ipconfig from a command prompt in JavaKit displays information about the TINI's current network configuration:

```
TINI /> ipconfig

Hostname          : tini00e254
Current IPv4 addr.: 192.168.111.3/24 (255.255.255.0)
(active)
Current IPv6 addr.: fe80:0:0:0:260:35ff:fe00:e254/64
(active)
Default IPv4 GW   : 192.168.111.1
Ethernet Address  : 00:60:35:00:e2:54
Primary DNS       :
Secondary DNS     :
```

```
DNS Timeout         : 0 (ms)
DHCP Server         : 192.168.111.1
DHCP Enabled        : true
DHCP Lease Ends     : Tue Apr 23 08:21:48 GMT 2002
                      (23 hr, 58 min, 33 seconds left)
Mailhost            : 0.0.0.0
Restore From Flash: Not Committed
```

Typing `help ipconfig` displays the command-line options supported for performing other functions related to the network configuration:

```
TINI /> help ipconfig
ipconfig [options]

Configure or display the network settings.
  [-a IP -m mask]     Set IPv4 address and subnet mask.
  [-n domainname]     Set domain name
  [-g IP]             Set gateway address
  [-p IP]             Set primary DNS address
  [-s IP]             Set secondary DNS address
  [-t dnstimeout]     Set DNS timeout (set to 0 for
                      backoff/retry)
  [-d]                Use DHCP to lease an IP address
  [-r]               Release currently held DHCP IP address
  [-x]                Show all Interface data
  [-h mailhost]       Set mailhost
  [-C]                Commit current network configuration
                      to flash
  [-D]                Disable restoration of configuration
                      from flash
  [-f]                Don't prompt for confirmation
```

For example, to set the static IP address 192.168.111.3 and a netmask of 255.255.255.0, type:

```
ipconfig -a 192.168.111.3 -m 255.255.255.0
```

To specify that the TINI should obtain its settings from a DHCP server, type:

```
ipconfig -d
```

Saving a Network Configuration

By default, the TINI stores its network configuration values in a special area of RAM whose contents are preserved on rebooting. In the DSTINIm400 module, the RAM has battery backup, so the contents also persist after powering down. There is still a chance that the configuration data will be lost, however, either due to battery failure, or if an application calls the `blastHeapOnReboot` method, which causes the RAM's contents to be erased on the next reboot, or if a user types `reboot -a` in JavaKit, which clears the heap and system memory before rebooting.

A solution is to store the network configuration in the DSTINIm400's Flash memory, in the area reserved for this information. This area is a portion of bank 47, which is a 64-kilobyte sector that stores both network configuration data and *slush.tbin* or another application loaded into Flash memory for running on startup. To store the network configuration data in Flash memory, execute the `ipconfig -C` command in JavaKit or call the TINI's `commitNetworkState()` method. A configuration committed to Flash memory persists after boot-up, powering down, and erasing of the RAM's contents.

It's possible for the TINI to override, or ignore, a committed configuration. To do so, execute the `ipconfig -D` command in JavaKit or call the TINI's `disableNetworkRestore()` method. The TINI will then behave as if the Flash memory had no stored parameters.

To change a configuration in Flash memory, you first need to erase bank 47 in the Flash memory. The easiest way to do this is to use JavaKit to reload slush or another *.tbin* application. To load slush, open a JavaKit session with the TINI. At the JavaKit prompt, type **B0**, press **Enter**, then type **F0** and press **Enter**. This clears the TINI's RAM. From the **File** menu, select **Load File**. Browse to the location of *slush_400.tbin* and click **Open**. When the JavaKit window displays **Load complete**, the file has been loaded into the Flash memory. You now should be able to execute `ipconfig -C` again to commit new network configuration parameters to Flash memory.

Banks 40–46 in the Flash memory store critical files such as the boot loader and files that implement the runtime environment. You don't want to corrupt these files, so use caution when executing commands that write to the Flash memory.

Sending UDP Datagrams

Now that you know something about how to configure the Rabbit and TINI modules for network communications, it's time to try an application. The first example is an embedded system that periodically sends datagrams to a remote host. To make it easy to detect missing or out-of-order datagrams in this example application, each datagram contains a byte with a sequence number. The sequence number increments on each send, resetting to zero after sending 255. A second byte in the datagram is the value of a port bit on the module. A timer determines how often to send the datagrams. The first example uses a Rabbit module and the second example uses a TINI.

A UDP communication takes place between two sockets. A socket is one end of a communication path on a network. Each socket has an IP address and a port number. In a typical application, the destination is programmed to receive UDP datagrams on a specific port. As explained later in this chapter, many standard application protocols have an assigned *well-known* port. Other applications are generally free to use any port number greater than 1023.

A destination may accept datagrams from any host or only from a specific host or hosts. The destination usually doesn't care what port the source sends from.

For a Windows application that receives the datagrams sent by the Rabbit and TINI modules, see Lakeview Research's Embedded Ethernet page at *www.Lvr.com*.

Rabbit Code

The Rabbit module's Dynamic C libraries include functions and constants for use in UDP communications. Rabbit Semiconductor also provides a variety of basic example programs that show how to do common tasks such and sending and receiving data using UDP and TCP. The Rabbit example code in this chapter is adapted from Rabbit Semiconductor's examples.

In the application, the firmware specifies the IP addresses and port numbers to use and sends a datagram periodically. A real-world application could perform additional tasks when not transmitting. As a debugging aid, in various locations in the code, a printf statement displays status messages in the STDIO window of Dynamic C's programming environment.

Initial Defines and Declarations

The firmware uses the TCPCONFIG 1 macro to configure the network interface to use the static IP address and netmask specified in the *tcp_config.lib* file, as described above. LOCAL_PORT is the port the Rabbit will use to send the datagrams. REMOTE_IP is the IP address of the computer the Rabbit will send datagrams to. REMOTE_PORT is the port on the remote computer that will receive the datagrams. In your application, you must set REMOTE_IP and REMOTE_PORT to appropriate values for your remote computer.

```
#define TCPCONFIG 1

#define LOCAL_PORT      5551
#define REMOTE_IP       "192.168.111.5"
#define REMOTE_PORT     5550
```

The MAX_UDP_SOCKET_BUFFERS constant sets the maximum number of socket buffers for the application. This application, which communicates with a single host, requires just one buffer:

```
#define MAX_UDP_SOCKET_BUFFERS 1
```

The #memmap xmem directive stores all C functions not declared as root in the extended memory area, rather than limiting storage to the 64 kilobytes of root memory.

```
#memmap xmem
```

The *dcrtcp.lib* file is the Dynamic C library that supports TCP/IP communications. Unlike other C compilers, the Dynamic C compiler doesn't use #include directives because its library system automatically provides the needed function prototypes and header information normally contained in included files. In place of #include, to enable using a library, Dynamic C requires a #use directive that names the file:

```
#use "dcrtcp.lib"
```

The mysocket variable is a Dynamic C udp_Socket structure that contains information about the UDP socket that will communicate with the remote host. The `sequence` variable contains the number the Rabbit will send to the remote host.

```
udp_Socket mysocket;
int sequence;
```

The main() Function

The application's `main()` function begins by calling `sock_init()` to initialize the TCP/IP stack. This call is required before calling any functions in *dcrtcp.lib*, ncluding any functions that use UDP or IP. If successful, the function returns zero. If the function doesn't return zero, the network isn't available and the program ends.

```
main()
{
  int return_value;
  sequence = 255;
  return_value = sock_init();
  if (return_value == 0) {
    printf("Network support is initialized.\n");
    }
   else {
      printf("The network is not available.\n");
      exit(0);
      }
```

A call to `udp_open()` opens the specified UDP socket, enabling communications. The call requires a pointer to the local socket (`&my_socket`), a local port number (`LOCAL_PORT`), a remote IP address (`resolve(REMOTE_IP)`) and port number (`REMOTE_PORT`) to communicate with, and either a function to call on receiving data or `NULL` to place received data in the socket's receive buffer. This application doesn't receive datagrams, so the parameter is `null`. The `resolve()` function converts an IP address string in dotted-quad format to the longword required by `udp_open()`.

If the remote IP address is zero, the socket connects to the IP address and port of the first received datagram on the socket. If the remote IP address is -1, the socket accepts datagrams from any remote host and port and sends all datagrams as broadcasts.

```
    if(!udp_open(&my_socket, LOCAL_PORT,
        resolve(REMOTE_IP), REMOTE_PORT, NULL)) {
```

```
      printf("udp_open failed.\n");
      exit(0);
      }
    else {
     printf("udp_open succeeded.\n");
    }
```

The `WrPortI()` function configures Port G, bit 6 as an output. This bit controls LED DS1 on the RCM3200 module's prototyping board. This application sends the state of bit 6 in the datagram.

```
  WrPortI(PGDDR, NULL, 0x40);
```

An endless `while` loop calls the `tcp_tick()` function and a costatement. The application must call `tcp_tick()` periodically to process network packets. Chapter 3 introduced Dynamic C's costatements. In this application, the costatement calls a routine that sends a datagram with a delay between each send. Dynamic C's `DelaySec()` function specifies the number of seconds to wait between datagrams. The application's `send_packet()` function sends the datagram.

```
  while(1) {
    tcp_tick(NULL);
    costate {
      waitfor(DelaySec(1));
      send_packet();
    }
  } // end while(1)
} // end main()
```

Sending a Datagram

The `send_packet()` function creates and sends a datagram. The `send_buffer` array holds the data to send. For each send, the application increments the sequence number and places the number in the first byte of the `send_buffer` array. The sequence number resets to zero after sending 255.

```
 int send_packet(void)
 {
   char send_buffer[2];
   int buffer_length;
   int return_value;
   int test_bit;
```

```
  sequence++;
  if (sequence > 255) {
    sequence = 0;
    }
  send_buffer[0] = (char)sequence;
```

The application then places the current value of Port G, bit 6 in send_buffer's second byte and toggles the port bit. (The application toggles the bit only so that the value changes with each send for this example application.)

The BitRdPortI() function reads the bit, and BitWrPortI() writes to the bit. Chapter 7 has more about these functions.

```
    test_bit = (BitRdPortI(PGDR, 6));
    send_buffer[1] = (char)test_bit;

  if (test_bit == 0) {
    BitWrPortI(PGDR, &PGDRShadow, 1, 6);
  } else {
    BitWrPortI(PGDR, &PGDRShadow, 0, 6);
  }
```

Dynamic C's udp_send() function sends the datagram. The function call requires a pointer to the local socket (&my_socket), a buffer with data to send (send_buffer), and the number of bytes in the buffer to send (sizeof(send_buffer). On success, udp_send() returns the number of bytes sent. On failure, the program closes and attempts to reopen the socket. If the call to udp_open() fails, the application ends.

```
  return_value = udp_send(&my_socket, send_buffer,
      sizeof(send_buffer);

  if (return_value < 0) {
    printf("Error sending datagram.  Closing and reopening
        socket.\n");
    sock_close(&my_socket);

    if(!udp_open(&my_socket, LOCAL_PORT,
        resolve(REMOTE_IP), REMOTE_PORT, NULL)) {
      printf("udp_open failed.\n");
      exit(0);
    }
  }
  else {
```

```
        printf("Sent: Message number %d \n", sequence);
    }
  return 1;
} // end send_packet()
```

TINI Code

TINI users can also use UDP to communicate with remote hosts. Java's `java.net.DatagramSocket` class includes methods for sending and receiving UDP datagrams.

As a debugging aid, in various locations in the code below and the other TINI applications in this book, `System.out.println` statements write status messages to the standard output stream. If you run the TINI application from a Telnet session, the status messages display in the Telnet window.

This and some of the other example applications in this book start an endless loop that runs the application until its process is killed or a reboot. To kill a process, type `ps` at the command prompt to obtain a list of the processes currently running and the number assigned to each:

```
ps
3 processes
1: Java GC (Owner root)
2: init (Owner root)
4: UdpSend.tini (Owner root)
```

To kill a specific process, type `kill` followed by the number of the process.

```
kill 4
```

The specified process then ends.

Imports and Initial Declares

The application imports `java.io` classes to support input and output operations, `java.net` classes to support networking functions, and the TINI-specific `BitPort` class to enable reading and writing to port bits.

```
import java.io.*;
import java.net.*;
import com.dalsemi.system.BitPort;
```

For this example, the `UdpSend` class implements the `Runnable` interface to enable the code that sends the datagrams to run in its own thread. Using a separate thread makes the code a little more complicated but also more useful because the program's main thread can perform other tasks at the same time.

The `testBit` variable is Port 5, bit 2 on the DSTINIm400's CPU. This bit controls LED1 on the module.

```
public class UdpSend implements Runnable {

    private BitPort testBit =
            new BitPort(BitPort.Port5Bit2);
    private byte[] dataToSend;
    private DatagramPacket udpPacket;
    private DatagramSocket udpSocket;
    private int delayTime;
    private int messageCount;
    private Thread datagramSender;
    private volatile boolean sendDatagrams;
```

Starting the Thread to Send Datagrams

The class's constructor has three parameters: the IP address and port of the computer to send datagrams to (`destinationInetAddress` and `destinationPort`) and the amount of time to delay between sending datagrams (`delayTime`). A `SocketException` is thrown if the socket can't be created.

```
public UdpSend(InetAddress destinationInetAddress,
        int destinationPort, int delayTime)
        throws SocketException {
```

The byte array `dataToSend` holds the data to send to the remote host. For this application, the datagrams are just two bytes.

```
byte[] dataToSend = new byte[2];
```

The `delayTime` variable that the `datagramSender` thread will use is set to the value of the `delayTime` parameter.

```
this.delayTime = delayTime;
```

Communications with the remote host use the `DatagramSocket` object `udpSocket`. The socket uses an available local port; the program code doesn't have to specify a port.

```
udpSocket = new DatagramSocket();
```

The datagrams sent to the remote host are stored in the `DatagramPacket` object `udpPacket`. The object specifies a byte array that contains the data to send (`dataToSend`), the length of the byte array (`dataToSend.length`), and the IP address and port number to send the datagrams to (`destinationInetAddress, destinationPort`).

```
udpPacket = new DatagramPacket(dataToSend,
    dataToSend.length, destinationInetAddress,
    destinationPort);
```

The `datagramSender` thread manages the sending of the datagrams. Using a separate thread enables the application to perform other tasks without having to wait for the thread's timer to time out. Setting the thread's `setDaemon()` property true creates the thread as a Daemon thread. The JVM exits when there are no user (non-Daemon) threads running. Calling the thread's `start()` method calls `UdpSend`'s `run()` method (below).

```
datagramSender = new Thread(this);
datagramSender.setDaemon(true);
datagramSender.start();
} // end UdpSend constructor
```

The main() Method

The `main()` method sets the values of three variables that may change depending on the application: the `delayTime` value in milliseconds and the values of `destinationIPAddress` and `destinationPort`. The `getByName` method of `InetAddress` converts the IP address in dotted-quad format to the `InetAddress` object required by the `DatagramPacket` object.

```
public static void main(String[] args)
    throws IOException {

int delayTime = 1000;

int destinationPort = 5550;
String destinationIPAddress = "192.168.111.5";

InetAddress destinationInetAddress =
    InetAddress.getByName(destinationIPAddress);
```

A call to the UdpSend constructor creates the myUdpSend object with the specified destination address, destination port, and delay time.

```
UdpSend myUdpSend =
    new UdpSend(destinationInetAddress,
    destinationPort, delayTime);
```

A while loop keeps the main thread alive. In this example application, the thread spends most of its time sleeping.

```
while(true) {
  try {
    Thread.sleep(1000);
  } catch (InterruptedException e) {
    System.out.print("InterruptedException: ");
    System.out.println(e);
  }
} // end while(true)
} // end main
```

Stopping the Sending of Datagrams

A stop() method enables program code to end the datagramSender thread and close the socket. Otherwise, the thread ends when no user threads are running.

```
public void stop() {
  sendDatagrams = false;
  datagramSender.interrupt();
  udpSocket.close();
} // end stop()
```

Sending Datagrams

The run() method executes when the main() method calls the datagram-Sender thread's start() method.

```
public void run() {
```

The sendDatagrams variable is initialized to true and messageCount is initialized to 255 so it wraps back to zero on the first message sent.

```
sendDatagrams = true;
int messageCount = 255;
```

A while loop repeatedly creates and sends a datagram, then waits delay-Time. The loop ends when an exception or the stop() method sets send-Datagrams false.

```
while (sendDatagrams) {
   try {
     createDatagrams();
```

DatagramSocket's send() method sends the datagram to the IP address and port specified in udpSocket.

```
udpSocket.send(udpPacket);
```

After sending a datagram, the program toggles the port bit whose value was sent in the datagram. BitPort's readLatch() method returns the last value written to the specified bit. (The application toggles the bit only so the value changes with each send for this example application.)

```
if (testBit.readLatch() == 0) {
   testBit.set();
} else {
   testBit.clear();
}
```

The thread then sleeps for the specified delay time. Calling the thread's interrupt() method causes an InterruptedException, whose catch block sets sendDatagrams false, ending the thread. An error when attempting to send a packet causes an IOException, whose catch block also sets sendDatagrams false, ending the thread.

```
     Thread.sleep(delayTime);

   } catch (InterruptedException e) {
     System.out.println("InterruptedException: ");
     System.out.println(e);
     sendDatagrams = false;

   } catch (IOException e) {
     System.out.print("IOException: ");
     System.out.println(e);
     sendDatagrams = false;
   }
 } // end while(sendDatagrams)
} // end run()
```

Creating the Datagram

The `createDatagram()` method stores the datagram's two bytes in the `dataToSend` byte array. The first byte is the `messageCount` variable, which increments on each send, resetting to zero after sending 255. The second byte is the value of Port 5, bit 2. The message is stored in the byte array `dataToSend`.

```
private void createDatagram() {
```

The message count in the datagram's first byte increments with each datagram, resetting to zero on 255.

```
if (messageCount == 255) {
    messageCount = 0;
} else {
    messageCount = ++messageCount;
}
```

```
dataToSend[0] = (byte)messageCount;
```

The datagram's second byte is the last value written to the `testBit` port bit.

```
dataToSend[1] = (byte)testBit.readLatch();
```

The `setData()` method of `DatagramPacket` stores the byte array in the `DatagramPacket` object. The `setLength()` method trims the datagram to match the length of the data. The size of `dataToSend` sets the datagram's maximum length.

```
udpPacket.setData(dataToSend);
udpPacket.setLength(dataToSend.length);
System.out.print("Message number: ");
System.out.println(messageCount);
} // end CreateDatagram()
```

```
} // end UdpSend
```

Receiving UDP Datagrams

The other side of UDP communications is receiving datagrams. The following applications are complements to the previous examples. A Rabbit and TINI program each wait to receive a datagram from a remote host, then display the contents of the datagram.

Rabbit Code

Much of the Rabbit code for receiving datagrams is similar to the code in the previous Rabbit example.

Initial Defines and Declarations

A TCPCONFIG 1 macro selects a network configuration from the *tcp_config.lib* file.

The MAX_UDP_SOCKET_BUFFERS macro specifies the number of socket buffers to allocate for UDP sockets. This application requires one socket buffer.

LOCAL_PORT specifies the port that the Rabbit will receive datagrams on. Generally, any port over 1023 is acceptable. The remote host will need to know this value when sending datagrams.

REMOTE_IP is the IP address of the host to receive datagrams from. Set this value to the IP address of the sending host. To accept datagrams from any host, set REMOTE_IP to zero. To accept only broadcast packets, set REMOTE_IP to 255.255.255.255.

```
#define TCPCONFIG 1
#define MAX_UDP_SOCKET_BUFFERS 1
#define LOCAL_PORT 5550
#define REMOTE_IP "192.168.111.5"
```

The #memmap directive stores all C functions not declared as root in the extended memory area, rather than limiting storage to the 64 kilobytes of root memory.

The *dcrtcp.lib* file is the Dynamic C library that supports TCP/IP communications.

```
#memmap xmem
#use "dcrtcp.lib"
```

The datagram_socket variable is a Dynamic C udpSocket structure.

```
udp_Socket datagram_socket;
```

Receiving a Datagram

The `receive_packet()` function checks for a received datagram and if there is one, writes its contents to Dynamic C's STDIO window. The `received_data` array holds the contents of the received datagram.

```
int receive_packet()
{
   static char received_data[128];
```

The `GLOBAL_INIT` section executes only once. The `memset()` function initializes the block of memory that will hold a received datagram.

```
#GLOBAL_INIT
{
    memset(received_data, 0, sizeof(received_data));
}
```

The `udp_recv()` function receives a datagram from the host specified in `datagram_socket`. The datagram is stored in `received_data`. If the return value is -1, there is no datagram and the function returns.

```
if (-1 == udp_recv(&datagram_socket, received_data,
      sizeof(received_data))) {
   return 0;
}
```

If there is a datagram, a `printf()` statement writes its contents to the STDIO window.

```
printf("Received bytes: %d, %d\n",received_data[0],
    received_data[1]);
return 1;
}
```

The main() Function

As in the previous Rabbit example, the `main()` function calls `sock_init()` to initialize the TCP/IP stack. If the return value isn't zero, the network isn't available.

```
main()
{
   int return_value;
   return_value = sock_init();
   if (return_value == 0) {
     printf("Nework support is initialized.\n");
```

```
    }
  else {
     printf("The network is not available.\n");
     exit(0);
     }

  printf("Opening UDP socket\n");
```

A call to udp_open() opens the specified UDP socket, enabling communications. The call requires a pointer to the local socket (&datagram_socket) and a local port number (LOCAL_PORT). The socket connects to the remote IP address in resolve(REMOTE_IP). The fourth parameter is zero to indicate that the socket will accept datagrams from any port on the remote host. To limit the datagrams to a specific source port at the remote host, this value can instead specify a port number. The final parameter is either a function to call on receiving data or NULL to place received data in the socket's receive buffer. The resolve function converts an IP address string in dotted-quad format to the longword required by udp_open.

```
  if(!udp_open(&datagram_socket, LOCAL_PORT,
      resolve(REMOTE_IP), 0, NULL)) {
    printf("udp_open failed!\n");
    exit(0);
  }
```

An endless while loop calls the tcp_tick() function to process network packets and the receive_packet() function to check for received datagrams.

```
  while(1) {
    tcp_tick(NULL);
    receive_packet();
  }
} // end main()
```

TINI Code

The java.net.DatagramSocket class includes methods for receiving UDP datagrams as well as sending them. The TINI's TINIDatagram-Socket class is a faster, memory-conserving replacement for Datagram-Socket. In the DatagramSocket class in Sun's JDK, the receive() method allocates a new InetAddress object on every receive, while TINI-

`DatagramSocket` overwrites the address instead of creating a new object. This example uses `TINIDatagramSocket`.

Initial Imports and Declarations

In addition to the `TINIDatagramSocket` class, the application imports `java.io` classes to support input and output operations, and `java.net` classes to support networking functions.

```
import java.io.*;
import java.net.*;
import com.dalsemi.tininet.TINIDatagramSocket
```

The `UdpReceive` class implements the `Runnable` interface so the code that waits for and receives datagrams can run in its own thread. The program's main thread can then perform other tasks at the same time.

```
public class UdpReceive implements Runnable {

    private TINIDatagramSocket udpSocket;
    private DatagramPacket udpPacket;
    private byte[] dataReceived;
    private Thread datagramReceiver;
    private volatile boolean receiveDatagrams;
```

Starting a Thread to Receive Datagrams

In the class's constructor, the `localPort` parameter specifies the local port to receive datagrams on. A `SocketException` is thrown if the socket can't be created.

The byte array `dataReceived` holds the data received from a remote host. Communications with the remote host use the `TINIDatagramSocket` object `udpSocket`. The socket uses a specific local port. The sending host must send the datagrams to this port.

The datagrams received from the remote host are stored in the `Datagram-Packet` object `udpPacket`. The object specifies a byte array to contain the received data (`dataReceived`) and the length of the byte array (`dataReceived.length`). For this example, the received datagrams contain just two bytes.

```
    public UdpReceive(int localPort) throws SocketException
```

```
    {
    byte[] dataReceived = new byte[2];
    udpSocket = new TINIDatagramSocket(localPort);

    udpPacket = new DatagramPacket(dataReceived,
        dataReceived.length);
```

The `datagramReceiver` thread manages the receiving of the datagrams. Using a separate thread enables the application to perform other tasks without having to wait for a datagram to arrive. Setting the thread's `setDaemon()` property true creates the thread as a Daemon thread, which ends when no user threads are running. Calling the thread's `start()` method calls `UdpReceive`'s `run()` method (below).

```
    datagramReceiver = new Thread(this);
    datagramReceiver.setDaemon(true);
    datagramReceiver.start();
    } // end UdpReceive constructor
```

The main() Method

The `main()` method sets the value of `localPort`, and a call to the `UdpReceive` constructor creates the `myUdpReceive` object with the specified port.

```
    public static void main(String[] args)
        throws IOException {

    int localPort = 5550;
    UdpReceive myUdpReceive = new
        UdpReceive(localPort);
```

A `while` loop keeps the `DatagramReceiver` thread alive. The loop spends its time sleeping. A real-world application could perform other functions here.

```
    while(true) {
      try {
        Thread.sleep(1000);
      } catch (InterruptedException e) {
        System.out.print("InterruptedException: ");
        System.out.println(e.getMessage());
      }
    } // end while(true)
  } // end main
```

Stopping the Receiving of Datagrams

A stop() method enables program code to end the datagramReceiver thread and close the socket. Otherwise, the thread ends when no user threads are running.

```
public void stop() {
   receiveDatagrams = false;
   datagramReceiver.interrupt();
   udpSocket.close();
} // end stop
```

Receiving Datagrams

The run() method executes when the main() method calls the datagram-Receiver thread's start() method.

```
public void run() {

   InetAddress senderAddress;
   receiveDatagrams = true;
```

A while() loop waits for datagrams until the stop() method sets receiveDatagrams false or an error occurs while receiving a datagram. The receive() method of TINIDatagramSocket returns on receiving a datagram. The getAddress() method returns the IP address of the sender. The getData() method returns a byte array with the datagram's contents.

A series of System.out.println statements writes the message and the sender's IP address to the console.

```
while (receiveDatagrams) {
   try {

      System.out.println("Waiting for datagram ...");
      udpSocket.receive(udpPacket);

      senderAddress = udpPacket.getAddress();
      dataReceived= udpPacket.getData();

      System.out.println("Received message: ");
      System.out.println(dataReceived[0]);
      System.out.println(dataReceived[1]);
      System.out.println();
      System.out.print("from: ");
      System.out.println
```

```
                        (senderAddress.getHostAddress());
            } catch (IOException e) {
```

If an error occurs while trying to receive a packet, `receiveDatagrams` is set to `false`, which ends the `while(receiveDatagrams)` loop and stops the thread.

```
            System.out.print("IOException: ");
            System.out.println(e.getMessage());
            receiveDatagrams = false;
        }
      } // end while(receiveDatagrams)
    } // end run()

  } // end UdpReceive
```

Exchanging Messages using TCP

With UDP, you can send a message at any time, to any computer, without first finding out if the remote computer is available to receive the message. With TCP, before exchanging data, one computer must request a connection to the other computer. The connection is between two sockets, with each socket defined by an IP address and port number.

The remote computer must respond to the request and the requesting computer must acknowledge receiving the response. When these events have occurred, a connection has been established and the computers can exchange other data. In a similar way, to close a connection, each computer sends a request to close and acknowledges the request to close received from the remote computer.

In the examples below, the embedded system's program waits for and responds to a request for a connection. When the connection has been established, the embedded system waits to receive data, reads a byte, increments it, sends it back to the remote host, and closes the connection. This code can server as a model for applications where a computer sends a request or command to an embedded system, which then returns a reply.

Rabbit Code

A Dynamic C application performs the TCP communications in the Rabbit module.

Initial Defines and Declarations

As in the Rabbit UDP example, the code begins by specifying a network configuration macro with TCPCONFIG and a local port for network communications. In this application, the Rabbit module accepts connection requests from any host and port, so there is no need to specify a remote IP address or port. The *dcrtcp.lib* file is the Dynamic C library that supports TCP/IP communications.

```
#define TCPCONFIG 1
#define LOCAL_PORT 5551
#memmap xmem
#use "dcrtcp.lib"

char server_buffer[255];
int bytes_read;
int return_value;
```

The server_socket variable is a Dynamic C tcp_Socket structure that specifies the socket to use for TCP communications.

```
tcp_Socket server_socket;
```

The function prototype for service_request() enables the main() function to call service_request() before it has been compiled.

```
void service_request();
```

The main() Function

The main() function begins by calling sock_init() to enable using TCP/IP functions. An endless while loop then alternates between executing the statements in a costatement that handles TCP communications and performing whatever other tasks the device is responsible for. Using a costatement for the TCP communications enables the device to do other things while waiting for a connection request or data from a remote host.

```
main() {
  int data_available;
```

209

```
return_value = sock_init();
if (return_value == 0) {
   while(1) {
```

In the costatement, Dynamic C's tcp_listen() function begins waiting for a connection request from a remote host to the specified local port. The call to tcp_listen() requires several parameters:

A pointer to a TCP socket (&server-socket).

The port number to listen on (LOCAL_PORT).

The remote computer's IP address (0 to accept requests from any IP address).

The port on the remote computer to communicate with (0 to communicate with any port).

Either a function to call when data is received or NULL to place received data in the socket's receive buffer (NULL).

Reserved parameter (0).

A waitfor() statement calls the application's connection_established() function. If a connection has been established with a remote host, the function returns 1 and program execution continues with the statements that follow. If there is no connection, the function returns 0 and program execution jumps to the costatement's closing brace. This gives other code in the while loop a chance to execute. When the code eventually loops back to the costatement, execution resumes at the waitfor() statement, which again calls the connection_established() function and continues in or exits the costatement as appropriate.

After a connection is established, a second waitfor() statement calls the application's check_for_received_data() function. The function returns 1 if there is a byte waiting to be read from the remote computer. If a byte is available or if the statement has been waiting for the number of seconds in DelaySec(), program execution continues with the statements that follow. Otherwise, program execution jumps to the costatement's closing brace and resumes at the waitfor() statement the next time through. The

`DelaySec()` function ensures that the `waitfor` statement eventually times out in case a remote host fails to send a data byte.

If a byte is available, a call to the application's `service_request()` function reads the byte and returns a response. This completes the communication, so the `sock_close()` function closes the connection and the costatement ends.

```
costate {
  tcp_listen(&server_socket,LOCAL_PORT,0,0,NULL,0);
  printf("Waiting for connection...\n");

  waitfor (connection_established());
  printf("Connection established. \n");

  waitfor (check_for_received_data() ||
      DelaySec(20));

  data_available = check_for_received_data();
  if (data_available > 0) {
    service_request();
    }
  else {
    printf("Timeout: the remote host provided no
        data. \n");
    }
  sock_close(&server_socket);
  printf("The connection is closed. \n");
} // end costate
```

If the call to `sock_init()` fails, the application ends without entering the `while(1)` loop.

```
  // Place code to accomplish additional tasks here.
  } // end while(1)
} // if (return_value == 0)

else {
  printf("The network is not available" \n");
  exit(0);
  }
} // end main()
```

Establishing a Connection

The connection_established function called in the costatement checks for a connection to a remote host. Dynamic C's sock_established() function returns 1 if a connection has been established to the specified socket and 0 if there is no connection. This code is in a separate function to enable calling it in a waitfor() statement.

It's possible that a connection may be established, data received, and the connection closed before the code has a chance to call sock_established(). To enable reading any data received if this occurs, the function also calls Dynamic C's sock_bytesready() function, which returns the number of bytes read or -1 if there are no bytes.

If sock_established returns 1 or if sock_bytesready() returns a value other than -1, connection_established() returns 0, indicating that either the connection is established or that the connection is now closed but there is at least one byte ready to be read. Otherwise the function returns 1.

Dynamic C's tcp_tick() function processes network packets and must be called periodically.

```
int connection_established() {
  tcp_tick(NULL);
  if (!sock_established(&server_socket) &&
      sock_bytesready(&server_socket) == -1) {
    return 0;
  }
  else {
    return 1;
  }
} // end connection_established()
```

Checking for Received Data

The check_for_received_data() function called in the main() function's costatement finds out if there is data available to be read from an existing connection. The sock_bytesready() function returns the number of bytes waiting to be read or -1 if no bytes are available. The check_for_received_data() function returns 1 if a byte is available and 0 if there are no bytes. A call to tcp_tick() processes network packets.

```
int check_for_received_data() {
  tcp_tick(&server_socket);
  if (sock_bytesready(&server_socket) == -1) {
    return 0;
  }
  else {
    return 1;
  }
} // end check_for_received_data
```

Reading and Responding to Received Data

The service_request() function reads a received byte and returns a response to the remote host. Dynamic C's sock_fastread() function reads bytes from a socket into a buffer and returns the number of bytes read or -1 on error. The function requires a pointer to a socket to read from (&server_socket), the byte array to place the data in (server_buffer), and the maximum number of bytes to read (sizeof(server_buffer)).

```
void service_request() {
  bytes_read = sock_fastread(&server_socket,
    server_buffer, sizeof(server_buffer));
```

If a byte was received, the code increments it, resetting to 0 on receiving a byte of 255.

```
if (bytes_read > 0) {
  printf("Byte received = %d \n", server_buffer[0]);
  if (server_buffer[0] == 255) {
    server_buffer[0] = 0;
  }
  else {
    server_buffer[0]=server_buffer[0] + 1;
  }
```

Dynamic C's sock_write() function writes the incremented byte to the socket, which causes the byte to be sent on the network to the remote host.

```
return_value = sock_write(&server_socket,
    server_buffer, 1);
if (return_value != -1) {
  printf("Byte sent = %d \n", server_buffer[0]);
  }
else {
  printf("Error writing to socket. \n");
  }
```

```
    }  // end if (bytes_read > 0)
    else {
      printf("Error reading from socket. \n");
    }
  } // end service_request()
```

TINI Code

The TINI can also function as a TCP server that receives and responds to requests to connect and exchange data. As in the UdpSend application in this chapter, the application runs in an endless loop. A `kill` command in a Telnet session ends the application.

Imports and Initial Declares

The application imports `java.io` classes to support input and output operations, and `java.net` classes to support networking functions.

```
import java.io.*;
import java.net.*;
```

The `TcpServer` class implements the `Runnable` interface so the code that does the network communications can execute in its own thread. This leaves the main thread free to do other things.

```
public class TcpServer implements Runnable {

    private ServerSocket server;
    private int readTimeout;
    private Thread serverThread;
    private volatile boolean runServer;
```

The main() Method

The class's `main()` method sets `localPort` to the port number clients will connect to and sets `readTimeout` to the number of milliseconds the server will wait to receive data after a remote host connects. The timeout is expressed in milliseconds. The `TcpServer` object `myTcpServer` uses the `localPort` and `readTimeout` values.

```
public static void main(String[] args)
    throws IOException {

    int localPort = 5551;
    int readTimeout = 5000;
```

```
TcpServer myTcpServer = new TcpServer
    (localPort, readTimeout);
```

A while loop executes while waiting for connection requests. In this example, the thread spends its time sleeping.

```
while (true){
  try {
    Thread.sleep(1000);
  } catch (InterruptedException e) {
    System.out.print("InterruptedException: ");
    System.out.println(e.getMessage() );
  }
  } // end while(true)
} // end main()
```

Initializing the Server

The constructor for the TcpServer class creates a thread to handle connection requests. The constructor's two parameters are the localPort and readTimeout values set in main().

```
public TcpServer(int localPort, int readTimeout)
    throws IOException {
```

A ServerSocket object (server) listens for connection requests on localPort, and on receiving a request, creates a socket object.

```
server = new ServerSocket(localPort);

System.out.print("The server is listening on port ");
System.out.println(localPort);
```

The readTimeout variable used in the run() method is assigned the value of the readTimeout parameter passed to the constructor.

```
this.readTimeout = readTimeout;
```

A separate thread (serverThread) handles connection requests. The thread's setDaemon() method is set to true so the server thread ends when no user threads are running. Calling the start() method calls the thread's run() routine.

```
serverThread = new Thread(this);
serverThread.setDaemon(true);
serverThread.start();
```

```
} // end TcpServer constructor
```

Waiting for Connection Requests

Calling serverThread's start() method causes the thread's run() method to execute. The run() method accepts connections and calls a method to handle each connection.

A while loop executes until the runServer variable is false, which occurs on an exception or if the class's stop() method sets runServer false.

```
public void run() {
  runServer = true;

  while (runServer) {
    try {
```

On accepting a connection request, the server's accept() method creates a socket for exchanging data with the connected host. The class's handleConnection() method manages communications with the socket.

```
      Socket socket = server.accept();

      try {
        handleConnection(socket);
      } catch (IOException e) {
        System.out.print("An error occurred while
            working with a socket: ");
        System.out.println(e.getMessage());
      } finally {
        try {
```

When handleConnection() returns or if there is an exception, the routine closes the socket to release any resources used by it. If there is an exception when attempting to close the socket, no action needs to be taken. If an exception occurs while attempting to accept a connection, runServer is set to false to stop the thread.

```
          socket.close();
        } catch (IOException e) {
        }
      }
    } catch (IOException e) {
```

```
        runServer = false;
      }
    }
  } // end run()
```

Stopping the Server

The stop() method provides a way to stop the server under program control by setting runServer false and closing the socket.

```
public void stop() {
   runServer = false;

   try {
     server.close();
   } catch (IOException e) {
   }
} // end stop()
```

Handling a Connection

The handleConnection() method handles a single connection with a remote host.

```
private void handleConnection(Socket socket)
    throws IOException {
  System.out.print("Connected to ");
  System.out.println(socket);
```

The socket timeout is set to the readTimeout value set in the main() method.

```
    socket.setSoTimeout(readTimeout);
```

An InputStream object reads data from the remote host, and an Output-Stream object writes to the remote host.

```
    InputStream in = socket.getInputStream();
    OutputStream out = socket.getOutputStream();
```

The InputStream object's read() method attempts to read a byte from the remote host.

If the byte is -1, the input stream is closed and no more communications can take place. Otherwise, the code increments the byte and writes the incremented value to the OutputStream object. To complete the communication, a call to the OutputStream object's flush() method causes the data to transmit immediately, and the output stream is closed.

```
try {
  int b = in.read();
  if (b != -1) {
    out.write(b + 1);
    System.out.print("Writing ");
    System.out.print(b + 1);
    System.out.print(" to remote host.");
    out.flush();
    out.close();
  }
} catch (InterruptedIOException ex) {
```

An InterruptedIOException indicates that the read attempt has timed out.

```
System.out.print("The remote host sent no data
    within ");
System.out.print(readTimeout / 1000);
System.out.println(" seconds.");
}
} // end handleConnection()
} // end TcpServer
```

UDP and TCP from PC Applications

A PC application can communicate with any embedded system that uses UDP or TCP, including the programs above. You can write the application using any of a number of programming languages, including Visual Basic .NET and Visual C#.

About Network Programming on a PC

Windows includes plenty of support that greatly simplifies network programming and troubleshooting. Windows includes drivers that support Ethernet communications and application programming interface (API) functions that enable applications to send and receive information over a network using TCP/IP and related protocols.

For example Visual Basic .NET applications that communicate with the Rabbit and TINI programs in this chapter, see my Embedded Ethernet page at www.Lvr.com.

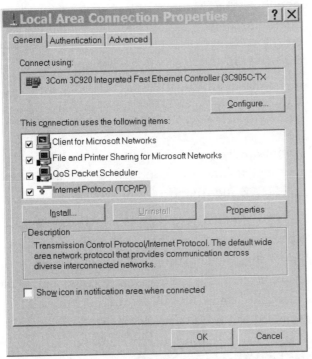

Figure 5-1: In Windows' Control Panel, Network and Connections enables installing TCP/IP support for a connection.

A custom application isn't the only way for a PC application to communicate over a network. Another option is to use a browser like Microsoft's Internet Explorer to request Web pages from computers in the network. Chapter 6 and Chapter 7 have more about how to serve Web pages from an embedded system.

To communicate over a network, a PC must have an Ethernet interface and a network connection to the embedded system the PC wants to communicate with, as described in Chapter 2.

If you access the Internet from your computer, you already have TCP/IP support installed. If you need to install TCP/IP, in Windows' Control Panel, click **Network and Connections** and right-click a connection (Figure 5-1).

If the **General** tab doesn't show Internet Protocol (TCP/IP), click the **Install** button to install it.

Using Visual Basic .NET

Network programming in Visual Basic .NET uses the `System.Net.Sockets` namespace, which includes several classes for use in network communications.

For UDP communications, at first glance, the `UdpClient` class appears to provide a convenient interface. `UdpClient` contains selected members of the `Socket` class and adds support for multicasting.

But `UdpClient` is limited in a way that makes it impractical for much beyond basic testing. `UdpClient`'s `Receive` method is synchronous, which means it blocks the program thread that calls `Receive` until a datagram arrives. If an application calls the `Receive` method and no datagram arrives, the thread that called `Receive` can do nothing but wait. You can place the `Receive` call in its own thread, leaving the main program thread free to perform other tasks while waiting, but there is no way to gracefully close a blocked thread if the data never arrives.

An alternative to `UdpClient` is the `Socket` class. By declaring a socket with `ProtocolType` set to `Udp`, you have access to all of the members of the `Socket` class, including the ability to use the `BeginReceive` and `EndReceive` methods in asynchronous data transfers. This means that the application doesn't have to wait for data to arrive. Instead, the program can call `BeginReceive` and continue to perform other operations. When data arrives, a callback routine runs and calls `EndReceive` to retrieve the data. And the program can close at any time.

For TCP communications, the `TcpClient` class is a little more flexible than `UdpClient`. The `SendTimeout` and `ReceiveTimeout` properties enable you to specify how long to wait for a response from a remote host before giving up. If you expect the remote host to be able to respond quickly most of the time, `TcpClient` may be suitable. Or as with UDP, you can use the `Socket` class for TCP communications.

In Depth:
Inside UDP and TCP

This section explains how UDP and TCP help get data to its destination. Knowing more about how the protocols work can help in selecting which protocol to use and in using the protocol effectively. Also included is a review of options for obtaining code to support UDP, TCP, and IP in embedded systems.

The Ethernet standard specifies a way to transfer information between computers in a local network. But Ethernet alone doesn't provide some things that many data transfers require. These include naming the port, or process, that is sending the data, naming the port that will use the data at the destination, handshaking to inform the source whether the destination received the data, flow control to help data get to its destination quickly and reliably, and sequence numbering to ensure that the destination knows the correct order for messages that arrive in multiple segments. The transmission control protocol (TCP) can provide all of these. The user datagram protocol (UDP) is a simpler alternative for data transfers that only require specifying of ports or error checking. Table 5-1 compares UDP and TCP.

Figure 5-2 shows the location of UDP and TCP in a network protocol stack. UDP and TCP communicate with the IP layer and the application layer. Some applications don't require UDP or TCP, and may communicate directly with the IP layer or the Ethernet driver.

About Sockets and Ports

Every UDP and TCP communication is between two endpoints, or sockets. Each socket has a port number and an IP address.

In an Ethernet frame, the Source Address and Destination Address fields identify the sending and receiving Ethernet interfaces. A UDP or TCP communication specifies the destination more precisely by naming a port at the destination. Each TCP communication also names a source port that identi-

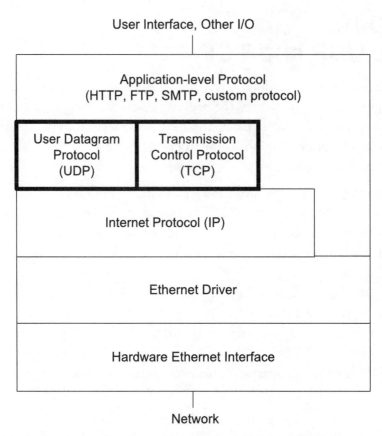

User Interface, Other I/O

| Application-level Protocol (HTTP, FTP, SMTP, custom protocol) |
| User Datagram Protocol (UDP) / Transmission Control Protocol (TCP) |
| Internet Protocol (IP) |
| Ethernet Driver |
| Hardware Ethernet Interface |

Network

Figure 5-2: In the network protocol stack, the TCP and UDP layers communicate with the IP layer and the application layer. Not all communications require TCP or UDP.

fies the provider of the data being sent. Each UDP communication has a source port, but UDP datagrams aren't required to include the source-port number in the header.

A socket's port isn't a hardware port like the ports that a CPU accesses using `inp` and `out` instructions. Instead, the port number identifies the process, or task, that is providing the data being sent or using the data being received.

You can think of a socket as one end of a logical connection between computers. Unlike a physical connection, where dedicated wires and electronic components form a link, a logical connection exists only in software. Data

Table 5-1: UDP and TCP are two popular protocols for exchanging data over local networks and the Internet.

Protocol	UDP	TCP
Name of unit transmitted	datagram	segment
Source port specified to remote host?	optional	required
Must establish a connection before transferring data?	no	yes
Supports error checking?	optional	required
Supports flow control?	no	yes
Supports handshaking?	no	yes
Supports sequence numbering?	no	yes
Supports broadcasting and multicasting?	yes	no

that travels between sockets that have a logical connection doesn't have to take the same physical path every time.

The Internet Assigned Numbers Authority (IANA) (*www.iana.org*) maintains a Port Numbers list that assigns port numbers to standard processes.

There are three groups of port numbers. Values from 1 to 1023 are called well-known ports, or contact ports, and are for use by system processes or programs executed by privileged users. Table 5-2 shows examples of a few common processes and their well-known ports.

Assigning a well-known port to a process makes it easy for a computer to know what port to use when it wants to communicate with a remote computer. For example, a computer requesting a Web page normally sends the request to port 80. The receiving computer assumes that messages arriving at port 80 will use the hypertext transfer protocol (HTTP) for requesting Web pages.

Ports from 1024 to 49151 are Registered ports. An entity can request a port number from the IANA for a particular use, and the IANA maintains a list of ports it has registered. Some of the Registered ports are assigned to companies. For example, ports 5190 through 5193 are assigned to America Online. Other assignments are to processes, such as Building Automation and Control Networks (bacnet) on port 47808. Networks that don't use the

Table 5-2: Examples of standard protocols and their assigned port numbers.

Protocol	Port Number
Domain Name Service	17
FTP data	20
FTP control	21
Telnet	23
SMTP	25
Network Time Protocol	53
Gopher	70
Finger	79
HTTP	80
POP2	109
POP3	110
Quote of the Day	123

ports in this group for their registered purposes are free to use these ports for any purpose.

Ports from 49152 through 65535 are dynamic and/or private ports. The IANA doesn't assign processes to these. A network may use these ports for any purpose.

In a communication between two hosts, the values of the source and destination ports don't have to be the same and usually aren't. The source typically selects any available local port and requests to communicate with a well-known port on the destination computer. On receiving the request, the destination computer may send a reply that suggests switching the communication from the well-known port to a private port at the destination. This keeps the well-known port available to receive other new communication requests.

For communications that don't use a well-known port, such as the examples in this chapter, the computers must agree ahead of time on what ports to transmit and receive on.

UDP: Just the Basics

UDP is a basic protocol that adds only port addressing and optional error detecting to the message being sent. There is no protocol for handshaking to acknowledge received data or exchange other flow-control information. UDP is a connectionless protocol, which means that a computer can send a message using UDP without first establishing that the remote computer is on the network or that the specified destination port is available to communicate. For these reasons, UDP is also called an unreliable protocol, meaning that using UDP alone, the sender doesn't know when or if the destination received a message.

The document that defines UDP is *RFC0768: User Datagram Protocol*. It's also approved standard STD0006.

A computer that wants to send a message using UDP places the message in a UDP datagram, which consists of a UDP header followed by the data payload containing the message. As Chapter 1 explained, the sending computer places the UDP datagram in the data area of an IP datagram. In an Ethernet network, the IP datagram travels in the data field of an Ethernet frame. On receiving the Ethernet frame, the destination computer's network stack passes the data portion of the UDP datagram to the port, or process, specified in the datagram's header.

In most respects, UDP is less capable than TCP, so UDP is simpler to implement and thus more suitable for certain applications. If needed, a communication can define its own handshaking protocol for use with UDP. For example, after receiving a message, a receiving interface can send a reply containing an acknowledge code or other requested information. If the sender receives no reply in a reasonable amount of time, it can try again. But if an application needs anything more than the most basic handshaking or flow control, you should consider using TCP rather than re-inventing it for use with UDP.

UDP has one capability not available to TCP, and that is the ability to send a message to multiple destinations at once, including broadcasting to all IP addresses in a local network and multicasting to a defined group of IP addresses. Broadcasting and multicasting aren't practical with TCP because the source would need to handshake with all of the destinations.

The UDP Header and Data

The UDP header contains four fields, followed by the data being transmitted. Table 5-3 shows the fields.

Source Port Number. The source port number identifies the port, or process, on the computer that is sending the message. The source port number is optional. If the receiving process doesn't need to know what process sent the datagram, this field can be zero. The field is two bytes

Destination Port Number. The destination port number identifies the port, or process, that should receive the message at the destination. The field is two bytes.

UDP Datagram Length. The UDP datagram length is the length of the entire datagram in bytes, including the header, with a maximum of 65535 bytes. The field is two bytes.

UDP Checksum. The UDP checksum is an optional error-checking value calculated on the contents of UDP datagram and a pseudo header. The pseudo header contains the source and destination IP addresses and the protocol value from the header of the IP datagram that will contain the UDP datagram when it transmits on the network (Table 5-4). The pseudo header doesn't transmit on the network. Including the information in the pseudo header in the checksum protects the destination from mistakenly accepting datagrams that have been misrouted. The checksum value is calculated in the same way as the IP header's checksum, described in Chapter 4. The field is two bytes.

A message that travels only within a local Ethernet network doesn't need the UDP checksum because the Ethernet frame's checksum provides error checking. For a message that travels through different, possibly unknown, networks, the checksum enables the destination to detect corrupted data.

Data. A UDP datagram can be up to 65,535 bytes, and the header is eight bytes, so a datagram can carry up to 65,527 bytes of data. In practice, the

Table 5-3: A UDP header has four fields.

Field	Number of Bits	Description
Source Port Number	16	The port, or process, that is sending the datagram.
Destination Port Number	16	The port, or process, the datagram is directed to.
UDP Datagram Length	16	The datagram length in bytes.
UDP Checksum	16	Checksum value or zero.

source computer usually limits datagrams to a shorter length. One reason to use shorter datagrams is that a very large datagram might not fit in the destination's receive buffer. Or the application receiving the data may expect a message of a specific size.

Shorter datagrams may also be more efficient. When a large datagram travels through networks with different capabilities, the Internet Protocol may fragment the datagram, requiring the destination to reassemble the fragments. All of the data will still probably get to its destination, but generally it's more efficient to divide the data at the source and reassemble it at the destination, rather than relying on IP to do the work en route.

The IP standard requires hosts to accept datagrams of up to 576 bytes. An IP header with no options is 20 bytes, and the UDP header is 8 bytes. So a UDP datagram with up to 548 data bytes and no IP options should be able to reach its destination without fragmenting.

Supporting UDP in Embedded Systems

Supporting UDP in an embedded system requires the ability to add a header to data to transmit and remove the header from received data, plus support for IP.

To send a datagram using UDP, a computer in an Ethernet network must do the following:

- Place the destination port number and datagram length in the appropriate locations in the UDP header. The source port number and checksum in the header are optional. Computing the checksum requires knowing the IP addresses of the source and destination.

Table 5-4: The checksum of a UDP datagram includes the values in a pseudo header containing these five values.

Field	Size (bytes)	Source
Source Address	4	IP header
Destination Address	4	IP header
Zero	1	(none)
Protocol	1	IP header
UDP Length	2	Length in bytes of the UDP datagram including the UDP header but excluding the pseudo header

- Append the data to send to the header.
- Place the UDP datagram in the data portion of an IP datagram. The IP datagram requires source and destination IP addresses and a checksum computed on the header.
- Pass the IP datagram to the Ethernet controller's driver for sending on the network.

To receive a datagram using UDP, a computer in an Ethernet network must do the following:

- Receive an IP datagram from the Ethernet controller's driver.
- Strip the IP header from the datagram. Calculate the IP checksum and compare the result with the received value.
- If the checksums match, strip the header from the UDP datagram. If using the UDP checksum, calculate its value and compare it to the received checksum.
- Use the destination port number to decide where to pass the received data.

As the examples at the beginning of the chapter showed, if you're using a module with UDP support, the details of creating the datagrams, extracting data from a received datagram, and dealing with the checksums are handled for you. The application code just needs to provide the IP addresses, port numbers, and data to send and call a function to send the datagram, or wait to receive data in a datagram addressed to a specific port.

TCP: Adding Handshaking and Flow Control

UDP provides the basics for transferring data between processes on different computers. But using UDP alone, the source doesn't know whether or not a destination received the data sent. TCP uses a system of sequence and acknowledgment numbers that enable the destination to acknowledge receiving specific data bytes. Using sequence numbers, a destination can place received messages in the order they were sent, even if they were received out of order. Sequence numbers also enable a destination to detect duplicate received data. For more efficient transfers of large amounts of data, TCP specifies a way for the source to match the amount of data sent with the ability of the destination to accept new data.

The document that defines TCP is *RFC0793: Transmission Control Protocol*. It's also an approved standard with the designation STD0007. Several additional RFCs contain proposed standards that enhance and improve the original standard.

TCP is a called a connection-oriented protocol because processes can't exchange data until they have exchanged communications to establish a connection with each other. TCP is called a reliable protocol because the handshaking, checksum, and sequence and acknowledge numbers enable the source to verify that data has arrived at its destination without error.

A TCP segment consists of a header optionally followed by a data payload. (A header might transmit without a data payload to send status or control information.) The term *segment* suggests that a single TCP segment is only a portion of a complete TCP data transfer, and in fact, every successful data transfer uses at least two segments. The source sends one or more segments containing data, and the destination sends one or more segments to acknowledge receiving the data. A single acknowledgment can acknowledge multiple segments. In contrast, each UDP datagram is an independent unit that requires no additional communication.

Like UDP, TCP uses port numbers to identify processes at the source and destination.

Before two processes can send and receive data using TCP, their computers must establish a connection by performing a 3-way handshake. On completing the handshake, each computer has acknowledged that the port specified in the handshake is available to receive communications from the specified port on the other computer. Either computer may then use the connection to send TCP segments to the other computer.

On receiving a data over an established connection, the destination responds by returning information about whether the data arrived without error, whether it's OK to send more data, and if so, the quantity of new data the destination is able to receive.

To close a connection, each computer sends a request to close the connection and waits for an acknowledgment of the request.

The TCP Header

The header of a TCP segment has ten required fields and one optional field. The header is at least 20 bytes. Data following the header is optional. Table 5-5 shows the fields.

Source Port Number. The source port number identifies the port, or process, on the computer that is sending the message. A TCP segment must include a source port number so the destination knows where to send the acknowledgment. This field is two bytes.

Destination Port Number. The destination port number identifies the port, or process, that should receive the message at the destination. This field is two bytes.

Sequence Number. The sequence number, also called the segment sequence number, identifies the segment. The sequence number enables the destination to acknowledge receiving the data in a specific segment. When a source sends a message that requires multiple segments, the sequence numbers enable the destination to place the segments in order even if they arrive out of order.

In the first segments sent when establishing a connection, each computer provides an initial sequence number. The TCP standard recommends select-

Table 5-5: A TCP header has 10 required fields and one optional field.

Field	Number of Bits	Description
Source Port Number	16	The port, or process, that is sending the datagram.
Destination Port Number	16	The port, or process, the datagram is directed to.
Sequence Number	32	Segment identifier.
Acknowledgment Number	32	Identifier of the last received byte.
Header Length	4	Length of TCP header in units of 32 bits.
Reserved	6	Zero.
Control Bits	6	URG: the segment is urgent ACK: the acknowledgment number is valid PSH: push the data to application right away RST: reset the connection SYN: synchronization is in progress FIN: the source has no more data to send
Window	16	The number of new bytes the source can accept.
Checksum	16	Checksum value.
Urgent Pointer	16	Sequence number of the last byte of urgent data
Options	0 or more	(optional) Can indicate the maximum segment size the source can handle.

ing this number by using the value of a counter that increments every four microseconds. Using a counter helps to prevent duplicate numbers if a connection closes, then reopens.

For segments that include data, the sequence number is also the number of the first data byte in the segment, with the following data bytes numbered in sequence. If the source sends another segment using the same connection, that segment's sequence number equals the previous segment's sequence number plus the number of data bytes in the previous segment. For example, assume that a source sends three segments, each with 100 data bytes, and the first segment's sequence number is 1000. The second segment's sequence number is 1100 (1000 + 100) and the third segment's sequence number is 1200 (1100 + 100).

If a sequence number reaches the maximum value of $2^{32}-1$, it wraps back to zero. This field is four bytes.

Acknowledgment Number. The destination computer returns an acknowledgment number to let the source know that a specific segment or segments were received. The field is valid when the ACK control bit described below is set to 1. The acknowledgment number equals the sequence number of the last received byte in sequence plus 1. This value is also the sequence number the destination expects in the next received segment. In returning an acknowledgment number, the computer is saying that it has received all of the data up to one less than the acknowledgment number.

For example, if we again assume that a source sends three segments, each with 100 data bytes, and the first segment's sequence number is 1000, on receiving the first segment, the destination could return a header with an acknowledgment number of 1100. On receiving the second segment (with a sequence number of 1100), the destination could return an acknowledgment number of 1200. On receiving the third segment, the returned acknowledgment number would be 1300.

The destination doesn't have to return a acknowledgment for every received segment. In the above example, the destination could wait until it received all three segments. It would then return a single segment with an acknowledgment number of 1300, indicating that all of the data bytes through 1299 have been received. But if the destination waits too long before acknowledging, the source will think the data didn't reach its destination and will resend.

In the above example, if the destination receives only the first and last segments, with segment numbers 1000 and 1200, it can return an acknowledgment number of 1100, but should wait to receive the middle segment, with the segment number 1100, before returning an acknowledgment number of 1300.

This field is four bytes.

Header Length. Because a TCP header's length can vary depending on the contents of the TCP Options field, the header includes a field that specifies the header's length. The value is in units of 32 bits, so all headers must be multiples of 32 bits, padded with zeros at the end if necessary. A header with no TCP Options field has a Header Length of 5, to indicate a header size of 160 bits, or 20 bytes. This field is four bits.

Reserved Field. This field is six bits, all zeroes.

Control Bits. The control-bits field is six bits. The bits provide information about the status of the connection, tell the destination something about when to process the data, and enable the source to inform the destination of a change in status of the connection. The following sections describe the meaning of each bit, in order as they appear in the header, when the bit is equal to 1.

URG. The segment is urgent. Urgent segments use the Urgent Pointer field described below.

ACK. The header contains a valid acknowledgment number. When establishing a TCP connection, each computer sets this bit in the first segment that acknowledges receiving a header containing a sequence number, and in all segments that follow in the connection.

PSH. The receiver should push, or send, the segment's data to the receiving application as soon as possible. If a computer normally waits for a buffer to fill before passing received data to an application, the PSH bit can advise the computer to pass data to the application right away, even if the buffer isn't full.

RST. Reset the connection. RST provides a way to recover if a connection becomes unsynchronized or invalid. A computer sends a segment with the RST bit set after receiving a segment that doesn't appear to be intended for the current connection, or if the connection has been closed. Receiving a segment with the RST bit set informs a computer that it should end the current connection and start over in establishing a connection. For example, if one computer in a connection crashes and restarts, the previous connection is no longer valid, but the other computer may not know this and may continue sending data. On receiving a segment for a closed connection, the destination returns a segment with RST set to let the source know that the computers need to re-establish the connection.

SYN. Synchronization is in progress. Synchronization is the process of performing the 3-way handshake to establish a TCP connection. The SYN bit is set to 1 until the handshake is complete, indicating the connection is established. In all of the segments that follow, the SYN bit is zero.

FIN. The source has no more data to send. The source may set this bit in the header of the segment containing the final data sent in a connection, or in a header that follows this segment.

Window. Window is the number of new bytes the receiving computer can accept. The value may change with each segment a computer sends, depending on how much buffer space is available. A source may use the received value in determining how much data to send in the next segment. The maximum window size is 65535 bytes. If a destination's window is zero, a source that wants to send data may send a single byte periodically to cause the destination to return an updated window value. This field is two bytes.

Checksum. TCP requires a checksum. The source and destination calculate the checksum on the contents of the TCP segment plus a pseudo header containing information from the IP header and the TCP segment length. Table 5-6 shows the values in the pseudo header. As with UDP, the pseudo header doesn't transmit on the network and including the pseudo header in the checksum protects the destination from mistakenly accepting datagrams that have been misrouted. The checksum value is calculated in the same way as the IP header's checksum, as described in Chapter 4. The field is two bytes.

Urgent Pointer. When the URG bit is set, the urgent pointer marks the end of the urgent data. The value is the sequence number of the last byte of urgent data, expressed as an offset from the segment's sequence number. For example, if the segment's sequence number is 1000 and the first 8 bytes are urgent data, the urgent pointer would be 8. A typical use for the urgent pointer is to enable a user to interrupt a process.

The wording of the original TCP standard left some confusion about whether the URG pointer points to the last byte of urgent data or the first byte following the urgent data. RFC 1122 clarifies by saying that URG should point to the last byte of urgent data. This field is two bytes.

Table 5-6: The checksum of a TCP segment includes the values in a pseudo header containing these five values.

Field	Size (bytes)	Source
Source Address	4	IP header
Destination Address	4	IP header
Zero	1	(none)
Protocol	1	IP header
TCP Length	2	Length in bytes of the TCP segment including the TCP header but excluding the pseudo header

TCP Options. The items in the TCP options field are optional, so this field is zero or more bytes.

The Maximum Segment Size option enables the receiving process to specify the maximum segment size the process can handle. A process uses this option only when establishing a connection, in a segment where the SYN bit is set. The option is four bytes, consisting of the byte 02h, followed by 04h, followed by two bytes that specify the maximum segment size.

The No Operation option provides a way to align options on a word boundary. The option is the single byte 01h.

The End of Option List option indicates that there are no more options in the field. This option is the byte 00h.

The complete TCP header must be a multiple of 32 bits. To achieve this, the end of the TCP Options field may be padded with zeros.

The Data Portion. Following the header is the optional data portion of the segment. The IP standard requires hosts to accept datagrams of up to 576 bytes. An IP header with no options is 20 bytes, and a TCP header with no options is also 20 bytes. So a TCP segment with up to 536 data bytes and no IP options or TCP options should be able to reach its destination without fragmenting.

Establishing a Connection

A TCP connection has two endpoints, one at the source and one at the destination. Each endpoint is a socket, with a port number and IP address.

Each TCP connection has a unique pair of sockets, but a single socket on a computer can have multiple connections, each to a different socket. For example, a computer's port 80 can have connections to a number of remote computers at the same time. A pair of computers can have multiple connections to each other at the same time, as long as no two pairs of sockets are identical.

To establish a connection, two computers must complete a 3-way handshake. Each communication in the handshake contains a TCP header. The computer that requests the connection is sometimes referred to as the TCP client, while the computer that receives the connection request is the TCP server. Once the connection has been established, either computer can transmit to the other at any time, although an application protocol may limit when the computers may transmit.

Figure 5-3 shows typical communications in a handshake between two processes, the client and server, using the following communications:

1. The client initiates the handshake by sending a segment containing an initial sequence number. In the example, the sequence number is 100. The acknowledgment number is zero, the SYN bit is 1, and the ACK and FIN bits are zero.

2. The server waits to receive a connection request. On receiving the segment from the client, the server responds by sending a segment containing its own initial sequence number and an acknowledgment number equal to the received sequence number + 1. In the example, the segment's sequence number is 500. The acknowledgment number is 101 (the received sequence number + 1). The SYN and ACK bits are 1, and the FIN bit is zero.

3. The client responds by sending a segment whose sequence number is 101, the received acknowledgment number. The acknowledgment number is

Request a Connection	
Sequence Number	100
Acknowledgment Number	0
SYN Bit	1
ACK Bit	0
FIN Bit	0

Acknowledge the Request	
Sequence Number	500
Acknowledgment Number	101
SYN Bit	1
ACK Bit	1
FIN Bit	0

Acknowledge the Response	
Sequence Number	101
Acknowledgment Number	501
SYN Bit	1
ACK Bit	1
FIN Bit	0

Figure 5-3: Establishing a TCP connection requires a 3-way handshake.

501, which is the received sequence number + 1. The SYN and ACK bits are 1, and the FIN bit is zero.

The connection is now established.

Sending and Receiving Data

Figure 5-4 shows an example of an exchange of data. The client sends a segment with a sequence number of 101, an acknowledgment number of 501, an ACK bit of 1, a SYN bit of zero, and eight bytes of data in the data portion of the segment. The ACK and SYN bits don't change for the remainder of the connection.

The server acknowledges receiving the 8 bytes of data by sending a segment with a sequence number of 501 and an acknowledgment number of 109. The data portion of this segment may also contain new data to be sent to the client, which the client acknowledges in another segment.

The segments sent when establishing a connection can include data as well. When this occurs, the destination must hold the received data until the connection is established.

A successful handshake tells the source computer that the data arrived at the destination computer's TCP layer. There is still room for error, however, because the handshake can't guarantee that the designated process at the destination computer received the data from the TCP layer. So to be absolutely sure that the destination's application received the data, you need a protocol at the application layer to provide the acknowledgment.

Closing a Connection

Closing a connection also requires handshaking. To close a connection completely, each computer sends a segment with the FIN control bit set to 1 to indicate that the computer has no more data to send. Each destination must acknowledge receiving the FIN. Figure 5-5 shows an example:

1. The client sends a segment with the FIN control bit set to 1. This indicates that the client will send no more data over this connection. The client may continue to receive from the server.

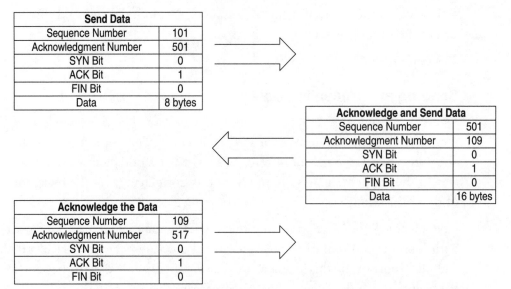

Send Data	
Sequence Number	101
Acknowledgment Number	501
SYN Bit	0
ACK Bit	1
FIN Bit	0
Data	8 bytes

Acknowledge and Send Data	
Sequence Number	501
Acknowledgment Number	109
SYN Bit	0
ACK Bit	1
FIN Bit	0
Data	16 bytes

Acknowledge the Data	
Sequence Number	109
Acknowledgment Number	517
SYN Bit	0
ACK Bit	1
FIN Bit	0

Figure 5-4: On receiving data, the receiver returns an acknowledgment number equal to the sequence number expected in the next segment.

Request to Close the Connection	
Sequence Number	109
Acknowledgment Number	517
SYN Bit	0
ACK Bit	1
FIN Bit	1

Acknowledge the Request and Request to Close	
Sequence Number	517
Acknowledgment Number	110
SYN Bit	0
ACK Bit	1
FIN Bit	1

Acknowledge the Request	
Sequence Number	110
Acknowledgment Number	518
SYN Bit	0
ACK Bit	1
FIN Bit	0

Figure 5-5: Closing a TCP connection also requires a 3-way handshake.

2. The server sends a segment acknowledging the received FIN. If the server has no more data to send, it sets its FIN bit to 1. Otherwise, the server continues to send data and sets the FIN bit to 1 when all of the data has been sent.

3. The client sends a segment acknowledging the received FIN. The connection is now closed.

Of course, it's possible that one of the computers will crash or be removed from the network before the closing handshake completes. In this case, the other computer may decide after a time to consider the connection closed and free the resources allocated to the connection.

Flow Control

A sending process may have multiple segments ready to send to a destination. Before sending each segment, the sending process could wait for an acknowledgment for the previous segment. But this isn't the most efficient way to transfer data if the destination has room to store the data in more than one segment.

For more efficient transfers, the sending process can use a received header's Window field to help determine how much data to send without waiting for an acknowledgment. The destination can adjust the size according to its current state by changing the contents of the Window field as needed in the headers it sends.

A received acknowledgment number tells the sender that the destination received all of the data with segment numbers up to one less than the acknowledgment number. If the sender receives no acknowledgment, it can resend the data. Typically, on sending a segment, the source temporarily stores the segment's data in a retransmission queue and starts a timer. On receiving an acknowledgment, the source deletes the data from the retransmission queue. If the source doesn't receive an acknowledgment by the time the timer times out, the source assumes that the destination didn't receive the segment and resends it, using the data in the retransmission queue.

The amount of time to wait before resending can vary with the network. Hosts often use the average round-trip time for a transmission in determining a timeout value.

Enhancing Performance

Over time, several methods have come into popular use to help make TCP data transfers more efficient. The methods limit how much data a sender can send in some situations, and may also eliminate the need to wait for a timeout before retransmitting. The methods are Slow Start, Congestion Avoidance, Fast Retransmit, and Fast Recovery. *RFC2581: TCP Congestion Control* documents the methods.

The methods all have to do with specifying the number of segments a source can transmit before receiving an acknowledgment. If a source waits for acknowledgment of the previous segment before sending the next segment, the source complies with the requirements of the approved and proposed standards. An embedded system that transfers data infrequently can use this simpler, if less efficient, approach.

Supporting TCP in Embedded Systems

Supporting TCP in an embedded system is more complicated than supporting UDP. In addition to adding and removing headers and supporting IP, the computer must perform the 3-way handshake to connect to a remote host, maintain sequence and acknowledgment numbers when exchanging data, handshake when closing a connection, and respond to detected errors.

To send a message using TCP, a computer in an Ethernet network must do the following:

- Establish a connection using the 3-way handshake.
- Use the received Window size to determine how much data the remote computer can accept.
- Place the source and destination port numbers, sequence number, acknowledgment number, header length, source window size, and checksum in the appropriate locations in the TCP header. Computing the checksum requires knowing the source and destination IP addresses.
- Place the data to send in the data portion of the segment.
- Place the TCP segment in the data portion of an IP datagram. The IP datagram requires source and destination IP addresses and computing a checksum on the header.
- Pass the IP datagram to the Ethernet controller's driver for sending on the network and start a timeout timer.
- Wait to receive an acknowledgment number that indicates that the remote computer received the data. If the acknowledgment doesn't arrive before a timeout, resend the segment.

To receive a datagram using TCP, a computer in an Ethernet network must do the following:

- Establish a connection using the 3-way handshake.
- Receive an IP datagram from the Ethernet controller's driver.
- Strip the IP header from the datagram. Calculate the checksum and compare with the received value.

- If the checksums match, strip the header from the TCP segment. Calculate the checksum and compare it to the received value.

- Examine the received acknowledgment number to find out if the segment is acknowledging receipt of previously sent data and if so, delete the acknowledged data from the retransmission queue.

- Compare the received sequence number to the expected value. If the numbers match, set the acknowledgment number to return to the sender in a TCP segment.

- Use the destination port number to decide where to pass the data.

In addition, at any time, either computer may request to close or reset the connection and the other computer should acknowledge the request and may request to close or reset the connection from the other end if appropriate.

As the examples at the beginning of the chapter showed, if you're using a module with TCP support, the details of creating the segments and dealing with the checksums and sequence and acknowledgment numbers are handled for you.

If you want to write your own code to support TCP, the book *TCP/IP Lean: Web Servers for Embedded Systems* by Jeremy Bentham (CMP Books) offers guidance on how to do it efficiently and effectively. The TCP standard is the ultimate reference on how the protocol works. For a very detailed, yet readable explanation of UDP, TCP, IP, and related protocols, see *TCP/IP Clearly Explained* by Pete Loshin (Morgan Kaufman).

6

Serving Web Pages with Dynamic Data

Chapter 5 showed how to use TCP and UDP to exchange messages containing application-specific data. Many standard application-level protocols also use TCP or UDP when exchanging information. One of the most popular of these is the hypertext transfer protocol (HTTP), which enables a computer to serve Web pages on request.

Because embedded systems almost always serve Web pages that contain dynamic, or real-time, information, this chapter begins with Rabbit and TINI examples that serve Web pages with dynamic content. Following the examples is an introduction to using HTTP and other protocols in serving Web pages.

Quick Start: Two Approaches

A Web browser such as Microsoft's Internet Explorer is a client application that uses HTTP to request Web pages from servers on the Internet or in a local network. The servers don't have to be PCs or other large computers. Even a small embedded system with limited memory can serve a page containing text and simple images, including pages that display real-time data and accept and act on user input.

A browser provides a user interface for requesting and displaying pages. The computers that request Web pages typically have full-screen displays, but for some applications, an embedded system with limited display capabilities can function as an HTTP client. If the requested pages are very simple, even a text-only display of a few lines might suffice. Or an embedded system might receive and process the contents of a Web page without displaying the page in a browser at all.

This chapter focuses on Web servers. With an Internet connection, a Web server can serve pages to any browser on the Internet. Or a server may be programmed to respond to requests only from specific IP addresses. A Web server in a local network may serve pages to selected computers or to any computer in the local network.

An embedded system that functions as a Web server generally has all of the following:

- Non-volatile memory to hold pages to be served.
- Support for TCP and IP. Requests for Web pages and the pages sent in response travel in the data portion of TCP segments.
- Support for HTTP. The server must be able to understand and respond to received requests for Web pages. The HTTP standard specifies the format for the requests and replies.
- A local-network or Internet connection. To serve pages on the Internet, the Web server must have an Internet connection. Any firewalls must be

configured so the system can receive HTTP requests, as described in Chapter 10.

- One or more pages to serve. The Web pages are files or blocks of text that use a form of encoding called hypertext markup language (HTML). The HTML encoding specifies the formatting of text and images on the page, including text size and fonts and the positioning of text and other elements on the page. The HTML code may include links to images that appear on the page, as well as links to other pages or resources. In serving a Web page with dynamic content, the software must have a way of inserting the dynamic content as the page is being served.

A variety of protocols and technologies can work along with HTTP and HTML to enable a server to provide Web pages that contain real-time data and respond to user input. This chapter includes two approaches to serving real-time data, and Chapter 7 covers ways that Web servers can respond to user input.

Serving a Page with Dynamic Data

Many Web pages are static, where the information on the page doesn't change unless someone edits the page's HTML file and uploads the new file to the server. Static Web pages are useful for presenting product information, articles, or other information that remains constant. But most embedded systems have little use for static pages, other than possibly presenting a home page with links to other pages. An embedded system that functions as a Web server will almost certainly want to display real-time information such as sensor readings or other up-to-the-minute information about the processes or environments the system is controlling or monitoring.

This section shows how the Rabbit and TINI modules introduced in Chapter 3 can serve Web pages that display dynamic data. Dynamic, or real-time, data includes any data that can change over time and can be different each time the page is served. An obvious example is a counter that displays the number of times the page has been accessed. Dynamic data may also include sensor or switch readings and time and date information. The supporting code included with the Rabbit and TINI (and additional sources in the case

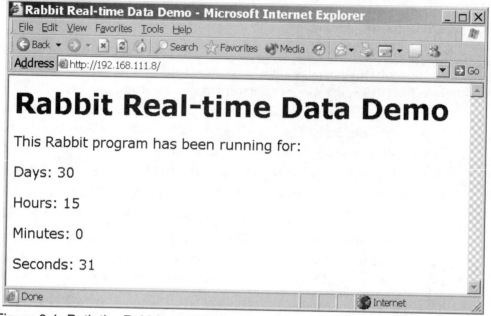

Figure 6-1: Both the Rabbit and TINI can serve pages that include dynamic, or real-time, data, such as the days, hours, minutes, and seconds displayed in these pages.

of Java servlets on the TINI) greatly reduces the amount of the programming required to serve Web pages with dynamic content.

The dynamic data served by the example applications in this chapter consists of a message that displays the amount of time the system or application has been up and running. Figure 6-1 shows an example page. The embedded system stores the number of days, hours, minutes, and seconds in variables. When serving the page, the server application inserts the current values of the variables in the appropriate places in the page. You can use the same techniques to create Web pages that display the current values of any variables in a system.

Although the result is the same, the Rabbit and TINI examples use different approaches to achieve the result. The Rabbit uses Server Side Include directives that instruct the server to insert the values of variables in the appropriate locations in the file being served. For the TINI, instead of storing the Web page in a separate file, the application creates the Web page as it's being sent, using a series of writes to send the page's contents to a TCP socket and inserting the values of variables in the designated locations in the page.

Rabbit Real-time Web Page

To serve its Web page, the Rabbit module uses HTTP functions and structures provided in Dynamic C to serve the Web page's file on request. The main program loop updates the time variables once per second.

Page Design

Listing 6-2 is the HTML code for Figure 6-1's Web page. The page uses HTML tags to advise the browser how to display the page's contents. Each tag consists of text enclosed by angle brackets (<>). The In Depth section of this chapter has more details about HTML tags and how to use them. For now, the relevant section of the code is the five lines that each begin with a paragraph tag (<p>).

A paragraph tag tells the browser to display the information that follows in a new paragraph. The first paragraph tag causes the browser to display the text, "This Rabbit program has been running for:".

Each of the four lines that follow contains a Server Side Include #echo directive that inserts the value of a variable on the page. A Server Side Include directive uses the same delimiters as an HTML comment. A comment, which is text that the browser ignores and doesn't display, is enclosed by <!-- and -->. On receiving a page that contains an HTML comment, the browser displays the page the same as if the comment and its delimiters weren't present.

Another use for comment delimiters is to enable a page to specify Server Side Include (SSI) directives that the server executes before serving the page to the browser. Before serving a page containing an SSI directive, the server executes the directive and replaces the delimiters and the text between them with the result of executing the directive. If for some reason the server doesn't support the directive, the server ignores the directive and the browser treats the directive as a comment, which isn't displayed.

```
<html>

<head>
<title>Rabbit Real-time Data Demo</title>
</head>

<body>

<h1>Rabbit Real-time Data Demo</h1>

<p>This Rabbit program has been running for:</p>
<p>Days:     <!--#echo var="days"--></p>
<p>Hours:    <!--#echo var="hours"--></p>
<p>Minutes: <!--#echo var="minutes"--></p>
<p>Seconds: <!--#echo var="seconds"--></p>

</body>

</html>
```

Listing 6-2: On serving this Web page, the server retrieves the current values of "days", "hours", "minutes", and "seconds" and inserts them in the page.

The #echo directive tells the server to replace the comment tag and its contents with the value of the named variable. For example, in the first directive, the server replaces <!--#echo var="days"--> with the value of the variable days on the server. If days equals 5, the browser receives and displays Days: 5.

The In Depth section of this chapter has more details about #echo and other Server Side Includes.

Serving the Page

The following is the complete application code the Rabbit requires to serve Figure 6-1's Web page.

Initial Defines and Declarations

As in Chapter 5's examples, TCPCONFIG specifies a macro that sets a network configuration stored in the file *tcp_config.lib*. Your program must specify an appropriate macro for your system and network configuration.

The #memmap directive stores all C functions not declared as root in the extended memory area.

```
#define TCPCONFIG 1
#memmap xmem
```

The application requires the *dcrtcp.lib* library, which supports TCP/IP and related protocols, and the *http.lib* library, which supports HTTP.

The #ximport directive retrieves a file from the PC being used for project development, stores the file's length and contents in the Rabbit's extended memory, and associates a symbol (index_html in the example below) with the file's address in memory. Application code uses the symbol to locate the file and determine its length. The path in the #ximport statement must match the location of the file in your development PC. The file *index.shtml* contains the text in Listing 6-2.

```
#use "dcrtcp.lib"
#use "http.lib"
#ximport "c:/rabbitserver/index.shtml" index_html
```

Four variables store the values for the units of time the Web page will display.

```
unsigned long days;
unsigned long hours;
unsigned long minutes;
unsigned long seconds;
```

Dynamic C's HTTP server uses two structures, HttpType and HttpSpec, which contain information relating to the files the Web server serves.

The HttpType structure matches file extensions with file types and specifies a handler to use with files with the named extensions. When sending a file in response to an HTTP request, the server must identify the file type in the Content-Type field of the HTTP header in the response. The file types are Multipurpose Internet Mail Extension (MIME) types defined in RFC 2045 through RFC 2049.

The server in this application supports a single Web page with the extension *.shtml*, which is the conventional extension for files that use SSI directives. Dynamic C's handler for pages with SSI directives is shtml_handler.

The HttpType structure below associates *.shtml* with the MIME type *text/html*, which is a text file that uses HTML encoding. Other MIME types include *text/plain, image/jpeg,* and *audio/mpeg.* The server's default file ("/") is associated with the first entry in the Http_types structure.

```
const HttpType http_types[] =
{
    { ".shtml", "text/html", shtml_handler}
};
```

The HttpSpec structure contains information about the files, variables, and structures that the Web server can access. Each entry in the structure has seven parameters, though not all entry types use all of the parameters. The structure in this example has entries for two files and four variables:

```
const HttpSpec http_flashspec[] =
{
  { HTTPSPEC_FILE, "/", index_html, NULL, 0, NULL, NULL},
  { HTTPSPEC_FILE, "/index.shtml", index_html, NULL, 0,
    NULL, NULL},

  { HTTPSPEC_VARIABLE, "days", 0, &days, INT32, "%d",
    NULL},
  { HTTPSPEC_VARIABLE, "hours", 0, &hours, INT32, "%d",
    NULL},
  { HTTPSPEC_VARIABLE, "minutes", 0, &minutes, INT32, "%d",
    NULL},
  { HTTPSPEC_VARIABLE, "seconds", 0, &seconds, INT32, "%d",
    NULL},
};
```

The HTTPSPEC_FILE entries associate the symbols defined in #ximport statements with the names of files that browsers may request from the server. These are the parameters for an HTTPSPEC_FILE entry:

Type. Indicates whether the entry is for a file, variable, or function. HTTPSPEC_FILE specifies that the entry is for a file.

Name. Names a file the Web server can access. This example has one file, *index.shtml*, with two entries to enable browsers to request the file by name (`"index.shtml"`) or as the default file to serve when no name is specified (`"/"`).

Data. Specifies the file's physical address. Both `HTTPSPEC_FILE` entries point to `index_html`, where the file *index.shtml* is stored.

Addr. Unused (`NULL`) for files.

Vartype. Unused (zero) for files.

Format. Unused (`NULL`) for files.

Realm. Names an `HttpRealm` structure that identifies a name and password required to access the file. `NULL` if unused.

The four `HTTP_VARIABLE` entries specify variables for the different units of time. These are the parameters for an `HTTP_VARIABLE` entry:

Type. Indicates whether the entry is for a file, variable, or function. `HTTPSPEC_VARIABLE` specifies that the entry is for a variable.

Name. Provides the name of a variable the Web server can access. The server's Web page displays the values of four variables: `"days"`, `"hours"`, `"minutes"`, and `"seconds"`.

Data. Unused (zero) for variables.

Addr. A short pointer to the variable.

Vartype. The type of variable. The options are 8-bit integer (`INT8`), 16-bit integer (`INT16`), 32-bit integer (`INT32`), 16-bit pointer (`PTR16`), and 32-bit floating-point value (`FLOAT32`). The `PTR16` type is useful for displaying strings.

Format. The `printf` specifier to use when displaying the variable. The specifier %d causes the variable to display as a decimal value.

Realm. Identifies a name and password to access the variable. `NULL` if unused.

The main() Function

The application's `main()` function begins by declaring variables related to time, calling `sock_init()` to initialize the TCP/IP stack, and calling `http_init()` to initialize the Web server. Calling `tcp_reserveport()` to reserve port 80 for the Web server is optional but can improve performance in two ways: by allowing a socket to be established even if the server can't exchange data yet and by shortening the waiting period for closing a socket.

```
main()
{
    unsigned long start_time;
    unsigned long total_seconds;

    sock_init();
    http_init();
    tcp_reserveport(80);
```

Dynamic C's SEC_TIMER variable contains the number of seconds since midnight on the morning of January 1, 1980. The program uses this value to measure how long the program has been running, beginning with an initial count stored in start_time when the program begins running:

```
    start_time = SEC_TIMER;
```

The program's endless while loop has two responsibilities. It calls http_handler(), which is required periodically to parse received requests and pass control to shtml_handler() or another handler specified in the HttpType structure. And a costatement updates the time variables once per second. (Chapter 3 introduced Dynamic C's costatements.)

When one second has elapsed, as specified in the waitfor(DelaySec(1)) statement, the program calculates the number of seconds it has been running by subtracting the start_time value from the current value of SEC_TIMER.

The program then divides the number of seconds into days, hours, minutes, and seconds:

To find the number of days, take the integer result of total_seconds divided by the number of seconds per day (86,400).

To find the number of hours, divide total_seconds by the number of seconds per hour (3600) to get the total number of elapsed hours. Eliminate any full days with modulus division by the number of hours per day (24).

To find the number of minutes, divide total_seconds by the number of seconds per minute (60) to get the total number of elapsed minutes. Eliminate any full hours with modulus division by the number of minutes per hour (60).

To find the number of seconds excluding full minutes, use the result of modulus division of `total_seconds` by the number of seconds per minute (60).

```
while (1) {
    http_handler();
    costate {
      waitfor(DelaySec(1));
      total_seconds = SEC_TIMER - start_time;
      days = total_seconds /86400;
      hours = (total_seconds /3600) % 24;
      minutes = (total_seconds /60) % 60;
      seconds = total_seconds % 60;
    }

    //Code to perform other tasks can be placed here.

  } // end while(1)

} // end main()
```

Dynamic C's HTTP server and SHTML handler code manage the serving of the Web page, including accepting requests to connect, returning the requested pages or other HTTP responses as appropriate, and closing connections.

In a real-world application, the main loop would probably perform other tasks as well. The costatement ensures that other tasks will get their turn even while waiting for the costatement's delay timer to time out.

Accessing the Web Server

When the Rabbit is running this code, you can request its Web page by entering the module's IP address in a browser's Address text box:

```
http://192.168.111.7
```

or by specifying the IP address and Web page:

```
http://192.168.111.7/index.shtml
```

If a domain name is assigned to the IP address, you can use that as well to request the page. On receiving a request for a page, the Rabbit's HTTP server appends an appropriate HTTP header to the top of the requested file and writes the header and file to the socket that requested it. The SHTML handler replaces the #echo directives on the page with the current values of days, hours, minutes and seconds. And the browser that requested the file displays Figure 6-1's Web page, which contains the time values.

Refreshing the page in the browser updates the displayed time. To update the display automatically at intervals, see Refreshing Pages Automatically later in this chapter.

TINI Real-time Web Page

To use a TINI to serve Web pages with dynamic content, you have a few choices. Your first thought might be to use the HttpServer class provided with the TINI's operating system. However, this built-in Web server can only serve static pages. Serving dynamic data would require changing the data in the stored pages whenever the content changes. It's more efficient to retrieve the dynamic data on request and insert it in the page as it's being served.

Another option is to install and run a server program that supports Java servlets. A servlet is a software component that can respond to user input and generate dynamic content for Web pages. In most cases, servlets are the most effective and time-saving way to enable a Web server to serve dynamic content. Chapter 7 has more about servlets and how to use them.

A third option is to write a basic Web server that uses the ServerSocket class and adds dynamic content as it serves its pages. For some low-volume applications that serve one or a few pages, this kind of home-brewed server can do the job without adding too much complexity. The example in this chapter uses the ServerSocket class to create a basic server that serves a page that displays the amount of time the TINI has been up and running. Whether or not you decide to use this approach, the code in this application is interesting as a demonstration of the responsibilities of a Web server.

The Web server responds to requests to connect to a specific port. When a connected host sends an HTTP request for a supported page, the server cal-

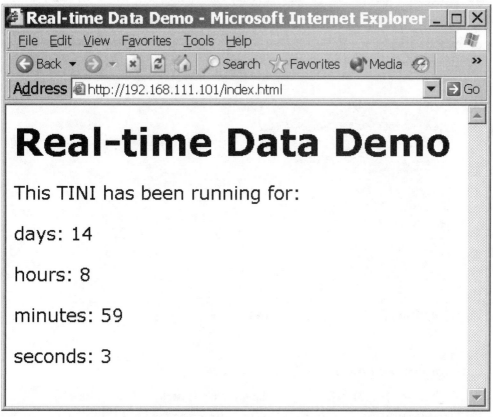

Figure 6-3: This Web page served by a TINI shows how long the TINI has been running since it booted up.

culates the values of variables the page contains, writes the contents of the page to the socket, and closes the socket.

Serving the Page

Figure 6-3 shows the Web page, and Listing 6-4 is the source code for the page as received by a browser. The program code below is an application that serves Figure 6-1's Web page. The code is very similar to the TcpServer example in Chapter 5, with the addition of code that parses requests and returns the Web page or error code.

255

```
<html>

<head>
  <title>Real-time Data Demo </title>
</head>

<body>
  <h1>Real-time Data Demo</h1>

  <p> This TINI has been running for:</p>
  <p>days: 14 </p>
  <p>hours: 8 </p>
  <p>minutes: 59 </p>
  <p>seconds: 3 </p>

</body>

</html>
```

Listing 6-4: The HTML code for Figure 6-3's Web page.

Imports and Initial Declarations

The code imports java.net classes for networking functions and java.io classes to support input and output functions. The TINI-specific TINIOS class includes an uptimeMillis() method the application uses to retrieve the number of milliseconds the TINI has been up and running.

```
import java.net.*;
import java.io.*;
import com.dalsemi.system.TINIOS;
```

The RealTimeWebPage class implements the Runnable interface so that the code that does the network communications can execute in its own thread. This leaves the main thread free to do other things.

```
public class RealTimeWebPage implements Runnable {

    private ServerSocket server;
    private int readTimeout;
    private Thread serverThread;
    private volatile boolean runServer;
```

The main() Method

The class's `main()` method sets `localPort` to the port number clients will connect on and sets `readTimeout` to the number of milliseconds the server will wait to receive data after a remote host connects. Port 80 is the default port for HTTP requests. The timeout is expressed in milliseconds. The `RealTimeWebPage` object `server` uses the `localPort` and `readTimeout` values.

```
public static void main(String[] args) throws
    IOException {
  int localPort = 80;
  int readTimeout = 5000;

  RealTimeWebPage server =
      new RealTimeWebPage(localPort, readTimeout);
```

An endless loop executes while waiting for connections. The thread spends its time sleeping, but could perform other tasks.

```
while (true){
  try {
    Thread.sleep(1000);
  } catch (InterruptedException e) {
    System.out.print("InterruptedException: ");
    System.out.println(e.getMessage() );
  }
} // end while(true)
} // end main
```

Initializing the Server

The constructor for the `RealTimeWebPage` class creates a thread to handle connection requests. The constructor's two parameters are the `localPort` and `readTimeout` values set in `main()`.

```
public RealTimeWebPage(int localPort, int readTimeout)
    throws IOException {
```

A `ServerSocket` object (`server`) listens for connection requests at `localPort`, and on receiving a request, creates a socket object.

```
server = new ServerSocket(localPort);
System.out.println("The server is listening on port "
    + localPort + ".");
```

The `readTimeout` variable used by the `run()` method below is assigned the value of the `readTimeout` parameter.

```
this.readTimeout = readTimeout;
```

A separate thread (`serverThread`) handles connection requests. Setting the thread's `setDaemon` method `true` creates the thread as a Daemon thread. The JVM exits when there are no user (non-Daemon) threads running. Calling the `start()` method calls the thread's `run()` routine.

```
serverThread = new Thread(this);
serverThread.setDaemon(true);
serverThread.start();
} // end RealTimeWebPage constructor
```

Waiting for Connection Requests

Calling `serverThread`'s `start()` method causes the thread's `run()` method to execute. The `run()` method accepts connections and calls a method to handle each connection.

```
public void run() {
```

An endless loop runs until the `runServer` variable is false, which occurs on an exception or if the class's `stop()` method sets `runServer` false.

```
runServer = true;
while (runServer) {
  try {
```

On accepting a connection request, the server's `accept()` method creates a socket for exchanging data with the connected host. The class's `handleConnection()` method manages communications with the socket.

When `handleConnection()` returns or if there is an exception, the method closes the socket to release any resources used by it. If there is an exception when attempting to close the socket, no action needs to be taken.

If an exception occurs while attempting to accept a connection, `runServer` is set to `false` to stop the thread.

```
Socket socket = server.accept();

try {
  handleConnection(socket);
} catch (IOException e) {
```

```
            System.out.print("IOException: ");
            System.out.println(e.getMessage());
          } finally {
            try {
              socket.close();
            } catch (IOException e) {
            }
          }
        } catch (IOException e) {
          runServer = false;
          System.out.print("IOException: ");
          System.out.println(e.getMessage());
        }
      } // end while(runServer);
    } // end run
```

Stopping the Server

The stopServer() method provides a way to stop the server under program control by setting runServer false and closing the socket.

```
public void stopServer() {
  runServer = false;
  try {
    server.close();
  } catch (IOException e) {
  }
} // end stopServer
```

Handling a Connection

The handleConnection() method handles a single connection with a remote host. The socket timeout is set to the readTimeout value set in the main() routine.

```
private void handleConnection(Socket socket)
    throws IOException {

  System.out.println("Connected to " + socket);
  socket.setSoTimeout(readTimeout);
```

An InputStream object reads data from the remote host, and a PrintStream object writes to the remote host.

```
InputStream in = socket.getInputStream();
  PrintStream out =
      new PrintStream(socket.getOutputStream());
```

The class's `processRequest()` method reads the received data and returns the requested web page or an error page.

When `processRequest` returns, the `Printstream` object's `checkError()` method flushes the output stream and returns true if an `IOException` other than `InterruptedIOException` has occurred or if the Printstream object's `setError()` method has been invoked.

```
try {
  processRequest(in, out);
  if (out.checkError()) {
    System.out.println("An error occurred while
        sending a web page.");
  } else {
    System.out.println("A response was sent.");
  }
} catch (InterruptedIOException e) {
  System.out.print("InterruptedIOException: ");
  System.out.println(e.getMessage());
  System.out.print("The connection timed out after
      receiving no data for : ");
  System.out.print(readTimeout / 1000);
  System.out.println(" seconds.");
}
} // end handleConnection
```

Processing a Request

The `processRequest()` method reads an incoming request and takes appropriate action.

```
private void processRequest(InputStream in,
    PrintStream out) throws IOException
{
```

The first step is to read the first four bytes from the `PrintStream` object.

```
int b1 = in.read();
int b2 = in.read();
int b3 = in.read();
int b4 = in.read();
```

This server supports GET requests only. The HTTP standard requires GET to be upper case, followed by a space. If the received bytes equal GET, followed by a space, the code reads any bytes that follow and stores them in the `StringBuffer` object `requestBuffer`. Reading the input stops on detecting a space character, a carriage return (\r), line feed (\n), or an end of file marker (-1).

```
if (('G' == b1) && ('E' == b2) && ('T' == b3) &&
    (' ' == b4)) {
  StringBuffer requestBuffer = new StringBuffer();
  int b = in.read();
  while ((b != -1) && (b != ' ') && (b != '\r') &&
      (b != '\n')) {
    requestBuffer.append((char)b);
    b = in.read();
  }
```

The StringBuffer object is converted to a String to enable examining its contents. The server accepts requests for the default page (indicated by "/") or for the file *index.html*. If there is a match with either of these, the class's sendWebPage routine returns the real-time Web page to the requesting host. If there isn't a match, a call to the sendErrorPage() method returns error code 404 and an error message to the requesting host.

```
String requestedPage = requestBuffer.toString();
String defaultPage = "/";
String indexPage = "/index.html";

if ((requestedPage.equals(defaultPage)) ||
    (requestedPage.indexOf(indexPage) != -1) ) {

  sendWebPage(out);

} else {
  sendErrorPage(out, "404 Not Found");
}
```

If "GET " wasn't received, the program checks to see if -1 was returned. If so, the input stream is closed, so there is nothing to return to the remote host. For any received data besides "GET " or -1, a call to the sendErrorPage() method returns error code 501 and the error message "Not Implemented" to the requesting host.

```
    } else {
      if ((b1 | b2 | b3 | b4) != -1) {
        sendErrorPage(out, "501 Not Implemented");
      }
    } // end if ('G'==b1||'E'==b2||'T'==b3||' '==b4)
  } // end processRequest
```

Sending the Web Page

The `sendWebPage()` method uses the `PrintStream` object to send the page containing real-time data.

```
private void sendWebPage(PrintStream out)
    throws IOException {
```

The page begins with the response's start line and HTML headers. A blank line (\r\n) after the HTTP header indicates the end of the header. The In Depth section of this chapter has more about these elements of a response.

```
out.print("HTTP/1.0 200 OK\r\n"
          + "Content-Type: text/html\r\n"
          + "\r\n");
```

A call to the TINIOS class's `uptimeMillis()` method returns the number of milliseconds that have elapsed since the TINI booted up. The page displays the time in days, hours, minutes, and seconds. To obtain the total number of seconds, divide `uptimeMillis()` by 1000.

```
long totalSeconds = TINIOS.uptimeMillis()/1000;
```

For the number of days, divide by the number of seconds per day:

```
long days = totalSeconds / 86400;
```

For the number of hours, divide by the number of hours per day and use modulus division to subtract any full days:

```
long hours = (totalSeconds /3600) % 24;
```

For the number of minutes, divide by the number of minutes per day and use modulus division to subtract any full hours:

```
long minutes = (totalSeconds / 60) % 60;
```

For the number of seconds, use modulus division to subtract any full minutes:

```
long seconds = totalSeconds % 60;
```

A series of `out.print` statements sends the page's contents to the requesting host. The page consists of blocks of static text, plus the values of the four variables inserted at the appropriate locations in the page. The `out.print` statements use the + operator to concatenate multiple String constants. This method keeps the code readable while limiting the number of writes to the

`PrintStream` object. The four variables each have their own `out.print` statements, however. This is because concatenating String variables uses large amounts of memory and processing power in the TINI. String constants don't have this effect, so concatenating these has no ill effects.

```
out.print("<html>"
          + "<head> <title> "
          + "Real-time Data Demo "
          + "</title> </head>"
          + "<body>"
          + "<h1> Real-time Data Demo</h1>"
          + "<p> This TINI has been running for:</p>"
          + "<p> days: ");
out.print(days);
out.print(" </p>"
         +"<p>"
          + "hours: ");
out.print(hours);
out.print(" </p>"
          + "<p>"
          + "minutes: ");
out.print(minutes);
out.print(" </p>"
          + "<p>"
          + "seconds: ");
out.print(seconds);
out.print (" </p>"
           + "</body>"
           + "</html>");
} // end sendWebPage()
```

Sending an Error Page

If the connected host sends a request for a non-existent page or a request other than GET, the `sendErrorPage` method uses a series of `out.print` statements to return an error code and a page that displays an error message. The `errorMessage` parameter contains the message.

```
private void sendErrorPage(PrintStream out,
    String errorMessage) throws IOException
{
```

The first text sent is the response's start line containing the error message and Content-Type header, followed by the required blank line.

```
out.print("HTTP/1.0 ");
```

```
out.print(errorMessage);
out.print("\r\n"
          + "Content-Type: text/html\r\n"
          + "\r\n");
```

Another series of `out.print` statements then sends a Web page that displays the error message.

```
out.print("<html>"
          + "<head><title>");
out.print(errorMessage);
out.print("</title></head>"
          + "<body>"
          + "<h1>");
out.print(errorMessage);
out.print("</h1>"
          + "</body>"
          + "</html>");
  } // end sendErrorPage
} // end RealTimeWebPage
```

Running the Server

As in the Rabbit example, you can request the TINI's Web page by entering its IP address, IP address and file name, or domain name (if available) in a browser's Address text box.

These examples show two different but equally useful ways to serve Web pages with dynamic data. Chapter 7 expands on this topic by showing two ways to create Web pages that can respond to user input in addition to displaying dynamic content.

In Depth:
Protocols for Serving Web Pages

The examples in this chapter showed how Web browsers use the hypertext transfer protocol (HTTP) to request Web pages, and the Web pages themselves are encoded using the hypertext markup language (HTML). In addition, some pages use server-side include (SSI) directives to enable a Web page to display dynamic data or to add other capabilities not available with HTML alone.

User Interface, Other I/O

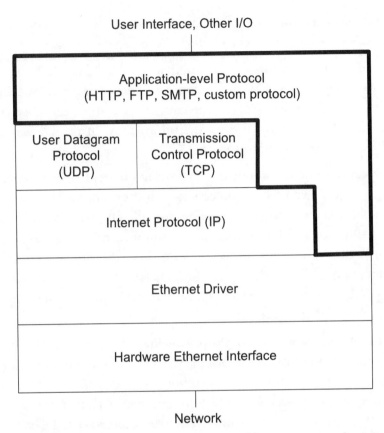

Figure 6-5: HTTP is an application-level protocol layer communicates with the Ethernet driver and either a UDP or TCP layer or the application layer.

This section has more details about HTTP, HTML, and SSI, with the focus on how embedded systems can use each in serving pages with dynamic content.

Using the Hypertext Transfer Protocol

HTTP is one of many standard application-level protocols used in network communications. Figure 6-5 shows the location of HTTP in a network protocol stack. Although in theory an HTTP communication can use any reliable protocol to reach its destinations on a network, in practice just about all network stacks pass HTTP communications through TCP and IP layers. An application that uses HTTP may be a Web browser, which requests Web pages, or a Web server, which returns Web pages on request.

Anyone who has browsed the Internet has used HTTP. When a browser sends a request for a Web page onto the network, the request contains a URL that identifies the location and file name of the page. Chapter 4 described how a network uses the information in the URL to determine where to route a communication.

On learning the IP address that is hosting the desired Web page, the client requests to open a TCP connection with the computer at that address. By default, Web servers serve pages on port 80. If a server is using a different port number, the URL specifies the number, as explained in Chapter 4. When the connection has been established, the browser sends a message containing an HTTP request for a page, and the receiving computer responds by serving, or sending, the Web page to the requesting computer over the TCP connection.

A benefit of using Web pages to provide information is that the browser interface is universal. If you place a Web server on the Internet, anyone with a browser and an Internet connection can view the server's pages. Search engines make it possible for users to find your page even if they don't know the IP address or domain name. Web pages don't have to be on the Internet, however. You can make a page available only within a local network. If desired, you can also restrict access by specifying what IP addresses can access a page or by requiring a password to access the page. In any case, you don't have to limit communications to users who are using specific hardware or software.

As the examples in Chapter 7 show, a server can also receive information from a browser. A Web page can enable users to send information to the computer that is serving a page, and the computer can use this information for any purpose.

HTTP Versions

HTTP version 1.1 is specified in *RFC 2616: Hypertext Transfer Protocol -- HTTP/1.1*. RFC1945 contains the previous versions, HTTP 1.0 and 0.9.

Version 1.1 adds capabilities for conserving network bandwidth, improving security and error notification, enabling clients to specify preferred languages or character sets, and allowing more flexible buffering by dividing data into chunks.

Many embedded systems serve small and simple Web pages. These systems may gain little benefit in supporting HTTP 1.1 and thus may use 1.0 for simplicity. HTTP 1.0 servers must also respond appropriately to requests from 0.9 clients. A browser that supports HTTP 1.1 should have no trouble communicating with a 1.0 server. Dynamic C's HTTP server complies with HTTP 1.0. The Tynamo Web server used in Chapter 7's TINI examples implements the required elements in HTTP 1.1.

Probably the main reason an embedded system might use HTTP 1.1 is its support for persistent connections, which can reduce the number of connections the server must open and close. With HTTP 1.0, each request requires a new connection. If a client requests a Web page that contains several links to images, the request for the page as well as each request for an image requires its own connection, which in turn requires the server and client to do the handshaking to open and close each connection. Requesting multiple pages within a short time also requires a new connection for each page. In contrast, with HTTP 1.1, the default behavior is persistent connections, where a connection is left open until either the client or server determines that the communication is complete or the server closes the connection after a period of no activity.

The RFC documents spell out the minimum capabilities that an HTTP server must have. The requirements vary with the HTTP version.

Elements of an HTTP Message

An HTTP message consists of an initial request or status line, optional message headers, a blank line, and an optional entity body. (HTTP 0.9 doesn't support status lines or headers.)

HTTP supports two types of messages, requests and responses. A client sends a request to ask a server for a resource, and the server returns a response containing the resource or status information.

Requests

An HTTP 1.0 request must contain at least two lines: the request line and a blank line. Some requests also have one or more message headers between the request line and the blank line, and some requests have an entity body following the blank line. Here is an example request for the file *index.html* from the host at *www.example.com*:

```
GET /index.html HTTP/1.0\r\n
Host: www.example.com\r\n
Accept: */*\r\n
Connection: close\r\n
\r\n
```

Each line in the request terminates in \r\n, which is a pair of escape sequences equivalent to a carriage return, or return to the beginning of the line (\r), followed by a line feed, or drop to a new line immediately below the current line (\n). Escape sequences provide a way of expressing text formatting commands such as these using plain text.

The Request Line

In the following request line:

```
GET /index.html HTTP/1.0
```

GET is a method that tells the server that the client is requesting a resource from the server. The HTTP/1.0 in the request line tells the server that the highest version of HTTP the client supports is 1.0.

/index.html is the name and path of the resource the client is requesting from the server. The "/" indicates that the file is in the server's root directory. The server's root directory may be, but doesn't have to be, the same as the root directory in the system's file system. For example, a server may define its root directory as */http-root*. Clients can then access files in */http-root* and its subdirectories (such as */http-root/images*), but not files in other directories under the system's root directory (such as */private*).

A GET request often contains only the file name and path, but an HTTP 1.1 server must also accept a request that contains a full URL such as this:

```
GET http://www.Lvr.com/index.html HTTP/1.1
```

On receiving a page that includes images, the client typically sends a GET request for each image.

In addition to the GET method, HTTP 1.0 and later define the HEAD and POST methods (Table 6-1). HEAD is similar to GET except that the server returns only the headers it would send in responding to a GET request for the resource, but not the resource itself. The POST method enables a client to send data to a resource on the server. The server passes the data received in the message body to the program, process, or other resource specified in the request line. The named resource uses the data. A common use for POST is to enable users to send data entered on a form to a CGI program, which processes the data and sends a response to the client. (Chapter 7 has more about CGI.) But a POST request can specify any resource, and the resource can use the data in any way.

The HTTP 1.1 standard says that all general-purpose servers must at minimum support the GET and HEAD methods.

HTTP 1.1 defines additional methods. One that embedded systems might use is PUT, which like POST, enables the client to send data to the server. But instead of naming a resource to receive the message body's data, a PUT request names a file or other entity where the server should store the message body's data. PUT can be useful for file transfers, where the request line names the file on the server where the server should store the received data.

HTTP 0.9 supports only the GET method, and the request line includes only the request and the URL, not the HTTP version. If no HTTP version is specified, the server should assume it's version 0.9.

Methods specified in requests must be upper case and followed by a space.

Headers

A message may contain headers between the request line and the blank line. A header can contain additional information about the request, such as the number of data bytes in the message body, or more general information, such as a date. Headers generally have the following format:

header_name: *data*

Table 6-1: Selected HTTP Methods Used in Requests

Method	HTTP Version Introduced In	Description
GET	0.9	Retrieve the specified Web page or other information
HEAD	1.0	Retrieve only the HTTP headers for the specified information (not the message body)
POST	1.0	Pass the information in the message body to the resource identified in the request line
PUT	1.1	Store the information in the message body in the file or other entity identified in the request line

The HTTP standard specifies valid header names and what data each header provides. For example, a client might include an Accept header in a request for a Web page to inform the server of what types of content the client can accept. In this example, the client accepts images in *.gif* and *.jpeg* formats:

```
Accept: image/gif, image/jpeg
```

This means that the client accepts all media types:

```
Accept: */*
```

If an HTTP 1.0 request includes data in the message body, the standard requires a Content-Length header that specifies the number of bytes in the message body:

```
Content-Length: 256
```

HTTP 1.1 also requires requests that include data in the message body to transmit the content length, but supports additional ways of doing so.

This HTTP 1.1 header:

```
Connection: close
```

indicates that the current connection is not persistent and should be closed after the response is sent. An HTTP 1.1 host that doesn't support persistent connections must send this header with every connection. HTTP 1.0 hosts don't support persistent connections or this header, which they can ignore if received.

An Authorization header enables a client to send authentication information such as a user name and password, usually after receiving a response with a WWW-Authenticate header, as described in Chapter 10.

An HTTP 1.1 request must include a Host header in each request. The Host header specifies the Internet host name (such as *www.Lvr.com*) of the resource being requested. The requirement for a Host header was added in the hope of conserving IP addresses by making it easier for a single IP address to support multiple host names. For example, a server might host both *www.example.com* and *www.Lvr.com* at the same IP address. On receiving a GET request for a default page, the server's HTTP software can examine the Host header to find out which host's page the client is requesting. Without the Host header, each host name needs its own IP address.

When a request is directed to a port other than the protocol's default port, the Host header includes this information as well:

```
Host: www.Lvr.com:5501
```

If a server doesn't have an Internet host name, the request must include a Host header with an empty value. The HTTP 1.1 standard says that when an HTTP 1.1 server receives an HTTP 1.1 request that doesn't include a Host header, the server must return a status code of 400 (Bad Request). HTTP 1.0 doesn't support the Host header, so HTTP 1.0 requests don't include it and 1.0 servers can ignore it if received.

The Message Body

The message body contains data the client is providing to the server, such as the data in a POST or PUT request.

Responses

On receiving an HTTP request, the server returns a response. An HTTP 1.0 response must contain at least two lines: a status line and a blank line to indicate the end of the headers. Some responses also have one or more message headers between the status line and the blank line, and some responses have a message body following the blank line. HTTP 0.9 servers return the message body only. Here are the status line and headers sent in reply to a request for a Web page:

```
HTTP/1.0 200 OK\r\n
Date: Wed, 09 Jul 2003 12:02:51 GMT\r\n
Content-Type: text/html\r\n
Content-Length: 432\r\n
\r\n
```

As with requests, each line in the response terminates with a carriage return and line feed (\r\n).

The Status Line

The status line contains the version of HTTP supported by the server and a status code and text phrase that give the result of the request. On success, this is the status line from an HTTP 1.0 server:

```
HTTP/1.0 200 OK
```

If the client requests a non-existent file, the response is this:

```
HTTP/1.0 404 Not Found
```

The HTTP standard includes a series of status codes and suggested text phrases to use with them.

Response Headers

A response can use headers to send additional information about a response or to return general information about the message or connection.

The HTTP 1.0 standard says that the header for a response that contains a message body should include a Content-Length field that gives the length of the message body in bytes:

```
Content-Length: 14092
```

If the Content-Length field isn't included, the closing of the connection determines the length of the message body.

A Date field indicates when the response message was generated (not when the Web page or other resource was created):

```
Date: Thu, 08 May 2003 02:45:58 GMT
```

If possible, servers should include a Date field in responses. However, a server that doesn't have a reasonably accurate clock must not include a Date field. The preferred format for the contents of the Date field is the *rfc1123-date* format specified in the HTTP 1.1 standard and RFC 1123. This format uses a fixed-length field for each element in the date. The example above uses this format. A computer that receives a response without a date can add a date to a received response if needed.

When a client requests a password-protected resource, the server can return a WWW-Authenticate header to request the client to provide a user name, password, or other authentication information before gaining access to the resource. Chapter 10 has more about using this header.

The HTTP standards specify the headers supported by each HTTP version.

Message Body

The message body contains any data the response wants to return to the client. In a response to a GET request, the message body contains the requested Web page or other resource.

Using HTTP with Other Client Applications

The main use for HTTP is for communicating with Web browsers, but other applications can send HTTP requests as well. For example, to retrieve and store information from a Web page, you could write an application that requests a page and then searches the response for desired information. A timer routine can trigger a page retrieval periodically.

Inside the Hypertext Markup Language

Related to HTTP is the Hypertext Markup Language (HTML) used in Web pages. HTML defines codes that specify how text and images appear on a Web page.

The HTML specification is available from the World Wide Web Consortium (W3C), at *www.w3.org*. The members of W3C are organizations interested in developing common protocols for the World Wide Web. HTML version 4.01 was released in 1999. Rather than continuing to update the

HTML specification, W3C has switched development to Extensible HTML (XHTML), a more flexible and powerful language whose roots are in HTML. For basic Web pages, you don't need anything beyond what's available in HTML. It's possible to create HTML Web pages that also comply with the XHTML specification.

Creating HTML Pages

You can create HTML pages using any text editor, including Windows Notepad. Or you can use a Web-design application such as Macromedia Inc.'s Dreamweaver, which enables you to create pages visually using toolbars and menus to add page elements and formatting. The application inserts the appropriate HTML code as needed. Some embedded systems serve very basic pages that require little in the way of fancy formatting or other features. When this is the case, using a text editor to create the pages is a reasonable choice. But even if you use a specialized application to create your pages, a little knowledge of HTML can be useful in ferreting out the inevitable problems that crop up.

The conventional extension for HTML-encoded files is *.html* or *.htm*.

This book provides only the most basic introduction to HTML. For more detail, refer to the specification or a book such as *HTML 4 for the World Wide Web* by Elizabeth Castro (Peachpit Press).

Using Tags

Figure 6-6 shows a basic Web page that displays text and an image. Listing 6-7 is the file that contains the HTML code for the page. HTML tags specify the text formatting and placement of the image. Each tag contains an HTML element enclosed in angle brackets (<>). Some elements have one or more required or optional attributes, which provide additional information about the element. For example, in this tag:

```
<input type="submit" value="Submit">
```

the element is `input`, and `type` and `value` are attributes that name the input type and the text the input button displays.

Figure 6-6: This basic Web page displays text and an image.

HTML elements and attributes are case-insensitive. However, elements and attributes in XHTML files must use lower case, so for XHTML compliance, use lower case for elements and attributes.

An HTML file can contain blank lines, indenting, and spaces between elements as needed for readability.

Everything between the HTML start (`<html>`) and end (`</html>`) tags is HTML-encoded text. The HTML start and end tags are optional.

The HTML-encoded text has two sections, the head and body.

The HEAD Section

The HEAD section contains information that doesn't display on the page. Everything between the `<head>` and `</head>` tags is in the HEAD section.

In the HEAD section, the `<title>` and `</title>` tags surround a title that displays in the browser window's title bar. The title also appears in the browser's Bookmarks or Favorites list if you add the page to the list.

```
<html>

<head>
  <title>Hello World</title>
</head>

<body>
  <h1> Hello <img src="earth.gif" alt="world"> </h1>
</body>

</html>
```

Listing 6-7: The HTML code for Figure 6-6's Web page.

The BODY Section

Everything between the `<body>` and `</body>` tags is in the BODY section, which contains the material that appears in the browser's main window.

Ordinary paragraph text on a Web page begins with the paragraph start tag (`<p>`). Each paragraph requires a start tag. HTML doesn't require closing paragraph tags (`</p>`), but XHTML does, so include closing tags for XHTML compliance.

Header tags provide a way to specify that paragraph text should display more prominently than ordinary text. In Figure 6-6, the word Hello is displayed as a level-1 header, enclosed by the tags `<h1>` and `</h1>`. A page can have up to six levels of headers (`<h1>` through `<h6>`). The font and size of the header text vary with the browser and how the user has configured it.

Many tags have required or optional attributes, which provide additional information to the command. The following tag tells the browser to request and display the image contained in the file *earth.gif*:

```
<img src="earth.gif" alt="world">
```

The `img` tag includes two attributes. A `src` attribute specifies the file name and the path to the file, relative to the Web site's root directory. For browsers that don't display images, the `alt` attribute specifies the text to display in place of the image.

The text that follows an attribute's equals sign is the attribute's value. In HTML, not all values need to be enclosed in quotation marks. XHTML requires quotation marks for all attribute values, so include the quotation marks for XHTML compliance.

Hyperlinks

The formatting of text and placement of images are useful in designing pages, but ultimately what made HTML and the Web popular was clickable hyperlinks to other pages. Here is an example:

```
<a href="http://www.w3.org">World Wide Web Consortium</a>
```

The <a> tag specifies that what follows is a link to another page. The text in quotes that follows the HREF attribute in the tag (http://www.w3.org in the example) names the URL to link to. The label that follows the <a> tag (World Wide Web Consortium in the example) is the text users will see on the Web page. The </a> tag ends the hyperlink.

The formatting that indicates a clickable link varies with the browser and how it's configured, but typically, links are underlined. With underlined links, for the above example, the browser would display only this label:

```
World Wide Web Consortium
```

Clicking the label causes the browser to send a request for the default Web page (since no file name is specified) at the host *www.w3.org*.

Using Tables to Format Text and Images

A popular way of formatting information on Web pages is with the use of tables. An HTML table specifies the placement of cells in rows and columns. Each cell can contain page elements such as text, an image, a hyperlink, or a combination. A table makes it easy to ensure that the page elements line up as intended on the page.

Figure 6-8 shows a Web page containing basic HTML table, and Listing 6-9 is the page's HTML code. Everything between these tags:

```
<table frame="border" border="2" rules="all">
</table>
```

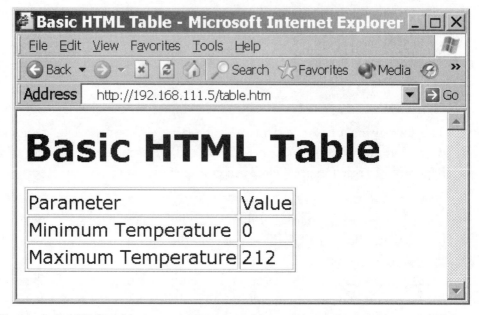

Figure 6-8: HTML tables provide a way of formatting information on a Web page.

is part of the table. In the `table` tag, the `frame="border"` attribute specifies that the table will display a border around its perimeter. The `border="2"` attribute specifies a border width of 2 pixels. The `rules="all"` attribute specifies that the rows and columns will display rules, or lines that delineate the rows and columns in the table.

Everything between `<tr>` and `</tr>` is in a table row. Everything between `<td>` and `</td>` is data that appears in a table cell in a row. Figure 6-8's table has three rows, with two cells in each row.

The HTML specification has more about tables and the options for formatting them.

Refreshing a Page Automatically

One limitation of Web servers is that the server won't send a page unless a client requests it. For example, a server may provide a Web page with current weather information. After a client has requested the page, the page dis-

```
<HTML>

<head> <title> Basic HTML Table </title> </head>

<body>

<h1> Basic HTML Table </h1>

<table frame="border" border="2" rules="all">

<tr>
<td> Parameter </td>
<td> Value </td>
</tr>

<tr>
<td> Minimum Temperature </td>
<td> 0 </td>
</tr>

<tr>
<td> Maximum Temperature </td>
<td> 212 </td>
</tr>

</table>

</body>

</html>
```

Listing 6-9: HTML code for 's Web page, which displays a table.

played in the browser doesn't update automatically if the conditions change. If a browser wants to continuously display the current conditions, it must periodically request a new, refreshed page.

You can request the latest version of a page by clicking the Refresh icon available on most browsers. It's also possible to add code that will cause a browser to refresh the page periodically without user intervention. Placing the following line of HTML code in a Web page's HEAD section will cause the browser to send a request for the page every 300 seconds:

```
<meta http-equiv="Refresh" Content="300">
```

The `Content` attribute specifies the number of seconds to wait before refreshing. Most browsers support this method of automatic refresh, though they may include an option to disable it.

Server Side Include Directives

A Server Side Include (SSI) directive requests a server to perform an action before serving a Web page that contains the directive. The capabilities of SSIs are limited but convenient for some applications. The Rabbit example earlier in this chapter used SSI directives to retrieve the values of variables to display on a Web page.

Server Side Includes were introduced by the Apache Group, which was formed to develop Apache HTTP Server, a popular open-source application used by many Web servers that run under UNIX, Windows, and other operating systems. Server Side Includes are now supported by many Web servers, including some embedded systems that function as Web servers. A server that supports Common Gateway Interface (CGI) programs is likely to support SSI as well. The documentation for the Apache HTTP Server includes documentation for SSI and is available from the Apache Software Foundation at *www.apache.org*.

Basics

As explained earlier in this chapter, in Web pages, SSI directives use the same delimiters as HTML comments (`<!--` and `-->`). Before serving a page that contains a directive supported by the server, the server executes the directive and replaces the delimiters and everything between them with the result of the directive. (Some directives, such as a `#config` directive that specifies formatting for other directives, have no result to display.)

Spacing is critical in SSI directives. There must be no space between the opening delimiter (`<!--`) and the directive's number sign (#), and there should be a space immediately preceding the closing delimiter (`-->`).

Because the server does all of the work of implementing the SSI directives, the requesting computer and its browser don't need to know anything about

SSI. The browser never sees the directives, just the results placed in the received Web pages.

Using Directives

Rabbit Semiconductor's Dynamic C supports three SSI directives: `#echo`, `#include`, and `#exec`.

#echo

The `#echo` directive inserts the current value of a variable in a requested Web page. If your server supports this directive, it's an obvious choice for displaying real-time information. To insert the value of the variable *temperature*, a Web page might contain this code:

```
<p>The temperature is <!--#echo var="temperature" --></p>
```

When the server serves the page, it retrieves the value of the temperature variable and replaces the `<!--` and `-->` delimiters and everything between them with this value. If the `temperature` variable equals 72, the paragraph appears on the page as:

```
The temperature is 72
```

The variable specified in the directive must be defined as an environment variable on the server. In Dynamic C, you define environment variables by adding an `HTTP_VARIABLE` entry for the variable in an `HttpSpec` structure, as shown in the Rabbit example earlier in this chapter. Other servers use different methods for defining environment variables.

In addition to displaying text, you can use `#echo` to display an image that reflects real-time status or conditions. In the example below, an HTML `img` tag causes the Web page to display the image contained in the file whose name is stored in the string variable `led1_image`:

```
<img src="<!--#echo var="led1_image" -->">
```

The server can set `led1_image` to different file names, such as `led_on.gif` and `led_off.gif`, depending on the current state of an LED at the server. On receiving a request for the Web page, the server inserts the current value of `led1_image`, and the Web page displays an image that matches the LED's current state.

The complement to #echo is #set, which sets the value of a variable. Dynamic C doesn't support #set, however.

#include

The #include directive causes the server to place the contents of the specified file in the Web page. The following #include directive:

```
<pre>
<!--#include file="myfile.txt" -->
</pre>
```

places the contents of *myfile.txt* in a Web page, at the location of the directive in the page. If the included file isn't HTML-encoded, precede the directive with an HTML <pre> tag, which tells the browser to maintain the line breaks and spacing in the file's contents. The </pre> tag ends the preformatted content.

#exec

The #exec directive can execute a command or CGI program and place the result in the Web page being served. In Dynamic C's implementation of #exec, the functions that the directive can execute must be specified in an HTTPSPEC_FUNCTION item in an HttpSpec structure.

The #exec directive can be a security risk if the system software doesn't have appropriate restrictions on what the directive can execute. For example, a Web site might display a guest book of comments from Web-site visitors. If a malicious visitor enters an #exec directive in the guest book, when a client requests the Web page containing the guest book, the server will parse the page for SSI directives and will attempt to execute the #exec directive, with possibly disastrous results.

Identifying Files that use Server Side Includes

The security issues with #exec directives suggest that there is good reason to limit which files a server parses for SSI directives. If the server doesn't look for directives, any directives that happen to be present won't execute and the browser will ignore them as HTML comments. Another reason to limit the files a server parses for SSI directives is to save the server from wasting time needlessly looking for directives on pages that don't have any.

The usual way to identify pages that use SSI is to give the filenames the extension *.shtml*, while plain HTML files use *.htm* or *.html*.

In Dynamic C, the HttpType structure specifies a handler to use with each supported file extension. In the Dynamic C example below, files with the extensions *.shtml* and *.html* each use a different handler. The *.shtml* handler parses the files for SSI directives, while the *.html* handler doesn't.

```
const HttpType http_types[] =
{
    { ".shtml", "text/html", shtml_handler},
    { ".html", "text/html", html_handler}
};
```

Other Web servers use other methods for specifying the handlers to use with different file types, but the concept is the same.

Chapter 6

7

Serving Web Pages that Respond to User Input

Chapter 6 showed how a Web page can use HTML to display text and images, including real-time data. Many embedded Web servers also need to display pages that can respond to user input. For example, a Web page might display a virtual control panel that enables users to start, stop, or modify processes controlled by an embedded system. Or a page might display a form that enables users to enter or select values for use in configuring or controlling a device.

'Two technologies for enabling Web pages to respond to user input are common gateway interface (CGI) programming and Java servlets. CGI programs and Java servlets can do the following:

- Retrieve the current values of variables and place them on a Web page to return to a client.

- Receive and act on data provided by a client who clicks a hyperlink or submits an HTML form.

- Do just about anything that an ordinary program is capable of, including making calculations, performing logical operations, and accessing I/O ports.

This chapter presents examples of devices that use CGI programming and Java servlets to enable Web pages to respond to user input. A Rabbit module uses CGI programming and a TINI uses Java servlets. The In Depth section of the chapter has more detail about what's involved in using these technologies, plus examples of how a server can serve forms and respond to form data submitted by users.

Quick Start: Device Controller

What method to use to enable a Web page to accept user input depends in part on the programming language and the system's capabilities. For the Rabbit, the HTTP server in Dynamic C's *http.lib* library supports Common Gateway Interface (CGI) programming. For the TINI, the addition of a servlet engine enables running servlets written in Java.

The browsers that display pages that request user input don't require any special capabilities. At the browser, a link or button that requests a server to take an action is just like any other hyperlink. A Web page that accepts user input on a form must support forms, but it's rare to find a browser these days without support for forms. On receiving the user's input, the server performs the processing and returns a Web page that may incorporate output from the program code the server has just executed.

The Device Controller's Web Page

The device-controller examples in this section use LEDs to represent processes the system is controlling. The examples can serve as prototypes for embedded systems that accept user input from Web pages for any purpose.

In the examples, the servers host a Web page that displays a virtual control panel (Figure 7-1). The Web page displays two LEDs and two buttons that

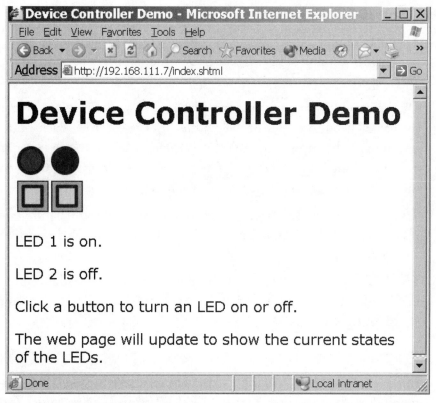

Figure 7-1: This Web page is a virtual control panel that enables users to turn LEDs on or off by clicking a button.

users can click to turn the LEDs on and off. Both the Rabbit and TINI can host this Web page, though they use different technologies to respond to the button clicks.

The images of LEDs on the Web page match the states of the LEDs in the embedded system at the time the browser requested the Web page. When a user viewing the page clicks a button, the Web server receives a message containing the name of a CGI function or servlet to execute. The server toggles the state of the selected LED and then either returns a Web page containing updated images and text or returns a code that advises the client to request an updated page.

Rabbit Device Controller

The first example uses the same RabbitCore RCM3200 module as the previous Rabbit examples. Listing 7-1 shows the HTML code for Figure 7-1's Web page.

On the page, the images of the two LEDs and their buttons are in table cells so that each button lines up below the LED it controls. Each button is a hyperlink. When a user viewing the page clicks a button, the server receives a message containing the text */led1toggle.cgi* or */led2toggle.cgi*. On the server, these file names are associated with CGI functions.

The page also uses SSI `#echo` directives, as described in Chapter 6, to display images of lit or unlit LEDs and text descriptions of the LEDs' states ("on" or "off").

The LEDs are controlled by bits 6 and 7 of Port G on the Rabbit 3000 CPU. The LEDS are included on Rabbit Semiconductor's prototyping board for the RCM3200.

Program Code

In the RCM3200, a Dynamic C program serves Figure 7-1's Web page and responds to button clicks that send HTTP requests to execute CGI functions. Much of the code is similar to the code in Chapter 6's Rabbit example.

Initial Defines and Declarations

As explained in Chapter 5, `TCPCONFIG` specifies a configuration that sets the IP address, netmask, and gateway IP address values:

```
#define TCPCONFIG 1
```

The CGI functions use the values in the `REDIRECTHOST` and `REDIRECTTO` constants to tell the client's browser what Web page to request to display the result of a button click. If the Rabbit is behind a router that uses NAT and if you want the Web page to be accessible beyond the local network, `REDIRECTHOST` must be the router's public IP address or domain name.

```
#define REDIRECTHOST    _PRIMARY_STATIC_IP
#define REDIRECTTO "http://" REDIRECTHOST "/index.shtml"
```

```html
<html>
<head>
  <title>Device Controller Demo</title>
</head>

<body>

<h1>Device Controller Demo</h1>

<table>
  <tr>
    <td> <img SRC="<!--#echo var="led1_image" -->"> </td>
    <td> <img SRC="<!--#echo var="led2_image" -->"> </td>
  </tr>
  <tr>
    <td> <a href="/led1toggle.cgi"> <img src="button.gif"> </a>
  </td>
    <td> <a href="/led2toggle.cgi"> <img src="button.gif"> </a>
  </td>
  </tr>
</table>

<p>LED 1 is <!--#echo var="led1_state" --> .</p>
<p>LED 2 is <!--#echo var="led2_state" --> .</p>

<p>Click a button to turn an LED on or off.</p>
<p>The Web page will update to show the current states of the
  LEDs.</p>

</body>
</html>
```

Listing 7-1: This Web page contains links to CGI programs that the Rabbit executes before serving Figure 7-1's page.

The #memmap xmem directive causes all C functions not declared as root to be stored in extended memory. The dcrtcp.lib library supports TCP/IP. The http.lib library supports HTTP functions.

```
#memmap xmem
#use "dcrtcp.lib"
```

```
#use "http.lib"
```

The #ximport directive retrieves a file from the PC being used for project development, stores the file's length and contents in the Rabbit's extended memory, and associates a symbol with the file's address in memory. This application uses one Web page and three image files. You must replace the file paths with paths that are valid for the files in your development PC.

```
#ximport "c:/rabbitserver/index.shtml"    index_html
#ximport "c:/rabbitserver/ledon.gif"      ledon_gif
#ximport "c:/rabbitserver/ledoff.gif"     ledoff_gif
#ximport "c:/rabbitserver/button.gif"     button_gif
```

An HttpType structure specifies the handler to use with different file extensions. If the handler is NULL, the server uses the default handler, which sends the file's contents unaltered. For the Device Controller application, the Web page uses the *.shtml* handler because the page contains SSI directives. Requests for files with *.cgi* and *.gif* extensions use the default handler. The structure below also specifies the default handler for HTML files.

```
const HttpType http_types[] =
{
    { ".shtml", "text/html", shtml_handler},
    { ".html", "text/html", NULL},
    { ".cgi", "", NULL},
    { ".gif", "image/gif", NULL}
};
```

The strings ledon_image and ledoff_image store the names of files that contain images of lit and unlit LEDs ("ledon.gif" and "ledoff.gif"). The string variables led1_image and led2_image each contain a file name for the image that matches the corresponding LED's state. The string variables led1_state and led2_state hold the text "on" or "off" as appropriate, to match the state of an LED.

```
const char ledon_image[] = "ledon.gif";
const char ledoff_image[] = "ledoff.gif";

char led1_image[15];
char led2_image[15];

char led1_state[4];
char led2_state[4];
```

Controlling the LEDs

Each LED has a function (led1toggle() and led2toggle()) that exe-cutes when the server receives a message indicating that a user has clicked that LED's button on the Web page. When called, the function receives a pointer to an HttpState structure that contains information about the cur-rent connection and request.

This is the code for LED1:

```
int led1toggle(HttpState* state)
{
  if (BitRdPortI(PGDR, 6) == 0) {
    // When the bit is 0, the LED is on, so turn it off.
    BitWrPortI(PGDR, &PGDRShadow, 1, 6);
    strcpy(led1_image,ledoff_image);
    strcpy(led1_state, "off");
    }
  else {
    // When the bit is 1, the LED is off, so turn it on.
    BitWrPortI(PGDR, &PGDRShadow, 0, 6);
    strcpy(led1_image,ledon_image);
    strcpy(led1_state, "on");
    }

  cgi_redirectto(state,REDIRECTTO);
  return 0;
}
```

Writing zero to a port bit that controls an LED turns the LED on, and writ-ing 1 to the port bit turns the LED off. The routine for LED1 reads the state of Port G, bit 6 and toggles the bit to the opposite state.

The BitRdPortI() function returns the value of a bit on one of the Rab-bit's internal ports. PGDR is Port G's data register, and 6 is the number of the bit to read.

The BitWrPortI() function writes a value to a bit in one of the Rabbit's internal ports. Again, PGDR is Port G's data register. The second parameter, PGDRShadow, is a variable that functions as a shadow register that contains the last value written to the register. Shadow registers are useful for storing the most recently written values to write-only registers. Program code can then learn a bit's value by reading the bit in the corresponding Shadow register. Port G has read/write access, but the `BitWrPortI()` function requires a shadow register. The function's third and fourth parameters are the value to write (1) and the bit number to write to (6).

After writing to the port bit, the routine stores a file name (`"ledon.gif"` or `"ledoff.gif"`, as appropriate) in `led1_image`, and stores `"on"` or `"off"` as appropriate in `led1_state`.

The call to the `cgi_redirectto()` function tells the server to return an HTTP response containing a response code that advises the client to request the URL stored in `REDIRECTTO`. In this application, the `REDIRECTTO` URL is the same *index.shtml* page the browser displayed when the user clicked a button. The newly retrieved page will contain updated images and text that reflect the current values of the LEDs. The statement `return 0` must follow the call to `cgi_redirectto()`.

The routine for LED2 is the same as the routine for LED1, except that it references LED2's port bit and variables:

```
int led2toggle(HttpState* state)
{
  if (BitRdPortI(PGDR, 7) == 0) {
    // When the bit is 0, the LED is on, so turn it off.
    BitWrPortI(PGDR, &PGDRShadow, 1, 7);
     strcpy(led2_image,ledoff_image);
       strcpy(led2_state, "off");
      }
  else {
    // When the bit is 1, the LED is off, so turn it on.
    BitWrPortI(PGDR, &PGDRShadow, 0, 7);
    strcpy(led2_image,ledon_image);
     strcpy(led2_state, "on");
    }

  cgi_redirectto(state,REDIRECTTO);
  return 0;
}
```

Specifying What the Web Server Can Access

As in Chapter 6's example, an `HttpSpec` structure contains information about the files, variables, and functions the Web server can access. The Web page and three image files each have an `HTTPSPEC_FILE` entry in the structure. When a browser requests the file *index.shtml* or the server's default file ("/"), the server serves the Web page stored at index_html. The four string variables that hold file names and LED state information each have an HTTPSPEC_VARIABLE entry. Two HTTPSPEC_FUNCTION entries associate the names of the CGI programs (/led1toggle.cgi and /led2toggle.cgi) with pointers to the functions led1toggle and led2toggle.

```
const HttpSpec http_flashspec[] =
{
   { HTTPSPEC_FILE, "/", index_html, NULL, 0, NULL, NULL},
    { HTTPSPEC_FILE, "/index.shtml", index_html, NULL, 0,
        NULL, NULL},
    { HTTPSPEC_FILE, "/ledon.gif", ledon_gif, NULL, 0,
        NULL, NULL},
    { HTTPSPEC_FILE, "/ledoff.gif", ledoff_gif, NULL, 0,
        NULL, NULL},
    { HTTPSPEC_FILE, "/button.gif", button_gif, NULL, 0,
        NULL, NULL},

    { HTTPSPEC_VARIABLE, "led1_image", 0, led1_image,
        PTR16, "%s", NULL},
    { HTTPSPEC_VARIABLE, "led2_image", 0, led2_image,
        PTR16, "%s", NULL},
    { HTTPSPEC_VARIABLE, "led1_state", 0, led1_state,
        PTR16,   "%s", NULL},
    { HTTPSPEC_VARIABLE, "led2_state", 0, led2_state,
        PTR16,   "%s", NULL},

    { HTTPSPEC_FUNCTION, "/led1toggle.cgi", 0, led1toggle,
        0, NULL, NULL},
    { HTTPSPEC_FUNCTION, "/led2toggle.cgi", 0, led2toggle,
        0, NULL, NULL},
 };
```

The main() Function

The program's main() function begins by writing to Port G's Data Direction Register (PGDDR) to configure bits 6 and 7 as outputs. Writing 1 to a bit in the register configures the corresponding port bit as an output. The program then reads the bits and stores the appropriate file names and text to use on the Web page to reflect the LEDs' states.

```
main()
{
```

```
WrPortI(PGDDR, NULL, 0xC0);

if (BitRdPortI(PGDR, 6) == 0) {
  strcpy(led1_image,ledon_image);
  strcpy(led1_state, "on");
} else {
  strcpy(led1_image,ledoff_image);
  strcpy(led1_state, "off");
}

if (BitRdPortI(PGDR, 7) == 0) {
  strcpy(led2_image,ledon_image);
  strcpy(led2_state, "on");
} else {
  strcpy(led2_image,ledoff_image);
  strcpy(led2_state, "off");
}
```

Before performing any network communications, the program must initialize the TCP/IP stack and Web server. As in Chapter 6's Rabbit example, calling tcp_reserveport() can improve the Web server's performance.

```
sock_init();
http_init();
tcp_reserveport(80);
```

The main program loop has just one task, calling http_handler(). In a real-world application, the main program loop would perform other tasks as well.

```
while (1) {
    http_handler();
    // Code to perform other tasks can be placed here.
}
} // end main
```

Using the Device Controller

When the RCM3200 module runs this program, any computer that can access the module over the network can request the Web page and view and control the LEDs. Clicking a button on the Web page causes the browser to send an HTTP request containing the name of a CGI function. The Rabbit executes the named function and returns a response code that advises the browser to refresh the page. In a similar way, you can enable users to control other processes on an RCM3200 or similar module via a Web page.

TINI Device Controller

To serve Figure 7-1's Device Controller Web page, a TINI can use Java servlets. Servlets are components that can place real-time data on a Web page and can receive and respond to user input, as well as performing just about any task that an ordinary program might do. A Web server that runs servlet code must have a servlet container, also called a servlet engine, which adds support for servlets to the Web server.

The servlet examples in this book are written for use with the Tynamo Web server, an HTTP server and servlet container from Shawn Silverman (*tynamo.qindesign.com*). Tynamo is free for development and educational use. Use in commercial products requires a license.

Another option for servlets on a TINI is Smart Software Consulting's TiniHttpServer (*www.smartsc.com*). TiniHttpServer is offered at no cost under the GNU General Public License. The source code is available.

For the latest information on licensing terms for both products, see their Web sites. The Web sites also have complete documentation, including links to the necessary files to download and instructions for building the servers and deploying them on a TINI module and other Java platforms.

The capabilities of any servlet engine will comply with the Java Servlet Specification, but the implementation details can vary with different products.

The Web Page

Listing 7-2 is the HTML source code for Figure 7-1's Web page when it has been served by a TINI using servlets. The Web page's HTML code isn't stored in a separate file. Instead, the servlet generates the page on request.

The HTML code is much the same as in Listing 7-1's code for the Rabbit, with differences only in how the dynamic data is handled.

```
<html>
<head>
  <title>Device Controller </title>
</head>

<body>
<h1> Device Controller Demo</h1>

<table>
<tr>
  <td><img src ="ledon.gif" ></td>
  <td><img src ="ledoff.gif" ></td>
</tr>

<tr>
  <td>
  <a href="/servlet/DeviceController?button1">
    <img src="button.gif"></a>
  </td>
  <td>
  <a href="/servlet/DeviceController?button2">
    <img src="button.gif" ></a>
  </td>
</tr>

</table>

<p>LED 1 is on.</p>
<p>LED 2 is off.</p>
<p>Click a button to turn an LED on or off.</p>
<p>The Web page will update to show the current states of the
  LEDs.</p>

</body>

</html>
```

Listing 7-2: When a browser requests Figure 7-1's Web page from a TINI module running the Tynamo Web server and the DeviceController servlet code in this chapter, the server inserts the file names and text descriptions to match the LEDs' states

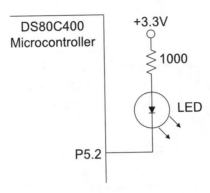

Figure 7-2: A port bit on the DSTINIm400 module controls an LED. A logic low turns the LED on.

The hyperlinks for the buttons each contain a string that names the servlet being requested. This Java statement sends the text required to place the image button.gif on a page and make it a hyperlink:

```
out.print("<p>
   <a href=\"/servlet/DeviceController?button1\">
   <img src=\"button.gif\">
   </a>"</p>);
```

In the hyperlink, /servlet/DeviceController matches a mapping in a configuration file for the Web server. The mapping tells the server to run the DeviceController servlet. Following the servlet mapping is a question mark and a query string (button1) that identifies the button that was clicked.

The server inserts the img tags ("ledon.gif", "ledoff.gif") and the text descriptions of the LEDs (LED 1 is on., LED 2 is off.) in the page each time the page is served. The images and text match the current states of the LEDs.

LED1 is D1 on the DSTINIm400 module and is controlled by Port 5, bit 2 on the DS80C400 microcontroller. Figure 7-2 shows the interface. A logic low on the port bit sinks current to turn the LED on, and a logic high cuts off the current and turns the LED off. The 1-kilohm pull-up resistor limits current through the LED. LED2 is an optional LED that can interface in the same way to Port 5, bit 3 on the '80C400.

(The DS-TINI-1 module includes an LED controlled by Port 3, bit 5 on the DS80C390 microcontroller. This interface is the reverse of the '80C400's circuit: a logic high turns the LED on, and a logic low turns it off.)

The Servlet

The Device Controller servlet is a Java class with methods that serve Figure 7-1's page and respond when users click the buttons on the page.

The class imports java.io classes to enable reading inputs and writing to outputs. Two additional packages support servlets. The javax.servlet package includes the Servlet interface and the abstract class Generic-Servlet, which implements the Servlet interface. The javax.serv-let.http package contains the abstract class HttpServlet, which adds support for HTTP and Web applications. The TINI-specific class com.dalsemi.system.BitPort enables accessing the port bits that control the TINI's LEDs.

The DeviceController class extends the HttpServlet class of the javax.servlet.http package.

```
import java.io.*;
import javax.servlet.*;
import javax.servlet.http.*;
import com.dalsemi.system.BitPort;

public class DeviceController
  extends HttpServlet
{
```

Two BitPort objects, led1 and led2, correspond to port bits on the '80C400 microcontroller The BitPort class's readLatch method returns the last value written to a port bit, which in turn indicates the state of the LED controlled by the bit. (To read a port bit configured as an input, use the read() method.)

```
BitPort led1 = new BitPort(BitPort.Port5Bit2);
BitPort led2 = new BitPort(BitPort.Port5Bit3);
```

Performing Tasks on Startup

The `GenericServlet` class includes an `init()` method that enables a servlet to perform tasks on startup. The `init()` method is called once, when the servlet starts, and is optional. In this example, `init()` sets the LEDs' port bits to turn the LEDs off.

```
public void init() throws ServletException {
   led1.set();
   led2.set();
} // end init()
```

Serving GET Requests

A received HTTP GET request causes the `DeviceController` class's `doGet()` method to be called. The `DeviceController` class overrides `HttpServlet`'s `doGet()` method with a method that serves the Device Controller Web page to the client. The `doGet()` method has two parameters: `request` is an `HttpServletRequest` object that contains the client's request, and `response` is an `HttpServletResponse` object that contains response information for the client.

A `ServletException` occurs if the server can't handle the GET request for some reason. An `IOException` occurs if there is an input or output error when the servlet is handling the GET request. The `doGet()` method throws `ServletExceptions` and `IOExceptions`.

```
public void doGet
   (HttpServletRequest request,
   HttpServletResponse response)
   throws ServletException, IOException {
```

The `getQueryString()` method of the `HttpServletRequest` object returns a string received from the client in the GET request. In this application, the query string is the text `button1` or `button2` that appears after the question mark in a button's hyperlink.

```
String query = request.getQueryString();
```

If the query string equals `"button1"`, indicating that Button 1 was clicked, the program calls the `toggle()` method to change the state of `led1`. The method returns `true` if the toggled LED is on and `false` if the LED is off.

If the query string doesn't contain `"button1"`, the program uses the `Bit-Port` class's `readLatch()` method to find out the last value written to `led1`'s port bit. If the last value written was zero, the LED is on and `ledOn` is set to `true`. If the last value written was 1, the LED is off and `ledOn` is set to `false`.

In the same way, depending on the contents of the query string, the program toggles or just reads the state of `led2`.

```
boolean led1On;
if ("button1".equals(query)) {
  System.out.println("Button 1 was clicked");
  led1On = toggle(led1);
} else {
  led1On = (led1.readLatch() == 0);
}

boolean led2On;
if ("button2".equals(query)) {
  System.out.println("Button 2 was clicked");
  led2On = toggle(led2);
} else {
  led2On = (led2.readLatch() == 0);
}
```

If there is no query string, such as when a user requests the page for the first time, the code reads the states of both LEDs and toggles neither.

Two `String` variables (`led1Image`, `led2Image`) hold the names of image files that correspond to the LEDs' states. Two additional `String` variables (`led1State`, `led2State`) hold the text `"on"` or `"off"` as appropriate for the LEDs. After reading the LEDs' states, the program sets the image and text strings to match the LEDs.

```
String led1Image;
String led1State;
if (led1On) {
  led1Image= "/ledon.gif";
  led1State = "on";
}
else {
  led1Image = "/ledoff.gif";
  led1State = "off";
}
```

```
String led2Image;
String led2State;
if (led2On) {
  led2Image= "/ledon.gif";
  led2State = "on";
}
else {
  led2Image = "/ledoff.gif";
  led2State = "off";
}
```

A call to the class's `sendWebPage()` method sends an updated Web page to the client. The method uses the `HttpServlet` response object and the four variables that indicate the LEDs' states and image files.

```
sendWebPage (response, led1Image, led2Image,
    led1State, led2State);
} // end doGet()
```

Toggling an LED

The `toggle()` method toggles the state of a `BitPort` object. The method returns a boolean value that indicates if the corresponding LED is on. The value is `false` if the last value written to the LED was 1 and the LED is off, and `true` if the last value written was zero and the LED is on.

```
private static boolean toggle(BitPort bitPort) {
  if (bitPort.readLatch() == 0) {
    bitPort.set();
    return false;
  } else {
    bitPort.clear();
    return true;
  }
} // end toggle()
```

Sending the Web Page

The `sendWebPage()` method writes a Web page to an output stream. The method uses the `HttpServlet` response object and four variables that the method inserts in the Web page. The method throws `IOExceptions`.

```
private void sendWebPage (HttpServletResponse response,
                        String led1Image,
                        String led2Image,
                        String led1State,
```

```
                                      String led2State)
       throws IOException {
```

The `setContentType()` method of the `HttpServletResponse` object sets the `Content-Type` field in the response's HTML header:

```
response.setContentType("text/html");
```

The `getOutputStream()` method of the `HttpServletResponse` object returns an instance of a `ServletOutputStream` object. The `ServletOutputStream` class extends the `java.io.OutputStream` class and provides an output stream for sending data to a client. You could use a `PrintWriter` object instead, but a `ServletOutputStream` object requires less processing, and thus is quicker. A series of `out.print` statements write the Web page's contents to the output stream. The servlet container automatically creates and writes an HTTP header that precedes the page's contents.

```
ServletOutputStream out = response.getOutputStream();
out.print("<html>"
        + "<head>"
        + "<title>Device Controller</title>"
        + "</head>"
        + "<body>"
        + "<h1>Device Controller</h1>");
```

Much of the HTML code is similar to the source code for the Web page in the Rabbit Device Controller example. The differences are in how the server gets the values of real-time variables and in how the server responds to button clicks.

The LED and button images are in a table to ensure they line up on the page. The variables `led1Image` and `led2Image` each contain a filename, `"ledon.gif"` or `"ledoff.gif"`, as appropriate, to indicate the images the browser should display for the LEDs.

Some of the text in the HTML code includes quotation marks. Because quotation marks are also the delimiters for a string, any quotation mark within a string must be preceded by a back slash (\). For example, many HTML tags include attributes enclosed by quotation marks, such as `<img src="ledon.gif">`

To write this line to the output stream, each quotation mark in the string must be preceded by a back slash: `out.print("<img src=\"ledon.gif\">");`

The back slash indicates that the quotation mark is part of the string and not the string's delimiter.

```
out.print("<table>"
     + "<tr>"
     + "<td>"
     + "<img src=\"");
out.print(led1Image);
out.print("\">"
     + "</td>"
     + "<td>"
     + "<img src=\"");
out.print(led2Image);
out.print("\">"
     + "</td>"
     + "</tr>");
```

In the hyperlinks for the button images, `/servlet/DeviceController` is a mapping that tells the server, via a configuration file, that `DeviceController` is a servlet. When a user clicks a button on the Web page, the browser returns either `button1` or `button2` to the TINI in the request's query string.

```
out.print("<tr><td>");
out.print("<a href=
     \"/servlet/DeviceController?button1\">
     <img src=\"/button.gif\"></a>");
out.print("</td><td>");
out.print("<a href=
     \"/servlet/DeviceController?button2\">
     <img src=\"/button.gif\" ></a>");
out.print("</td></tr></table>");
```

In addition to the LEDs' images, two lines of text indicate the states of the LEDs. The variables `led1State` and `led2State` each hold the text "on" or "off" as appropriate, and `out.print` statements write the text to the output stream.

```
out.print("<p>LED 1 is ");
out.print (led1State);
out.print(".</p>"
```

```
        + "<p>"
        + "LED 2 is ");
out.print (led2State);
out.print(".</p>"
        + "<p>"
        + "Click a button to turn an LED on or off."
        + "<p>"
        + "The Web page will update to show the
            current states of the LEDs."
        + "</p>"
        + "</body>"
        + "</html>");
```

The servlet container flushes and closes the output stream when the request has been serviced, so there's no need to do so in the servlet.

Loading and Running Servlets

In writing an ordinary Java program for use on a TINI, you compile the program to one or more *.class* files and use the TINIConvertor utility to convert the file(s) to a *.tini* file. You can then use an FTP program to copy the file to the TINI. Or you can use the build utility Ant to automate the process of creating and copying the files. When the file or files have been transferred to the TINI, you can run the program from a Telnet session by typing java, followed by the name of the *.tini* file.

With servlets, things are more complicated. The Tynamo Web server functions both as a Web server, which responds to HTTP requests, and as a servlet container, which contains and manages the servlets. A variety of configuration files contain information about the servlets and Web server. The Ant utility is the recommended way to compile, convert, and deploy the Web server and servlets on the TINI.

With Ant, you can compile your *.java* files and create the file *webserver.tini*, which contains both the object code required to respond to HTTP requests and the code for your servlets.

If you use another servlet container, such as TiniHttpServer, the details will vary, but the information about how to use Ant, TiniAnt, and the configuration files are likely to be similar.

Required Components

These are the required components for creating and running servlets on a TINI with the Tynamo Web server:

- A TINI module, to run the Tynamo Web server.
- The Java SDK, for program development, from *java.sun.com*.
- The Tynamo Web server, to support servlets, from *tynamo.qindesign.com*.
- Ant, a Java-based build tool, from *jakarta.apache.org*.
- TiniAnt, a plug-in that integrates TINI's build process into Ant, from *tiniant.sourceforge.net*.
- The *NetComponents.jar* library, with FTP and Telnet support for deploying the Web server on the TINI. The NetComponents distribution is available from *www.saverese.org*.

The Tynamo Web server uses four configuration files. You must edit at least three of these to provide information that is specific to your development PC and your servlets. The *build.properties* file contains the locations and names of various files and directories on the development computer. The *servlets.props* file contains information about the servlets. The *deploy.properties* file contains your TINI's IP address and other information that the Ant utility uses in copying the Web server's files to the TINI. The *webserver.props* file enables you to specify a default directory, home page, and other properties of your server. (Many servers can use the default *webserver.props* file, with no editing.) You can edit these files in any text editor.

Below is more information about each of these files, followed by instructions for how to use the files in compiling, converting, and deploying files to the Web server.

Creating a build.properties File

The *build.properties* file is in the home directory of the Tynamo distribution. The file contains the locations and names of the TINI's home directory and the servlets on the development computer. The Ant utility uses the information in the file in building the TINI's executable file. Listing 7-3 is an example *build.properties* file.

```
#example build.properties file
tini.path=C:/tini1.11
src.paths=/myservlets
src.files=DeviceController.java, FormResponse.java
include.servletReloading=false
dependency.files=
dependency.groups=
dependency.classpath=
reflect.classes=DeviceController, FormResponse
```

Listing 7-3: The build.properties file contains information that Ant uses in compiling the servlets.

For each of the following items, edit the existing text by inserting the information that applies to your system and servlets. Use forward slashes as separators even if the operating system of your developement computer (such as Windows) uses back slashes. Ant converts to back slashes as needed.

Set `tini.path` equal to the location of the TINI SDK on the development computer:

```
tini.path=/tini1.11
```

Set `src.paths` equal to the location of the source code for your servlets on the development computer:

```
src.paths=/myservlets
```

If there are multiple locations, separate the paths with colons or semicolons:

```
src.paths=/myservlets;/test
```

Set `src.files` equal to the names of your servlets, separating multiple names with commas or spaces:

```
src.files=DeviceController.java, FormResponse.java
```

Set `reflect.classes` equal to the full class name of each servlet, separating multiple names with commas or spaces:

```
reflect.classes=DeviceController, FormResponse
```

Three dependency entries can contain information about the classes that a servlet uses, or depends on. Not every servlet requires dependency information.

A `dependency.files` entry specifies the name and location of a file that contains dependency information for one or more servlets. An example entry is:

```
dependency.files=examples/servlet_examples_dep.txt
```

Below is the information provided in the dependency file for Tynamo's example servlet `RequestInfoServlet`:

```
RequestInfoServlet=
com.qindesign.servlet.example.RequestInfoServlet;
com.qindesign.servlet.example.Common
```

The `RequestInfoServlet` entry has two values separated by a semicolon. The first value is the full name of the servlet's class. The second value informs the build process that the servlet depends on the `com.qinde-sign.servlet.example.Common` class.

Creating a servlets.props File

The *servlets.props* file is in the *bin* directory of the Tynamo installation and must contain information required by the servlet container to run your servlets. The file provides information about each servlet supported by the server. Listing 7-4 is an example *servlets.props* file for the servlets `Device-Controller` and `FormResponse`.

A servlet name identifies the servlet in the file. The servlet names in the example are `DeviceController` and `FormResponse`. A mapping specifies how clients can request to run the servlet and has the following format:

servlet_name.**mapping**=*mapping*

where *servlet_name* is a servlet name and *mapping* is the text that clients can use to request the servlet from the server.

The following mapping enables clients to request to run the servlet `Device-Controller` by typing the TINI's IP address or domain name followed by `/servlet/DeviceController` in a browser's Address text box:

```
DeviceController.mapping=/servlet/DeviceController
```

For example, if the IP address is 192.168.111.9, the user would enter the following:

```
DeviceController.mapping=/servlet/DeviceController
DeviceController.class=DeviceController

FormResponse.mapping=/servlet/FormResponse
FormResponse.class=FormResponse
```

Listing 7-4: The servlets.props file contains configuration information for your servlets.

```
http://192.168.111.9/servlet/DeviceController
```

The `servlets.props` file must also specify the full class name of the class that implements the `javax.servlet.Servlet` interface for each servlet. The class name is the name of the servlet's class in the source code, preceded by its package name, if any. This information uses the following format:

servlet_name.**classname**=*class*

where *servlet_name* is the servlet name and *classname* is the class name. In the example, the class name for the servlet `DeviceController` is also `DeviceController`. In this case it's redundant, but other classes might use a different name for the class name and servlet name.

If the servlet is in a package, the class name must specify the package name as well, as in this example:

```
Shutdown.class=com.qindesign.servlet.ShutdownServlet
```

The optional `initParams` entry can specify one or more initialization parameters to use when the servlet starts:

```
Shutdown.initParams=passwd=shut:down
```

The optional `loadOnStartup` entry can specify that the servlet should load when the server starts, rather than on first use:

```
Shutdown.loadOnStartup=true
```

The number sign (#) indicates a comment, which the server ignores:

```
# Shutdown servlet
```

The example *servlets.props* file included with the Tynamo Web server has additional examples.

Creating a deploy.properties File

The *deploy.properties* file simplifies the process of transferring files to a TINI. Listing 7-5 shows an example.

Four `deploy` properties contain information about the TINI. The `server` property is the TINI's IP address. The `userid` and `password` properties are the user ID and password required to log onto the TINI's FTP server. The `rootdir` property is the directory the deploy process should use as the root directory on the TINI when transferring files. The deploy process creates the directory if it doesn't exist.

Setting Web Server Properties

The *webserver.props* file enables you to specify properties of the server. The default file will work with no changes, but you can edit the entries if you wish. To use a default directory other than */web/http-root* for files on the server, edit this entry with the desired directory path.

```
server.rootDir=/web/http-root
```

To use a default home page other than *index.html*, edit this entry with the desired default file's name:

```
server.welcomeFile=index.html
```

The entries in the provided file show additional options you can change.

Running the Web server

When you've obtained the necessary components and have written a servlet such as the DeviceController servlet above, these are the steps required to use Tynamo to run the servlet on a TINI:

1. Install Ant and TiniAnt on your development PC, following the instructions provided with each, including setting the recommended environment variables to identify file locations.

2. As described above, edit *build.properties, servlets.props, deploy.properties,* and *webserver.props* with the appropriate information for your TINI and servlets.

```
deploy.server=192.168.111.2
deploy.userid=root
deploy.password=tini
deploy.rootdir=/web
```

Listing 7-5: The deploy.properties file contains information specific to the TINI that will run the Web server.

3. Build *webserver.tini* with Ant. Open a window with a command prompt. Under Windows XP, click **Start**, then **Run**, and enter **cmd** in the **Open:** text box that appears. Change to Tynamo's home directory and enter **ant**. This runs the file *ant.bat* included with the Ant distribution. Ant uses the information in *build.properties* and Tynamo's *build.xml* file to locate the needed files, compile, and convert the result to the file *webserver.tini*. The file contains the executable code for the servlet container and the servlets the Web server can run.

4. Copy any static HTML files, images, or other files the Web server will need to access to the appropriate directories under the Tynamo's home directory on the development computer. The *webserver.props* file specifies the root directory for these files. The default is *http-root*.

5. From a command prompt in Tynamo's home directory, enter ant deploy. This runs *ant.bat* again, but this time runs the deploy task instead of the default build task. (Tynamo's *build.xml* file specifies the default task.)

The deploy task copies the Web server's files to the TINI. Using the default settings, the files copied are the following files under Tynamo's home directory:

\bin\webserver.tini (the Web server application)
\bin\WebServer (a script to run the Web server)
\bin\webserver.props (configuration information about the Web server)
\bin\servlets.props (information about the servlets)
\bin\mimeTypes.props (MIME definitions for file types)
\http-root* (all files in this directory)

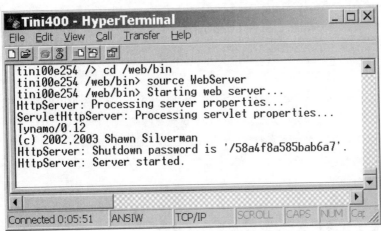

Figure 7-3: You can run the Tynamo server from a Telnet session with the TINI.

6. To run the Web server, in a Telnet session, at a command prompt in the root directory, enter the following command:

```
source web/bin/WebServer
```

This executes the WebServer script, which contains the following text:

```
java /web/bin/webserver.tini /web/bin/webserver.props &
```

On running the Web server, the Telnet window displays something like the text in Figure 7-3. And the TINI is ready to run the servlets named in servlets.props.

Serving Other Files

The default configuration of the Tynamo Web server treats any request not handled by a servlet as a request for a file under the */web/http-root* directory. Examples of such requests include requests for image files or static HTML files. If the request doesn't specify a valid servlet or file name, the default configuration serves the page *index.html* if available in the specified directory.

The default home page can contain a hyperlink to the Device Controller servlet:

```
<a href="/servlet/DeviceController">Device Controller</a>
```

311

Save the Web page as *index.html* and copy the file to the TINI's */web/http-root* directory. Then users who enter the TINI's IP address alone or the IP address followed by */index.html* will see the Web page with the link to the servlet.

To redirect the user's browser to request the servlet automatically from the home page, include this META tag in the Web page's HEAD section:

```
<meta http-equiv="Refresh" content="0;
    url=/servlet/DeviceController">
```

In Depth:
Using CGI and Servlets

The examples above showed how Web pages can use CGI functions and servlets to enable users to click hyperlinks to run program code on the server and view the result in a Web page. This section has more detail about CGI and servlets, including additional examples that show how embedded systems can use forms to accept text input from users.

CGI for Embedded Systems

The common gateway interface (CGI) defines a protocol that enables users to click a link or button on a Web page to request a server to execute program code. A CGI program can perform just about any function on the server. After running the requested program, the server returns a result in an HTTP response.

Support for CGI programming has been around since the earliest days of the Web. The first Web server to implement CGI was the NCSA HTTPD server from the National Center for Supercomputing Applications. NCSA publishes a CGI Specification at *http://hoohoo.ncsa.uiuc.edu/cgi/*. Many embedded systems that support networking also include support for CGI. The Dynamic C library *http.lib* is an example.

CGI programming doesn't require a particular programming language. On large servers, the Perl language has long been popular. Perl programs are typically scripts that require an interpreter to execute, and large servers generally have a Perl interpreter. A small embedded system isn't likely to have a Perl interpreter, so CGI programs for embedded systems are often written in C.

A Web server that runs CGI programs must be able to do the following:

- Identify a received HTTP request that references a CGI program to execute.
- Locate and run the requested CGI program.
- Return an HTTP response.

The response the server returns after running a CGI program often includes an HTTP redirection code that advises the browser to request a page containing an acknowledgment or a refreshed page with updated data.

Some CGI programs process data submitted by a client on a form. When a client submits a request that contains form data, the server must be able to pass the data to the CGI program that will use the data.

For security reasons, a server may provide a way to enable, disable, or limit support for CGI.

CGI Requests

A client can request a server to run a CGI program by sending an HTTP request containing the name of a CGI program on the server. In the Device Controller example in this chapter, the buttons on the Web page are hyperlinks that each contain a program name:

```
<a href="/led1toggle.cgi"> <img src="button.gif"> </a>
```

Clicking the image of the button causes the browser to request the server to run the program (or function) *led1toggle.cgi*.

Text hyperlinks are another way to request a server to run CGI programs. The following HTML code causes the text "Turn off LED1" to appear on a Web page as a hyperlink:

```
<a href="/led1off.cgi"> Turn off LED1> </a>
```

Clicking the hyperlink causes the browser to request the server to run the program *led1off.cgi*.

Servers also use CGI programming in accepting input from a Web page containing a form. Clicking a form's **Submit** button causes the form's data to be sent to the server in an HTTP GET or POST request. The server can be configured to respond to the request by running CGI code that processes the form data and returns a response.

Identifying and Running CGI Programs

CGI code may be an interpreted script, a compiled program, or a function within a program.

Large servers often store all CGI programs in a directory such as *cgi-bin*. Or a server may identify CGI programs by a *.cgi* extension in the program name. In Dynamic C, CGI programs can be functions declared as `HTTPSPEC_FUNCTION` items in an `HttpSpec` structure. Or an application can use the form-handling capabilities in Dynamic C's server utility library (*zserver.lib*) to process form data.

Returning a Response

A CGI program must return an HTTP response to the request that caused the server to run the program. Like other HTTP responses, the response includes a status line, response headers, and if appropriate, a message body. The response can provide requested information or acknowledge that submitted data was received. To enable a user to view the result of executing a CGI program, a response may contain a redirection code that advises the user's browser to refresh the current Web page.

In this chapter's Device Controller application for the Rabbit module, after a user clicks a button on the Web page, the browser requests a refreshed copy of the page so the user can see the LEDs' current states. To cause the browser to request to refresh the page, the server returns a response containing the following code in the response line, with the desired file name and path in a `Location` header:

```
Http 1.0 302 Found
Location: http://192.168.111.7/index.shtml
```

On receiving this response code in reply to a GET request, the browser sends a new GET request for the specified file. In case a browser doesn't support automatic redirection, many responses include a message body that displays a hyperlink to the file in the Location field and text that advises the user to click the link to view the file.

Servlets for Embedded Systems

For displaying real-time data and responding to user input, Java programmers can use servlets, as introduced in the TINI example in this chapter. A servlet is a Java class that adds capabilities to a server.

A Web server that runs servlet code must have a container, or servlet engine, to manage the servlets. The container provides network services for sending and receiving requests, decodes requests, and formats responses. For security, a container can also place restrictions on the execution of servlets.

A browser that requests a Web page served by a servlet doesn't require support for Java or servlets. When a browser sends a URL to a server, the browser doesn't have to know or care whether the URL identifies a static Web page or a servlet. The text that the browser sends to the server identifies the servlet. In the DeviceController example, the images of buttons are hyperlinks that users can click to request the server to run the servlet DeviceController:

```
<a href="/servlet/DeviceController?button1">
  <img src="button.gif"></a>
```

A mapping in the server's configuration file identifies /servlet/Device-Controller as a servlet, and button1 following the question mark is the query string that the browser returns to the server along with the requested URL.

On receiving a request for a servlet, the server runs the servlet code. The servlet can generate dynamic data, insert the data into a Web page, and write the Web page's contents to an output stream for sending to the client. A servlet can also do just about anything an ordinary Java program can do, such as making calculations, performing logical operations, and reading and writing to files or ports.

The document that defines servlets and their behavior is the Java Servlet Specification, available from *java.sun.com*.

On receiving an HTTP request containing the name of a servlet to run, the server passes the request to the servlet container. The container examines the request to determine which servlet to call. The container then calls the servlet, passing two objects: a request object with information about the request and a response object that will contain information about the response. A response object may supply an `OutputStream` or `PrintWriter` object that the servlet uses to respond to the request. The servlet runs, performing its programmed function and returning a response to the request.

The `HTTPServer` class in the TINI's `com.dalsemi.tininet.http` package supports static Web pages only. The Tynamo Web server and TiniHttpServer are more powerful alternatives that add support for servlets.

Receiving Form Data

In addition to providing information on Web pages, servers can receive information from users by hosting Web pages that contain forms. A form can contain text boxes or other elements where users can enter data or make selections. When the user clicks a form's **Submit** button, the browser sends the form data to the server in an HTTP GET or POST request. The server can use the data in any way. An embedded system might use a form to request configuration data, collect information about users, or request passwords. The server may return a page that acknowledges receiving the data or a response that redirects the user's browser to another page.

As Chapter 6 showed, the HTML standard includes tags and attributes for creating forms on a Web page. The examples below show how to host forms on Rabbit and TINI modules.

Figure 7-4 shows a form that enables the user to enter maximum and minimum temperatures for use in an alarm system. When a user clicks **Submit**, the browser sends the temperature values to the server in an HTTP request. On receiving the values, the server either returns the Web page in Figure 7-5 or a response that instructs the user's browser to request the page.

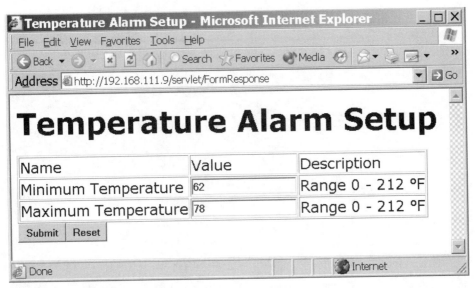

Figure 7-4: This Web page contains a form that enables users to enter values for use by the server.

A server could use the temperature values to configure a temperature alarm system. In a similar way, you can use forms in just about any application where the server wants to collect information via a Web page.

Listing 7-6 is the HTML code for the form. Every form has three elements: form tags that define the start and end of the form, one or more controls that enable users to provide data to the server, and a **Submit** button that enables users to send the data to the server. In addition, most forms include descriptive text and a **Reset** button that returns the inputs to the values they contained when the page was served (before the user made any changes).

In Listing 7-6, the opening tag of the form is:

```
<form action="/" method="post">
```

The FORM tag's action attribute names the URL where the browser will submit the form data when a user clicks the **Submit** button. In this example, the URL is "/", which refers to the server's default file. The method attribute's "post" value may be lower case in the HTML file. When the

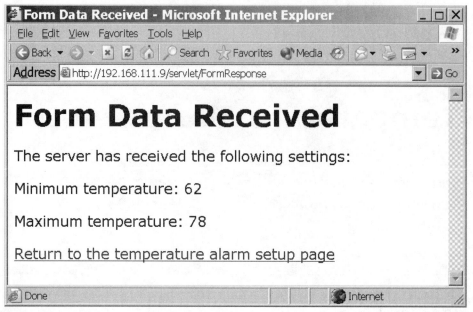

Figure 7-5: A server might return a page like this to acknowledge receiving form data from a user.

browser sends a request, POST is upper case as required by the HTTP standard.

The `method` attribute specifies whether the browser will use an HTML GET or POST request to send form data to the server. In a GET request, the browser appends the data to the URL being requested. In a POST request, the browser places the data in the body of the request.

The form's closing tag is `</form>`. Everything between the form's opening and closing tags is part of the form.

Listing 7-6's form uses an HTML table to format the information in the form. Each variable has a name, value, and description in the table. The names and descriptions are plain text, except for the degree symbol. The HTML code `&deg;` causes the browser to display a degree symbol.

The `input` tags determine the contents of the cells in the Value column. This example `input` tag has four attributes:

```
<input type="text" name="maximum_temperature"
```

```
<html>
<head><title>Temperature Alarm Setup</title></head>

<body>
<h1>Temperature Alarm Setup</h1>

<form action="/" method="POST">

<table border>

<tr>
<td>Name</td>
<td>Value</td>
<td>Description</td>
</tr>

<tr>
<td>Minimum Temperature</td>
<td><input type="text" name="minimum_temperature"
    value="72" maxlength="3"></td>
<td>Range 0 - 212 &deg;F</td>
</tr>

<tr>
<td>Maximum Temperature</td>
<td><input type="text" name="maximum_temperature"
    value="78" maxlength="3"></td>
<td>Range 0 - 212 &deg;F</td>
</tr>

</table>

<p>
<input type="submit" value="Submit">
<input type="reset" value="Reset">
</p>

</form>
</body>
</html>
```

Listing 7-6: HTML source code for Figure 7-4's form.

```
maxlength="3" value="80">
```

The value of the `type` attribute is set to `"text"` to specify that the input is a single-line text box or other input control for entering text. The `name` attribute identifies the control on the form. The `maxlength` attribute is the maximum number of characters a user may enter in the text box. The `value` attribute is the default data the text box displays.

In addition to text, a variety of other controls use `input` tags, including check boxes, radio buttons, passwords, **Submit** buttons, and **Reset** buttons. Every `input` tag must have a `value` attribute. All types except text (the default) must have a `type` attribute, and most tags require a `name` attribute. The other attributes needed vary with the input type and the application's requirements.

Two additional `input` tags in Listing 7-6 add **Submit** and **Reset** buttons to the form. For each, the `type` attribute specifies the button type and a `value` attribute specifies the text to display on the button. When a form has just one **Submit** button and one **Reset** button, the `type` attribute identifies the buttons and there's no need for `name` attributes to further identify the buttons.

Forms on a Rabbit

The RCM3200 RabbitCore module can host Figure 7-4's form. In the Device Controller example earlier in this chapter, an `#ximport` directive loads a file containing the Web page's HTML source code into the Rabbit-Core's memory. For forms, instead of providing an HTML file containing the form to serve, you can use functions in Dynamic C's server utility library, *zserver.lib*, to create a form from information provided in the application.

An advantage of using *zserver.lib* to create forms is its automatic handling of errors in user input according to limits you specify. A limitation of using *zserver.lib* is the need to use its 3-column table format, unless you modify the library's display handler.

The following code shows how an RCM3200 module can serve the Temperature Alarm form and response.

Initial Defines and Declarations

Again, much of the configuration code is similar to the code in previous examples. TCPCONFIG specifies a macro that sets a network configuration stored in the file *tcp_config.lib*. Your program must specify an appropriate macro for your system and network configuration, as described in Chapter 5.

```
#define TCPCONFIG 1
```

Because of the need for forms support, this program uses the ServerSpec structure defined in *zserver.lib*, which includes support for basic forms, instead of the HttpSpec structure in *http.lib*. When HttpSpec is unneeded, the HTTP_NO_FLASHSPEC directive saves code space.

```
#define HTTP_NO_FLASHSPEC
```

The FORM_ERROR_BUF directive is required for forms. The directive reserves memory for a buffer used in form processing and must be large enough to hold the name, value, and four additional bytes for each form variable.

```
#define FORM_ERROR_BUF 256
```

On receiving form data, the server redirects the client's browser to the URL specified in FORM_RESPONSE_REDIRECTTO. In this application, the URL points to a file that acknowledges receiving the form data. REDIRECTHOST is the _PRIMARY_STATIC_IP address defined in *tcp_config.lib*.

```
#define REDIRECTHOST _PRIMARY_STATIC_IP
#define FORM_RESPONSE_REDIRECTTO
   "http://" REDIRECTHOST "/formresponse.shtml"
```

All C functions not declared as root go to extended memory. The *dcrtcp.lib* library supports IP and TCP. The *http.lib* library supports HTTP functions.

```
#memmap xmem
#use "dcrtcp.lib"
#use "http.lib"
```

The #ximport directive loads a file from the development PC into the Rabbit's Flash memory. The directive associates the symbol form_response_shtml with the file's address in memory.

```
#ximport "c:/rabbitserver/formresponse.shtml"
   form_response_shtml
```

The `HttpType` structure specifies the handler to use with different file extensions. Web pages that contain SSI directives have the extension *.shtml* and use Dynamic C's SHTML handler. Plain HTML pages use the default HTML handler.

```
const HttpType http_types[] =
{
    { ".html", "text/html", NULL},
    { ".shtml", "text/html", shtml_handler}
};
```

Responding to Submitted Data

On receiving form data, the `form_response()` function executes and calls the `cgi_redirectto()` function. This function causes the server to return an HTTP response that redirects the client's browser to the Web page named in `FORM_RESPONSE_REDIRECTTO`.

```
int form_response(HttpState* state)
{
   cgi_redirectto(state, FORM_RESPONSE_REDIRECTTO );
   return 0;
} // end form_response()
```

The main() Function

The program's `main()` function creates the form, initializes the TCP/IP stack and Web server, and enters an endless loop that processes received HTTP requests and can perform any other tasks the system is responsible for.

The *zserver.lib* library includes a `ServerSpec` structure that has information about the files, functions, and variables that the server can access. The library contains functions that access elements in the structure. One of the items in the `ServerSpec` structure is an array of `FormVar` structures that hold information about a form's variables. This application has two form variables, so it defines an array (`setup`) that contains two `FormVar` structures. The `form`, `function`, and `var` variables are values returned by `ServerSpec` functions.

```
void main(void) {
  FormVar setup[2];
```

```
int form;
int function;
int var;
```

The `maximum_temperature` and `minimum_temperature` variables are the form variables that users can change.

```
int maximum_temperature;
int minimum_temperature;
maximum_temperature = 212;
minimum_temperature = 0;
```

Creating the Form

A series of `ServerSpec` functions sets up the form and configures the server to serve the form and the page sent in response to receiving form data.

Adding a Web page. The `sspec_addxmemfile()` function names the Web page that users will see after submitting form data:

```
sspec_addxmemfile ("formresponse.shtml",
   form_response_shtml, SERVER_HTTP);
```

The function has three parameters:

`"formresponse.shtml"` is the name of the file containing the Web page on the server.

`form_response_shtml` is the location where the `#ximport` directive stored the file.

`SERVER_HTTP` indicates that the file is valid for Dynamic C's HTTP server. (Dynamic C also supports `SERVER_FTP`).

The function returns the location of the file in the `ServerSpec` structure or -1 on failure.

Adding a Form. The `sspec_addform()` function adds a form to the `ServerSpec` structure:

```
form =
   sspec_addform ("setup.html", setup, 2, SERVER_HTTP);
```

The function has four parameters:

`"setup.html"` is the name of the form's Web page on the server.

`setup` is the `FormVar` array defined earlier.

2 is the number of entries in the `setup` array.

`SERVER_HTTP` indicates that the form is valid for Dynamic C's HTTP server.

The value returned, `form`, is the form's location in the `ServerSpec` array.

The `sspec_setformtitle()` function sets the title the form will display:

```
sspec_setformtitle(form, "Temperature Alarm Setup");
```

The function has two parameters:

`form` is the value returned by `sspec_addform()`.

`"Temperature Alarm Setup"` is the title.

The function returns zero on success or -1 on failure.

Adding a Function. The `sspec_addfunction()` function adds a function to the list of objects the Web server recognizes.

```
function = sspec_addfunction("form_response",
    form_response, SERVER_HTTP);
```

The function has three parameters:

`"form_response"` is the function's name.

`form_response` is a pointer to the function.

`SERVER_HTTP` indicates that the function is valid for Dynamic C's HTTP server.

The `function` value returned is the function's location in the `ServerSpec` structure or -1 on failure.

Adding a Function to Call on Receiving Form Data. The `sspec_setformepilog()` function names the function that the server will call after receiving form data from a client:

```
sspec_setformepilog(form, function);
```

The function has two parameters:

`form` is the value returned by `sspec_addform()`.

`function` is the value returned by `sspec_addfunction()`.

The function returns zero on success or -1 on failure.

Specifying Form Variables

Another series of ServerSpec functions adds variables to the form and sets a name, description, number of characters, and range for each.

Adding a Variable. The `sspec_addvariable()` function adds a variable to the `FormVar` array in the `ServerSpec` structure. This is the function call for the first variable:

```
var = sspec_addvariable("maximum_temperature",
    &maximum_temperature, INT16, "%d", SERVER_HTTP);
```

The function has five parameters:

`"maximum_temperature"` is the variable's name on the form.

`&maximum_temperature` is a pointer to the variable.

`INT16` is the variable type.

`"%d"` specifies the output format on the form as a decimal number.

`SERVER_HTTP` indicates that the variable is valid for Dynamic C's HTTP server.

The value returned, `val`, is the function's location in the `ServerSpec` structure or -1 on failure.

The `sspec_addfv()` function adds a variable in a `FormVar` array to the form.

```
var = sspec_addfv(form, var);
```

The function has two parameters:

`form` is the value returned by `sspec_addform()`.

`var` is the value returned by `sspec_addvariable()`.

The value returned, `var`, is the index of the added form variable or -1 on failure.

Associating a Name with a Variable. The `sspec_setfvname()` function sets the name the form will display for the variable.

```
sspec_setfvname(form, var, "Maximum Temperature");
```

The function has three parameters:

`form` is the value returned by `sspec_addform()`.

`var` is the value returned by `sspec_addfv()`.

`"Maximum Temperature"` is the name to display on the form.

The function returns zero on success or -1 on failure.

Adding a Variable Description. The `sspec_setfvdesc()` function sets a variable description that the form will display:

```
sspec_setfvdesc(form, var, "Range 0 - 212 &deg;F");
```

The function has three parameters:

`form` is the value returned by `sspec_addform()`.

`var` is the value returned by `sspec_addfv()`.

`"Range 0 - 212 &deg;F"` is the text the form will display in the Description column for the `"Maximum Temperature"` variable.

The function returns zero on success or -1 on failure.

Setting a Variable's Maximum Length. The `sspec_setfvlen()` function sets the maximum number of characters the form will accept and display for a variable's value:

```
sspec_setfvlen(form, var, 3);
```

The function has three parameters:

`form` is the value returned by `sspec_addform()`.

`var` is the value returned by `sspec_addfv()`.

`3` is the maximum number of characters.

The function returns zero on success or -1 on failure.

Setting a Variable's Range. The `sspec_setfvrange()` function sets a variable's minimum and maximum allowed values.

```
sspec_setfvrange(form, var, 0, 212);
```

The function has four parameters:

`form` is the value returned by `sspec_addform()`.

`var` is the value returned by `sspec_addfv()`.

`0` is the minimum value the server will accept for the variable.

`212` is the maximum value the server will accept for the variable.

If a user enters a value outside the specified range, the server adds an error message to the form and redirects the user's browser to the form so the user can change the value. The function returns zero on success or -1 on failure.

Adding More Variables. In the same way, calls to these functions add the minimum_temperature value to the form:

```
var = sspec_addvariable("minimum_temperature",
    &minimum_temperature, INT16, "%d", SERVER_HTTP);
var = sspec_addfv(form, var);
sspec_setfvname(form, var, "Minimum Temperature");
sspec_setfvdesc(form, var, "Range 0 - 212 &deg;F");
sspec_setfvlen(form, var, 3);
sspec_setfvrange(form, var, 0, 212);
```

Accessing the Form

The sspec_aliasspec() function enables requesting the form in alternate ways. In this example, in addition to requesting the file *setup.html* by its file name, users can request the file "index.html" or the default Web page at the IP address ("/").

```
sspec_aliasspec(form, "index.html");
sspec_aliasspec(form, "/");
```

Starting the Server

When the form has been created, the program is ready to initialize the TCP/IP stack and the Web server. As in the previous Rabbit HTTP example, calling tcp_reserveport() gives improved performance.

```
sock_init();
http_init();
tcp_reserveport(80);
```

The program's main loop calls http_handler() and can perform any other tasks the RCM3200 is responsible for. For example, for this application, the main loop might monitor temperatures and generate an alarm when a temperature is outside the minimum and maximum range specified on the form.

```
while (1) {
    http_handler();
}
```

```
} // end main()
```

Listing 7-7 is the HTML source code for the *formresponse.shtml* file in Figure 7-5. The page acknowledges receiving the form data and uses SSI #echo directives to display the temperature values received from the client.

When the RCM3200 module is running this program, users can access the form by entering the module's IP address or domain name in a browser's Address text box. Clicking the form's **Submit** button sends the temperature values to the RSM3200, which reads the values and either stores the values and returns an acknowledgment or returns an error message if either of the values is outside the accepted range.

Forms on a TINI

A TINI can serve Figure 7-4's form using the Tynamo Web server or another Web server with support for servlets. Listing 7-8 is the source code for the form when served by a TINI running a servlet. The only difference between the HTML code in Listing 7-6 and the form served by the TINI is the form tag's action attribute. For the TINI, form tag is:

```
<form method=POST action="/servlet/FormResponse">
```

When a user clicks the **Submit** button, the browser submits the form data to the servlet FormResponse on the server. The server's configuration file identifies /servlet/FormResponse as a servlet.

Requesting the Servlet

When the Tynamo Web server and FormResponse servlet are loaded into a TINI, users can request the TINI to run the servlet by entering the TINI's IP address or domain name followed by /servlet/ and the servlet's name:

```
http://192.168.111.9/servlet/FormResponse
```

Or the TINI can contain a static Web page with a link to the servlet:

```
<A HREF="/servlet/FormResponse">View the Form</A>
```

The FormResponse servlet serves the form with the current values of minimum_temperature and maximum_temperature inserted. On receiv-

```
<html>
<head>
  <title>Form Data Received</title>
</head>

<body>
  <h1>Form Data Received</h1>

  <p> The server has received the following settings: </p>
  <p> Maximum temperature: <!--#echo
      var="maximum_temperature"--></p>
  <p> Minimum temperature: <!--#echo
      var="minimum_temperature"--></p>
  <P><a href="index.html">Return to the temperature alarm setup
      page</a></p>
</body>

</html>
```

Listing 7-7: HTML code for Figure 7-5's Web page when served by a Rabbit module. SSI directives retrieve the temperature values received when the client submitted the form.

ing new values from a client, the servlet returns a Web page that acknowledges receiving the values.

On receiving an HTTP GET request for the FormResponse servlet, the servlet returns a Web page that displays the current minimum and maximum temperature settings and enables users to change the values by typing new ones and clicking **Submit**. On receiving form data in a POST request, the servlet checks for valid data. If the submitted data is valid, the servlet returns a page that acknowledges receiving the data. If the data isn't valid, the servlet returns the form with an error message and a request to retry.

The Servlet

As in the previous TINI example, to support servlets and HTTP, the program imports javax.servlet and javax.servlet.http classes for serv-

```
<html>
<head>
  <title>Temperature Alarm Setup</title>
</head>

<body>
  <h1>Temperature Alarm Setup</h1>

  <form method=POST action="/servlet/FormResponse">

  <table border>

  <tr>
    <td>Name</td>
    <td>Value</td>
    <td>Description</td>
  </tr>

  <tr>
    <td> Maximum Temperature </td>
    <td><input type="text" name="maximum_temperature"
        value=80></td>
    <td>Range 0 - 212 &deg;F</td>
  </tr>

  <tr>
    <td> Minimum Temperature </td>
    <td><input type="text" name="minimum_temperature"
      value=60></td>
    <td>Range 0 - 212 &deg;F</td>
  </tr>

  </table>

  <p></p>
  <p><input type="submit" value="Submit">
     <input type="reset" Value="Reset"></p>

  </form>
  </body>
  </html>
```

Listing 7-8: HTML source code for Figure 7-4's Web page using a servlet.

let support and `java.io` classes to support input and output functions. The `FormResponse` servlet extends the `HttpServlet` class.

```
import java.io.*;
import javax.servlet.*;
import javax.servlet.http.*;

public class FormResponse extends HttpServlet {
```

A DELAY_TIME constant determines how often the servlet executes a periodic task. The servlet uses the default values DEFAULT_MIN_TEMPERATURE and DEFAULT_MAX_TEMPERATURE if values previously set by the user aren't available. The *setup.bin* file stores the setup parameters from the setupParameters array. The timer thread enables the TINI to perform a task at timed intervals.

```
private static final int DELAY_TIME = 6000;
private static final int DEFAULT_MIN_TEMPERATURE = 0;
private static final int DEFAULT_MAX_TEMPERATURE = 212;
private static final String SETUP_FILE = "setup.bin";
private int[] setupParameters;
private volatile Thread timer;
```

The PeriodicTask class implements the Runnable interface so that the code that performs the periodic task can execute in its own thread. The class's run() method executes when FormResponse's init() method calls the start() method of the timer thread.

In this example, the run() method contains an endless loop that waits for the number of milliseconds in DELAY_TIME to elapse, then writes the minimum and maximum settings to the console. In a real-world application, the run() method might perform tasks such as communicating with a temperature controller or monitor that uses the minimum and maximum values.

```
private class PeriodicTask implements Runnable {

  public void run() {
    while (timer != null) {
      try {
        Thread.sleep(DELAY_TIME);
        System.out.print ("Minimum temperature = ");
        System.out.println (setupParameters[0]);

        System.out.print("Maximum temperature = ";
        System.out.println(setupParameters[1]);

      } catch (InterruptedException ex) {
```

```
        }
      }// end while (timer != null)
    } // end run()
  } // end PeriodicTask
```

The server calls `destroy()` after it takes a servlet out of service and all pending requests have either completed or timed out. A servlet should provide a `destroy()` method if it has acquired resources that won't otherwise be destroyed. In this example, the `destroy()` method stops the timer thread started by `PeriodicTask`'s `run()` method. Another reason to use a `destroy()` method is to save any data that the `init()` method might need next time and will otherwise be destroyed.

A call to `super.destroy()` calls the `destroy()` method of `Generic-Servlet` and writes a message to the log. The `destroy()` method then sets the `timer` thread to `null` and calls the thread's `interrupt` method. This generates an `InterruptedException` in `PeriodicTask`'s run method and terminates the thread.

```
public void destroy() {
  super.destroy();
  timer = null;
  timer.interrupt();
} // end destroy()
```

Servicing GET and POST Requests

The `doGet()` method calls the `sendSetupPage()` method, which returns a Web page with a form that enables users to view the current minimum and maximum temperature values and submit new ones. The parameters required for `sendSetupPage` are an `HttpServletResponse` object and either an error message to display on the page or `null` if there is no error message.

```
public void doGet( HttpServletRequest request,
    HttpServletResponse response)
    throws ServletException, IOException
{
  sendSetupPage (response, null);
} // end doGet()
```

The `doPost()` method receives and responds to data submitted on the form. On receiving values, the method checks to see if the values are within the specified ranges. If they are, the servlet returns a page that acknowledges receiving the data and stores the values in a file. If the values aren't acceptable, the servlet returns the form with an error message.

String variables hold the temperature values submitted on the form. Accepted values are stored as integers in the `setupParameters` array.

```
public void doPost(HttpServletRequest request,
  HttpServletResponse response)
    throws ServletException, IOException
{
  String minimumTemperature = null;
  String maximumTemperature= null;
  String errorMessage = null;
  int intMinimumTemperature = setupParameters[0];
  int intMaximumTemperature = setupParameters[1];
```

Calls to the `getParameter()` method of the `HttpServletRequest` object return the temperature values the client submitted on the form. The `Integer.parseInt` method converts the strings to integers. The server uses the integer values in determining whether the values are in the allowed ranges. An application that uses the values is also likely to want them in numeric form, rather than as strings.

For each value, the code tests to find out if the value is within the specified range. If not, an `errorMessage` string describes the problem.

```
minimumTemperature =
  request.getParameter("minimum_temperature");
if (minimumTemperature != null) {
  try {
    intMinimumTemperature =
      Integer.parseInt(minimumTemperature);
    if (intMinimumTemperature > 212 ||
      intMinimumTemperature < 0) {
      errorMessage = "Please try again: minimum
        temperature must be between 0 and 212.";
    }
  } catch (NumberFormatException e) {
    log("Invalid minimum temperature: ");
    log("minimumTemperature");

  }
} // end if (minimumTemperature != null)
```

```
maximumTemperature=
    request.getParameter("maximum_temperature");
if (maximumTemperature!= null) {
  try {
    intMaximumTemperature =
        Integer.parseInt(maximumTemperature);
    if (intMaximumTemperature > 212 ||
        intMaximumTemperature < 0) {
      errorMessage = "Please try again: maximum
          temperature must be between 0 and 212.";
    }
  } catch (NumberFormatException e) {
    log("Invalid max. temperature: ";
    log(maximumTemperature);


  }
} // end if (maximumTemperature!= null)
```

The code also checks to be sure that the minimum value submitted is less than the maximum. If not, an errorMessage string describes the problem.

```
if (intMinimumTemperature >= intMaximumTemperature) {
  errorMessage = "Please try again: the minimum
    temperature must be less than the maximum
    temperature.";
} // end if
```

The method then writes a Web page to the client. If the submitted values are acceptable, they're stored in the setupParameters array and a call to the sendAcknowledgementPage() method returns a Web page that acknowledges receiving the values. If the submitted values aren't acceptable, they aren't saved and a call to sendSetupPage() returns the form with the error message to advise the client to retry.

```
if (errorMessage == null) {
  setupParameters[0] = intMinimumTemperature;
  setupParameters[1] = intMaximumTemperature;
  log("New minimum temperature: " +
    minimumTemperature);
  log("New maximum temperature: " +
    maximumTemperature);
  sendAcknowledgementPage(response);
} else {
  sendSetupPage(response, errorMessage);
}
} // end  if (errorMessage == null)
```

Performing Tasks on Startup

The GenericServlet class includes an init() method that enables a servlet to perform tasks on startup. The init() method is called once, when the servlet starts, and is optional. In this example, init() calls the getSetupParameters() method to initialize the setup parameters and creates a thread that performs a periodic task.

```
public void init() throws ServletException {
    setupParameters = new int[2];
    getSetupParameters();
    timer = new Thread(new PeriodicTask());
    timer.start();
    System.out.println("The timer has started.");
    log("Timer started");
} // end init()
```

Saving and Retrieving Data in a File

The getSetupParameters() method retrieves the setup parameters from a file, if the file is available. Otherwise, the method uses the default values. A FileInputStream object attempts to read the parameters from the file whose name is stored in SETUP_FILE. The parameters are the first two values in the file.

```
private void getSetupParameters() {
    try {
        DataInputStream in = new DataInputStream
            (new FileInputStream(SETUP_FILE));
        int intMinimumTemperature = in.readInt();
        int intMaximumTemperature = in.readInt();
        setupParameters[0] = intMinimumTemperature;
        setupParameters[1] = intMaximumTemperature;
        try {
            in.close();
        } catch (IOException ex) {
        }
    } catch (FileNotFoundException ex) {
        log("Setup file not found");
        setupParameters[0] = DEFAULT_MIN_TEMPERATURE;
        setupParameters[1] = DEFAULT_MAX_TEMPERATURE;
    } catch (IOException ex) {
        log("Error reading from setup file", ex);
        setupParameters[0] = DEFAULT_MIN_TEMPERATURE;
        setupParameters[1] = DEFAULT_MAX_TEMPERATURE;
```

```
      }
   } // end getSetupParameters
```

The saveSetupParameters() method saves new setup parameters in the file whose name is stored in SETUP_FILE. A FileOutputStream object writes the values to the file. The parameters are the first two bytes in the file.

```
private void saveSetupParameters() {
   try {
      DataOutputStream out = new DataOutputStream
         (new FileOutputStream(SETUP_FILE));
      out.writeInt(setupParameters[0]);
      out.writeInt(setupParameters[1]);
      out.flush();
      out.close();
   } catch (IOException ex) {
      log("Error writing to setup file", ex);
   }
} // end saveSetupParameters
```

Acknowledging Received Form Data

The sendAcknowledgementPage() method sends a Web page to the client to acknowledge receiving submitted form data. The doPost method calls sendAcknowledgementPage() if the submitted data was accepted. A call to saveSetupParameters() stores the new data in a file. The setContentType() method of the HttpServletResponse object sets the Content-Type field of the HTML header in the returned. page. A ServletOutputStream object writes the Web page to the client.

The Web page displays the received values and also includes a hyperlink that enables the user to return to the setup page.

As in the previous TINI example, all quotation marks (") in the HTML code of the page being sent must be preceded by a back slash (\).

```
private void sendAcknowledgementPage
   (HttpServletResponse response)
      throws IOException
{
   saveSetupParameters();
   response.setContentType("text/html");
   ServletOutputStream out = response.getOutputStream();
   out.print ("<html>"
         + "<head>"
```

```
        + "<title> Form Data Received </title>"
        + "</head>"
        + "<body>"
        + "<h1> Form Data Received </h1>"
        + "<p>"
        + "The server has received the following
            settings:"
        + "</p>"
        + "<p>"
        + "Minimum temperature: ");
    out.print (setupParameters[0]);
    out.print ("</p>"
        + "<p> Maximum temperature: ");
    out.print (setupParameters[1]);
    out.print ("</p>"
        + "<p>"
        + "<a href=\"/servlet/FormResponse\">"
        + "Return to the temperature alarm setup page</a>"
        + "</p>"
        + "</body>"
        + "</html>");
} // end sendAcknowledgementPage
```

Sending the Form

The sendSetupPage() method sends a Web page containing a form where the client can enter minimum and maximum temperature settings. The method uses the HttpServeletResponse object and the error message, if any, generated on examining previously submitted values.

The method calls getSetupParameters() to retrieve the values to display on the form. The setContentType() method of the HttpServletRe-sponse object sets the Content-Type field of the HTML header in the returned page. A ServletOutputStream object writes the Web page to the client.

```
    private void sendSetupPage(HttpServletResponse
      response, String errorMessage)
        throws IOException
    {
      getSetupParameters();
      response.setContentType("text/html");
      ServletOutputStream out = response.getOutputStream();
      out.print ("<html>"
          + "<head>"
```

```
          + "<title>Temperature Alarm Setup</title>"
          + "</head>"
          + "<body>"
          + "<h1>Temperature Alarm Setup</h1>"
          + "<form method=POST action=
              \"/servlet/FormResponse\">"
          + "<table border>"
          + "<tr>"
          + "<td>Name</td>"
          + "<td>Value</td>"
          + "<td>Description</td>"
          + "</tr>"
          + "<tr>"
          + "<td> Minimum Temperature </td>"
          + "<td><input type=\"text\" name=
              \"minimum_temperature\" maxlength=3 value=");
     out.print (setupParameters[0]);
     out.print (">"></td>"
          + "<td>Range 0 - 212 &deg;F</td>"
          + "</tr>"
          + "<tr>"
          + "<td> Maximum Temperature </td>"
          + "<td><input type=\"text\" name=
              \"maximum_temperature\" maxlength=3 value=");
     out.print (setupParameters[1]);
     out.print (">"></td>"
          + "<td>Range 0 - 212 &deg;F</td>"
          + "</tr>"
          + "</table>");
     if (errorMessage != null)
       {
       out.print ("<p>" + errorMessage + "</p><p>");
       }
     out.print ("<input type=\"submit\"
         value=\"Submit\">"
          + "<input type=\"reset\" Value=\"Reset\">"
          + "</form></body>"
          + "</html>");
   } // end sendSetupPage()

 } // end FormResponse
```

8

E-mail for Embedded Systems

E-mail's primary use, of course, is to enable humans to send and receive messages over a network. But many embedded systems can make good use of e-mail as well. E-mail can be a convenient way for an embedded system to exchange information with humans or even communicate with other embedded systems with no human intervention at all.

For example, a security system can be programmed to send a message when an alarm condition occurs. Or a data logger might send a message once a day with the logger's readings for the previous 24 hours. In the other direction, an embedded system might receive e-mail containing new configuration settings or other commands, requests, or data.

E-mail has a couple of advantages over other methods of communication. Recipients can retrieve and read their messages whenever they want. And if the information isn't time-critical, the sender might find it easier or more efficient to place the information in an e-mail and send it off when convenient, rather than having to respond in real time to requests for the information. Another advantage is that an account with e-mail access alone can be less expensive than an account that supports hosting a Web server or performing other TCP/IP communications.

A down side to e-mail is that recipients might not receive information as quickly as needed if they don't check their e-mail regularly or if an e-mail server at either end gets backed up and delays delivery.

This chapter begins with examples that show how a Rabbit and TINI can send and receive e-mail messages. The In Depth section has more about obtaining and using e-mail accounts for embedded systems and the protocols used to exchange e-mail on the Internet.

Quick Start: Sending and Receiving Messages

The examples that follow demonstrate how a Rabbit and TINI can send e-mail using the Simple Mail Transfer Protocol (SMTP) and receive e-mail using the Post Office Protocol 3 (POP3).

Dynamic C includes support for e-mail protocols in Rabbit modules. A TINI can send e-mail using Java's URL class and a protocol handler that takes care of many of the details involved in communicating with an SMTP server. For receiving e-mail, a TINI can use TCP/IP to establish a connection with a mail server's socket and exchange e-mail using the protocols supported by the server.

Sending e-mail requires the name of an SMTP server that will accept the e-mail and deliver or forward it toward its recipient. As discussed later in this chapter, the SMTP server may be at the ISP that provides the embedded system's Internet connection or at the host for the embedded system's domain name.

In a similar way, receiving e-mail requires the name of the POP3 server at the ISP or domain host that stores e-mails sent to the embedded system's mailbox. To access the mailbox, the embedded system generally must provide the account's user name and password.

The hosts of the SMTP and POP3 servers can provide the server names to use in communicating with the servers.

If the program code contains a domain name rather than an IP address for an SMTP or POP3 server, the embedded system must have a specified DNS server to request the corresponding IP address from. See Chapter 5 for more about using DNS servers with a Rabbit or TINI.

The example applications send e-mails that contain unchanging text messages and write the contents of received e-mails to the console (the STDIO window in Dynamic C or a Telnet session for the TINI). In real-world applications, the embedded system can place any kind of information in the e-mails to send and can use the information in received e-mails in any way.

Sending an E-mail from a Rabbit

Dynamic C's *smtp.lib* library contains functions that greatly simplify the code required to program a Rabbit module to send e-mail. The firmware defines strings for the sender's e-mail address, the recipient's e-mail address, the Subject line, and the message body. The smtp_sendmail() function then uses these values in initializing the data structures used in sending the e-mail in the format expected by the SMTP server. The smtp_mailtick() function handles communications with the mail server, and smtp_status() returns a status code when the e-mail has been sent or an error occurs.

The code that follows is an application that sends an e-mail.

Initial Defines and Declares

As explained in Chapter 5, the firmware selects a network configuration from *tcp_config.lib*.

```
#define TCPCONFIG 1
```

SENDER is the rabbit's e-mail address and SMTP_SERVER is the name of the SMTP server that will accept the e-mail and forward it toward its recipient.

You must change these values to values appropriate for your device's e-mail account and SMTP server.

```
#define SENDER      "rabbit1@Lvr.com"
#define SMTP_SERVER "mail.example.com"
```

In initiating communications with an SMTP server, the client sends a HELO command that identifies the client. By default, the Rabbit firmware sends the Rabbit's IP address as an identifier. Some mail servers require a domain name rather than an IP address. For communicating with these servers, SMTP_DOMAIN can set a domain name to send.

```
#define SMTP_DOMAIN "Lvr.com"
```

The SMTP_DEBUG macro causes all communications with the server to be displayed in the Dynamic C's STDIO window. This feature can be very helpful in debugging.

```
#define SMTP_DEBUG
```

As in the previous examples, the #memmap directive causes all C functions not declared as root to be stored in extended memory. The code requires the *dcrtcp.lib* library to support TCP/IP and the *smtp.lib* library for SMTP communications.

```
#memmap xmem
#use dcrtcp.lib
#use smtp.lib
```

Creating the Message

Variables hold the recipient's e-mail address, the e-mail's subject line, and the message body. The create_message() function sets the contents of these elements for the e-mail to be sent.

```
char recipient[64];
char subject[64];
char body[256];

void create_message() {
  strcpy(recipient, "jan@lvr.com");
  strcpy(subject, "Hello from Rabbit");
  strcpy(body, "Rabbit test message.");
}
```

Sending the Message

The `main()` routine calls the `create_message` function to compose the message then calls `sock_init()` to initialize the TCP/IP stack. The `smtp_sendmail()` function initializes internal data structures with the strings in `create_message()`. A `while` loop calls `smtp_mailtick()` repeatedly to perform communications with the SMTP server. When the server returns a value other than `SMTP_PENDING`, the `while` loop ends and the STDIO window displays the status message returned by `smtp_status()`.

```
void main()
{
  create_message();
  sock_init();

  smtp_sendmail(recipient, SENDER, subject, body);

  while(smtp_mailtick()==SMTP_PENDING)
    continue;

  switch (smtp_status())
  {
    case SMTP_SUCCESS:
     printf("The message has been sent.\n");
     break;
    case SMTP_TIME:
     printf("Timeout error. Message not sent.\n");
       break;
    case SMTP_UNEXPECTED:
     printf("Invalid response from mail server.
       Message not sent.\n");
       break;
    default:
       printf("Error. Message not sent.\n");
  }
} // end main()
```

Additional Options

The default timeout value for communications with the SMTP server is 20 seconds. The `SMTP_TIMEOUT` macro can specify a different number of seconds:

```
#define SMTP_TIMEOUT 30
```

To send a message body from a memory location instead of a string, use Dynamic C's `smtp_sendmailxmem()` function in place of `smtp_sendmail()`. Instead of a string containing the message body, the function requires the message body's starting location in memory and the message length.

Sending an E-mail from a TINI

One way to send an e-mail from a TINI is to write or obtain an SMTP client program that establishes a connection with an SMTP host and sends commands and data as needed to communicate with the host. Another option is to use the `java.net.URL` class with a protocol implementer for the URL *mailto* scheme. (See Chapter 4 for more about URL schemes.) The protocol implementer automatically handles many of the details of SMTP communications.

The TINI software supports *mailto* via `com.dalsemi.protocol.*` and `com.dalsemi.protocol.mailto.*` classes. The source code that supports *mailto* is in the file *ModulesSrc.jar*, in the \src directory of the TINI distribution. The following SendEmail program uses *mailto* to send an e-mail.

Imports and Initial Declares

The class imports `java.io` classes for input and output functions and `java.net` classes for networking functions. The `com.dalsemi.protocol.mailto.*` classes are required to support the URL class's *mailto* protocol.

The TINI's From address shouldn't change, so it's stored in the static string `MAILFROMADDRESS`. You'll need to change this value to match the address of your TINI's mailbox.

```
import java.io.*;
import java.net.*;
import com.dalsemi.protocol.mailto.*;

public class SendEmail {

   final String MAILFROMADDRESS = "tini1@Lvr.com";
```

Creating the Message

The `main()` method sets the values of three strings used in an e-mail: the recipient's e-mail address (`mailToAddress`), the Subject line (`message-Subject`), and the message body (`messageBody`). These values are passed to the `SendEmail` object `mySendEmail`.

```
public static void main(String args[])
{
   String mailToAddress = "jan@Lvr.com";
   String messageSubject = "Hello from TINI";
   String messageBody = "Test message.";

    SendEmail mySendEmail = new SendEmail(mailTo,
         subject, message);

} // end main()
```

The constructor for `SendEmail` calls the class's `send()` method to send an e-mail using the three values specified in `main()`.

```
SendEmail(String mailToAddress, String messageSubject,
     String messageBody) {
   send(mailToAddress, messageSubject, messageBody);
} // end SendEmail constructor
```

Sending the E-mail

The `send()` method does the work of sending the e-mail. The `mailURL` object is a URL object that contains the sender's and recipient's e-mail addresses in this format:

`mailto:`*mailToAddress*`?from=`*mailFromAddress*

where *mailToAddress* is the receiver's e-mail address and *mailFromAddress* is the TINI's e-mail address.

```
private void send(String mailToAddress,
     String messageSubject, String messageBody) {

   try {

      URL mailURL = new URL("mailto:" + mailToAddress +
          "?from=" + MAILFROMADDRESS);
```

The `mailConnection` object represents a connection to the SMTP server that will receive the e-mail being sent to the address in `mailTo`. The `openConnection()` method prepares to communicate with the SMTP server.

```
Connection mailConnection =
    (Connection)mailURL.openConnection();
mailURL.openConnection();
```

A `Printstream` object writes to the connection.

```
PrintStream output = new
    PrintStream(mailConnection.getOutputStream());

System.out.println("Sending the email...");
```

In sending an e-mail, the From and To headers are added automatically using the strings in `MAILFROMADDRESS` and `mailToAddress`. The application provides the Subject line, the required blank line (\r\n) between the end of the headers and the beginning of the message body, and the message body. The required period on a line by itself, which indicates the end of the message, is added automatically on calling the `Printstream` object's `close()` method.

```
output.print("Subject: ");
output.print(messageSubject);
output.print("\r\n\r\n");
output.print(messageBody);
output.print("\r\n");

output.close();
System.out.println("The message has been sent.");
```

A `MalformedURLException` error occurs on attempting to create a URL object with incorrect URL syntax or an unsupported scheme. An `IOException` occurs on an error writing to the `PrintStream` object.

```
} catch (MalformedURLException e) {
System.err.print("MalformedURLException: ");
System.err.println(e.getMessage());
} catch (IOException e) {
System.err.print("IOException: ");
System.err.println(e.getMessage());
}
} // end send()

} // end SendEmail
```

Adding the MAILTO Dependency to the Build

Building the SendEmail application requires a few additional considerations to enable using the *mailto* protocol handler. The build process requires `com.dalsemi.protocol` and `com.dalsemi.protocol.mailto` classes in *modules.jar*.

When compiling *SendEmail.java* to *SendEmail.class*, you must include the location of *modules.jar* in the bootclasspath. Here is an example command line (which you can place in a batch file) for compiling *SendEmail.java* to *Send.Email.class*:

```
javac -bootclasspath ..\..\bin\tiniclasses.jar;
    ..\..\bin\modules.jar SendEmail.java
```

When converting *SendEmail.class* to *SendEmail.tini,* use the BuildDependency utility instead of TiniConvertor. Like TiniConverter, BuildDependency converts *.class* files to *.tini* files, but BuildDependency can also specify dependencies. Here is an example command line for converting *SendEmail.class* to *Send.Email.tini*:

```
java -classpath ..\..\bin\tini.jar;%classpath%
BuildDependency -f SendEmail.class -o SendEmail.tini
-d ..\..\bin\tini.db -add MAILTO -p ..\..\bin\modules.jar
```

The `-add` option adds the MAILTO dependency to the project, and the `-p` option names the location of `modules.jar`.

BuildDependency is in the file *tini.jar.* To view the available options, run BuildDependency with no parameters.

Specifying the SMTP Host

To send an e-mail, you need to name an SMTP host that will receive and deliver or forward the e-mail being sent. The SendEmail application above doesn't contain this information. There are two ways to provide it. You can set the mail host in the ipconfig utility, using the `-h` option. For example:

```
ipconfig -h mail.example.com
```

Or you can provide the name in the command line that runs the program. For example:

```
java -Dmail.host=mail.example.com SendEmail.tini &
```

where *mail.example.com* is the name of the SMTP server.

A mail host specified in the command line overrides a mail host set in ipconfig.

To prevent having to type a long command line each time you run the program, create a text file that contains the command-line text, copy the file to the TINI, and run the command line by typing:

```
source filename
```

where *filename* is the name of the text file.

Receiving E-mail on a Rabbit

For retrieving e-mail from a server, Dynamic C includes the *pop3.lib* library. As with sending e-mail, the support library greatly simplifies the application code required to receive an e-mail. The following program demonstrates how a Rabbit can retrieve an e-mail. The program displays the messages in the STDIO window.

Initial Defines and Declares

As explained in Chapter 5, a TCPCONFIG macro selects a network configuration from *tcp_config.lib*. POP_HOST is the URL or IP address in dotted-quad format of the POP3 mail host for the rabbit's mailbox. POP_USER and POP_PASS are the user name and password for the rabbit's e-mail account. You must change these values to values appropriate for your system's e-mail account.

```
#define TCPCONFIG 1

#define POP_HOST   "mail.example.com"
#define POP_USER   "rabbit1"
#define POP_PASS   "embedded"
```

The POP_PARSE_EXTRA macro is optional, but convenient. It performs additional processing of received messages, storing the contents of the To, From, and Subject fields and the message body in separate strings.

```
#define POP_PARSE_EXTRA
```

As in the other Rabbit applications, the #memmap directive causes all C functions not declared as root to be stored in extended memory. The *dcrtcp.lib* library supports TCP/IP and the *pop3.lib* library supports POP3 communications.

```
#memmap xmem
#use "dcrtcp.lib"
#use "pop3.lib"

int current_message;
```

Processing and Displaying Messages

The store_message() function is a callback function that receives and processes downloaded messages. The function has several parameters with information about a received message. The message_number value is the number of the message in the series of messages being retrieved. The to, from, and subject strings contain the contents of the corresponding fields in an e-mail's header. The body_line string contains a line of text in the message body, and body_length is the length of body_line.

The function is called when headers or a line of text in a message body have been received.

```
int store_message(int message_number, char *to,
    char *from, char *subject, char *body_line,
    int body_length)
{
```

Statements in a program's #GLOBAL_INIT section are called only once, on program startup. In this example, the #GLOBAL_INIT section initializes the current_message variable.

```
#GLOBAL_INIT
    {
        current_message = -1;
    }
```

If the message number of a retrieved message (message_number) is different than the stored value in current_message, the function sets current_message equal to message_number and displays the message's headers in the STDIO window.

If `message_number` is the same as `current_message`, the headers have already been displayed, so there's no need to repeat them.

```
if(current_message != message_number) {
   current_message = message_number;
   printf("MESSAGE <%d>\n", current_message);
   printf("FROM: %s\n", from);
   printf("TO: %s\n", to);
   printf("SUBJECT: %s\n", subject);
}
```

The function writes a line of the message body to the STDIO window and returns.

```
   printf("%s\n", body_line);
   return 0;
}
```

Retrieving Messages

The program's `main()` function calls `sock_init()` to initialize the TCP/IP stack and then calls `pop3_init()` to specify the callback function that will process the contents of received e-mails.

```
void main()
{
   static long mail_host_ip;
   static int response;

   sock_init();
   pop3_init(store_message);
```

A call to resolve(POP_HOST) returns a `long` value containing the IP address of the specified mail host.

```
   printf("Resolving the mail host's name...\n");
   mail_host_ip = resolve(POP_HOST);
```

The `pop3_getmail()` function initiates retrieving e-mail for the account specified by POP_USER and POP_PASS from the server specified in `mail_host_ip`. The function calls `pop3_tick()` repeatedly until it returns a response other than POP_PENDING to indicate that the mail retrieval is complete or has returned an error code.

```
   pop3_getmail(POP_USER, POP_PASS, mail_host_ip);
   printf("Receiving e-mail...\n\n");
```

```
while((response = pop3_tick()) == POP_PENDING)
    continue;
```

A `switch` block displays a message that describes the result returned by `pop3_tick()`, and the program ends.

```
switch(response)
{
  case POP_SUCCESS:
  printf("\nThe messages have been retrieved.\n");
  break;
 case POP_TIME:
  printf("Timout error.\n");
  break;
 case POP_ERROR:
  printf("General error.\n");
  break;
 default:
   printf("Undefined error.\n");
}
} // end send_email
```

Additional Options

Two additional macros, POP_DEBUG and POP_NODELETE, can be useful in some situations.

For debugging, calling POP_DEBUG causes all communications with the POP3 server to display in Dynamic C's STDIO window.

```
#define POP_DEBUG
```

After downloading an e-mail message, the Rabbit normally sends a POP3 DELE command to request the server to delete the message on the server. After calling POP_NODELETE, the Rabbit no longer sends the DELE command, and most servers will retain the messages after the Rabbit has downloaded them.

```
#define POP_NODELETE
```

If the application doesn't require the contents of the From, To, and Subject in separate strings, don't define POP_PARSE_EXTRA and provide only these three parameters to the callback function: the message number, a pointer to a line of text, and the length of the text.

Receiving E-mail on a TINI

A TINI can also retrieve e-mail from a POP3 server. However, the TINI has no built-in support for POP3 communications. One option is to obtain a module with POP3 support. Or you can provide the support by writing an application that sends and responds to POP3 commands. The following application connects to a mail server, downloads any messages in the mailbox, and writes the status information and the messages to `System.out` for viewing in a Telnet session. The In Depth section of this chapter has more details about the POP3 commands the application sends.

Imports and Initial Declares

The program imports `java.net` classes for networking functions and `java.io` classes to support the input and output functions. The `java.util` package contains the `StringTokenizer` class used in reading received responses from the mail server.

The default port for POP3 servers is 110.

You must change the `USERNAME`, `PASSWORD`, and `MAILHOST` strings to match the user name, password, and the POP3 mail host for the TINI's mailbox. The mail host can be a domain name such as *mail.example.com* or an IP address in dotted-quad format.

```
import java.io.*;
import java.net.*;
import java.util.*;

public class ReceiveEmail {

  public static final int POP3PORT = 110;

  private final String USERNAME = "tini1";
  private final String PASSWORD = "ethernet";
  private final String MAILHOST = "mail.example.com";

  private BufferedReader input;
  private PrintWriter output;
  private Socket pop3Socket;

  private String mailHost;
  private String userName;
```

```
private String password;
```

The Constructor

The class's constructor uses the values passed to it to set corresponding variables.

```
public ReceiveEmail(String mailHost, String userName,
    String password) {
  this.mailHost = mailHost;
  this.userName = userName;
  this.password = password;
} // end ReceiveEmail constructor
```

Requesting Messages

The main() method sets the deleteOnServer variable and calls the retrieveEmails() method, which carries out the class's purpose. Set deleteOnServer true to request the mail server to delete messages after downloading, or false to request the server to retain the messages.

```
public static void main(String[] args) {

  boolean deleteOnServer = false;
  ReceiveEmail myReceiveEmail = new ReceiveEmail
      (MAILHOST, USERNAME, PASSWORD);
  myReceiveEmail.retrieveEmails(deleteOnServer);

} // end main()
```

The retrieveEmails() method calls routines to log on to the mail host, get the number of messages waiting, and read and display the messages.

The Socket object pop3Socket connects to the specified mail server's POP3 port. The Socket class's setSoTimeout() method enables setting a timeout in milliseconds for waiting for data from the POP3 host. A timeout causes a java.io.InterruptedIOException.

```
private void retrieveEmails(boolean deleteOnServer) {

  int socketTimeout = 10000;
  String response;
  try {
    System.out.print("Connecting to ");
    System.out.println(MAILHOST);
    pop3Socket = new Socket(MAILHOST, POP3PORT);
```

```
pop3Socket.setSoTimeout(socketTimeout);
```

Reading Messages

A `BufferedReader` object reads input from the mail host, and a `Print-Writer` object writes to the mail host. `PrintWriter`'s `autoFlush` property is set to `true` to cause each `println` to automatically flush the output buffer, sending the text to the server.

On establishing a connection, the mail server returns +OK.

```
input = new BufferedReader(new InputStreamReader
    (pop3Socket.getInputStream()));
output = new PrintWriter
    (pop3Socket.getOutputStream(), true);

response = input.readLine();
if (response.startsWith("+OK")) {
  System.out.println("Connected to the mail host.");
```

If the connection was established, the `logOntoMailHost()` method attempts to log on. On success, the `getNumberOfMessages()` method returns the number of messages in the mailbox. If one or more messages are available, the `getMessages()` method retrieves them. The `closeConnectionWithServer()` method closes the connection with the mail host and is in a `finally` block to ensure that it executes before the method ends.

```
    if (logOntoMailHost()) {

      int numberOfMessages = getNumberOfMessages();
      if (numberOfMessages > 0) {
        getMessages(numberOfMessages, deleteOnServer);
      } else {
        System.out.println("No messages in mailbox.");
      }

    } else {
      System.out.print("Error in connecting to the
          mail host: ");
      System.out.println(response);
    }

  } // end if (response.startsWith("+OK"))
```

```
  } catch(IOException e) {
    System.err.print("IO exception: ");
    System.err.println(e.getMessage());
  } finally {
    closeConnectionWithServer();
  }
} // end retrieveEmails
```

Logging onto the Mail Host

The `logOntoMailHost()` method uses the provided user name and password to attempt to log on to the mail host and gain access to the user's mailbox. The POP3 protocol defines USER and PASS commands for providing these values. When a command succeeds, the mail host returns +OK. The method returns `true` if the logon was successful and `false` if it failed.

```
private boolean logOntoMailHost() throws IOException {

  String response;

  output.println("USER " + USERNAME);
  response = input.readLine();

  if (!(response.startsWith("+OK"))) {
    System.out.print("Password error: ");
    System.out.println(response);
    return false;
  }

  output.println("PASS " + PASSWORD);
  response = input.readLine();

  if (!(response.startsWith("+OK"))) {
    System.out.print("User name error: ");
    System.out.println(response);
    return false;
  }

    System.out.println("Logged on to the mail
        server.");
    return true;
} // end logOntoMailHost
```

Getting the Number of Messages

The `getNumberOfMessages()` method sends a POP3 STAT command to retrieve the number of messages in the mailbox and the number of bytes in the messages.

The response to the STAT command begins with +OK, followed by the number of messages and the total number of bytes in the messages. The String-Tokenizer object st extracts tokens, consisting of the text up to a delimiter such as a space or new-line character. The `hasMoreTokens()` method indicates whether a token is available for reading. If the first token equals +OK, the tokenizer extracts the tokens that follow. The method returns the number of messages or -1 on an error.

```
private int getNumberOfMessages() throws IOException {
    int numberOfMessages = 0;
    int numberOfBytes = 0;

    String response;
    output.println("STAT");
    response = input.readLine();
    System.out.println("STAT response = " + response);

    StringTokenizer st = new StringTokenizer(response);
    if (st.hasMoreTokens()) {
        if (!(st.nextToken().equals("+OK"))) {
            return -1;
        }
    }

    if (st.hasMoreTokens()) {
        numberOfMessages =
            Integer.parseInt(st.nextToken());

        if (st.hasMoreTokens()) {
            numberOfBytes =
                Integer.parseInt(st.nextToken());
        }
    }

    System.out.print("The mailbox has " );
    System.out.print(numberOfMessages);
    System.out.print(" messages in ");
    System.out.print(numberOfBytes);
    System.out.println(" bytes.");
```

```
        return numberOfMessages;
    } // end getNumberOfMessages
```

Retrieving and Displaying Messages

The getMessages() method retrieves the messages, displays them, and if deleteOnServer is true, requests the mail host to delete the retrieved messages when the connection closes.

```
    private void getMessages(int numberOfMessages,
        boolean deleteOnServer) throws IOException {
    String response;

        System.out.println ("Retrieving e-mail...");
```

A for loop steps through each message up to numberOfMessages, retrieving each in turn.

```
    for(int messageNumber = 1; messageNumber <=
        numberOfMessages; messageNumber++) {

    System.out.print("Retrieving message ");
    System.out.print(messageNumber);
    System.out.print(" of ");
    System.out.print(numberOfMessages);
```

The POP3 RETR command requests a specific message from the mail host. If the mail host's response begins with +OK, the BufferedInput object reads lines from the mail host until detecting a period on a line by itself, which indicates the end of the message.

A message body that contains a line with only a period will have an additional period added to the beginning of the line. The startsWith() method checks to see if the response string begins with a period. If it does, the substring() method removes the first period.

The received lines are written to the standard output stream and display in the window of a Telnet session.

```
        output.print("RETR ");
        output.println(messageNumber);

        response = input.readLine();
```

```
    if (!(response.startsWith("+OK"))) {
      System.out.print("Error reading response: ");
      System.out.println(response);
      return;
    }

    response = input.readLine();
    while(!response.equals(".")) {
      if (response.startsWith(".")) {
        response = response.substring(1);
      }
      System.out.println(response);
      response = input.readLine();
    }
```

If deleteOnServer is true, a POP3 DELE command followed by the message number requests the mail host to delete the just-retrieved message on the server.

```
    if(deleteOnServer) {
      output.print("DELE ");
      output.println(messageNumber);

      response = input.readLine();
      if (!(response.startsWith("+OK"))) {
        System.out.print("Error deleting messages: ");
        System.out.println(response);
        return;
      }
    }
  } // end for loop

  return;
} // end getMessages()
```

Closing the Connection

The closeConnectionWithServer() method closes the connection with the mail server. A POP3 QUIT command informs that server that communications are complete, and the socket's close() method closes the connection.

```
  private void closeConnectionWithServer() {
    if(pop3Socket != null) {
      try {
        output.println("QUIT");
```

```
        pop3Socket.close();
        System.out.println("The connection with the mail
            server is closed.");

      } catch(IOException e) {
        System.err.print("IO exception: ");
        System.err.println(e.getMessage());
      }
    }
  } // end closeConnectionWithServer()

} // end ReceiveEmail
```

In Depth:
E-mail Protocols

The examples above showed how embedded systems can use SMTP and POP3 to send and receive e-mail. This section has more about the protocols and how to use them in embedded systems.

How E-mail Works

To send and receive e-mails on the Internet, an embedded system (or any computer) must have the following:

* A connection to the Internet.

* An e-mail account with an address in the form *user_name@domain*. In the e-mail address *rabbit1@Lvr.com*, *Lvr.com* is the domain that hosts the e-mail account and *rabbit1* is the user name that identifies the owner of the account in the domain. The user also selects a password required to gain access to the account's mailbox.

* Access to incoming and outgoing mail servers. The incoming mail server accepts and stores e-mail addressed to the account and enables the user to retrieve received messages. The outgoing mail server accepts and delivers or forwards any mail the user sends.

* Support for TCP/IP and the protocols used by the mail servers in sending and retrieving e-mail. Two widely supported protocols are the Simple Mail Transfer Protocol (SMTP) for sending e-mail to a server that will

forward the e-mail toward its recipient and the Post Office Protocol Version 3 (POP3) for retrieving received e-mail from a mailbox on a server.

E-mail Accounts for Embedded Systems

An e-mail account used by an embedded system is no different from an e-mail account that anyone might use. However, in obtaining e-mail accounts, there are considerations that are specific to embedded systems.

Embedded systems tend to have limited processing power and fewer resources compared to larger computers. This means that e-mail communications should use protocols that aren't overly complex, to avoid overwhelming system resources. And second, embedded systems are likely to use their e-mail without human intervention, so they need to use protocols that enable composing, sending, retrieving, and reading messages entirely under firmware control. In other words, a Web-based e-mail account designed for users who will log onto a Web page and click through various screens to view and send messages isn't the best choice for an embedded system. An account that enables the embedded system to communicate using POP3 and SMTP commands alone is a better choice for most embedded applications.

If your embedded system will receive e-mails, you want to take special care to ensure that the e-mail address remains private. Don't give the account an easily guessed user name such as *info* or *webmaster*. And don't post the address on a Web page, because spammers will harvest the address and inundate the account with e-mails that the embedded system will have to plow through to find any valid correspondence.

Domain Hosts and ISPs

In many cases, the user or manager responsible for an account contracts with an ISP to provide everything required for Internet access, including an Internet connection, the option to set up one or more e-mail addresses, and the ability to send and receive e-mail using the ISP's mail servers. With this type of account, the ISP provides the domain name in the e-mail address and the user selects a user name that is unique to the domain.

But a user (which can be an embedded system) can also have different sources for Internet access and an e-mail account. Businesses and other entities that own a domain name often contract with a domain-hosting company for e-mail services, including the ability to create multiple e-mail addresses for the domain. Embedded systems in the domain *Lvr.com* might have the e-mail addresses *rabbit1@Lvr.com*, *rabbit2@Lvr.com*, and so on. The domain host provides a mail server that accepts and stores e-mail sent to the domain's e-mail addresses and enables the owners of the e-mail addresses to retrieve the messages on request.

ISPs generally have local connections for their customers, but a domain host doesn't have to be located physically near the computers that use the domain's e-mail accounts. To retrieve a domain's e-mail, a user may use a local ISP to gain access to the Internet and then communicate over the Internet with the domain host's mail server.

If your domain host and ISP are different entities, you need to decide which provider's mail host to use for sending e-mail. Sometimes you have a choice. In other cases, only one mail server, either at the ISP or at the domain host, will work.

The first issue in deciding what mail host to use is that the computer sending the e-mail and the mail host receiving it must support the same protocol. Embedded systems are likely to use SMTP, while some ISPs support only Web-based e-mail or other proprietary protocols.

If the sending computer's ISP doesn't have an available SMTP server to communicate with, the embedded system might be able to use a mail server at the domain host instead.

However, some domain hosts have implemented security measures that senders of e-mail need to be aware of. The security is needed because SMTP doesn't support authentication of users using passwords. A local ISP can require computers to identify themselves on connecting by providing a user name and password or a hardware identifier such as the Ethernet address of a network card or modem. The ISP can use this information to determine whether a connected computer is authorized to use the ISP's mail server.

An SMTP mail server at a domain host accessed via the Internet doesn't have information about the users who are accessing the server. Allowing anyone to use an SMTP server leaves the server open to abuse. So some hosts have implemented a type of authorization called POP-before-SMTP. This method requires a user to obtain temporary authorization to send e-mail by first checking the account for incoming e-mail. After checking for e-mail, the user is authorized to use the provider's server to send e-mail for a limited time, such as 15 minutes. After the authorization expires, the user needs to check for incoming e-mail again to regain authorization to send e-mail. If your domain host uses POP-before-SMTP authorization, your embedded system will need to comply with this protocol in order to send e-mail.

Another problem with accessing external mail servers is that some ISPs block all traffic to port 25, which is SMTP's default port, to prevent users from sending e-mail via external SMTP servers. If your ISP follows this practice and you want to use your domain host's SMTP server, check with the domain host to see if you can access their server on another port.

When you sign up for an e-mail account that uses POP3 and SMTP, the host provides the names of its incoming and outgoing mail servers. For example, the POP3 server for incoming mail might be *mail.example.com* and the SMTP server might be *smtp.example.com*. You select a user name and password, and you or the provider specifies the domain name in the e-mail address. On a PC, you can typically view the server names in your e-mail program, under **Accounts, Options**, or a similar menu item.

In the same way, an embedded system uses an account's user name, domain name, password, and servers in sending and receiving e-mail. The system's firmware can compose messages to send and parse received messages to extract the desired information.

Using the Simple Mail Transfer Protocol

The Simple Mail Transfer Protocol (SMTP) defines a reliable and efficient way of transferring e-mail to a server. Its command-and-reply protocol is basic enough to be feasible for small systems to support.

To send an e-mail, an SMTP client sends a series of commands to establish communications with an SMTP server and then sends the e-mail message for the server to deliver to its recipient or forward to another server for delivery. On receiving a command from a client, the server returns a reply code and may return a reply message or additional requested information. SMTP communications typically use TCP, but TCP isn't required.

The document that defines SMTP is RFC 2821: *Simple Mail Transfer Protocol.*

A Typical Transaction

Below is a typical session where a client establishes a connection, sends an e-mail, and closes the connection.

1. The client and server establish a TCP connection with the server's SMTP port.

Server: 220

2. The client identifies itself to the server.

Client: HELO Lvr.com
Server: 250

3. The client provides the e-mail address of the sender.

Client: MAIL FROM <rabbit1@Lvr.com>
Server: 250

4. The client provides the e-mail address of the recipient.

Client: RCPT TO: <jan@example.com>
Server: 250

5. The client sends the e-mail's contents, including headers and ending with a period on a line by itself.

Client: DATA
Server: 354
Client: From: rabbit1@Lvr.com
Client: To: jan@example.com
Client: Subject: Hello from Rabbit
Client: (blank line between e-mail header and message body)

Client: Rabbit test message.
Client: .
Server: 250

6. The client notifies the server that it's ready to close the session.

Client: QUIT
Server: 221

7. The client and server close the TCP connection.

SMTP Commands and Reply Codes

SMTP supports eleven commands for establishing communications, sending e-mail, requesting information about the server, and closing communications. Some commands have required or optional parameters. For example, with a HELO command, the client provides its domain name or IP address. After receiving a command, the server returns a 3-digit reply code. Many servers also include a text message after the reply code. For example, on receiving a QUIT command, a server at *example.com* might reply with the following reply code and text message:

```
221 example.com closing transmission channel
```

Some commands, such as HELP, request information, which the server provides following the reply code.

The SMTP standard says that the commands aren't case sensitive, but in violation of the standard, some mail servers require commands to be upper case, so using upper case is safest.

Each command and reply ends in the pair of ANSI characters 0Dh 0Ah, which is a carriage return/line feed pair, often abbreviated as CRLF. In print functions in program code, this pair is often expressed as \r\n.

The Commands

The following are the eleven SMTP commands, with an explanation and example for each:

DATA

Purpose: Announces that all of the data that follows, up to the end-of-mail indicator, is the e-mail message.

Parameters: none

Reply code on success: 354, then 250 after receiving the end-of-message indicator (a period on a line by itself).

Example:

Client: `DATA`

Server: `354`

Client: `Hello,`

Client: `This is a test message.`

Client: `.`

Server: `250 OK`

EHLO

Purpose: Opens communications, identifies the client, and requests information about the server. In a multi-line reply, all but the last line have a hyphen after the reply code. Some older servers support only HELO, not EHLO. Clients may use HELO, though EHLO is recommended.

Parameters: the client's domain name or IP address in dotted-quad format

Reply code on success: 250

Example:

Client: `EHLO Lvr.com`

Server: `250-example.com greets Lvr.com`

Server: `250-8BITMIME`

Server: `250-SIZE`

Server: `250-DSN`

Server: `250 HELP`

EXPN

Purpose: requests the server to verify that the parameter identifies a mailing list and returns the e-mail addresses of the list's members. In a multi-line reply, all but the last line have a hyphen after the reply code. Servers aren't required to support this command.

Parameter: *<the mailing list to expand>*

Reply code on success: 250 or 252

Example:

Client: `EXPN example-list`

Server: `250-<jsmith@example1.com>`
Server: `250 <rjones@example2.com>`

HELO

Purpose: Opens communications and identifies the client.
Parameter: the client's domain name or IP address in dotted-quad format
Reply code on success: 250
Example:
  Client: `HELO 192.0.2.1`
  Server: `250 OK`

HELP

Purpose: Requests additional information. Servers aren't required to support this command.
Parameter: [*string that names a HELP topic*]
Reply code on success: 211 or 214
Example:
  Client: `HELP`
  Server: `211` *help information*

MAIL

Purpose: Initiates a transaction that sends e-mail to the server.
Parameter: `FROM:` <*sender's e-mail address*>
Reply code on success: 250
Example:
  Client: `MAIL FROM: <tini1@Lvr.com>`
  Server: `250 OK`

NOOP

Purpose: No operation. Verifies that the server is receiving commands.
Parameter: none
Reply code on success: 250
Example:
  Client: `NOOP`
  Server: `250 OK`

QUIT

Purpose: Requests the server to close the connection.

Parameter: none
Reply code on success: 221
Example:
  Client: `QUIT`
  Server: `221 example.com closing transmission channel`
  Client and Server then close the connection.

RST

Purpose: Requests the server to cancel the current transaction and reset all buffers and state tables relating to the transaction. If the server hasn't yet acknowledged the end-of-data indicator for a message, the server discards all information relating to the message.
Parameter: none
Reply: 250
Example:
  Client: `RST`
  Server: `250 OK`

RCPT

Purpose: Identifies the e-mail's recipient.
Parameters: `TO:` *<sender's e-mail address>*
Reply code on success: 250 or 251
Example:
  Client: `RCPT TO: <rabbit1@Lvr.com>`
  Server: `250 OK`

VRFY

Purpose: Requests the server to verify that the parameter identifies the user or mailbox.
Parameter: the user's e-mail address
Reply: 250 *<user's e-mail address>*
Example:
  Client: `VRFY tini1`
  Server: `250 <tini1@Lvr.com>`

The Reply Codes

Table 8-1 lists the reply codes an SMTP server can return. If the reply code begins with 2, the command was successful. If the reply code begins with 3, the command was successful and the server is waiting for additional data. If the reply code begins with 5, the server didn't accept the command or carry out the requested action and the client needs to take action to correct the command before retrying.

Requirements for an SMTP Client

If your embedded system uses SMTP client code such as Dynamic C's *smtp.lib* or a *mailto* protocol handler in Java, you generally don't have to worry about the details of programming the SMTP transactions. If you're programming at a lower level, the client's program code must meet the requirements of the SMTP standard. In addition, every e-mail message must meet certain requirements.

The Client

Every SMTP client must be capable of the following:

1. The client must send the appropriate commands for establishing communications, sending e-mail, and closing communications. The minimum commands to send a message are HELO or EHLO, followed by MAIL, RCPT, DATA, and QUIT. The commands must be sent in this order.

2. The client must read received reply codes and take appropriate action, which may include retrying the command or closing the session.

3. The client must implement a timeout for receiving a reply from a command. The SMTP standard recommends timeout values ranging from 2 to 10 minutes for different operations. For example, the minimum recommended timeout for receiving a reply after sending an end-of-message indicator is 10 minutes, to allow the server time to process the message. Clients can specify other reasonable timeout values, however. If a server fails to respond and a timeout occurs, about all the client can do is close the connection and retry.

Table 8-1: An SMTP server returns one of these reply codes after receiving a command.

Reply Code	Description
211	System status or reply to HELP command.
214	Help message.
220	*domain* Service ready.
221	*domain* Service closing transmission channel. (Reply to QUIT command.)
250	Requested mail action okay and completed.
251	User is not local. Will forward to *forward path*.
252	Cannot verify user, but will accept message and attempt delivery.
354	Start the mail input.
421	*domain* Service not available, closing transmission channel.
450	Requested mail action not taken: mailbox not available (busy).
451	Requested action aborted: local error in processing.
452	Requested action not taken: insufficient system storage.
500	Syntax error, command not recognized.
501	Syntax error in parameters or arguments.
502	Command not implemented.
503	Bad sequence of commands.
504	Command parameter not implemented.
550	Requested action not taken: mailbox not available.
551	User not local; please try *forward path*.
552	Requested mail action aborted: exceeded storage allocation.
553	Requested action not taken: mailbox name not allowed (incorrect syntax).
554	Transaction failed.

4. The client must be sure that the message doesn't include a line with a period on a line by itself, which is the end-of-message indicator. If the message contains a line that begins with a period, the sender must add another period to the beginning of the line. On receiving a line of message text, an e-mail client checks to see if the line begins with a period. If it does, and if the line contains one or more additional characters, the receiver strips the period at the beginning of the line, returning the message line to its original contents.

For many embedded systems, received messages have a standard, application-specific format, and the format can be defined so that a message body never contains a period on a line by itself. In this case, the client doesn't have to worry about checking for message lines that begin with periods.

Messages

In addition to the requirements for the server, RFC standards specify requirements for e-mail messages.

The SMTP standard specifies maximum lengths that all SMTP servers must support. A user name may be up to 64 characters. A domain name may be up to 255 characters. A line in a message may be up to 1000 characters, including the two end-of-line characters. And a message may be up to 64 kilobytes. Servers must support at least these "minimum maximums," and can support larger maximums.

The document *RFC 2822: Internet Message Format* specifies the format for text messages sent as e-mail. A message consists of the following elements in order:

headers
blank line
message body

Each header field has the following format:

field_name:field_body\r\n

where *field_name* is the field's name (such as From), *field_body* is the field's contents (such as rabbit1@Lvr.com), and \r\n signifies a CRLF sequence.

The two header fields required by the specification are From and Date. From identifies the sender. Date is the date that the sender put the message into its final form. Other headers such as To and Subject are optional. Dynamic C's SMTP client automatically inserts From, To, and Subject headers using the parameters provided to the smtp_sendmail() and smtp_sendmailxmem() functions.

Not every embedded system that wants to send e-mail includes a real-time clock for obtaining Date information. A message without a Date field will reach its recipient as long as the recipient's software doesn't care that the field is missing.

The recommended format for the Date field is:

```
Date: <day> <month> <year> <time of day> <time zone>
```

or

```
Date: <day of week>, <day> <month> <year> <time of day> <time zone>
```

The month and optional day of the week are given as 3-letter abbreviations. The time is in hours and minutes since midnight. The year must use four digits. The time zone should be local.

For example,

```
Date:  11 Oct 2003 14:52 CST
```

or

```
Date: Mon, 5 Jun 2003 12:01 EST
```

For information on standard ways to send non-text information such as images or audio, see the MIME specifications in RFC 2045, 2046, and 2049.

Performance Issues

If your device has time-critical tasks to perform at the same time as it's sending e-mail, it's best to place the code that communicates with the SMTP server in its own thread or task, so the CPU can do other things while waiting for the server to respond.

Sending E-mail with a URL

Another option for sending e-mail is to use a URL with the *mailto* scheme. Chapter 4 introduced URLs and schemes such as *http*, *ftp*, and *mailto*. The scheme identifies the protocol that a browser or other software will use in sending the request specified in the URL.

When you click a typical *mailto* link on a Web page, the browser creates a new e-mail message in the PC's default e-mail program and fills in the To:

header with the `mailto` address. A user can then compose and send a message to that address.

As the TINI example in this chapter showed, embedded systems can use the *mailto* protocol to send e-mail messages created in firmware. In Java, the URL class represents a URL, and a protocol implementer for the *mailto* scheme handles the details of communicating with an SMTP server. A basic URL that uses the *mailto* scheme has the following form:

```
mailto:tini1@Lvr.com
```

RFC 2368: The mailto URL scheme extends the *mailto* URL scheme defined in RFC1738. Under RFC2368, a *mailto* URL can also contain one or more headers and even the message body. For example, to include a From: address, use this format:

```
mailto:jan@Lvr.com?from:tini1@example.com
```

A question mark separates the recipient's e-mail address and the From: header.

Use & to concatenate additional headers and the message body. For example:

```
mailto:jan@Lvr.com?from:tini1@example.com&
    subject:greeting&body:hello%20from%20TINI!
```

Characters that are reserved in HTML and in this URL scheme must be encoded. Encode a space (as in the message body above) as `%20`. Encode a question mark (?) as `%3`, an ampersand (&) as `&amp`, a percent sign (%) as `%25`, and a line break in the message body as `%0D%0A`.

Using the Post Office Protocol

SMTP enables a computer to send e-mail. A complementary protocol is the Post Office Protocol Version 3 (POP3), which enables a computer to download e-mail from a server.

The standard that defines POP3 is *RFC 1939: Post Office Protocol - Version 3*, the third edition of the protocol first described in RFC 918.

As with SMTP, in a POP3 communication, a client sends a series of commands to a server and the server returns a response to each command. POP3 communications travel in TCP segments. The default port for POP3 communications is 110.

The POP3 standard defines twelve commands. Some commands have required or optional parameters that follow the command.

Every POP3 response begins with a status indicator: +OK on success and -ERR to respond to a command that is not recognized, not implemented, or has incorrect syntax. For some commands, requested information may follow the status indicator, and a server may provide additional text to explain the status. The status indicators are always upper case.

The POP3 standard defines three states in a session. After a TCP connection has been established and the server has sent a greeting, the session is in the Authorization state. After the client identifies itself and the server has acquired resources associated with the client's mailbox, the session is in the Transaction state. In this state, the client has exclusive access to the mailbox and the client can request services from the server. After the client has sent a QUIT command, the session is in the Update state. The server releases resources associated with the client, deletes messages marked for deleting, and returns a response. The client and server then close the TCP connection.

A newer and more flexible alternative to POP3 is the Interactive Mail Access Protocol (IMAP) defined in RFC 1730. IMAP enables a user to select messages to download, move files among multiple mailboxes on the server, and share a mailbox with other clients. IMAP also has more efficient handling of MIME attachments. For the needs of a typical embedded system, however, POP3's capabilities are sufficient and easier to implement.

A Typical POP3 Transaction

Below is a typical session where a client establishes a connection, retrieves an e-mail, and closes the connection.

1. The client and server establish a TCP connection with the server's SMTP port.

  Server: +OK

2. The client sends a user name.

Client: USER tini1
Server: +OK

3. The client sends a password.

Client: PASS ethernet
Server: +OK

4. The client requests a listing of the number of messages in the mailbox and the total number of bytes in the messages.

Client: STAT
Server: +OK 1 856

5. The client requests to retrieve message 1.

Client: RETR 1
Server: +OK
Server: *the message contents*
Server: .

6. The client notifies the server that it's ready to close the session.

Client: QUIT
Server: +OK

7. The client and server close the TCP connection.

POP3 Commands

The following are POP3's twelve commands. The commands are case-insensitive. All servers must support seven of the commands and the rest are optional, as noted.

APOP

Purpose: requests user authentication using a method that doesn't require transmitting an unencrypted password. To obtain the required MD5-digest-string parameter, the client applies the MD5 algorithm described in RFC 1321 to the timestamp in the server's greeting and a secret string shared by the client and server. For a specific mailbox, a server generally supports either PASS or APOP.
Servers required to support: no

Parameters: *user_name <MD5_digest_string>*
Reply on success: +OK
Example:
 Client: APOP jan *<16-byte string in hexadecimal format>*
 Server: +OK

DELE

Purpose: requests to mark a message for deleting. Normally, users will want to delete retrieved messages to prevent filling the mailbox and retrieving the same messages over and over. A server may also delete retrieved messages automatically, even if the client doesn't send a DELE command, or a server may delete messages that have been retrieved but not deleted after a specified time limit.
Servers required to support: yes
Parameters: *message_number*
Reply on success: +OK
Example:
 Client: DELE 4
 Server: +OK message 4 deleted

LIST

Purpose: requests a scan listing containing the number of bytes in the requested message or all messages if no message number is specified.
Servers required to support: yes
Parameters: [*message_number*]
Reply on success: +OK *number_of_message number_of_bytes*
If there are multiple messages, the server returns a multi-line reply.
Example:
 Client: LIST 2
 Server: +OK 2 130

NOOP

Purpose: no operation. Indicates that the connection to the server is valid.
Servers required to support: yes
Parameters: none
Reply on success: +OK
Example:
 Client: NOOP

Server: +OK

PASS

Purpose: Provides a password for authentication. For a specific mailbox, a server generally supports either PASS or APOP.
Servers required to support: yes
Parameters: *password*
Reply on success: +OK
Example:
  Client: PASS embedded
  Server: +OK

QUIT

Purpose: requests the server to delete all messages marked for deleting and close the connection.
Servers required to support: yes
Parameters: none
Reply on success: +OK
Example:
  Client: QUIT
  Server: +OK

RSET

Purpose: unmark any messages marked for deleting
Servers required to support: yes
Parameters: none
Reply on success: +OK
Example:
  Client: RESET
  Server: +OK

RETR

Purpose: requests a message.
Servers required to support: yes
Parameters: *message_number*
Reply on success: +OK *number_of_bytes* followed by the message and ending in a period on a line by itself
Example:

Client: RETR 5
Server: +OK 212 octets
      message contents
      .

STAT

Purpose: requests a drop listing containing the number of messages in the mailbox and the total number of bytes in the messages.
Servers required to support: yes
Parameters: none
Reply on success: +OK *number_of_messages number_of_byte*s
Example:
  Client: STAT
  Server: +OK 2 508

TOP

Purpose: requests a message's headers plus the specified number of the message's top lines.
Servers required to support: no
Parameters: *message_number number_of_lines_to_receive*
Reply on success: +OK
Example:
  Client: TOP 2 3
  Server: +OK
  Server: From: tini2@Lvr.com
  Server: To: controlcenter@Lvr.com
  Server: Subject: Status Report
  Server: Date: 28 Jul 2003 10:21 CST
  Server: Subject: HighTemp=101
  Server: Subject: LowTemp=13
  Server: Subject: MedianTemp=56
  Server: .

UIDL

Purpose: requests a unique-id listing for one or all messages. The unique id is a string specified by the server and consisting of one to 70 characters in the range 21h to 7Eh. The value identifies a message in the user's mailbox and persists across sessions.

377

Servers required to support: no
Parameters: [*message_number*]
Reply on success: +OK *message_number unique_id*
If there is no message number, the server returns a multi-line reply with information about each message in turn.
Example:
  Client: UIDL 3
  Server: +OK 3 *unique-id for message 3*

USER

Purpose: provides a user name for authentication.
Servers required to support: no
Parameters: *user_name*
Reply on success: +OK
Example:
  Client: USER tini1
  Server: +OK

Requirements for a Client

Every POP3 client must be capable of the following:

1. The client must send the appropriate commands for establishing communications, retrieving e-mail, and closing communications. The minimum commands to check for mail and retrieve messages from a mailbox protected with a user name and password are USER, PASS, STAT, RETR, and QUIT. The commands must be sent in this order.

2. The client must read received replies and take appropriate action on receiving an -ERR reply.

3. The POP3 standard doesn't talk about timeouts, but a client application will probably want to time out and close the connection if the server fails to respond to a command within a reasonable time.

4. A line of message text that begins with a period transmits with an extra period at the beginning to prevent the line from appearing as an end-of-message indicator. In receiving a line that begins with a period, the client should check to see if the line contains one or more additional charac-

ters. If it does, the client should strip the first period from the line and consider the line part of the message, not the end-of-message indicator.

Some embedded application can define a standard, application-specific format that doesn't allow a period on a line by itself in received messages. In this case, the client doesn't have to worry about checking for message lines that begin with periods.

Messages

As explained earlier in this chapter, RFC standards specify requirements for e-mail messages. The receiver of an e-mail can use the standard header fields to filter messages by sender or subject.

Performance Issues

If your device has time-critical tasks to perform at the same time it's receiving e-mail, it's best to place the code that communicates with the POP3 server in its own thread or task so the CPU can do other things while waiting for the server to respond.

Chapter 8

9

Using the File Transfer Protocol

The previous chapters have shown several ways that an embedded system can send and receive information on networks. The options have included applications that send messages using UDP and TCP, Web pages with dynamic content, and e-mail. Another possibility that some systems can find useful is the File Transfer Protocol (FTP), which defines a way for computers to send and receive information stored in files.

This chapter includes examples that show how the Rabbit and TINI can function as FTP servers and FTP clients, followed by details about FTP and its capabilities.

Quick Start:
FTP Clients and Servers

The Rabbit and TINI modules each include FTP support that helps in using a module as an FTP client or server. For the Rabbit, Dynamic C's *ftp.lib* and *ftp_server.lib* libraries provide functions for transferring information in files. For the TINI, support is available in the URL and URLConnection classes and in the TINI's FTPClient and FTPserver classes.

A Rabbit or TINI client application can communicate with just about any FTP server, in a local network or on the Internet. And you can use just about any standard FTP client application or a command-line interface to access files hosted by a Rabbit or TINI FTP server.

The example applications send text files and write the contents of received files to the console (the STDIO window in Dynamic C or a Telnet session for the TINI). In real-world applications, the embedded system can place any kind of information in the files to send and can use the information in received files in any way.

Rabbit FTP Client

The following examples show how a Rabbit can exchange files with an FTP server. A Dynamic C application can use one of two sources for files to send and receive. Many basic applications can store the files in buffers in root memory. For transferring large amounts of data, for generating a file's contents on request, or for processing received data on receipt, a data-handler callback function can receive requested files or generate files to send.

Retrieving a File

This example shows how a Rabbit module can retrieve a file, store its contents in a buffer, and write the contents of the file to Dynamic C's STDIO window.

Initial Defines and Declares

As explained in Chapter 5, a `TCPCONFIG` macro selects a network configuration.

```
#define TCPCONFIG 1
```

Various parameters enable communicating with a specific FTP server. You must change `REMOTE_HOST`, `REMOTE_USERNAME`, `REMOTE_PASSWORD`, `REMOTE_FILE`, and `REMOTE_DIR` to values appropriate for the FTP server your Rabbit will communicate with.

`REMOTE_HOST` is the domain name or IP address of the remote FTP server. `REMOTE_PORT` is the port on the FTP server to connect to. Set this value to zero to connect to the default port for the FTP control connection (21). `REMOTE_USERNAME` and `REMOTE_PASSWORD` are the user name and password that enable access to a user area on the FTP server.

```
#define REMOTE_HOST     "ftp.example.com"
#define REMOTE_PORT     0
#define REMOTE_USERNAME "embedded"
#define REMOTE_PASSWORD "ethernet"
```

Additional values specify the directory to change to on connecting to the FTP server (`REMOTE_DIR`) and the name of the file the Rabbit will retrieve (`REMOTE_FILE`). Set `REMOTE_DIR` to `"/"` to specify the server's root directory.

```
#define REMOTE_DIR      "/usr/embedded/"
#define REMOTE_FILE     "testfile.txt
```

If `USE_PASSIVE` is defined, `PASSIVE_FLAG` is set to `FTP_MODE_PASSIVE`, which causes the Rabbit to request to use FTP's passive mode in opening the data channel for file transfers. Passive mode can be useful when communicating through a firewall. The In Depth section of this chapter has more on passive mode.

```
#define USE_PASSIVE

#ifdef USE_PASSIVE
  #define PASSIVE_FLAG  FTP_MODE_PASSIVE
#else
  #define PASSIVE_FLAG  0
#endif
```

The `#memmap xmem` directive causes all C functions not declared as root to be stored in extended memory. The *dcrtcp.lib* library supports TCP/IP, and *ftp_client.lib* supports FTP client communications.

```
#memmap xmem
#use "dcrtcp.lib"
#use "ftp_client.lib"
```

The `file_buffer` array holds the retrieved file and should be large enough to hold any file being requested.

```
char file_buffer[2048];
```

The main() Routine

The `main()` routine begins by calling `sock_init()` to initialize the TCP/IP stack. The `retrieve_file()` function then requests a file from the remote FTP server. If `retrieve_file()` fails, it returns 1 and the program ends with an error code of 1. On success, the `main()` routine returns zero.

```
int main()
{
   int return_value;
   return_value = sock_init();
   if (return_value == 0) {
     printf("Network support is initialized.\n");
     }
   else {
     printf("The network is not available.\n");
     exit(2);
   }

   if (retrieve_file()) {
     exit(1);
   }
   return 0;
} // end main()
```

Requesting a File

The `retrieve_file()` function requests the file and returns zero on success.

```
int retrieve_file()
{
```

```
longword file_size;
int byte_in_file;
int return_value;
```

```
printf("Preparing to download %s...\n", REMOTE_FILE);
```

The `ftp_client_setup()` function initiates the request for the file. Nine parameters provide the information required to request the transfer. The `REMOTE_HOST`, `REMOTE_USERNAME`, `REMOTE_PASSWORD`, `REMOTE_FILE`, `REMOTE_DIR`, and `file_buffer` parameters are defined above.

The `FTP_MODE_DOWNLOAD` constant specifies that the Rabbit wants to retrieve (rather than send) a file. A logical OR of this value with `PASSIVE_FLAG` causes the Rabbit to request to use passive mode if `USE_PASSIVE` was defined earlier. The `sizeof(file_buffer)` parameter is the length of the buffer that will contain the retrieved file.

```
return_value = ftp_client_setup(
   resolve(REMOTE_HOST),
   REMOTE_PORT,
   REMOTE_USERNAME,
   REMOTE_PASSWORD,
   FTP_MODE_DOWNLOAD|PASSIVE_FLAG,
   REMOTE_FILE,
   REMOTE_DIR,
   file_buffer,
   sizeof(file_buffer));
```

The function returns zero on success. The function fails if the host address is zero, if `sizeof(file_buffer)` is negative, or if there are no available socket buffers to open an internal control socket to the FTP server. If the function fails, the program ends with an exit code of 1.

```
if (return_value != 0) {
   printf("FTP setup failed.\n");
   exit(1);
}
```

The `ftp_client_tick()` function manages communications with the FTP server. The function returns zero while pending, 1 on success, and a value from 2 to 6 to indicate an error. The program loops until the function returns a non-zero value.

```
printf("Looping on ftp_client_tick()...\n");
while( 0 == (return_value = ftp_client_tick()) );
```

On success, a call to the `ftp_client_xfer()` function returns the size of the file retrieved. Dynamic C's STDIO window displays the file size and the contents of the file.

On failure, a `printf()` statement displays an error message. A call to `ftp_last_code()` returns the most recent message code returned by the FTP server.

```
if( 1 == return_value ) {
   file_size = ftp_client_xfer();
   printf("The file has been received.
     File size: %d bytes.\n", file_size);

   printf("Contents of file:\n");
   for (byte_in_file = 0; byte_in_file <=
        (file_size - 1); byte_in_file++)
   printf("%c",file_buffer[byte_in_file]);
   printf("\n");
   return 0;
} else {
   printf("FTP download failed: status = %d, last code =
        %d\n", return_value, ftp_last_code());
   return 1;
}
} // end retrieve_file
```

Sending a File

In a similar way, a Rabbit can use the *ftp.lib* library to send a file to an FTP server.

Initial Defines and Declares

Much of the program code is similar to the previous example, including these initial statements that provide system-specific and application-specific information for the transfer and name the libraries the program uses. You must change REMOTE_HOST, REMOTE_USERNAME, REMOTE_PASSWORD and REMOTE_DIR to values appropriate for the FTP server your Rabbit will communicate with.

```
#define TCPCONFIG 1
#define REMOTE_HOST      "ftp.example.com"
#define REMOTE_PORT      0
#define REMOTE_USERNAME  "embedded"
```

```
#define REMOTE_PASSWORD  "ethernet"
#define REMOTE_DIR       "/usr/embedded/"
#define REMOTE_FILE      "testfile.txt"
#define USE_PASSIVE

#ifdef USE_PASSIVE
  #define PASSIVE_FLAG    FTP_MODE_PASSIVE
#else
  #define PASSIVE_FLAG    0
#endif

#memmap xmem
#use "dcrtcp.lib"
#use "ftp_client.lib"
```

The `file_buffer` array holds the data that the Rabbit will transfer in a file. This example uses a small 10-byte buffer.

```
char file_buffer[10];
```

The main() Function

The `main()` function calls `create_file()` to place data in the array that will be sent as a file to the FTP server. A call to `sock_init()` initializes the TCP/IP stack. If the initialization fails, the program ends with an error code of 2. The `send_file()` function sends the file. If the attempt to send the file fails, the program ends with an error code of 1. On success, the program returns zero.

```
int main()
{
  int return_value;
  create_file();

  return_value = sock_init();
  if (return_value == 0) {
    printf("Network support is initialized.\n");
    }
  else {
    printf("The network is not available.\n");
    exit(2);
  }
  if (send_file())
    exit(1);
  return 0;
} // end main()
```

Creating the File

For this example, the data in the file is the string `"test data"`, terminating in a null character (`\0`). Of course, a file can contain any text or binary data.

```
create_file(void) {
   file_buffer[0]='t';
   file_buffer[1]='e';
   file_buffer[2]='s';
   file_buffer[3]='t';
   file_buffer[4]=' ';
   file_buffer[5]='d';
   file_buffer[6]='a';
   file_buffer[7]='t';
   file_buffer[8]='a';
   file_buffer[9]='\0';
} // end create_file
```

Sending the File

As in the `retrieve_file()` function in the previous example, the `send_file()` function calls `ftp_client_setup()`, followed by `ftp_client_tick()`.

```
int send_file(void)
{
   int return_value;
   printf("Calling ftp_client_setup() to upload %s...\n",
       REMOTE_FILE);
```

The parameters for `ftp_client_setup()` are the same as in the previous example except for the last value, which contains the size of the file being transmitted rather than the size of the buffer for a received file.

```
return_value = ftp_client_setup(resolve(
   REMOTE_HOST),
   REMOTE_PORT,
   REMOTE_USERNAME,
   REMOTE_PASSWORD,
   FTP_MODE_UPLOAD|PASSIVE_FLAG,
   REMOTE_FILE,
   REMOTE_DIR,
   file_buffer,
   sizeof(file_buffer));
```

```
if (return_value != 0)  {
  printf("FTP setup failed.\n");
  exit(2);
}
```

The `ftp_client_tick()` function returns 0 while the transfer is in progress. When the function returns 1, the transfer has completed successfully. If the function returns a value greater than 1, the transfer has failed. A message in Dynamic C's STDIO windows displays the result.

```
printf("Looping on ftp_client_tick()...\n");
while( 0 == (return_value = ftp_client_tick()) );

if( 1 == return_value ) {
  printf("FTP upload completed successfully.  %d
      bytes.\n", ftp_client_filesize());
  return 0;
} else {
  printf("FTP upload failed: status = %d, last code =
      %d\n", return_value, ftp_last_code());
  return 1;
}
} // end send_file()
```

TINI FTP Client

To request files from an FTP server, a TINI can use Java's URL and URLConnection classes with the *ftp* URL scheme. Applications that need to transfer files in both directions can use the TINI's FTPClient class.

Requesting a File in a URL

Java's URL and URLConnection classes provide support for requesting resources from remote hosts in URLs. Chapter 8 showed how a Java program can use a URL with a *mailto* protocol handler to send an e-mail. In a similar way, you can use a URL with an *ftp* protocol handler to request a file from an FTP server. The FTP capabilities are one-way only. A client can request files but can't send them.

The FtpUrlReceiver class below shows how a TINI can use the URL and URLConnection classes to request a file. The source code to support requesting files in URLs is in com.dalsemi.protocol.ftp.Connection.java in the file *ModulesSrc.jar* in the \src directory of the TINI distribution.

Imports and Initial Declares

The FtpUrlReceiver class imports java.io classes to support input and output functions and java.net classes to support networking functions.

```
import java.io.*;
import java.net.*;
```

A series of constant strings provide default values to use in connecting to the remote host and requesting a file. USERNAME and PASSWORD are the user name and password required to log onto the server. REMOTEHOST is the IP address or domain name of the FTP server. FILENAME is the requested file. You must change these values to match the parameters appropriate for your FTP server and requested file.

```
public class FtpUrlReceiver {

    public static final String USERNAME = "embedded";
    public static final String PASSWORD = "ethernet";
    public static final String REMOTEHOST = "192.168.111.5";
    public static final String FILENAME = "testfile.txt";
```

The FtpUrlReceiver class's constructor requires values for a remote host, user name, and password. The port variable can specify a port to use for the FTP control connection. If this value is -1, the connection uses the default port of 21. The type variable can specify a transfer type of ASCII (a) or binary (i).

```
    private String remoteHost;
    private String userName;
    private String password;
    private int port = -1;
    private String type = "a";
```

The Constructor

The class's constructor uses the passed values to set the corresponding variables.

```
    public FtpUrlReceiver(String remoteHost,
        String userName, String password) {
        this.remoteHost = remoteHost;
```

```
      this.userName = userName;
      this.password = password;
   } // end FtpUrlReceiver constructor
```

Reading a File

The class's main() method creates the FtpUrlReceiver object ftp. A call to the class's getFile() method returns the InputStream object inStream, which contains the received file. A BufferedReader object, in, reads the file from the InputStream object. On reading a received line of text, a System.out.println() statement writes the line to the default output stream. A received null indicates the end of the input stream. The close() method closes the BufferedReader object when the file has been read.

```
   public static void main(String[] args) {
       try {
           FtpUrlReceiver ftp = new
               FtpUrlReceiver(REMOTEHOST, USERNAME,
               PASSWORD);

           InputStream inStream = ftp.getFile(FILENAME);

           BufferedReader in = new BufferedReader(new
               InputStreamReader(inStream));
           String line;
           System.out.println("Reading " + FILENAME + ":");
           while ((line = in.readLine()) != null) {
             System.out.println(line);
           }
           System.out.println();

          in.close();

       } catch (IOException e){
         System.err.print("IO exception: ");
         System.err.println(e.getMessage());
       }
   } // end main()
```

Setting the Port and Transfer Type

The setPort() method can set the port to a value other than the default FTP control port of 21. Zero indicates the default port.

```
public void setPort(int port) {
    this.port = port;
} // send setPort()
```

The `setType()` method can set the transfer type. Use `"a"` to indicate ASCII and `"i"` to indicate binary.

```
public void setType(String type) {
    this.type = type;
} // end setType()
```

Requesting a File

The `getFile()` method creates and sends a URL to request a file from the FTP server. The URL object `url` contains the request for the file and uses the values defined earlier. If the port variable is greater than zero, the URL specifies a port. If using the default port, the URL doesn't need to specify a port value. The In Depth section of this chapter has more about the syntax of the URL.

```
public InputStream getFile(String fileName)
    throws IOException {
  URL url = new URL("ftp://"
        + userName
        + ":" + password
        + "@" + remoteHost
        + ((port >= 0) ? (":" + port) : "")
        + "/" + fileName
        + ";type=" + type);
```

The `URLConnection` object `conn` reads from the FTP server referenced in the URL object. The URL object's `openConnection()` method creates the `URLConnection` object, which represents a connection to the named FTP server.

The `getInputStream()` method returns an input stream that reads from the connection to the server.

```
URLConnection conn = url.openConnection();
return conn.getInputStream();

} // end getFile()
} // end FtpUrlReceiver
```

Building the Application

As with the TINI e-mail applications in Chapter 8, building the FtpUrlReceiver application requires a few additional considerations to enable using the *ftp* protocol handler. The build process uses the `com.dalsemi.protocol.*` and `com.dalsemi.protocol.ftp.*` classes in *modules.jar*.

When compiling *FtpUrlReceiver.java* to *FtpUrlReceiver.class*, you must include the location of *modules.jar* in the bootclasspath. Here is an example command line (which you can place in a batch file):

```
javac -bootclasspath ..\..\bin\tiniclasses.jar;
    ..\..\bin\modules.jar FtpUrlReceiver.java
```

When converting *FtpUrlReceiver.class* to *FtpUrlReceiver.tini*, use the Build-Dependency utility in place of TiniConvertor. Here is an example command line:

```
java -classpath ..\..\bin\tini.jar;%classpath%
    BuildDependency -f FtpUrlReceiver.class
    -o FtpUrlReceiver.tini -d ..\..\bin\tini.db
    -add FTP -p ..\..\bin\modules.jar
```

The `-add` option adds the `FTP` dependency to the project, and the `-p` option names the location of `modules.jar`.

Requesting a File with FTPClient

If you need more abilities than the `URL` and `URLConnection` classes provide, the TINI's `FTPClient` class is an option. The source code for `FTPClient` is in `com.dalsemi.protocol.ftp.FTPClient.java` in the file *ModulesSrc.jar* in the *\src* directory of the TINI distribution. The class supports file transfers in both directions. The TINI's slush shell uses this class to implement an FTP client controlled via the command line.

The following example uses the `FTPClient` class to request a file from an FTP server.

Imports and Initial Declares

The `FTPClientReceiver` class imports `java.io` classes to support input and output functions. The `com.dalsemi.protocol.ftp.FTPClient` class supports communications with FTP servers.

A series of constant strings provide default values to use in connecting to the remote host and requesting a file. USERNAME and PASSWORD are the user name and password required to log on to the server. REMOTEHOST is the IP address or domain name of the FTP server. FILENAME is the requested file. You must change these values to match the parameters appropriate for your FTP server and requested file.

```
import com.dalsemi.protocol.ftp.FTPClient;
import java.io.*

public class FtpClientReceiver {
    public static final String USERNAME = "embedded";
    public static final String PASSWORD = "ethernet";
    public static final String REMOTEHOST =
        "192.168.111.5";
    public static final String FILENAME = "testfile.txt";
```

The FtpClientReceiver class's constructor requires values for a remote host, user name, and password. The port variable can specify a port to use for the FTP control connection. If this value is zero, the connection uses the default port of 21. The type variable can specify a transfer type of ASCII (a) or binary (i).

```
private String remoteHost;
private String userName;
private String password;
private int port = 0;
private String type = "a";
```

The main() Method

The main() method creates the FtpClientReceiver object ftp using the parameters provided and calls the doGetFile() method to retrieve the file.

```
public static void main(String[] args)
    throws IOException {

    FtpClientReceiver ftp = new
        FtpClientReceiver(REMOTEHOST, USERNAME,
        PASSWORD);
    ftp.doGetFile(FILENAME);
} // end main()
```

The Constructor

The constructor uses the passed values to set the corresponding variables.

```
public FtpClientReceiver(String remoteHost,
   String userName, String password) {
      this.remoteHost = remoteHost;
      this.userName = userName;
      this.password = password;
} // end FtpClientReceiver constructor
```

Setting the Port and Transfer Type

The setPort() method can set the port to a value other than the default
FTP control port of 21. A negative value indicates the default port.

```
public void setPort(int port) {
    this.port = port;
} // end setPort()
```

The setType() method can set the transfer type. Use "a" to indicate
ASCII and "i" to indicate binary.

```
public void setType(String type) {
    this.type = type;
} // end setType()
```

Requesting a File

The doGetFile() method uses FTPClient's methods to log onto the
server, read responses, and request a file. For each command sent, a Sys-
tem.out.println() statement writes the returned response to the standard output stream.

The FTPClient object client specifies a non-default port if needed.

```
public void doGetFile(String filename)
    throws IOException {

    FTPClient client;
    if (port >= 0) {
      client = new FTPClient(remoteHost);
    } else {
      client = new FTPClient(remoteHost, port);
    }
```

The `userName()` and `password()` methods send the user name and password to log onto the server.

```
try {
    client.userName(userName);
    System.out.println
        (client.getResponseString());

    client.password(password);
    System.out.println
        (client.getResponseString());
```

The `ascii()` and `binary()` methods can specify whether to use ASCII or binary mode for the transfer. FTPClient also supports the methods `dir()` and `list()`. Both of these request a directory listing from the server.

```
if ("a".equalsIgnoreCase(type)) {
    client.ascii();
} else if ("i".equalsIgnoreCase(type)) {
    client.binary();
}
System.out.println
    (client.getResponseString())
```

An FTP file transfer uses two TCP connections, or channels: a control channel for commands and a data channel for the file being transferred. FTPClient's `passiveConnection()` method sends a PASV command to request to use FTP's passive mode. In passive mode, the client, rather than the server, opens the data channel. FTPClient also supports the `dataConnection()` method, which uses the EPSV command to request to use extended passive mode. If the server responds that it doesn't support extended passive mode, the `dataconnection()` method sends a PORT command that specifies a port number the server should use for the data channel. The In Depth section of this chapter has more on the passive modes and PORT command.

```
client.passiveConnection();
System.out.println
    (client.getResponseString());
```

The `retr()` method sends an FTP RETR command that requests the specified file. A `BufferedReader` object reads the file, and `System.out.println()` statements write the file's contents to the standard output stream. A received null indicates the end of the input stream. The `close()` method closes the `BufferedReader` object when the file has been read.

After sending the file, the server closes the data channel. A call to `FTPClient`'s `close()` method sends an FTP QUIT command to request the server to close the control channel, which ends the session. The call to `close()` is in a `finally` block to ensure that the method is called before the `doGetFile()` method ends.

```
            client.retr(filename);
            System.out.println
                (client.getResponseString());

            BufferedReader in = new BufferedReader(
                new InputStreamReader
                (client.getDataStream()));

            String line;
            System.out.println("File contents:");
            while ((line = in.readLine()) != null) {
                System.out.println(line);
            }
            System.out.println();

            in.close();
        } finally {
            client.close();
        }
    } // end doGetFile()
} // end FtpClientReceiver
```

Building the Application

The FTPClientReceiver application uses the `com.dalsemi.protocol.ftp.FTPClient` class in *modules.jar*. So as in the previous example, when compiling *FtpClientReceiver.java* to *FtpClientReceiver.class*, you must include the location of *modules.jar* in the bootclasspath. Here is an example command line:

```
javac -bootclasspath ..\..\bin\tiniclasses.jar;
    ..\..\bin\modules.jar FtpClientReceiver.java
```

Use the BuildDependency utility to convert *FtpClientReceiver.class* to *FtpClientReceiver.tini*. Here is an example command line:

```
java -classpath ..\..\bin\tini.jar;%classpath%
    BuildDependency -f FtpClientReceiver.class
    -o FtpClientReceiver.tini -d ..\..\bin\tini.db
    -add FTP -p ..\..\bin\modules.jar
```

The -add option adds the FTP dependency to the project, and the -p option names the location of *modules.jar.*

Sending a File with FTPClient

In a similar way, a TINI can also use the FTPClient class to send a file to an FTP server. The FTPClientSender class imports java.io.* classes to support input and output functions. The com.dalsemi.protocol.ftp.FTPClient class supports communications with FTP servers.

Constant strings provide default values for the user name, password, and server's IP address. The FILENAME constant is the file to request from the server. You must change these values to match the parameters appropriate for your FTP server and requested file.

```
import com.dalsemi.protocol.ftp.FTPClient;
import java.io.*;

public class FtpClientSender {
    public static final String USERNAME = "embedded";
    public static final String PASSWORD = "ethernet";
    public static final String REMOTEHOST =
        "192.168.111.5";
    public static final String FILENAME = "testfile2.txt";
```

The FtpSender class's constructor requires values for a remote host, user name, password, and port, which is zero to specify the default port of 21. The type variable can specify a transfer type of ASCII (a) or binary (i).

```
    private String remoteHost;
    private String userName;
    private String password;
    private int port = 0;
    private String type = "a";
```

The main() Method

The main() method creates the FtpClientSender object ftp using the parameters provided and calls the doSendFile() method to send the file.

```
public static void main(String[] args)
    throws IOException {

    FtpClientSender ftp = new FtpClientSender
        (REMOTEHOST, USERNAME, PASSWORD);
    ftp.doSendFile(FILENAME);
} // end main()
```

The Constructor

The constructor for `FtpClientSender` uses the passed values to set the corresponding variables.

```
public FtpClientSender(String remoteHost,
    String userName, String password) {
    this.remoteHost = remoteHost;
    this.userName = userName;
    this.password = password;
} // end FtpClientSender constructor
```

Setting the Port and Transfer Type

The `setPort()` method can set the port to a value other than the default FTP control port of 21. Zero indicates the default port.

```
public void setPort(int port) {
    this.port = port;
} // end setPort()
```

The `setType()` method can set the transfer type. Use a to indicate ASCII and i to indicate binary.

```
public void setType(String type) {
    this.type = type;
} // end setType()
```

Sending a File

The `doSendFile()` method uses `FTPClient`'s methods to log onto the server, read responses, and send a file. For each command sent, the console displays the returned response.

The method creates the `FTPClient` object `client`, specifying a non-default port if needed.

```
public void doSendFile(String filename)
    throws IOException {

    FTPClient client;
    if (port >= 0) {
        client = new FTPClient(remoteHost);
    } else {
        client = new FTPClient(remoteHost, port);
    }

    try {
```

The `userName()` and `password()` methods send the user name and password to log onto the server.

```
        client.userName(userName);
        System.out.println
            (client.getResponseString());

        client.password(password);
        System.out.println
            (client.getResponseString());
```

The `ascii()` and `binary()` methods can specify whether to use ASCII or binary mode for the transfer. The `passiveConnection()` method requests to use passive mode for the transfer.

```
        if ("a".equalsIgnoreCase(type)) {
            client.ascii();
        } else if ("i".equalsIgnoreCase(type)) {
            client.binary();
        }
        System.out.println
            (client.getResponseString())

        client.passiveConnection();
        System.out.println
            (client.getResponseString());
```

For sending the file, the client can choose between two FTP commands. APPE requests the server to append the data being transferred to an existing file of the same name. STOR requests the server to replace any data in an existing file of the same name with the new data. With both commands, if the file doesn't exist, the server creates the file. The `issuecommand()` method can send either of these commands (or other FTP commands).

```
client.issueCommand
    ("APPE " + FILENAME + "\r\n");
//client.issueCommand
    ("STOR " + FILENAME + "\r\n");
System.out.println
    (client.getResponseString());
```

An `Outputstream` object writes data to the file. A call to the class's `write-File()` method writes the data to the `OutputStream` object. After writing the file, the output stream is flushed to send the data immediately, then closed.

After sending the file, FTPClient closes the data channel. A call to `FTPClient`'s `close()` method sends an FTP QUIT command to request the server to close the control channel, which ends the session. The call to `close()` is in a `finally` block to ensure that the method is called before the `doSendFile()` method ends.

```
OutputStream output =
    client.getOutputStream();
writeString(output, "test data\r\n");
output.flush();
output.close();
System.out.println
    ("The file has been transferred.");

} finally {

client.close();

}
} // end doSendFile()
```

Writing a String to the Output Stream

The `writeFile()` method writes the contents of a string to an `OutputStream` object. The `stringToWrite` variable is the contents of the file to write to the server. The `String` class's `getBytes()` method converts the string to a byte array for passing to the `OutputStream` object.

```
private void writeString(OutputStream output, String
stringToWrite) {
    try {
        output.write(stringToWrite.getBytes());
    } catch (IOException e){
```

```
          System.err.println("IO exception: " +
  e.getMessage());
        }
  } // end writeString()
} // end FtpClientSender
```

Building the Application

The FTPClientSender application uses the com.dalsemi.proto-col.ftp.FTPClient class in *modules.jar*. So as in the previous example, when compiling *FtpClientSender.java* to *FtpClientSender.class*, include the location of *modules.jar* in the bootclasspath. Here is an example command line:

```
javac -bootclasspath ..\..\bin\tiniclasses.jar;
    ..\..\bin\modules.jar FtpClientSender.java
```

Use the BuildDependency utility to convert *FtpClientSender.class* to *FtpClientSender.tini*. Here is an example command line:

```
java -classpath ..\..\bin\tini.jar;%classpath%
    BuildDependency -f FtpClientSender.class
    -o FtpClientSender.tini -d ..\..\bin\tini.db
    -add FTP -p ..\..\bin\modules.jar
```

The -add option adds the FTP dependency to the project, and the -p option names the location of *modules.jar*.

Rabbit FTP Server

Dynamic C's *ftp_server.lib* library provides support for an FTP server that can enable clients to request to exchange files with a Rabbit module. The files can be stored in root memory, in the extended memory area, or in Flash memory or battery-backed RAM.

The example below shows how the Rabbit can create and serve files and enable clients to send files to the server. You can communicate with the server using any standard FTP client application or a command-line interface.

Initial Defines and Declares

As explained in Chapter 5, the firmware selects a network configuration from *tcp_config.lib*.

```
#define TCPCONFIG 1
```

A series of `define` statements configures the file system and FTP server.

The FTP server uses Dynamic C's *filesystem mk II*, also called FS2, for storing information in named files in Flash memory or battery-backed RAM. Defining FORMAT resets the list of files in the user block area of Flash or battery-backed memory. This statement needs to execute only the first time the program runs, to put the file system in a known state.

```
#define FORMAT
```

The `FTP_USE_FS2_HANDLERS` macro enables FS2 support in the default functions for the file handler and enables clients to write files to the file system.

```
#define FTP_USE_FS2_HANDLERS
```

The `FS_MAX_FILES` macro specifies the maximum number of files supported by the file system.

```
#define FS_MAX_FILES 50
```

The `FS2_USE_PROGRAM_FLASH` macro specifies how many kilobytes of program Flash memory the file system can use.

```
#define FS2_USE_PROGRAM_FLASH 32
```

The `FTP_CREATE_MASK` macro provides the `servermask` parameter for the `sspec_addfsfile()` function, which makes files available to the FTP server. The default is SERVER_FTP | SERVER_WRITABLE, which specifies the FTP server and enables authorized users to delete and overwrite files on the server.

```
#define FTP_CREATE_MASK SERVER_FTP | SERVER_WRITABLE
```

A portion of the user block in memory holds a structure that associates the names of files with the files' locations. The `FTP_USERBLOCK_OFFSET` macro specifies the offset in the user block where the structure will be stored. The default is zero. Change this value if your application uses the default portion of the user block for another purpose. The `sizeof(server_spec)` function returns the structure's size.

```
#define FTP_USERBLOCK_OFFSET 0
```

The `SSPEC_MAXSPEC` macro specifies the maximum number of files supported by the FTP server. The default is 10.

```
#define SSPEC_MAXSPEC 10
```

The `FTP_EXTENSIONS` macro enables support for the FTP DELE (delete) command.

```
#define FTP_EXTENSIONS
```

As in the previous examples, the `#memmap xmem` directive causes all C functions not declared as root to be stored in extended memory, and the code requires the *dcrtcp.lib* library to support TCP/IP. This example also requires the *fs2.lib* library to support the FS2 file system and *ftp_server.lib* to support the FTP server's functions.

```
#memmap xmem
#use "fs2.lib"
#use "dcrtcp.lib"
#use "ftp_server.lib"
```

Starting the FTP Server

The `main()` routine performs initialization functions and starts the FTP server.

```
void main()
{
   File private_file;
   File public_file;
   FSLXnum ext;
   int file;
   int user;
   long len;
   static char create_file1_buffer[127];
   static char create_file2_buffer[127];
```

The `fs_get_flash_lx()` function returns a *logical extent number* that indicates the preferred Flash-memory device for FS2 files. The preferred device is the second Flash memory if one is available, and otherwise is the reserved area in the program Flash memory.

To use a portion of the program Flash memory for the file system, you must define two constants. In *rabbitbios.c* (in the *bios* directory of the Dynamic C distribution), set XMEM_RESERVE_SIZE to the number of bytes to reserve for the file system in the program Flash. And in your application, before the statement #use "fs2.lib", define FS2_USE_PROGRAM_FLASH to equal the number of kilobytes the file system will use. The application uses the smaller of the two values. (This application sets FS2_USE_PROGRAM_FLASH to 32 kilobytes above.)

To use battery-backed RAM for the file system, use the fs_get_ram_lx() function in place of fs_get_flash_lx(). To use the non-preferred Flash memory for the file system, use the fs_get_other_lx() function.

```
ext = fs_get_flash_lx();
```

The fs_init() function initializes the file system.

```
fs_init(0, 0);
```

If the FORMAT macro is defined in the applicaiton, the file system and user block are initialized to known states. The lx_format() function formats the file system extent, deleting any files that were present. The writeUser-Block() function initializes the user block in memory to zeros. Don't execute this block of code if you want to preserve files already in memory.

```
#ifdef FORMAT
  lx_format(ext, 0);
  len = 0;
  writeUserBlock(FTP_USERBLOCK_OFFSET, &len,
      sizeof(long));
#endif
```

The application creates two FS2 files and stores text in each. File 1 is public_file and contains the text "public file". File 2 is private_file and contains the text "private file".

```
  sprintf(create_file1_buffer, "public file");
  fcreate(&public_file, 1);
fwrite(&public_file, create_file1_buffer,
    strlen(create_file1_buffer));
fclose(&public_file);

  sprintf(create_file2_buffer, "private file");
  fcreate(&private_file, 2);
```

```
fwrite(&private_file, create_file2_buffer,
    strlen(create_file2_buffer));
fclose(&private_file);
```

The `ftp_load_filenames()` function loads the data structure that keeps track of the locations of the files. On success, `ftp_load_filenames()` returns zero and a call to `ftp_save_filenames()` saves the data structure to the user block. Even if there are no file names defined yet, saving the data structure puts it in a known state.

```
if (ftp_load_filenames() < 0) {
    ftp_save_filenames();
}
```

The application uses Dynamic C's `ServerSpec` structure defined in *zserver.lib* and introduced in Chapter 7. The `sauth_adduser()` function defines a user who can access files on the server. A file can be accessible to a specific user or users, or to any user.

To make a file accessible to all users, define a user with the user name of `anonymous` and an empty string (`""`) for a password. The `SERVER_FTP` parameter names the server that the user can access. The `ftp_set_anonymous()` function specifies the user name for files that anyone can access.

The `sspec_addfsfile()` function enables the FTP server to access the FS2 files created earlier. The function associates the file name *public.txt* with file 1 on the FTP server. The `sspec_setuser()` function enables the anonymous user defined above to access the file.

```
user = sauth_adduser("anonymous", "", SERVER_FTP);
ftp_set_anonymous(user);

file = sspec_addfsfile( "public.txt", 1, SERVER_FTP ) ;
sspec_setuser(file, user );
```

In a similar way, the following statements define a user with the user name rabbit1 and password `embedded`. The `sauth_setwriteaccess()` function enables rabbit1 to send files to the server in addition to requesting files. Rabbit1 can access file 2 on the server as the file *private.txt*. This file isn't available to anonymous users.

```
user = sauth_adduser("rabbit1", "embedded",
```

```
         SERVER_FTP);
  sauth_setwriteaccess(user, 1);

  file = sspec_addfsfile( "private.txt", 2, SERVER_FTP );
  sspec_setuser(file, user );
```

A call to `sock_init()` initializes the TCP/IP stack. A call to `ftp_init(NULL)` initializes the FTP server using the default handlers. As explained in Chapter 6, calling `tcp_reserveport()` can improve the server's performance. The `FTP_CMDPORT` constant is 21, the default FTP command port.

An endless loop calls `ftp_tick()` to process FTP requests as needed.

```
  sock_init();
  ftp_init(NULL);

  tcp_reserveport(FTP_CMDPORT);

  while(1) {
    ftp_tick();
  }
} // end main()
```

TINI FTP Server

The TINI software includes an FTP server. When the *.startup* file in the TINI's */etc/* directory contains this line:

```
setenv FTPServer enable
```

the slush shell runs the FTP server on start up. This is the server you use to transfer *.tini* programs to the TINI. You can use the same server to transfer files in both directions for any purpose using a standard FTP client application.

The TINI's `FTPServer` class assumes that slush is present and uses some of its commands. For example, on receiving an FTP LIST command from a client, the server tries to invoke slush's `ls` command. Other slush commands that the FTP server might call include `cd`, `cd ..`, `del`, `ls`, `ls -l`, `md`, `move`, and `rd`. If you want to use the TINI's FTP server in your application, the TINI will need to also be running slush or another shell that implements the above commands.

The source code for the FTP server is in the `com.dalsemi.shell.server.ftp` classes `FTPServer.java`, `FTPSession.java`, and `FTPInputStream.java`. These are in the file *APIsrc.jar* in the \src directory of the TINI distribution.

In Depth:
Inside the File Transfer Protocol

The File Transfer Protocol defines a standard protocol for transferring files between computers. The main documents that define FTP are *RFC 959: File Transfer Protocol (FTP) and RFC 1123: Requirements for Internet Hosts -- Application and Suppo*rt.

Requirements

An embedded system can function as an FTP client or server. A client initiates communications with a server and sends requests to transmit or receive files. In most cases, an embedded system that needs to exchange files with a single PC should function as a client. Many embedded systems don't have a lot of resources to spare, and running an FTP server that is always available requires processing time and memory. Running a server also puts the system at a greater security risk because any computer in the network might be able to gain access to the system's files. But if the embedded system needs to make its files available to anyone on the network, or if the files need to be available to other computers at all times, the system will need to function as a server.

A computer that uses FTP must have a file system, which enables the system to store information in named entities called files. Files are of course useful in desktop computers, where you select files to run programs, view documents and images, and perform other tasks.

Embedded systems can support file systems as well. A small embedded system may just store data in specified locations in memory, with no need to place the data in named files. But for many embedded systems, a file system provides a useful structure for accessing information, both locally and over a network.

For example, a system can store collected data or configuration settings in files. A system functioning as an FTP client can initiate communications periodically with a remote computer to request to send or receive files. A system functioning as an FTP server can make its files available on request and can allow remote computers to send files that the system will use. The user that communicates with the embedded system can be a human using an FTP program or a process that functions without human intervention. For example, a PC can be programmed to retrieve a file once a day from an embedded system.

In PCs, the file system includes the ability to store files in a directory structure and to specify attributes such as whether a file is write-protected or accessible to certain users. Under Windows XP, from the **My Computer** folder, you can browse the directories and view file names and attributes. (In the **View** menu, click **Choose Details** to specify what information to display and click **Details** to view the information.) The TINI supports a similar file system, which you can browse from the slush shell using commands such as `ls -l` and `cd`.

A very basic file system might just consist of a structure with a series of entries that each store the name, starting address in memory, and length of a file. In Dynamic C, entries in an `HttpSpec` or `ServerSpec` structure can specify files that are accessible to a Web or FTP server. Each entry includes a file name, the address in memory where the file's length and contents are stored, and optional security information.

On a PC, you can perform FTP transfers using an FTP client application such as WS_FTP from Ipswitch, Inc. Two other ways to perform FTP transfers are from a command prompt and from a browser. To use the command-line interface, enter `ftp` at a command prompt and enter ? for a list of commands. The browser interface is explained later in this chapter. Ipswitch and others also offer applications that enable a PC to function as an FTP server.

Transferring a File

To transfer a file, an FTP session uses two channels, or communications paths, one for control information and one for the file being transferred. Each channel has a separate TCP connection.

On the server, the default port for the control channel is 21 and the default port for the data channel is 20. The client can use any available port or ports. The default for the client is to use the same port for both the control and data channels. However, transfers that use FTP's stream mode, which requires a new data connection for each file, should send a PORT command to specify a new, non-default port for each file transfer.

Requesting a new port for each transfer prevents problems due to TCP's timeout requirements. When a connection closes, TCP requires a timeout before the same connection can be reused. The timeout prevents a new connection that is identical to a recently closed connection from receiving data intended for the previous connection. When transferring multiple files in a single session, if a transfer tries to use the same port as the previous connection, the port may be unavailable because thes timeout for the previous connection hasn't expired. Specifying a different port for each data connection eliminates the problem. Other alternatives are to use the block or compressed transfer modes, which don't require a new data connection for each file.

These are typical steps in sending a file to a server in stream mode, where the file's contents are sent without a header or any assumed structure for the file's data:

1. The client opens a control channel between any available local port and port 21 on the server. The client sends commands to establish communications and request to send a file.

2. The server opens a data channel between the server's port 20 and the port the client is using for the control channel.

3. The client sends the file's contents, closes the data channel, and requests the server to close the control channel.

4. The server closes the control channel.

In a similar way, these are the steps in receiving a file from a server in stream mode:

1. The client opens a control channel between any available local port and port 21 on the server. The client sends commands to establish communications and request a file.

2. The server opens a data channel between the server's port 20 and the port the client is using for the control channel. The server sends the file and closes the data channel.

3. The client requests the server to close the control channel.

4. The server closes the control channel.

A client that is communicating from behind a firewall may find that the firewall blocks the server's request to open the data connection. To get around this limitation without having to reconfigure the firewall, the client can send a command that requests a passive transfer process (PASV or EPSV), where the client, rather than the server, opens the data connection. The client must send the command to request a passive transfer preceding each transfer.

When a client specifies the location of a file on a server, the location is relative to the directories that the server makes available to the client. This location can differ from the file's absolute location in the computer. For example, a computer functioning as a server may allow the user to access the directory */ftp/user1* and its subdirectories. The server's root directory for that user is then */user1*. To access a file at */ftp/user1/data/test.txt*, the client would specify the location on the server as */data/test.txt*, which is the file's location relative to the user's root directory.

Commands

The FTP standard defines required and optional commands for FTP servers to support.

All of the commands and symbols that represent parameter values are case-insensitive. A command ends with CRLF.

Minimum Implementation

RFC 959 specifies the commands that a minimum implementation of FTP must support, and RFC 1123 updates this list with additional commands. The implementation specified by RFC 1123 is more capable in handling communications between computers that may use different operating systems, file systems, and firewall protection.

However, RFC 1123 says that computers whose operating system or file system doesn't allow or support a command aren't obligated to add support for it. So for example, an embedded system whose file system doesn't support subdirectories can run an FTP server that doesn't support MKD, CWD, or other commands that manipulate directories.

In reality, which commands a system's software needs to support depends in part on how the system will use FTP. On a PC, a user that needs to exchange files with varied FTP servers will want an FTP client application that is as capable and flexible as possible. And an FTP server that is available to varied clients will want to support a large command set. But an embedded system that exchanges files only with known FTP clients or servers can have a more minimal implementation. If the transfers are only with known servers or clients and are controlled entirely by software at both ends, the commands can be known, predictable, and thus limited.

The following commands are the minimum implementation required by RFC 1123, plus EPSV and EPRT, which have additional support for IP v6 addresses. The commands included in RFC 959's smaller subset are noted as well.

ACCT *account*

The ACCT command identifies a user account. A server may require an ACCT value to log on, or a system may use accounts to grant specific privileges (to store files, for example) at any time after logging on.

APPE *pathname*

With the APPE command, the client requests the server to append the received data to the named file if it exists, and otherwise to create the file and store the received data in it.

CDUP

The CDUP command requests to change to the current directory's parent directory.

CWD *pathname*

The CWD command requests to change the working directory to the directory specified in *pathname*.

DELE *pathname*

The DELE command requests to delete the file specified in *pathname* on the server.

EPSV

The EPSV command requests the server to wait for the client to open the data connection instead of having the server open the connection. The server responds to this request with code `227 entering extended passive mode`, followed by the port number where the server will listen for the client. The format of the response is:

Entering Extended Passive Mode (|||*port_number*|)

where *port_number* is the number of the port the server will be listening on. The recommended delimiter character is ASCII 124 (|). The first two fields are place holders for future use and must be empty. The format is similar to the format of the argument passed with EPRT, described below.

This command is defined in *RFC 2428: FTP Extensions for IPv6 and NATs.* Also see the PASV command. Many servers support PASV, but not EPSV.

EPRT

The EPRT command enables the client to provide an extended address for the data connection.

The format of EPRT is:

EPRT |*net-prt*|*net-addr*|*tcp-port*|

where:

net-prt is an Address Family Number from the list maintained by IANA. IP Version 4 is 1; IP Version 6 is 2.

net-addr is the IP address. IP Version 4 addresses use dotted quad notation. IP Version 6 addresses use the representation described in *RFC 2373: IP Version 6 Addressing Architecture.*

tcp-port is the number of the TCP port where the host is listening for a connection.

This command is defined in *RFC 2428: FTP Extensions for IPv6 and NATs.* Also see the PORT command. Many servers support PORT, but not EPRT.

HELP [*command name*]

The HELP command requests text that explains how to use the server or how to use an optional command provided as a parameter with the command.

LIST [*pathname*]

The LIST command requests the server to send a list of files in the directory specified in *pathname* or information about the file specified in *pathname*. If there is no parameter sent with the command, the server returns information about the current directory.

MKD *pathname*

The MKD command requests to create a directory specified in *pathname* on the server.

MODE *mode*

The MODE command specifies a transfer mode: stream (s), block (b), or compressed (c). In stream mode, the default, the data has no assumed format. In the optional block and compressed modes, the data begins with a header that enables the receiver to determine when a transfer is complete, so there's no need to close the data connection after each transfer to indicate end of file. Compressed mode also enables sending compressed data for faster transfers.

RFC 959's minimum implementation requires support for stream mode.

NLST [*pathname*]

The NLST command requests the server to send a list of file names in the directory specified in *pathname*.

NOOP

The NOOP command performs no function except to elicit a response that confirms that the server is responding to commands.

RFC 959's minimum implementation includes support for NOOP.

PASS *password*

With the PASS command, the client specifies the password for the user name. If the user name is anonymous, the password conventionally is the user's e-mail address.

PASV

The PASV command requests the server to wait for the client to open the data connection instead of having the server open the connection. The server responds to this request with the code 227 entering passive mode, followed by the IP address and port number where the server will listen for the client. This information uses the same format as the PORT command. Passive mode can be useful when communicating through firewalls. Also see EPSV.

PORT *host-port*

The PORT command enables the client to specify an IP address and port number the client will use for the data connection. The *host-port* parameter consists of four decimal numbers that represent the four bytes that make up a 32-bit IP address, followed by the two bytes of the port address. The parameter uses the format *h1,h2,h3,h4,p1,p2*, where *h1* is the high byte in the IP address followed by the next three bytes in order and *p1* is the high byte in the port number, followed by the low byte.

For example, to request to use port 53249 (D001h) at IP address 192.168.111.100, the command would be PORT 192,168,111,100,208,1. (The decimal value 53249 equals D001h. D0h is 208 in decimal, so the decimal values of the two bytes are 208 and 1.)

415

As explained above, issuing a PORT command before establishing a data connection can prevent problems due to TCP's timeout requirements. Transfers that use passive or extended-passive mode don't require a PORT command because the server waits for the client to connect on the port the server has specified.

RFC 959's minimum implementation includes support for PASV.

PWD

The PWD command prints the name of the current working directory.

QUIT

With the QUIT command, the client requests the server to close the control connection. If the data connection is open, the server will wait for it to close before closing the control connection.

RFC 959's minimum implementation includes support for QUIT.

RETR *pathname*

A client uses the RETR command to request a file from the server. The *pathname* parameter specifies the file's path, if needed, and name.

RFC 959's minimum implementation includes support for RETR.

RMD *pathname*

The RMD command requests to remove a directory specified in *pathname* on the server.

STAT [*path*]

The STAT command requests status information. If the command has no parameter, the server returns the current values of all transfer parameters and the status of connections. If the command includes a path, the command returns a directory listing for the path, as in a LIST command, but using the control connection.

STOR *pathname*

A client uses the STOR command to request to send a file to the server. The *pathname* parameter specifies the file's path, if needed, and name. If the file doesn't already exist on the server, the server creates the file. If the file does exist on the server, the server overwrites the file.

RFC 959's minimum implementation includes support for STOR.

STRU

The STRU command specifies the structure of the data's contents. The file structure (f), which is the default, makes no assumptions about the structure of the data. With the record structure (r), the data is assumed to consist of sequential records in a prescribed format.

RFC 959's minimum implementation includes support for the file structure and support for the record structure if the file system supports records.

SYST

The SYST command returns text that indicates what operating system the server is running. Standard text to use for popular operating systems is available at *www.iana.org/assignments/operating-system-names*. The options include WIN32 and more specific designations such as WINDOWS-98 and WINDOWS-CE.

TYPE

The TYPE command can specify how text characters are encoded in the files being transferred. In ASCII Non-print (AN), which is the default, a character is represented by a byte containing a 7-bit NVT-ASCII code, with the most significant bit set to zero. The Telnet standard (*RFC 854: Telnet Protocol Specification*) defines the NVT-ASCII character set, which includes codes for carriage return (CR) and line feed (LF). Non-print means that the data isn't required to include vertical-format information such as CRLF or page breaks. Other FTP types are EBCDIC and Image.

RFC 959's minimum implementation includes support for ASCII Non-print type.

USER *username*

In the USER command, *username* identifies the client requesting access to the server's resources. When a server is available to any client, *username* is anonymous.

RFC 959's minimum implementation includes support for USER.

Additional Commands

RFC 959 defines additional commands and valid reply codes, and RFC 2228: *FTP Security Extensions* adds more. On receiving an unrecognized command, a server returns reply code 502 (Command not implemented).

Requesting a File with a URL

A computer that only needs to receive files, but not send them, can use a URL to communicate with an FTP server. The URL standard (RFC 1738) defines an *ftp* scheme for URLs. The scheme is:

ftp://*user:password@host*[*:port*]*/url-path*

where

> *user* is the user name to gain access to the FTP server.
>
> *password* is the user's password. If the URL doesn't supply a password, a browser may prompt for it.
>
> *host* is the host's IP address in dotted-quad format or a domain name.
>
> *port* is the port to connect to on the server. The port is 21 if not specified.
>
> *url-path* is the location and name of the file being requested.

The url-path is in the form:

> [*cwd1/cwd2/...cwdn*]*/filename*[*;type*=typecode]

where *cwd1*, *cwd2*, and so on are any directories required to specify the location of the file on the server, *filename* is the name of the file being requested, and an optional *typecode* specifies the type of resource being requested. A typecode of a means ASCII Non-print, which is the default if not specified. A typecode of i is Image (binary), and d means directory. Requesting a URL for an ASCII or image file causes the client to send a RETR command for the named file. Requesting a URL that names a directory causes the client to send an NLST command to request a list of files in the specified directory.

The browser or other software that supports the FTP scheme opens a connection with the specified host, and sends the appropriate FTP commands to retrieve the file or list of file names.

In Java, an instance of the URL class represents a URL. As the TINI example in this chapter showed, an instance of the URLConnection class can communicate with a resource that a URL references, such as an FTP server.

Chapter 9

10

Keeping Your Devices and Network Secure

If your device connects to the Internet, you need to pay attention to network security. Many devices that connect only to local networks can benefit from security measures as well.

Without effective security, an unauthorized user may do any of the following:

- View your data, device firmware, or the contents of any files.
- Alter or erase files.
- Install and run program code on your device.
- Submit Web-page form data that causes the device to malfunction or has other unintended consequences.
- Spy on transmissions to and from your device.
- Gain access to other computers in the local network.

- Clog your network with repeated attempts to communicate, preventing authorized users from accessing the device and other computers in the local network and possibly preventing the device from performing the tasks it's responsible for.

Fortunately, there are steps you can take to prevent these activities. Not every device needs to implement every security measure. What steps to take depend on the device, its capabilities and responsibilities, the local network the device resides in, and any connections the device has to networks outside the local network.

In some ways, embedded systems are often inherently more secure than a PC with a familiar operating system and plenty of resources to exploit. If your device's firmware is in a one-time-programmable (OTP) ROM, you don't have to worry about preventing malicious users from overwriting the firmware. If your device serves Web pages that contain no private information, there's no need to encrypt the data being sent. But in most cases, there are risks you need to protect against, to ensure that your device continues to operate as it should and to ensure that the security of other computers in the local network aren't compromised.

One way to limit who has access to a resource is to require a user name and password before serving the resource. This chapter shows how you can use HTTP's Basic Authentication to protect resources with user names and passwords. The In Depth section details four steps that will go a long way to ensuring the security of your devices and the local networks they reside in.

Quick Start: Limiting Access with Passwords

For many applications, it's desirable to limit access to certain Web pages by requiring users to enter a valid user name and password. HTTP 1.0 supports Basic Authentication, which enables a server to require a valid user name and password before returning a Web page.

Basic Authentication is sufficient protection for some applications, and many networking libraries and packages for embedded systems support it.

Figure 10-1: On receiving a request for Basic Authentication, browsers display a window like this to enable users to enter a user name and password.

Using Basic Authentication

When a client requests a Web page protected with Basic Authentication, the server requests the client to authenticate, or prove that the client is authorized to receive the resource. The server does this by returning an HTTP header with the error code 401 (Unauthorized) and a WWW-Authenticate field that names the type of authentication required. Here is an example:

```
HTTP/1.0 401 Unauthorized\r\n
Date: Mon, 14 Apr 2003 12:05:15 GMT\r\n
WWW-Authenticate: Basic realm="Embedded Ethernet" \r\n
\r\n
```

The WWW-Authenticate field names two values: the authentication scheme, or method, to use (Basic in the example) and the realm the scheme applies to ("Embedded Ethernet"). On returning a valid user name and password in the format required by the named authentication scheme, a client can access resources within the named realm. A server can support multiple realms, with each allowing access to a different set of users.

On receiving a header requesting Basic Authentication, the client's browser typically displays a window that requests the user to enter a user name and password. Figure 10-1 shows an example. The window displays the name of the page's realm, so when naming a realm, use something meaningful to end users. For added security, most browsers display dots in place of the password's characters when they're entered. When the user has entered the requested information and clicks OK, the browser sends an authorization request containing the password and user name. The request travels in an HTTP GET request that includes an Authorization request with the encrypted user name and password:

```
GET / HTTP/1.0\r\n
Authorization Basic ZW1liZWRkZWQ6ZXRoZXJuZXQ/r/n
/r/n
```

On receiving the GET request, the server decrypts the user name and password. If both are valid for the specified realm, the server returns the Web page originally requested. If not, the server typically returns another response with error 401 and a request to authenticate. Most browsers display the authentication window again, but after receiving a third request to authenticate, some browsers give up and don't re-display the window. Opening a new browser window typically allows the user to try again, however.

The encryption used in Basic Authentication is the Base64 Content-Transfer-Encoding method described in *RFC 1521: MIME (Multipurpose Internet Mail Extensions) Part One: Mechanisms for Specifying and Describing the Format of Internet Message Bodies*, minus the specified limit of 72 characters per line.

In the encoding, the data to transmit is first divided into 24-bit chunks. Each chunk is then divided into four 6-bit numbers. A table provided in the standard assigns a character in the BASE64 alphabet to each 6-bit value (0 to 63). The BASE64 alphabet includes upper- and lower-case letters, numerals, and a few additional characters. For example, binary 000000 in BASE64 is the character *A*, and binary 011010 (26 decimal) is the character *a*.

In a request for Basic Authorization, the client converts a string in this format:

user_name:*password*

to BASE64. The resulting characters transmit in the Authorization field of the HTTP header.

For example, if the user name is embedded and the password is ethernet, the string to encrypt is:

```
embedded:ethernet
```

Each character is a byte, so there are 17 bytes, which equal 22 6-bit values with four bits left over. To obtain an integral number of 6-bit values, pad the end with two zeroes. Encrypting the user name and password gives this 23-character string:

```
ZWliZWRkZWQ6ZXRoZXJuZXQ
```

The result must be an integral multiple of 24 bits. When needed, add one or two equal signs (=) to the end of the string to lengthen it. The example above requires one equal sign.

The BASE64 encryption can be easily decrypted by anyone spying on a transmission. It's also possible for a determined hacker to keep trying different user names and passwords until something works. The In Depth section of this chapter describes Digest Authentication, which is more complex but more secure and thus more suitable for some applications.

Basic Authentication on the Rabbit

Rabbit Semiconductor's *http.lib* library includes support for Basic Authentication. Chapter 6's example introduced the HttpSpec structure, which contains an HTTP_FILE entry for each file a Rabbit's Web server can access. Each entry can also specify a realm for password-protecting the file.

To protect a file, the application must include an HttpRealm structure with one or more user names and passwords, and the file's HTTP_FILE entry must specify the realm, as in the following example application.

Initial Defines and Declares

Much of the code that configures and initializes the Rabbit is the same as in previous examples in Chapter 6 and Chapter 7, so I'll skip extended explanations of these statements.

Figure 10-2: On receiving a valid user name and password, the application returns the requested Web page.

```
#define TCPCONFIG 1
#memmap xmem
#use "dcrtcp.lib"
#use "http.lib"
```

An #ximport directive imports a Web page (*index.html*) that displays a message on successful authentication.

```
#ximport "c:/rabbit/passworddemo/index.html"
    index_html
```

Figure 10-2 shows an example Web page. In a real-world application, this page would display the protected contents.

The HttpRealm structure myrealm contains a single entry that defines an authorized user with a user name ("embedded"), password ("ethernet"), and realm name ("Lakeview Research"):

```
const HttpRealm myrealm[] =
{
    {"embedded", "ethernet", "Lakeview Research"}
};
```

The single entry in the HttpType structure associates the file extension *.html* with the handler for files of type text/html.

```
const HttpType http_types[] =
{
    { ".html", "text/html", NULL}
};
```

The HttpSpec structure contains information about the file the server serves. The two entries enable clients to request the file by name ("/index.html") or as the default file served on entering the server's IP address alone ("/") in a browser's Address text box.

```
const HttpSpec http_flashspec[] =
{
    { HTTPSPEC_FILE, "/", index_html, NULL, 0, NULL,
      myrealm},
    { HTTPSPEC_FILE, "/index.html", index_html, NULL,
      0, NULL, myrealm}
};
```

The main() Function

The main() function initializes the TCP/IP stack and the HTTP handler and calls tcp_reserveport() to enable establishing a connection even if no sockets are available. An endless while loop then calls http_handler() repeatedly to handle any incoming requests.

```
main()
{

    sock_init();
    http_init();
    tcp_reserveport(80);

    while (1) {
        http_handler();
    }
} // end main()
```

When the program is running and a client requests *index.html* or the server's default file, the server returns an authentication request. On receiving an authentication request from the client with the required encrypted user name, password, and realm, the server returns the Web page *index.html*.

In a similar way, you can use Basic Authentication in Rabbit applications that use forms and the *zserver.lib* library, as described in Chapter 7. Rabbit Semiconductor has an example application that illustrates Basic Authentication with forms.

Basic Authentication on the TINI

For the TINI, Web servers that support Java servlets, such as the Tynamo Web server and TiniHttpServer, typically support Basic Authentication as well. The following `BasicAuthentication` servlet for the Tynamo Web server requires clients to provide a valid user name and password before the servlet will serve its Web page to the client.

Initial Imports

As in the previous example, the name of the realm is "Lakeview Research," the user name is "embedded," and the password is "ethernet."

In addition to the `java.io.IOException`, `javax.servlet`, and `javax.servlet.http` classes, the servlet imports the `AuthenticatedHttpServlet` class from Tynamo's `com.qindesign.servlet` package.

```
import java.io.IOException;
import javax.servlet.ServletOutputStream;
import javax.servlet.ServletException;
import javax.servlet.http.HttpServletRequest;
import javax.servlet.http.HttpServletResponse;
import com.qindesign.servlet.AuthenticatedHttpServlet;

public class BasicAuthentication extends
    AuthenticatedHttpServlet {
```

Methods

The `getRealm()` method returns the name of the realm. The class must support this method.

```
public String getRealm(HttpServletRequest req) {
    return "Lakeview Research";
}
```

The `isAuthorized()` method is passed a realm, user name, and password and checks to see if these match the values supported by the servlet. The class must support this method.

```
public boolean isAuthorized(String realm,
    String username, String password) {
  return "Lakeview Research".equals(realm) &&
      "embedded".equals(username) &&
```

```
    "ethernet".equals(password);
} // end getRealm()
```

The doGet() method functions like the doGet methods in previous examples, except that it is called only after a GET request has been authorized. In this example, the method returns a Web page containing a single line of text informing the client that the user name and password are valid. In a real-world application, this page would display the protected information.

```
protected void doGet(HttpServletRequest req,
    HttpServletResponse resp)
    throws ServletException, IOException {
  resp.setContentType("text/html");
  ServletOutputStream out = resp.getOutputStream();
      out.println("<P>Valid username and password
      detected.");
} // end doGet()
```

In a similar way, the servlet can respond to authorized POST requests. This example just calls the doGet() method.

```
protected void doPost(HttpServletRequest req,
   HttpServletResponse resp)
       throws ServletException, IOException {
     doGet(req, resp);
} // end doPost()
```

The doUnauthorizedGet() method is like doGet(), except that it's called when an authorization attempt fails. The method writes the contents of a Web page to a ServletOutputStream object. The Web page contains an error message and a link that requests the servlet again to give the user another chance.

Users may not see this Web page every time they send a request that fails authentication. On receiving an HTTP response with error code 401 (Unauthorized), many browsers display the authentication window again and ignore the Web page returned in the response. But if the browser gives up after three tries, or if the user closes the authentication window without clicking OK, the browser may display the Web page.

```
protected void doUnauthorizedGet(HttpServletRequest
    req, HttpServletResponse resp)
    throws ServletException, IOException {
  resp.setContentType("text/html");
```

```
                    ServletOutputStream out = resp.getOutputStream();
                    out.print("<P>Invalid username or password.");
                    out.print("<P><A HREF=
                        \"/servlet/BasicAuthentication\">Try
                        again</A>");
                } // end doUnauthorizedGet()
```

In a similar way, the servlet can respond to unauthorized POST requests. This example just calls the doUnauthorizedPost() method.

```
        protected void doUnauthorizedPost (HttpServletRequest
            req, HttpServletResponse resp)
                    throws ServletException, IOException {
            doUnauthorizedGet(req, resp);
        } // end doUnauthorizedPost
```

```
    } end BasicAuthentication
```

When this servlet has been compiled and the Tynamo Web server is running, requesting the servlet */servlet/BasicAuthentication* at the TINI's IP address will cause Figure 10-1's window to display. On receiving a GET request with the user name "embedded" and password "ethernet" using Basic Authentication, the doGet() method returns the Web page with protected content to the client.

In Depth:
Four Rules for Securing Your Devices and Local Network

Paying attention to the following four rules will go a long way in ensuring that your device, data, and local network are as secure as possible from security risks:

1. Use a **firewall** and configure it with the most restrictive settings that allow your device to perform the communications it requires.

2. Restrict access to individual protected resources with **user names and passwords**.

3. **Validate** data provided by users to ensure the contents won't cause harm.

4. **Encrypt** data that must remain private.

For each of these, you need to review the risks as they apply to your device, then take actions as needed to reduce or eliminate the risks. The actions will vary with the device, the firmware, and the security needs of the computers in any local network the device attaches to.

Use a Firewall

A firewall is the first line of defense against unauthorized access to the resources of your device and local network. Chapter 4 introduced firewalls and explained the need to configure them to allow a device to function as a server on the Internet. This chapter has more about firewalls, including how to select and use a firewall to provide the maximum protection for your device and local network while still allowing necessary communications to pass through the firewall.

Three ways for an embedded system to obtain firewall protection are a dedicated firewall device, firewall software running on a PC in the same local network as the embedded system, and firewall firmware in the device itself. A dedicated device is the easiest to use. Firewall software in a PC has the advantage of costing nothing if you have a PC available and running that can function as a firewall for a local network. Firmware that performs the function of a firewall in the device can be an option in some cases where you need to protect a single device.

Firewall Basics

A firewall device is an embedded system that connects between a local device or network and the Internet or other networks the local computer(s) communicate with. The firewall typically has multiple LAN ports for connecting local computers and hubs and a single WAN port that connects to the outside world. The local computers are said to be *behind the firewall*. Everything the WAN port can communicate with is *outside the firewall*. In smaller networks, the WAN port often connects to a cable or DSL modem that connects to an ISP. Every communication to or from a computer outside the firewall must go through the firewall to reach a computer in the local network. The firewall's configuration determines which communications can pass through the firewall.

Firewalls are mainly concerned with restricting incoming communications, though in some cases, a firewall may also block outgoing communications that appear to be fraudulent, such as an outgoing datagram with a non-local Source Address.

Many firewall devices are multi-function devices that also perform the functions of a hub and a router with network address translation (NAT). (See Chapter 4 for more about NAT.) The hub enables multiple computers to connect to the firewall. To add more computers, you can connect another hub to one of the local ports as described in Chapter 2.

In a similar way, a Windows XP PC configured to use Internet Connection Sharing (ICS) can protect a local network, including embedded systems, by enabling Windows XP's Internet Connection Firewall. The PC must have two network interfaces. An Ethernet interface connects the PC to the local computers protected by the firewall. A second Ethernet interface or an interface to a modem connects the PC to the world outside the firewall. The Internet Connection Firewall has configuration options similar to those for a dedicated firewall device.

A firewall's configuration determines which IP datagrams the firewall will allow to pass through to the local network. Most firewall devices support a password-protected Web interface for setting the configuration. To configure the firewall device, you need a network-connected PC or other computer that enables you to view and enter information on the Web pages, but once the firewall is configured, the device protects the network without requiring a connected PC. For added security, many firewalls enable you to restrict access to the configuration pages to computers in the local network only.

The specifics of how to configure a firewall vary with the manufacturer and model, but the general concepts are the same for all firewalls. The basic rule for configuring a firewall is to block all communications through the firewall except those that you explicitly want to allow.

Functioning as a Client

Some embedded systems can function strictly as clients that request resources from or send data to other computers but don't have to accept communications from hosts the client hasn't initiated communications with. For example, a system that uses the Internet only to send periodic sensor readings to remote computers doesn't need to accept communications from computers other than the ones the system sends the reading to. The firewall can examine each datagram received from outside the firewall. If the information in the headers shows that the datagram's source and destination match those of a valid, currently active connection, the datagram can pass through to the local network. If not, the firewall drops the datagram and may return a response indicating that the data was refused.

To help in deciding whether to allow a received datagram to pass to the local network, the firewall may maintain and consult a table that contains an entry for each connection. When a local computer sends a TCP segment or UDP datagram to a remote host and port, a firewall can create a table entry that allows incoming traffic from that remote host and port to pass to the specified local host and port. For TCP connections, the firewall deletes the entry when the TCP connection is closed as indicated by the FIN or RST flag. For UDP, which doesn't use formal connections, the firewall can use a timeout to decide when to delete the entry. TCP connections can also use a timeout as a backup for cases where the connection doesn't close properly.

As Chapter 9 explained, in FTP transfers, by default the server requests to open a TCP connection for a transfer's data channel. If the client's firewall blocks requests to open a connection, the client can request to use passive or extended passive mode, where the client computer opens the connection using a port number provided by the server.

Hosting a Server

If a local computer needs to be able to serve resources to requesting computers outside the firewall, you need to configure the firewall to allow the requests to pass through the firewall while preventing other, unwanted traffic from entering the local network.

A firewall may allow several options for restricting incoming traffic. For example, a local network might include an embedded system that hosts a Web server on port 80, the default port for HTTP communications. Configuration options for allowing incoming HTTP requests include the following, from most restrictive to least restrictive:

- Allow incoming IP datagrams that don't belong to an established connection only if they contain TCP segments that contain HTTP requests that are directed to port 80, and forward the TCP segments to a specified host. This is the most secure option. A datagram passes through the firewall only if the datagram contains a TCP segment, the contents of the segment's Destination Port Number field is 80, and the contents of the segment's data area indicate that the message is an HTTP request. Not all firewall devices are capable of filtering in this much detail. Also, additional fragments in a fragmented datagram won't have a TCP or HTTP header to examine, so the firewall needs to have a mechanism that allows additional fragments to pass through the firewall.

- Allow incoming IP datagrams that don't belong to an established connection only if they contain TCP segments directed to port 80. Forward the TCP segments to a specified host and port. This option is like the previous one except that it doesn't examine the contents of the TCP segment's data area to verify that it contains an HTTP request.

- Allow all incoming IP datagrams that don't belong to an established connection and forward their contents to a specified host. This is the least secure option, but it can be sufficient for some applications. For example, the specified host may be an embedded system that accepts only HTTP requests from specific IP addresses, ignoring all other communications.

Other configuration options a firewall might have include these:

- Specify remote IP addresses that a local host can receive traffic from. This option is useful if your embedded system communicates only with a specific IP address or series of IP addresses.

- Allow only specified computers to communicate with computers outside the firewall. Or block specified computers from communicating with computers outside the firewall. These options enable you to allow an embedded system to communicate on the Internet while protecting other computers in the local network that don't need Internet access. The firewall may enable you to identify the computers by IP address or by Ethernet hardware address. Using hardware addresses can be useful if the IP addresses are assigned dynamically and are subject to change.

- Block any outgoing communication where the Source Address of the datagram isn't a local address. (A firewall with NAT support will translate the local address to the firewall's public IP address when sending the datagram on the Internet.) This option can prevent some malicious software from using your local computers to access the Internet.

- Allow a host behind the firewall to communicate without firewall protection. The host is said to reside in a "demilitarized zone" (DMZ) and must have its own public IP address.

Embedded Firewalls

If you have a device that connects to the Internet by itself, without connecting to a local network, you may be able to provide adequate protection in the device firmware, without requiring a separate firewall device. This is especially true if the device requires only specific and limited Internet access. For example, if the device communicates with a single IP address over a specific user port, the firmware can ignore all other network communications. For other applications, requiring all users to enter a user name and password before accessing the device's resources (as in the Basic Authentication examples earlier in this chapter) may provide adequate protection.

Restrict Access with User Names and Passwords

A firewall enables you to control which local resources are available on the Internet and which IP addresses can access those resources. But firewalls filter only on the information in IP and other headers. They can't identify specific, authorized users who may be using IP addresses that the firewall doesn't know about ahead of time.

A solution is to provide authorized users with a password and to require users to enter the password before accessing a resource. For additional security and to identify who is accessing the resources, you can require a user name in addition to a password. Each user name and password combination can be unique to a user, so different users can have different access. The accepted passwords and user names may be hard-coded into the firmware, with authorized users informed of the values to use. Or you may want to allow users to obtain access to a resource by filling out a form that requires selecting a user name and password. The form can request additional information as well.

Two words you'll encounter relating to password protection are *authentication* and *authorization*. A user who wants to access a protected resource must provide authentication, or proof that the user has permission to access the resource. On receiving a valid user name and password, the server grants authorization, or permission, to access the resource.

Basic Authentication and Digest Authentication

The examples at the beginning of this chapter showed how to use Basic Authentication to require a user name and password before accessing a resource.

A more secure option than Basic Authentication is Digest Authentication. To access a resource protected with Digest Authentication, the user must provide a *message digest,* which is a 32-character ASCII hex string created from information provided by both the client requesting the resource and the server that is hosting the resource. The information that goes into creating the message digest includes a *nonce* value that the server returns in response to a request for a protected resource, a user name, a password, a realm, and the request. The default method for obtaining the message-digest string is the MD5 algorithm described in *RFC 1321: The MD5 Message-Digest Algorithm.*

The nonce value provided by the server typically incorporates a time stamp and an Etag value that identifies the resource being requested. The time stamp enables the server to allow access for a specified time before requiring re-authentication. A server can use the Etag value to prevent replay attacks, where an unauthorized user requests an updated version of a resource previously returned to an authorized user.

Rabbit Semiconductor's Dynamic C includes functions that support Digest Authentication on Web servers hosted by Rabbit modules. Some older Web browsers don't support Digest Authentication.

HTML Passwords

For very basic password protection, HTML's password box can do the job. A password box on a Web page is just like a text box except that the TYPE attribute of HTML's input tag is "password":

```
<input type = "password" name=mypassword maxlength=20>
```

When a user types a password in the box, the browser displays a dot for each character typed. When the user clicks the form's **Submit** button, the browser sends the password to the server without encrypting it. Unlike Basic Authentication, which many servers support automatically, the use of this type of password box is application-specific. The server must provide program code to check the password and take appropriate action.

Additional Password Considerations

Be sure to limit access to any files that store user names and passwords so they aren't easily viewable by unauthorized users. And be aware that password protection only limits who can request a resource. The resource itself isn't encrypted when traveling on the network.

As previous chapters have shown, user names and passwords can also control access to e-mail mailboxes and files on an FTP server.

Validate User Data

Another way a device's resources can be at risk is via data received from a client, such as data submitted on a form. Users can cause harm due to malicious behavior or carelessness.

Limiting Input Range

When enabling users to enter data to be used in configuring or controlling a device, it's always a good idea to limit valid inputs to a reasonable range. For example, in a system that controls heating and cooling for a house, you may want to allow inputs only between, say, 50 and 80 degrees Fahrenheit. That way, if someone mistakenly types a thermostat setting of 0 instead of 60, the system can display an error message instead of attempting to implement the setting.

Limiting Input Length

On a form, input tags that enable users to enter text should always have a `maxlength` attribute that limits the number of characters a user can send. This line of HTML code creates an input box called temperature and allows the user to enter up to three characters:

```
<input type= "text" name="temperature" maxlength=3>
```

Limiting the length helps to ensure that the received value doesn't extend beyond the amount of memory reserved for the value on the server.

SSI Vulnerabilities

Chapter 6 introduced SSI directives. A couple of directives can have unintended consequences. The `#exec` directive can request the server to execute program code, and the `#include` directive can request the contents of a file to be included in a requested resource. If your server supports these directives but they're unneeded by applications, it's best to disable them if possible. In any case, to guard against unauthorized release of data or execution of program code, anything stored in the device that should remain private should be in an area unavailable to unauthorized users.

The Rabbit's *http.lib* library supports `#include` and an `#exec cmd` directive, which can execute a function named in an `HTTPSPEC_FUNCTION` entry in the application's `HttpSpec` structure.

Encrypt Private Data

The fourth rule for securing network resources is to encrypt data that must remain private. Basic and Digest Authentication encrypt passwords. It's also possible to encrypt any data exchanged between two computers.

Encrypting and decrypting large amounts of data can take up a lot of CPU cycles and time. On small embedded systems, the challenge is to obtain the needed security without overwhelming the system's resources. Options such as AES encryption and stand-alone firewalls that support Virtual Private Network protocols are two possible solutions for embedded systems.

AES (Rijndael) Encryption

In 1997, the U.S. National Institute of Standards and Technology (NIST) began a search for a new encryption standard that was royalty-free, easy to implement even on small embedded systems, and able to withstand attack. In 2001, Federal Information Processing Standard (FIPS) 197 designated the Rijndael algorithm the winner of the search. The algorithm was named the government's Advanced Encryption Standard (AES) to use for sensitive but unclassified information. Entities other than the U.S. Government are welcome to use the algorithm as well, of course.

Rabbit Semiconductor's Dynamic C offers a library module with support for the Rijndael Advanced Encryption Standard (AES) cipher.

Virtual Private Networks

Another option for securing network data is a virtual private network (VPN). The computers at each end of the VPN can use authentication and encryption to ensure that the data is secure from spying and to block all other traffic from entering the VPN.

The program code required to implement a VPN can be too complex and time-consuming to develop for a small embedded system. However, just about any system can communicate over a VPN by connecting to a relatively inexpensive firewall device with VPN support.

VPNs use IP Security (IPsec) protocols for encryption and authentication. A variety of RFC documents cover the protocols. A good place to start is with *RFC 2411: IP Security Document Roadmap.*

To establish a VPN, a computer at each end of the network must have software that knows how to use the required protocols to establish a connection to the other end. Windows XP includes an IPSec Security Manager that enables PCs to communicate over a VPN. For embedded systems, the easiest way to support VPN is to connect the system to a firewall device that supports VPNs.

Firewalls that support VPNs typically include a variety of configuration options. At the local network, you can enable a single IP address, an entire subnet, or a user-specified range of addresses within a subnet to access the VPN. You can specify that the local network will accept VPN communications from a specified IP address or domain name, or from any requesting host.

To use encryption, both ends of the VPN must agree on the type of encryption to use and they must share a key that enables each end to encrypt and decrypt network traffic. Encryption options include AES and the older methods 3DES and DES. Authentication options include MD5 and the more secure 160-bit Secure Hash Algorithm (SHA).

When both ends have been configured, the devices can communicate and attempt to establish the VPN. When the VPN has been established, the two devices can use encryption to transfer data securely.

Secure Sockets Layer Encryption

Many Web browsers support the Secure Sockets Layer (SSL) protocol for encrypting data such as the credit-card numbers customers send to on-line retailers. SSL uses public-key cryptography, which uses separate keys for encrypting and decrypting. The computer requesting the encrypted data generates a public key for encrypting and a private key for decrypting. The sender of the data uses the public key in encrypting the data. Decrypting requires the private key, which only the receiving computer has access to.

SSL encryption is very secure but requires more resources than many small embedded systems can provide. Netburner is one company that offers SSL support for its products, which use Motorola's 32-bit ColdFire processors.

Chapter 10

Index

Index

Index